Municipal Management Series

Managing Small Cities and Counties: A Practical Guide

The International City/County Management Association is the professional and educational organization for appointed administrators and assistant administrators in local government. The purposes of ICMA are to enhance the quality of local government and to nurture and assist professional local government administrators in the United State and other countries. To further its mission, ICMA develops and disseminates new approaches to management through training programs, information services, and publications.

Local government managers—carrying a wide range of titles—serve cities, towns, counties, councils of governments, and state/provincial associations of local governments. They serve at the direction of elected councils and governing boards. ICMA serves these managers and local governments through many programs that aim at improving the manager's professional competence and strengthening the quality of all local governments.

The International City/County Management Association was founded in 1914; adopted its City Management Code of Ethics in 1924; and established its Institute for Training in Municipal Administration in 1934. The Institute, in turn, provided the basis for the Municipal Management Series, generally termed the "ICMA Green Books."

ICMA's interest and activities include public management education; standards of ethics for members; the *Municipal Year Book* and other data services; urban research; and newsletters, a monthly magazine, *Public Management*, and other publications. ICMA's efforts toward the improvement of local government management—as represented by this book—are offered for all local governments and educational institutions. ■

Municipal Management Series

Managing Small Cities and Counties: A Practical Guide

Published for the
ICMA Training Institute

By the International
City/County Management
Association

Edited by

James M. Banovetz
Drew A. Dolan
John W. Swain

Municipal Management Series

Managing Small Cities and Counties: A Practical Guide
Advanced Supervisory Practices
Effective Communication
The Effective Local Government Manager
Effective Supervisory Practices
Emergency Management: Principles and Practice for Local Government
Housing and Local Government
Local Government Police Management
Management of Local Planning
Management of Local Public Works
Management Policies in Local Government Finance
Managing Fire Services
Managing Human Services
Managing Local Government: Cases in Decision Making
Managing Municipal Leisure Services
The Practice of Local Government Planning
The Practice of State and Regional Planning
Service Contracting: A Local Government Guide

Library of Congress Cataloging-in-Publication Data

Managing small cities and counties: a practical guide / edited by James M. Banovetz, Drew A. Dolan, John W. Swain.
p. cm.—(Municipal management series)
Rev. ed of: Small cities and counties. ©1984.
Includes bibliographical references and index.
ISBN 0-87326-093-7
1. Municipal services—United States—Management. I. Banovetz, James M. II. Dolan, Drew Anderson. III. Swain, John W. IV. Small cities and counties. V. Series.
HD4605.M25 1994
352.7—dc20 94-14625
CIP

Printed in the United States of America.

05 04 03 02
8 7 6 5 4 3

Foreword

Because the majority of North Americans live in small communities, ICMA's mission—to enhance the quality of local government—means focusing in particular on smaller cities and counties, villages, and towns. In 1975 ICMA published the *Small Cities Management Training Program*, a set of twelve booklets that collectively dealt with the management problems of small communities. This training program was followed in 1984 by the book *Small Cities and Counties: A Guide to Managing Services*.

Like the training program, the book was designed to encourage team building by giving department heads the information they needed to understand one another's managerial problems and to build closer working relations. It was also intended to provide a general survey of local government operations that would be useful to all local government administrators. In addition, the book was designed to help newly elected officials understand the workings of local government and the problems and policy issues they might face.

Ten years later, it is more important than ever for ICMA to help smaller communities maintain and improve their services: 95 percent of all U.S. cities serve fewer than 25,000 people, and 74 percent of counties serve populations of under 50,000.

Smaller community governments have always had the task of delivering services to their residents. But today's governments play an increasingly complex and challenging role as they attempt to meet their community's needs. Small governments today face many of the same problems as larger ones: a shrinking tax base, reduced federal and state aid, citizen opposition to both increases in taxes and cuts in services, unfunded federal mandates, a more diverse population, greater human service needs, global competition. They must promote economic development and at the same time manage growth and ensure a healthy, safe, and pleasing environment.

To help smaller communities meet their present and future challenges, ICMA has developed this second edition of *Small Cities and Counties* under the title of *Managing Small Cities and Counties: A Practical Guide*. The second edition has been developed with the same overall aims as the first edition; all the material from the first edition has been comprehensively revised to reflect current management concerns and issues. As in the first edition, the editors and authors have illustrated their discussion of management and policy issues with examples of innovative practices from a wide range of smaller cities and counties.

Creating this book was a cooperative effort that involved a number of people. We extend our special thanks to James M. Banovetz for his leadership on this project and to him and his co-editors, Drew A. Dolan and John W. Swain, for their expertise, hard work, patience, and flexibility throughout the book's development.

The following individuals reviewed the first edition and contributed valuable suggestions for its revision: David S. Arnold, former editor, Municipal Management Series, ICMA; Stephen Hintz, University of Wisconsin, Oshkosh; and Robert B. Morris, former village manager, Glencoe, Illinois.

We are grateful to our editorial committee for their dedicated and valuable work in suggesting revisions to the first edition and in reviewing the manuscripts prepared for the second edition. The members of this committee were Neal G. Berlin, City Manager, Arvada, Colorado; Dee Bruemmer, Assistant City Administrator, Davenport, Iowa; William P. Buchanan, County Manager, Sedgwick County, Kansas; Edwin C. Daley, City Manager, Winchester, Virginia; Velga Drillis-Eizis, Village Administrator, Orland Hills, Illinois; Richard L. Escalante, City Manager, Farmers Branch, Texas; Lee Gilmour, County Administrator, County of Glynn, Georgia; Robert S. LaSala, Deputy County Administrator for Growth Management, County of Sarasota, Florida; J. Thomas Lundy, County Manager, Catawba County, North Carolina; and Gerald Seals, County Administrator, County of Greenville, South Carolina.

We would like to thank the chapter authors, not only for their contributions but also for their responsiveness, patience, and cooperation during the stages leading to publication. In addition, the author of Chapter 14 wishes to thank Jean Van Devanter White, Director, Office of Public Affairs, Fairfax County, Virginia, for her assistance.

A number of ICMA staff members contributed to the project: Barbara Moore, Director of Publications; Verity Weston-Truby, who oversaw the project; Eileen Hughes, who copyedited the manuscript; Dawn M. Leland, who coordinated production, with assistance from Brian Derr; Jane Pellicciotto, who designed the book; and Phyllis Brown, who provided administrative assistance and input the manuscript for production. We also wish to thank freelance designer Lynne Hofman, who created the layout.

William H. Hansell, Jr.
Executive Director, ICMA
Washington, D.C.

Preface

The nation's political leaders, the media, and scholars tend to think about government in terms of big governments—the political institutions found in Washington, D.C., state capitals, and large cities. It is their performance and the behavior of their leaders that shape the American image of government.

But Americans obtain most government services from the governments of the communities in which they live. For most Americans, this means that their services come from smaller governments—those in suburbs, communities beyond metropolitan areas, or rural counties. Not all community governments are responsible for the same services, but each is charged with the duty of protecting the health, welfare, and safety of its residents. Thus, these governments have ultimate responsibility for the quality of life in their respective communities. This responsibility is growing in magnitude, particularly as the national and state governments are forced by fiscal retrenchment to reduce their level of support for local government.

This book has been written for and about these smaller communities and their governments. Because their decisions and activities have such a major impact on people's lives, the nation's counties, cities, villages, boroughs, and towns must be managed efficiently and effectively. A central theme of this book is that the task of efficient and effective management increasingly requires a level of managerial knowledge and specialized expertise comparable to that required to direct the affairs of a very large and complex business. Indeed, community governments, even those of modest size, are relatively large and complex organizations.

The first edition of this book, *Small Cities and Counties: A Guide to Managing Services,* was published in 1984. In 1991, ICMA established an editorial committee to review the first edition and recommend the changes needed to update the book. The contributions of that committee have been invaluable.

Although this second edition has a table of contents much like the first, and indeed has many of the same chapter authors, it represents a complete and detailed reworking of the material. A chapter on emergency planning has been added to the book; the chapters on planning, economic development, public works, leisure services, budgeting and financial management, communication, and intergovernmental relations are entirely new; the chapter on the office of the clerk has been rewritten to equalize the emphasis on county and city clerks; and the other chapters have all been substantially reworked to ensure current, state-of-the-art treatment of the subject matter.

Those of us who worked on this second edition owe sincere thanks to Ross Clayton, Charles K. Coe, Robert H. Goodin, Howard A. Gudell, Charles B. Hetrick, Ronald B. Hoskins, Cristy A. Jensen, Rebecca Roberts McCarthy, John F. Shirey, Russell L. Smith, Burton Sparer, Gerald C. Sprecher, Richard L. Ulrich, Clarence B. Walker, and Carol B. Zar, whose words and thoughts from the first edition gave us our points of departure for this second effort.

A book like this cannot take shape without the contributions of many people. ICMA staff help has been absolutely outstanding. So, too, has been the help of June M. Kubasiak of my staff at Northern Illinois University, who managed the communications and paper flows between editors, committee members, and authors throughout the preparation of both editions. Finally, the Maxine Goodman Levin College of Urban Affairs at Cleveland State University supported my work throughout the development of this edition.

Drew A. Dolan, Center for Urban and Public Affairs at Wright State University, and John W. Swain, Department of Political Science at the University of Alabama, Tuscaloosa, joined with me to co-edit this second edition. With their backgrounds in county and other rural local governments, they have added immensely to the richness of the insight into the daily operations of small cities and counties.

The first edition of this book was dedicated to local government leaders: to those whose primary responsibility is to cope with the changes that constantly assail local communities. It is such leaders who must anticipate changes, develop goals and objectives regarding the future of their communities, and then manage the forces of change to achieve those goals and objectives. It is to these leaders that Americans have entrusted the quality of life in their communities, and it is to these leaders that this book is again dedicated.

James M. Banovetz
DeKalb, Illinois

Table of Contents

PART I Providing Community Government

PART II Building a Better Community

PART IV Managing Government

PART I

Providing Community Government

INTRODUCTION

The City is the People, the title of a book by urbanologist Henry Churchill, reminds local leaders of a very central reality: communities are not collections of land, streets, buildings, or public institutions; they are collections of people. And community governments—those of cities, counties, and villages—exist to serve people.

Government at any level provides a mechanism through which people can work together to improve the quality of their lives. Community governments are the principle mechanism through which people can improve the quality of life in their own neighborhoods. As such, community governments are very important to people—perhaps more important than any other level of government. It is, after all, in their own neighborhoods that people spend most of their lives; that is where they live, work, go to school, and fill most of their leisure hours.

Because they are so important, community governments have a major responsibility—a responsibility to work *with* people. People are not, after all, simply objects to be served by community government; people are the source of the values, objectives, and even many of the ideas and much of the energy that guide and direct government activity.

This book is about improvement in the quality of neighborhood life. It is about the way in which community governments can work with people to help them make their neighborhoods safer, healthier, and more pleasant places to be.

The three chapters that form the first part of the book are about the nature and function of community government. Chapter 1 underscores the importance of community governments by noting that they are the "governments of last resort" for their residents; they are the governments that ultimately must provide the help and services that most affect the quality of daily life. The chapter describes the context in which community governments operate today: the attitudes of people, the complexity of government, the demands for service, the concern about taxes, and the changes with which community governments must cope. It also discusses strategies for coping with change and the importance of professionalism in the management of government operations.

Community governments derive their powers—the limits on what they can and cannot do—from the law. Indeed, their very existence is established and controlled by the law. Chapter 2 discusses the vital link between the law and community government. Besides identifying the sources of authority for these governments, it also describes the forms of county and municipal governments and discusses some of the more common legal problems that they face.

The third chapter describes one of the oldest and least acknowledged offices in the community government, that of city or county clerk. Its duties are critical to effective government operation: the office of clerk maintains records, issues licenses and permits, and sometimes sets the agenda for legislative meetings. But perhaps more important, it is charged with major responsibilities for managing the interface between government and citizens: this office conducts elections; it is the first stop for citizens seeking information about government; it is charged with providing public notice of meetings of the legislative body and other boards and commissions; and it ensures compliance with laws providing public access to government records.

The theme implicit in each of these chapters is that of the importance of serving the people who constitute the community.

The Challenges of Community Government

At the end of the twentieth century, city and county governments find themselves in a position similar to the one they occupied a hundred years earlier. They have again become the governments of last resort in confronting the problems of the society they serve. However, despite the similarity in their past and present positions, community governments have undergone cataclysmic changes, particularly in the last fifty years. They have experienced a vast expansion of their service responsibilities, a 360-degree change in public support, and major alterations in their mode of operation.

When the twentieth century began, community governments had primary responsibility for "people problems," which were handled by the police, fire, parks, health, welfare, and public works departments. To be sure, community governments were limited in their ability to deal with these problems—by the laissez-faire attitudes of society as well as by the strict constructionism applied by the courts in interpreting their powers—but they were the last, and only governmental, resort of those in need.

Now, at the twentieth century's end, community governments again find themselves the last resort of their residents. Faced with mounting budget deficits and resistance to higher taxes, national and state governments have begun to disengage themselves from responsibility for people in need. In some instances (e.g., Medicaid and community mental health services) they have cut back their financial support, leaving local governments to make up the difference. In others, (e.g., education and general assistance) state governments have mandated local action but failed to provide enough funds to cover the added costs.

Community services are provided by many agencies besides local governments. Private not-for-profit agencies frequently provide such services as hospitals and cultural programs, and public-private partnerships often are used to provide such services as solid waste disposal; water, electric, and gas utilities; and a variety of human service programs. Some private firms now even assume direct responsibility for some public services, such as education programs. Still, it is the community government that must coordinate such efforts; the community government must endure public pressure when such programs are the targets of criticism; community governments must respond to the void left when other service providers abandon their role. Community governments must assume the ultimate responsibility—and any residual bills—for maintaining the quality of life in their neighborhoods.

This responsibility has grown in the last half-century, during which social, economic, and political changes have occurred that required community governments to undertake more services—services such as economic development, comprehensive planning, neighborhood renewal, housing, mental health programs, programs for senior citizens, day care, and drug counseling. In some cases, these services have been established in response to the escalating political activity of well-informed and vocal citizen groups, but most have been provided in response to federal and state pressures and funded by grant programs. The pressures continue because, although the disengagement of the national and state governments has meant less financial support, it has produced no reduction in federal and state mandates, regulations, or political interference.

Citizen attitudes toward government have also changed profoundly. At the beginning of the twentieth century, people were suspicious of government power; the citizens agreed with Thomas Jefferson's notion that "that government governs best which governs least." As the century progressed, however, attitudes about government began to change as Franklin D. Roosevelt brought the nation out of the Great Depression and won history's largest military conflict. The voters elected John F. Kennedy and Lyndon B. Johnson on platforms calling for active government involvement in all aspects of community life. Factors such as the war in Vietnam, the civil disobedience of the sixties and seventies, and Watergate—together with escalating public spending, budget deficits, and taxation—restored public skepticism of government.

The public is unwilling to cut back; voters regularly re-elect a Congress whose leadership is committed to more services for more people.

The result, as the end of the twentieth century approaches, has been popular ambivalence. On one hand, the public demands a return to limited government, with lower taxes, reduced budget deficits, and less government regulation. Voters elected Jimmy Carter in 1976, Ronald Reagan in 1980 and 1984, and George Bush in 1988 on platforms calling for governmental retrenchment. Yet, at the same time, the public is unwilling to cut back governmental services; voters regularly re-elect a Congress whose leadership is committed to more services for more people. The election of Bill Clinton in 1992 reflected this ambivalence: Clinton's election campaign promised a more active government but also pledged to reduce the budget deficit without raising taxes on the middle class.

In local communities, where government deficits are legally prohibited, this ambivalence has resulted in public pressure to produce "more with less." This pressure has added to the demand for more intergovernmental coordination; it has produced new methods for evaluating public services; it has given rise to searches for "reinventing government," "total quality control in government," and "customer service government"; and thus it has increased the need for the professionalization of those who manage and deliver community services.

Professional advice

Faced with a faltering state and local economy and recognizing the debilitating effect of tough times on the collective attitude and disposition of the community, the city manager of Portland, Maine (65,000), proposed that the city build a stadium to bring a professional baseball team to the community. With this as a goal, community residents worked together on an application to authorize a Double A team for Portland starting in the spring of 1994. The effort served to encourage the entire community to lift itself out of the economic recession.

Source: Nadeen M. Daniels, Assistant City Manager, Portland, Maine, 1993.

The demand for professionally competent administrative leadership in community governments arose early in the century and increased exponentially during the second half. It started with a demand for professional managers in cities; that demand soon extended to counties; more recently it has led to the creation and widespread use of city and county administrators; and ultimately it extended beyond top management levels to encompass supervisory personnel as well.

Professionalization has proven its value: it helped change the poor public image under which government labored.

Professionalization has affected the delivery of services and the formulation of policy as well. Managers and administrative officers do not have the power to vote in council and board meetings, but they are available to identify problems, gather information, suggest alternatives, and offer advice to elected officials. In the current information age, knowledge is power, and the presence of an educated, experienced, professional adviser has increased the ability of elected mayors, presidents of county boards, and council and board members to influence and alter the economic and social forces affecting their communities. This increased professionalization has proven its value: it has helped change the poor public image under which government had labored. A 1990 federal government survey found that at that time local government was more highly regarded by the public than either the federal or state level of government.[1] The accompanying sidebar shows two different formats in which professionals have been particularly successful.

Two major forms of government: two types of professional management

Professional local government administrators serve in two kinds of government forms:

The council-manager form: The mayor and council appoint a chief executive officer who serves at the council's pleasure, directs administrative operations, appoints administrative officers, advises the council on matters of policy, and answers to the council for the performance of all administrative departments. The manager has neither a vote nor a veto in council meetings.

Managers see themselves as facilitators; they play key roles in policy development and implementation.

The administrator form: Either the mayor or the mayor and council appoint a chief administrative officer who serves at the pleasure of the appointing authority. The CAO's powers vary; administrative powers may be identical to those of a manager in council-manager form.

Administrators see themselves as coordinators; they implement policy under the leadership of the chief elected official.

Adapted from Eric Anderson, "Two Major Forms of Government: Two Types of Professional Management," in *Municipal Year Book 1989* (Washington, DC: ICMA, 1989), 25.

In order to help increase the professional competence of community government leaders, this book summarizes the management problems and challenges encountered in service departments and offices. This chapter sets the stage for the discussion by looking at community governments—those governing cities, counties, villages, and towns—in order to understand their importance in the American federal system and the professional manager's role in them. Subsequent chapters describe the services that governments provide, the challenges that communities must confront, and the skills needed by managers to fulfill their role.

The thesis of this book is that community governments will be more successful in responding to the challenges of the future if they inspire their employees to attain higher levels of professional competence and to increase their effectiveness by working together to solve community problems.

Community government today

Although large cities (e.g., New York, Boston, Seattle) and metropolitan counties (e.g., Dade County, Cook County, and Los Angeles County) receive the most public attention, the majority of Americans live in smaller communities, mainly those with a population of less than 50,000. These communities are important, not just because there are so many of them and their governments serve so many people, but because their governments operate at the neighborhood level. They deliver the public services that people use in their daily lives.

The importance of smaller local governments in the American system is shown by the figures in Table 1–1. Nine of ten American counties and 99 percent of American cities serve communities with fewer than 100,000 people; nearly half of all counties and 95 percent of cities serve communities of fewer than 25,000 people. In short, small and medium-sized communities dominate the American local government scene.

Table 1–1 Number and population of community governments (cities and counties) in the United States, 1987.

Classification[a]	Counties No.	Counties %	Cities No.	Cities %
All communities				
Units	3,042	100.0	19,200	100.0
Population	217,397	100.0	149,864	100.0
Under 100,000 population				
Units	2,644	86.9	19,017	99.0
Population	68,687	31.7	87,923	58.7
Under 50,000 population				
Units	2,257	74.2	18,732	97.6
Population	41,408	19.1	68,401	45.7
Under 25,000 population				
Units	1,401	46.0	18,171	94.6
Population	19,587	9.1	49,015	32.7

[a] All population figures are 1986 estimates and are shown in thousands.

Historical perspective

The community has long been recognized as the source of grass-roots democracy in the United States; here, the slogan of the 1960s, "Power to the people," is realized. Government is operated by community residents, less on the basis of party politics than on that of face-to-face contact between friends and neighbors. Here, the business of government is transacted in a local community building, but it is also transacted in the shopping centers, church halls, and living rooms of those who are directly affected by government action. Here, an elected representative is contacted, not by sending a letter to some distant capital, but by stopping the representative on the street or by calling him or her at home.

The preference for small communities

The potential for personal, face-to-face contact and the vitality it brings to government affairs have reinforced the desire of the American people to keep local governments small, even in the midst of large metropolitan regions. Small-community government continues, even in large urban areas, because that is the way the people want it.

Americans have always wanted their local governments to be small and accessible. This preference was at work in the Midwest, for example, when county boundaries were being established. The rule of thumb was that each county had to be small enough so that a farmer living anywhere in the county could travel by horse and wagon from farm to county seat, transact business, and return home between the morning and evening barnyard chores.

Growth in the number of local governments

In the face of continuous population growth, the preference for small governments has inevitably resulted in the creation of a large number of local governments. That number peaked at more than 150,000 units during the first half of the twentieth century, before school-district mergers and the elimination of townships in several states brought the number down to approximately 80,000. Although the number of counties has remained relatively constant, the number of municipalities—cities, villages, and towns—has continued to increase; thus, the number of community governments has continued to increase.

The demand for more services has had the most influence on the increase in the size of community governments.

As urban populations became more dense and the need for certain services, such as regional transportation, extended beyond existing government boundary lines, a new form of government—the special district—came into existence to provide specialized services to defined geographic areas. Special districts were usually made independent of the existing county and municipal governments and typically were organized to perform only a single function, such as to provide transportation, sewage disposal, or parks. The number of such units of government has increased dramatically, especially in the 1987-1992 period: nationally, they increased by 168 percent between 1952 and 1992, but 29 percent of that increase (3,599 new special districts or 10.9 percent of all special districts) took place between 1987-1992. Figure 1–1 on page 8 shows why this growth in the number of governments occurred.

Growth in local service responsibilities

The demand for more services—a result of increased population density, growing social awareness and public concern, and federal and state mandates—has had the most influence on the increase in the size and scope of community governments. Spending by these governments increased 3,197 percent, from $65 to $2,143 per capita, from the end of World War II in 1946 to 1989.[2]

Another way to look at the increase in the activity of local governments is to study the changes in the kinds of service provided. Historically, communities were responsible for basic community support services: public safety, streets and highways, cemeteries, public utilities, and libraries. During the first half of the twentieth century, land use planning, low-income housing, urban renewal, and health programs joined the list. In the last half of the century, a whole new set of service programs has been added.

Community governments now find themselves responsible for a mix of services. They provide juvenile centers, meals-on-wheels, senior citizen centers, human relations commissions, housing, child day-care centers, drug counseling and rehabilitation programs, community mental health centers, legal aid programs, emergency hot lines, job training programs, and tax increment financing districts to promote economic development. In many states, such services constitute the most rapidly expanding area of county government expenditures.

Some of these new services are provided directly by government; others are provided by community-based, not-for-profit agencies or by public-private partnerships. Even when the community government is not the direct service provider, it is expected to coordinate the efforts of these agencies and partnerships and to give them financial assistance. Counties, in particular, are expected to play this role. Another equally significant trend affecting counties has been the expansion of their obligations to include many of the services traditionally associated with

Figure 1–1 New kinds of local government were superimposed on the existing government structure in response to changing local concerns and needs for services.

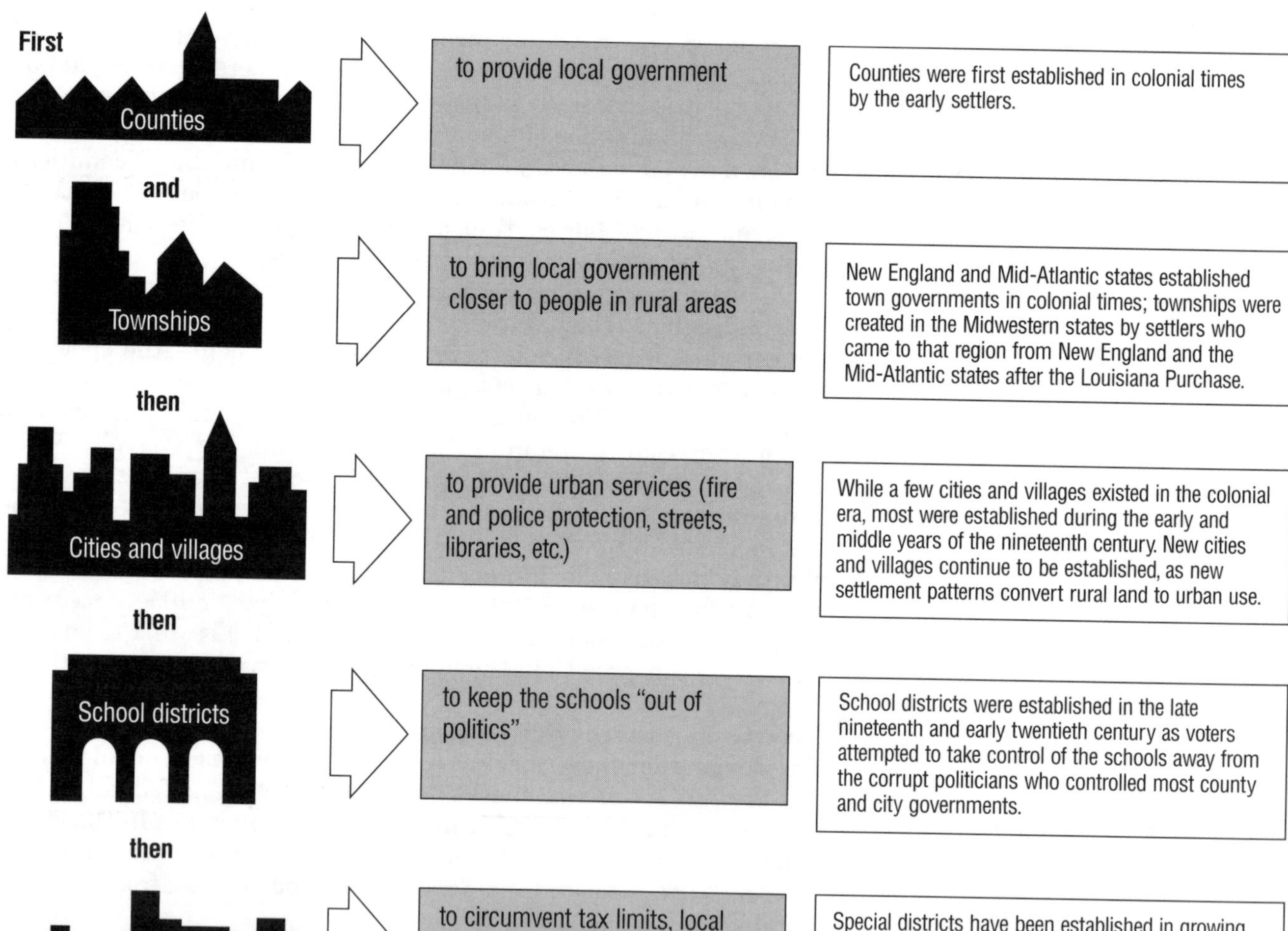

First
Counties
to provide local government
Counties were first established in colonial times by the early settlers.
and
Townships
to bring local government closer to people in rural areas
New England and Mid-Atlantic states established town governments in colonial times; townships were created in the Midwestern states by settlers who came to that region from New England and the Mid-Atlantic states after the Louisiana Purchase.
then
Cities and villages
to provide urban services (fire and police protection, streets, libraries, etc.)
While a few cities and villages existed in the colonial era, most were established during the early and middle years of the nineteenth century. New cities and villages continue to be established, as new settlement patterns convert rural land to urban use.
then
School districts
to keep the schools "out of politics"
School districts were established in the late nineteenth and early twentieth century as voters attempted to take control of the schools away from the corrupt politicians who controlled most county and city governments.
then
Special districts
to circumvent tax limits, local powers, geographic boundary limitations, and other restrictions
Special districts have been established in growing numbers since the mid-twentieth century. They are sometimes created to provide services over a geographic area that is different from the boundaries of existing local governments and sometimes to create additional governments that will have added tax and borrowing powers.
equal
1 Great proliferation in the number of local governments
2 Lack of uniformity in local government boundaries
3 Problems of service coordination
4 Voter confusion and apathy
5 High taxes and government spending

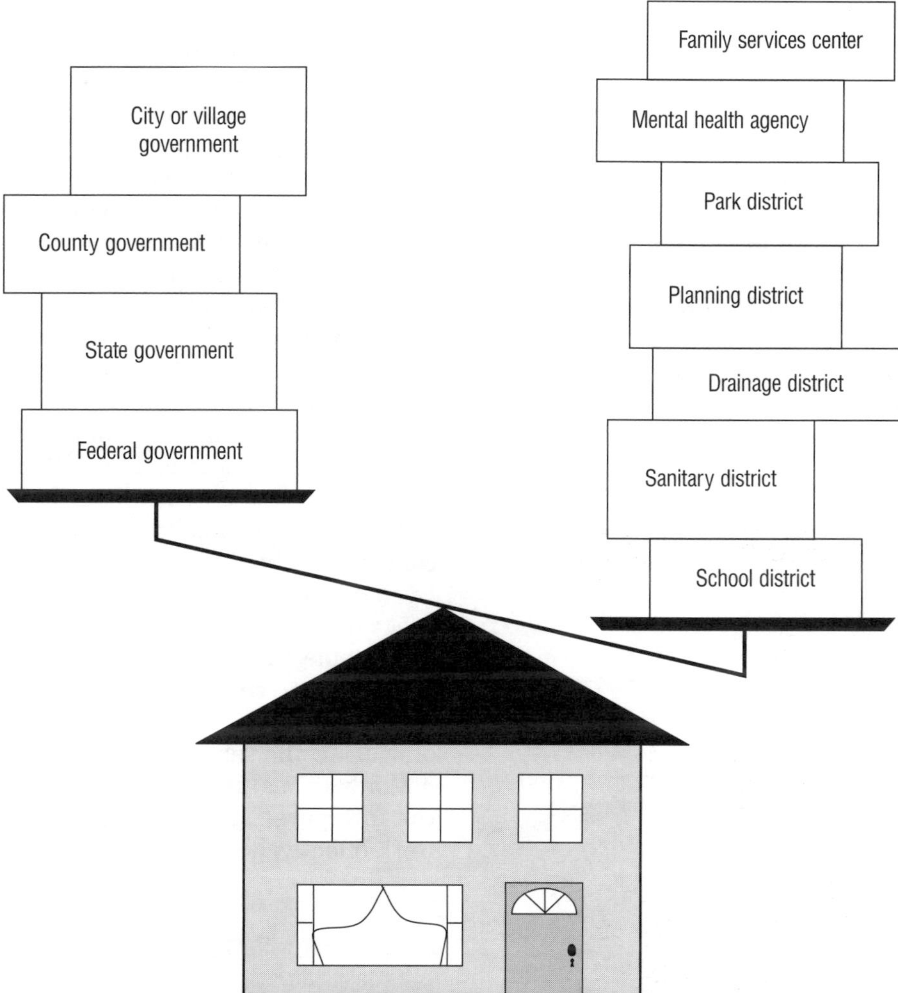

Figure 1–2 The house is John Q. Citizen's domain, a piece of property that is served (some would say overloaded) by many governments. The typical citizen has little understanding of the complex system of governments that affect his or her life, including a wide range of special districts that are almost invisible.

cities and villages. As their populations urbanize, more and more counties have been asked to provide for fire protection, communicable-disease control, zoning, code enforcement, and legal aid.

Today's intergovernmental complexity

Delivering local public services through a system involving counties, municipalities, school districts, special districts, not-for-profit agencies, and public-private partnerships has a number of consequences. Some of these are related to the difficulties citizens have in understanding the system; others stem from the labyrinth of overlapping jurisdictional boundaries.

The citizen's view of local government

The typical resident has only a rough understanding of the sometimes bewildering service delivery system. It is not unusual, for example, for a citizen's home to be served by a county government, a city or a village government, one or more school districts (in some states, separate school districts exist for elementary schools, secondary schools, and community colleges), as many as a dozen or more special districts, and any number of public-private agencies. Figure 1–2 illustrates the citizen's perspective: the drawing portrays some of the governments and other public agencies that may serve any given piece of residential property.

The complexity of the system varies from state to state. Most states have a highly fragmented system: Illinois, for example, is served by 6,627 units of local government. Some states have relatively few units of local government; Hawaii has only 18. Table 1–2 lists the number of local governments serving each state.

It is not unusual for voters to elect individuals to fill more than a hundred offices in any given four-year period.

Figure 1–2 also portrays how John Q. Public's burdens grow in direct proportion to the complexity of the system. As the number of units of government increases, so too does the number of offices to be filled by election. It is not unusual for voters in some communities to elect individuals to fill more than a hundred national, state, and local government offices in any given four-year period. Voters cannot hold local government officials accountable when they cannot understand the system or keep track of the elective offices that exist.

Finally, as the number of governments increases, John Q. Citizen becomes more and more confused about which government is responsible for what service. It is difficult to know, for example, whether a particular road is maintained by the village, the township, the county, or the state. Are welfare services provided by the city, the township, the county, or whom? Which government provides meals for the elderly? Even experts on government have trouble determining the answers to these questions.

Unable to understand the local government system, typical rural residents see county officials as those responsible for all of their local services; residents of urban areas look at their city, village, or town officials in the same fashion. Therefore, officials must become proficient not only in making their own governments work, but also in promoting the intergovernmental coordination needed to make the entire system work effectively.

Breakfast with city council

Confronted by referenda results and private reports that showed that voters were alienated from government, the Littleton, Colorado (33,600), city council developed an Outreach program to complement existing city communication initiatives. The council began a series of monthly Breakfast with City Council meetings to which personal invitations were sent to selected community residents and business people. The sessions are used to introduce city officials and staff and to present topics of special interest to each audience. The majority of the time is reserved for an open forum in which officials can respond to citizens' questions and concerns. An optional tour of government offices is included. The breakfasts are free to attendees, but the cost to the city has been minimal. In the program's first two years, nearly 4,000 people were invited to one of the breakfasts.

The city council also sponsors a series of monthly Neighborhood Meetings at which staff members make presentations on upcoming projects planned for the neighborhood. Again, a majority of the time is devoted to an open forum for discussion of residents' questions and concerns. In the first two years, over 13,000 households were personally invited to participate in one of the forums.

Source: Kelli Narde, Assistant to the City Manager, Littleton, Colorado, 1993.

Overlapping boundaries

Not only is the typical community served by many different official entities, but they usually do not have common boundaries. School boundaries rarely coincide with city or village boundaries; a city may be located in parts of two or more counties; a park district may serve several villages; and a planning authority may serve several counties

State	All government units	Local governments				
		County	Municipal	Township	School district	Special district
United States	86,743	3,043	19,296	16,666	14,556	33,131
Alabama	1,134	67	440	-	129	497
Alaska	176	12	149	-	-	14
Arizona	598	15	86	-	228	268
Arkansas	1,437	75	489	-	324	584
California	4,495	57	460	-	1,080	2,897
Colorado	1,826	62	266	-	180	1,317
Connecticut	575	-	30	149	17	378
Delaware	281	3	57	-	19	201
District of Columbia	2	-	1	-	-	1
Florida	1,041	66	390	-	95	489
Georgia	1,321	157	536	-	185	442
Hawaii	21	3	1	-	-	16
Idaho	1,105	44	199	-	116	745
Illinois	6,810	102	1,282	1,433	997	2,995
Indiana	2,976	91	566	1,008	310	1,000
Iowa	1,904	99	953	-	445	406
Kansas	3,918	105	627	1,355	324	1,506
Kentucky	1,345	119	438	-	177	610
Louisiana	461	61	301	-	66	32
Maine	799	16	22	468	88	204
Maryland	416	23	155	-	-	237
Massachusetts	851	12	39	312	86	401
Michigan	2,727	83	534	1,242	587	280
Minnesota	3,616	87	854	1,804	477	393
Mississippi	898	82	294	-	176	345
Missouri	3,368	114	933	324	553	1,443
Montana	1,305	54	128	-	544	578
Nebraska	2,997	93	534	452	842	1,075
Nevada	212	16	18	-	17	160
New Hampshire	531	10	13	221	168	118
New Jersey	1,625	21	320	247	550	486
New Mexico	494	33	99	-	94	267
New York	3,319	57	620	929	714	998
North Carolina	954	100	518	-	-	335
North Dakota	2,795	53	366	1,351	284	740
Ohio	3,534	88	942	1,317	665	521
Oklahoma	1,822	77	589	-	614	541
Oregon	1,487	36	240	-	340	870
Pennsylvania	5,397	66	1,022	1,548	516	2,244
Rhode Island	128	-	8	31	4	84
South Carolina	705	46	270	-	91	297
South Dakota	1,803	64	310	971	184	273
Tennessee	960	93	339	-	14	513
Texas	4,919	254	1,171	-	1,101	2,392
Utah	635	29	228	-	40	337
Vermont	690	14	50	237	278	110
Virginia	461	95	230	-	-	135
Washington	1,796	39	268	-	296	1,192
West Virginia	708	55	231	-	55	366
Wisconsin	2,752	72	583	1,267	430	399
Wyoming	576	23	97	-	56	399

Table 1–2 Number of governmental units by state, 1992.

and all of the local governments located within those counties. Conversely, several school districts might serve different parts of a single city; a drainage district might serve only a portion of a county; and a street-lighting district might serve only the commercial area of a city or village.

When all of these differences are aggregated, the result resembles the situation shown in Figure 1–3. Note, for example, the situation in Community MF in the figure: MF lies in parts of three different counties, four different school districts, and a planning district. It has its own park district, which does not serve residents in the neighboring communities. Community MK lies in two counties and three school districts; it has kept its portion of County CD from being served by the planning district that serves the balance of the county.

Figure 1–3 does not overstate the problem; in fact, it understates it. Figure 1–3 does not show boundaries for townships; it shows only one kind of school district, although many states have two or three (e.g., some states have separate districts for elementary and secondary schools; many have special districts for community colleges); and it does not list most of the special districts (e.g., sanitary district, water supply district,

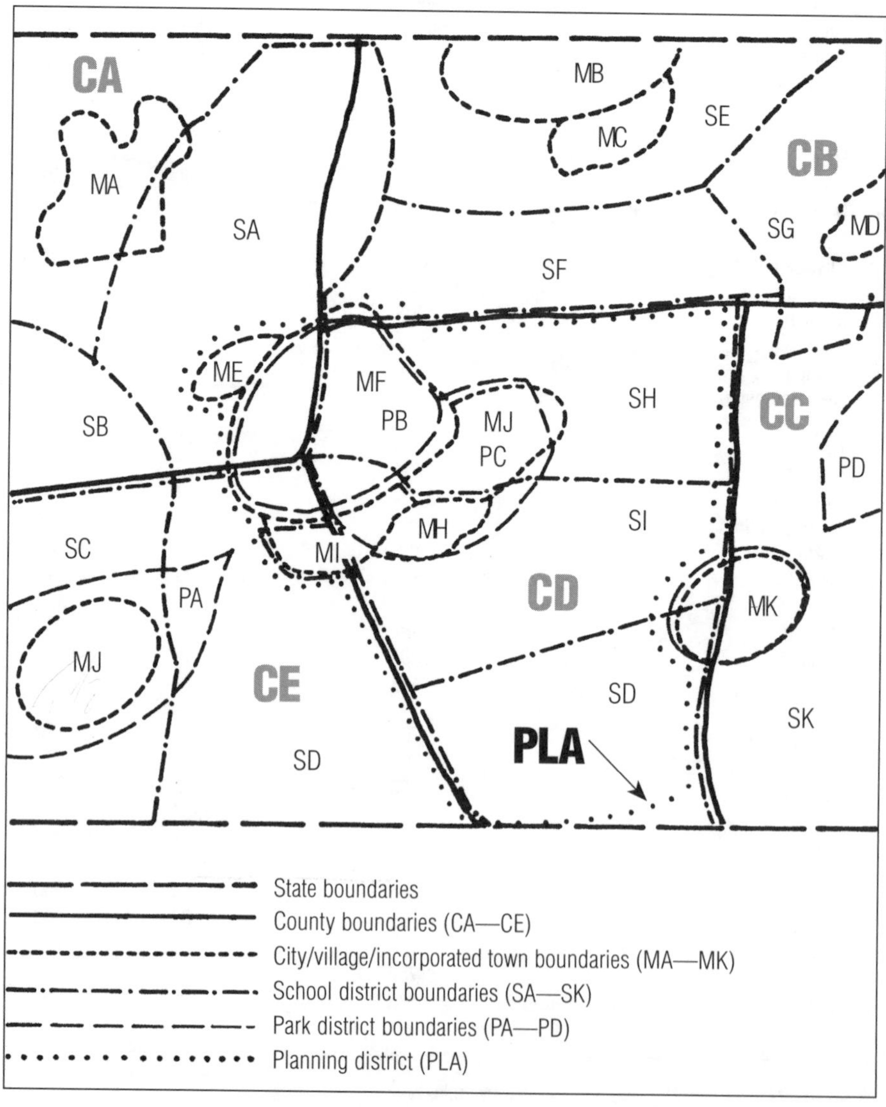

Figure 1–3 Governmental boundaries at local levels: a typical, simplified pattern.

mosquito abatement district, rural economic development districts) that might normally be expected to be found in such an area.

Such boundary fragmentation poses many special problems for the local official. Some of these are financial, because the property tax resources of the area are artificially divided among the local governments. Others result from the service delivery systems. Residents in the County CA portion of Community MF will receive a different set of county-provided human services than will their neighbors living in the County CB portion of MF. Because ME residents do not have a park district, they will attempt to use parks in MF, increasing the congestion in MF parks without paying any of the costs of maintaining them.

The proliferation of governments and their services has made government more difficult to manage.

Other problems will exist. For example, radio frequencies for emergency services will have to be coordinated; property tax assessment ratios in different counties must be equalized; and intergovernmental controls must be exercised over the use of water and the disposal of wastes. In short, the work of many different local officials must be coordinated to provide effective government services to the region. Such coordination is discussed more fully in Chapter 15.

Thus, the proliferation of governments and their services has made government more difficult to manage. Developments anticipated for the future promise to pose even greater challenges.

Community government in the future

One has only to look at the past to know that change profoundly affects local government. The world today is very different from the world of 1980, when few homes, businesses, or community governments had seen a personal computer. It is even more different from the world of 1960, when the electronics revolution was still unknown to most people. Futurists are unanimous in declaring that the pace of change is continually increasing. Thus, future changes may be even more dramatic and traumatic than those of the past—for local governments as well as for the rest of society. It is impossible to know what life will be like in 2020, but it is safe to predict that it will be very different from life in 1995.

Yet most community leaders in 2020 will be people who were born and raised before 1995. To adjust to the changes in store will require leaders of the highest caliber who have the education and skills to manage and utilize vast amounts of electronically stored and processed information. Most of all, it will require leaders who can anticipate and prepare for change.

Predictions of future changes are usually made for four different time periods. The first of these is five years into the future, a time frame in which community government is relatively fixed, because the trends that affect the next five years are already known and occurring. A second time frame, eight to twelve years into the future, is more difficult to predict, but the opportunity to affect this period is much greater. Major community projects—such as utility-line extensions, public buildings, and parks—can be planned, constructed, and put into use within this time frame. A third time frame is the more distant future, twelve to twenty-five years from the present. It is even harder to predict, but long-range plans may still be made. Finally, because some municipal facilities—such as public buildings, streets, and utility lines—heavily influence private development and land use and have an estimated life of forty years or more, thought must also be given to the future beyond the twenty-five-year limit. This period is extremely hard to predict, but it is nonetheless affected by present-day decisions. Planning is discussed in Chapter 4.

The forces of change

Each of these time periods will be affected by forces that are already in place. Future changes can be predicted by studying the consequences of changes that have already occurred, and strategies for shaping the future must be based on these anticipated changes.

Six kinds of on-going change seem particularly applicable to community governments: economic change, demographic change, change in urban population patterns, technological change, political change, and ideological change.[3] Details on likely changes are summarized in the accompanying sidebar. The challenge of leadership is not to prevent such changes, but to develop strategies to minimize their negative consequences and maximize their potential benefits.

Categories of change

Economic change
Resource scarcities
Slower economic growth
Slower government growth
Crisis in worker skills
Economic globalization

Demographic change
More retired persons
Fewer school children
More Hispanic citizens
Smaller households
Less stable households
Independence of women
AIDS crisis

Urban change
Population shifts to South and West
Population movement from metro to rural regions
Slower rate of suburban sprawl
Decline in importance of central city
Rise in importance of smaller communities

Technological change
Communication changes
Computers
High technology
Artificial intelligence

Political change
Increased service demand
Taxpayer resistance
Official accountability
More emphasis on ethics
Stronger executives
More minority voters

Ideological change
Increased conservatism
Increased citizen distrust of government
Loss of citizen confidence in government
Quality of life concerns displace emphasis on community growth

Economic change

The nation's rate of economic growth is expected to diminish as resources become more scarce and the federal government takes action to cut defense spending and eradicate the budget deficit. These changes will ultimately produce a healthier national economy, but the short-term impact on government spending and services and on the growth of tax revenues that accompanies economic growth may be severe. During the early 1990s, the short-term outlook was for an era of increased government austerity and retrenchment. Chapter 5 discusses economic development strategies.

A fundamental reality of the 1990s and beyond is the globalization of the world economy. Increasingly, major industries manufacture products on a global scale, locating industrial facilities wherever they can take maximum advantage of favorable economic conditions to obtain raw materials, employ labor and industrial technologies at the lowest cost, and ship products efficiently to a world market. They move capital and jobs from place to place solely on the basis of economic competitiveness.

As the ICMA FutureVisions Consortium has noted, such trends

will have an enormous impact on local governments. . . . Agile local governments that sense trends can reap significant benefits for citizens and businesses of the community, but 'business-as-usual' communities are likely to find themselves losers in the high-stakes game of economic resources.[4]

Demographic changes

Important changes are occurring in the population of the United States. The most significant is the change in age: the number of people aged sixty-five and over will increase by ten million between 1970 and 2000, while the school-age population, people under nineteen years of age, will drop from 38 percent to 30 percent of the U.S. population. For communities, this shift has many implications, not the least of which is a change in emphasis from schools to community facilities for elderly residents. Observers have already noted that organized older citizens are quickly overtaking local interest groups such as the PTA in exerting effective pressure on local governments.

A local government's ability to tap the potential of an increasingly diverse labor pool will determine its operating success.

Increasingly, a local government's ability to tap the potential of, and manage, an increasingly diverse labor pool will determine its operating success. Blacks, Hispanics, and Asians will account for the greatest percentage of growth in the nation's labor force, and the Hispanic population will increase steadily and become the largest minority group in the nation. The dramatic increase in the participation of women in the workforce will continue, with its accompanying demands for changes in work patterns, improved day care, and more sensitivity to family obligations. Governments that develop the managerial sensitivity to work effectively with the variety of people in these growing labor pools will find an improved supply of potential workers. Governments that respond to the growing diversity of their citizenry will also enjoy improved community relations. Different groups have different values, different expectations regarding the role of government, and different needs for public services. The ability to respond appropriately to these differences can build citizen support for community government.

The ongoing atomization of American life—the pattern of smaller and less-stable households—will make itself felt in increased crime, drug addiction, antisocial behavior, and personal insecurity. These problems will have profound consequences for communities, including demands for more community mental health services, more services for troubled families, shelters for battered women and abused children, crisis counseling programs, and food and shelter for the homeless.

Finally, the AIDS crisis will begin to affect communities in ways not yet understood. More than 1 percent of the American population is now estimated to be infected with HIV, and approximately 95 percent of these people will eventually develop AIDS and die from it. AIDS is currently the tenth leading cause of death in the United States. Worse, the incidence of AIDS is increasing: the number of cases diagnosed in the United States in 1990 was 700 percent higher than in 1985. The rapid spread of the disease will disrupt society, require more treatment systems and facilities, and affect the workforce. Already, experts claim that many more local government employees than imagined suffer from the disease.[5]

Although these demographic trends bring added problems and challenges, they also appear in some cases to add strength to the local sense of community. Throughout the nation, agencies that depend on volunteers report that people are becoming more willing to get involved through voluntary action to help those in need.

The 1970s also saw migration from urban to rural areas, a trend that could re-emerge in the 1990s.

Changes in urban population patterns

Multiple population shifts have been under way in the last decades of the twentieth century, affecting local governments in both urban and rural areas. People have been moving from the older Northeastern and Midwestern metropolitan areas toward the South, Southwest, and West, and they have been migrating from the central cities to suburban neighborhoods. New concentrations of population have arisen along transportation corridors and around subregional commercial and industrial centers, increasing the need for urban services in rural areas. The 1970s also saw migration from urban to rural areas, a trend that could re-emerge in the 1990s. Central cities still serve as the center of activities for larger areas, and efforts to rebuild their infrastructures and develop new community facilities will continue. These cities will continue to be the residence primarily of unemployed, poor, and elderly citizens, but efforts to rebuild them do attract a small but steady number of affluent people with small households and few children.

Small and medium-sized communities, especially those along transportation corridors in rural areas, are likely to play a more important role in American life. All will experience substantial changes; some will confront sharp pressures for growth while others decline.

Technological changes

Changing technology will alter service delivery demands and techniques, offering many new tools for improving local government administration. Good government will be government that uses state-of-the-art microprocessing technology: data banks for storing information; information processing systems and simulation techniques to aid and improve decision making; and telecommunications systems that improve communication with citizens and within and between governments themselves.

Computerized communication

To facilitate communication between city hall and council members, Englewood, Colorado (30,000), installed computers in the homes of the city manager and the seven city council members. With the computers and word processing software on a network, the council members can work and communicate with each other around the clock. The system has made communication faster and more efficient and allows council members to work during hours most convenient to them.

Source: *The Guide to Management Improvement Projects in Local Government,* vol. 16, no. 2 (Washington, DC: ICMA, 1992), no. CCR-9.

To get the full benefit of new technologies, governments will have to invest in training to build employee competence in applying them. The workforce of the future must be far more educated and sophisticated than the present workforce. Some futurists have predicted that by the year 2010 virtually every job in the nation will require some skill with information-processing technology.

Because of these changes, governments must upgrade the priority given to funding for training. It can no longer be one of the first items to be cut from strained budgets; continuous staff training will increasingly make the difference between government effectiveness and ineffectiveness.

Political changes

As the baby boomer generation has moved into mid-life and taken control of elective offices, its members have found disillusionment and frustration. Raised on the notion that they could make a difference in public policy (consider, for example, the impact of their demonstrations on the war in Vietnam and on the civil rights movement), they have come to local elective office intent on making a difference, only to experience a feeling of powerlessness. Four trends have contributed to that feeling among local government officials:

1. Pervasive intervention of the federal government in services and activities that once were solely the responsibility of the local governments. The federal government mandates local governments to take certain actions, but provides no dollars to help finance such actions. As a result, local officials, faced with unfunded mandates, must raise taxes or cut spending on other programs. From the view of local officials, the federal government gets credit for addressing a problem, but they get the blame for the fiscal consequences.

Figure 1–4 On October 27, 1993, many local government officials joined in National Unfunded Mandates Day to protest federal mandates. Here, mayors from SMAC (Suburban Mayors Action Coalition) in Cook County, Illinois, attend a press conference.

2. Increasing involvement of the courts as the final arbiter in thousands of decisions that once were thought to be entirely legislative.
3. Interference by state legislatures in local matters through the passage of mandates, requiring specific kinds of programs and actions by local officials. In some states, the cost of meeting state legislative mandates consumes over 60 percent of local tax dollars.
4. "Whipsaw" of public opinion, caused by powerful but contradictory forces. The public demands both more services and tax cuts. Failure to deliver both simultaneously too often leads to public perception that government officials are inept.

Many observers wrongly believe that the level of federal government intervention is diminishing. For verification, they point to the loss of federal revenue sharing and declining federal financial assistance to local governments. However, as Figure 1–5 demonstrates, the loss of revenue-sharing dollars represented only a temporary cutback in federal aid levels; by the early 1990s such aid was again showing a continuing increase in both real and constant dollars. Furthermore, with cutbacks in defense spending, the prospect for still higher levels of federal aid appeared promising. Yet, an increase in aggregate aid levels for all local governments does not mean that such aid is increasing for each local government. Changes in aid patterns have caused many local governments to experience a net loss in federal aid in both real and constant dollars.

Another trend deserves note. Evidence is mounting that voters are becoming increasingly disillusioned with Congress. Such disillusionment in the past has led to a stronger presidency and stronger executive offices in state and local government as well. Whether or not this happens, there is evidence that the office of mayor and county board president is growing in stature and influence.[6]

Figure 1–5 Federal grants in aid to state and local governments, 1970–1993.

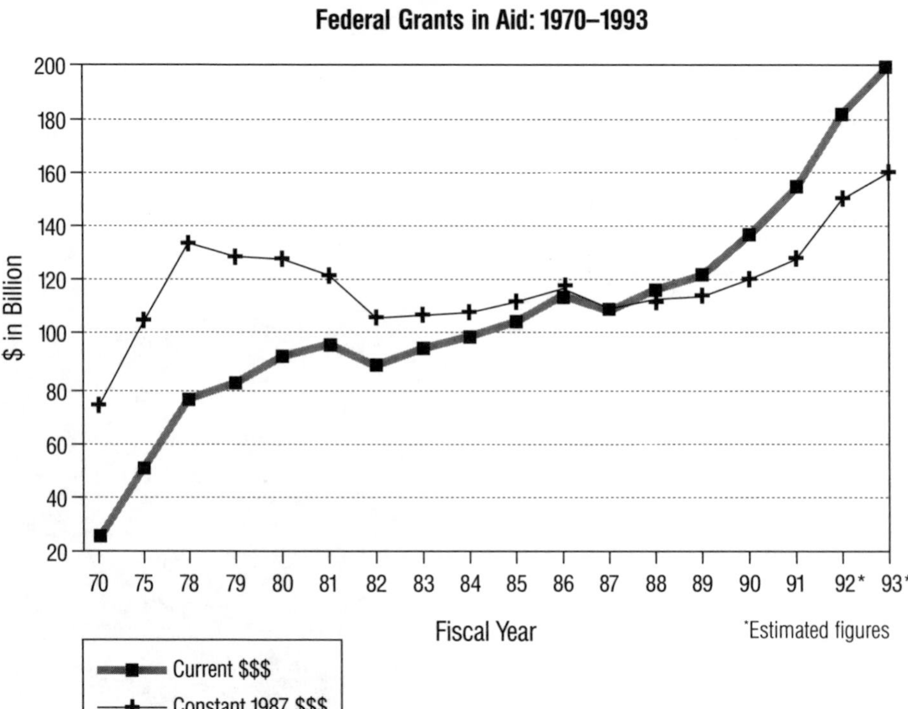

Ideological changes

There have been a number of indications that the United States became more conservative during the 1970s and 1980s. The election victories of Jimmy Carter, Ronald Reagan, and George Bush, all of whom ran on conservative platforms, attest to the trend. In 1992, none of the leaders of the Democratic party's liberal wing even ventured a campaign for the party's nomination. Conservatism was also reflected in the increasing resistance of local taxpayers to referendums calling for tax, borrowing, and spending increases. Candidates for executive and legislative office at all levels routinely predicated their campaigns on pledges of no tax increases.

Voters not only became more conservative, but increasingly distrustful of government. Vietnam, Watergate, and numerous smaller crises have left their mark on the American political scene. One consequence has been greater voter concern with the ethics of public officials. The public questioning of the personal integrity of presidential nominees Gary Hart and Bill Clinton and Supreme Court nominee Clarence Thomas reflected a growing concern with official behavior, which has extended to the behavior of local officials as well.

Strategies for coping with change

Many suggestions have been advanced to help local governments cope with change. They have in common the notion that government cannot just react to change, but that it must become proactive in developing and implementing new strategies, indeed new concepts in governing, if the public is to be served adequately in the future.

Reinventing government

Public attention has been focused in recent years on strategies recommended for "reinventing government." The concept was first popularized by authors David Osborne and Ted Gaebler in their best-selling book of that name;[7] it was quickly adopted by President Bill Clinton as the theme for his administration's efforts, led by Vice-President Al Gore, to modernize and streamline the federal government.[8] Borrowed from the activities of forward-looking community governments, the concept underlying these efforts has been the notion that government should change its approach to problem solving from a preoccupation with methods to an emphasis upon accomplishment, and from a focus upon service delivery to a role as catalytic agent to enlist community members and the private sector in the effort to create better communities. As Peter Drucker has argued, communities need "a government that is strong because it confines itself to decision and direction and leaves the 'doing' to others. . . This is not a government that 'does'; it is not a government that 'administers'; it is a government that governs."[9]

The doctrine of reinventing government offers much that is worthy of consideration by those who would change government for the better. Certainly government needs to become more concerned with results and less focused on methods. Government service agencies ought to operate at a level of efficiency and effectiveness competitive with private sector firms performing the same functions. Government operations must be customer-oriented and directed at problem prevention rather than just problem resolution. Government budgeting should focus on service accomplishment rather than cost inputs, and private sector resources and energies should be harnessed to public service whenever possible.

Rightsizing government

Corvallis, Oregon (44,757), used reinventing government models to compact services and move toward rightsizing government. Over five years, the city reduced its budget by 34 percent, increased salaries by 35 to 40 percent, and avoided corresponding diminution in services. The city saved over $1 million by increasing the use of volunteers by more than 50 percent and determined that compacting of services could reduce taxes by up to $1.50 per thousand dollars of assessed valuation without service cutbacks.

Source: Gerald Seals, City Manager, Corvallis, Oregon, 1992.

Local government's ability to "reinvent" itself is limited by its democratic obligation to be responsive to voter demands and to provide services equally to all.

Care must be taken, however, not to confuse the purpose of government with the purpose of private enterprise. The latter exists to produce a profit; government exists to serve the public in a manner that is both efficient and responsive. For government, responsiveness is not simply a matter of customer satisfaction; it also requires equity in service delivery for all constituents, regardless of income level, purchasing power, race, sex, or physical ability. Government must serve those who cannot afford its products with the same energy and quality as it serves those who can and will pay. Government is compelled to provide its employees with adequate retirement programs and health insurance coverage; the private sector excuse that such fringe benefits adversely affect its cost competitiveness cannot be accepted when government is the employer. Most government services exist because they cannot be provided profitably by private enterprise; taxation is the mechanism through which such services are subsidized.

Local government's ability to "reinvent" itself thus is limited by its democratic obligation to be responsive to changing voter demands and to provide services equally and equitably to all.

Building the essential community

Recognizing the need for local governments to develop strategies for coping with change and to plan for the future, ICMA formed its Committee on Future Horizons in the late 1970s. In the book entitled *The Essential Community: Local Government in the Year 2000,* the committee suggested that community governments in the years ahead must *nurture* their communities by (1) cutting operating costs; (2) more closely regulating services to achieve basic sufficiency, using the pricing mechanism where possible to help achieve that goal; (3) reducing their dependence on federal aid; (4) becoming more involved in lobbying federal and state legislatures to minimize the tendency of such bodies to impose new service obligations and expenditure requirements on community governments; and (5) altering their mix of services to better serve a population that is growing older, is more diverse in its cultural background, and has more single-parent families.[10]

Future visions

Ten years later, the ICMA FutureVisions Consortium continued the work of the Committee on Future Horizons. It identified the major changes that are having—and will continue to have—an impact on community governments, and it recommended strategies for dealing with them. These recommendations are summarized below.[11] (Where appropriate, references are provided to chapters in this book where more information about the topic is provided.)

The information revolution As more information flows more easily through the community and the local government organization, leaders must practice networking and power sharing and use them to facilitate better decision making. They should provide better processes for articulating community priorities; organize the community around its central issues; improve the government's communication skills; and play a greater civic education role in the community. (See Chapter 14.)

Rapid technological change Adjustment to technological changes will require personal readiness to welcome and embrace such change and to explore ways to apply it in everyday activities. It will also require a bias for action, creating a climate that encourages risk by those experimenting with the new technology, encouraging nontraditional and cross-sectoral relationships in using the technologies, and focusing on the simplifying virtues of the new methods. (See Chapters 5, 6, 9, 10, 11, and 13.)

The shift from representative to participatory democracy This will result from an unprecedented degree of citizen involvement in governing processes. Such citizen initiative will require new forums for citizen interaction, new opportunities for citizen involvement, and more effort to help elected officials in their efforts to achieve community consensus. (See Chapter 14.)

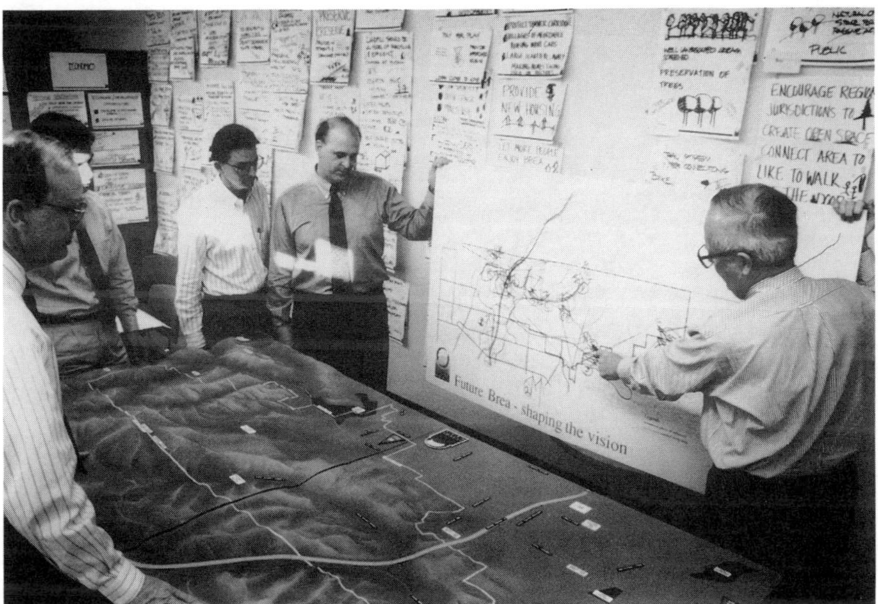

Figure 1–6 The city of Brea, California, initiated a process called Shaping the Vision to reach community consensus on citizens' hopes for the future of an unincorporated land area of 7.4 square miles.

Regional problem solving Increasingly, local governments face problems that cannot be addressed by single jurisdictions. Local communities are advised to create new regional solutions, not new government entities, to address common issues; to identify methods for regional tax sharing and service delivery; to foster economic development through regional cooperation in order to compete successfully in the international marketplace; and to organize around issues to bring the greatest local expertise to bear on problem solving. (See Chapter 15.)

Consensus on community goals Increased citizen involvement and special interest politics will make consensus building more difficult—and more essential. Recommended strategies include anticipating problems and seeking input from diverse community groups; identifying strategies to offset the negative consequences of certain services and activities (for example, a neighborhood may agree to accept a solid waste disposal site if it receives royalties); and helping citizens better understand their service needs.

Changing demographics The increasing number of elderly people and an increasingly diverse population will require local governments to rethink and redesign service programs and priorities. Other strategies include making better use of elderly citizens as a labor resource, promoting better education within the community, and anticipating immigration trends so that the community can respond positively to the diversity that immigration brings. (See Chapters 7, 8.)

Education and training Because so many community problems can be traced to educational inadequacies, community governments will have to become more proactive in working with educational agencies to provide mid-life education and retraining opportunities, to develop improved programs for dealing with at-risk youth, and to promote the social service and mental health intervention needed to assist those, and especially those youth, with serious family problems. (See Chapter 8.)

Diversity and the workforce Communities and their governments must become more understanding of diversity and more ready to respond to its requirements, whether that diversity results from different cultural backgrounds or new and emerging life-styles. Strategies to cope with this trend include the development of innovative work alternatives (Chapter 13); programs to celebrate the variety of cultures in the community; and development of greater sensitivity to cultural conventions, attitudes, and traditions.

Globalization and economic development Suggested strategies for responding to this trend include encouraging regional economic development efforts (Chapter 5), looking for more flexible sources of revenue to underwrite the cost of local services, and lobbying state governments to relax restrictions on local governments' ability to tax and enter into creative partnerships (Chapter 12).

Public and private sector relationship Strategies to utilize the private sector more effectively in service delivery and problem solving include forming new partnerships with the private and not-for-profit sectors in which the local government holds an equity interest and underwrites some of the risk in joint ventures; using innovative carrot/stick strategies in dealing with developers; increasing use of special assessments to fund special developments or services; and utilizing debt instruments to leverage private sector help in addressing infrastructure and technology issues. (See Chapters 4, 12, 15.)

The citizen as customer Economic constraints will require local governments to make difficult political decisions about levels of service. Rather than dictate what services a neighborhood will receive, community governments will need to involve citizens in the choice. This means that governments must offer service choices, through which individual neighborhoods can define their desired level and mix of services, create procedures for involving citizens in the choice, and develop incentives and disincentives that will help bring service demands into line with resources.

The environment Concern about environmental issues will continue, requiring community governments to direct growth in line with community concerns and examine service delivery systems with regard to their environmental impact. (See Chapters 4, 6, 7, 15.)

Health services Community governments will be forced to spend more time on health issues, both as employers and as providers of health services. This will require them both to encourage the development of local medical facilities and improve traditional health agency functions to take account of demands emanating from life-style changes. (See Chapter 8.)

Police services Increasing community pressures of all kinds will impose new burdens on police forces already hard pressed to cope with rising crime. Changes in police personnel and recruitment policies, training, technologies, and patrolling strategies will be required to meet these demands. (See Chapter 10.)

Leisure services Changing demographic and life-style patterns will require a more flexible leisure services system, sensitive to diverse needs. Some new facilities—such as ice rinks, golf courses, and zoos—can be developed on a regional basis. (See Chapter 7.)

Housing Changes in life-styles, income levels, and demographics will continue to require changes in styles, prices, and location of housing units. Responses will require adjustments in land use patterns, zoning codes, subdivision developments, and housing styles adapted to changing human needs. (See Chapters 4, 8.)

Infrastructure Community infrastructure continues to be linked to community development, economic growth, and community well-being. Deteriorating infrastructure and the decline of intergovernmental grants for infrastructure development and maintenance means that creative new strategies will be needed to finance infrastructure development. Creative financing, technological improvements, and capital planning will have to be blended into a long-term program to sustain infrastructure quality. (See Chapters 6, 12.)

These diverse strategies will not be effectively implemented with the management skills learned and developed in the past. The accompanying sidebar lists some of the important skills that will be essential for managers in the future.

Important skills and attributes for the local government manager

Consensus builder
Educator on community issues
Translator/interpreter of community values
Problem solver
Process leader
Convener of interested parties and diverse community groups

Team builder/mentor
Source of empowerment
Change agent
Champion of new technologies
Facilitator of conflict resolution
Bearer of ethical standards
Champion of leadership development within the community

Source: Amy Cohen Paul, *Future Challenges, Future Opportunities: The Final Report of the ICMA FutureVisions Consortium* (Washington, DC: ICMA, 1991).

Responsibility for coping with change

The future is everybody's business. The responsibility for anticipating the future, planning for it, and implementing strategies designed to cope with it is shared by elected officials, the chief administrative officer, department heads, and staff.

It is ultimately the responsibility of elected officials to see that the members of the management team work well together.

Elected officials

Elected officials have a special concern for the future. Because their primary function is to make the community a better place in which to live, it is their responsibility both to fashion the policies needed to cope with change and to set the tone for forward thinking—for assessing the impact of present decisions on the future—among citizen groups and government employees alike. Elected officials who are concerned only with the period of time until the next election—or who look only for the easiest possible solutions to problems—discourage government workers concerned with the future, depress attempts at long-range planning, and leave the community at the mercy of the forces of change.

Elected officials also have two specific responsibilities with respect to change. The first is to see that the administrative staff has the professional training, motivation, desire, and opportunity to anticipate and prepare for change. The second is to work cooperatively with each other and with the administrative staff to address planning issues. It is ultimately the responsibility of elected officials to see that the members of the management team work well together.

Chief administrative officer

The chief administrative officer also has a primary responsibility for the future:

> *In the decades ahead, building and managing flexible and responsive local governments—organizations that anticipate and react effectively to changing conditions—will be a principal challenge facing local government managers. Indeed, the ability to identify, articulate, and interpret the implications of change for the local environment may become a defining competency of the local government management profession.*[12]

To implement the strategies for dealing with change identified by the FutureVisions Consortium and in the concept of "reinventing government," he or she will need to develop the skills and attributes listed in the sidebar on page 23.The chief administrative officer must also (1) set an example for both elected officials and senior administrative staff through his or her concern for the future; (2) see that information is compiled about the effects of change on the community and about the probable future effects of proposed policy changes on service programs and the quality of community life; (3) ensure effective communication among elected officials, department heads, and the public regarding the potential impact of present and proposed policies on the future of the community; and (4) be aware of technological developments of potential importance to the community and search for ways to use these developments to improve public services and lower their costs.

Department heads

Department heads are the people with principal responsibility for the delivery of services. Presumably, they are experts in their respective fields, whether the field is law enforcement, public works, park management, human services, personnel management, or another area of specialization. It is the department heads' job to understand the impact of change on their respective areas and on the services they deliver. Further, they must serve as expert advisers to political leaders, the chief administrator, and the public regarding the impact of change on the services for which they are responsible.

Summary
From the community's perspective, the responsibility for coping with change is best met when each official fulfills his or her assigned role. For the elected official, this means staying in touch with community values, aspirations, and preferences. For the administrative official, this means keeping abreast of information regarding the forces of change and the effect of those forces on his or her area of responsibility and developing the knowledge and experience needed to deal with change. In short, for the administrative official, this means continuous effort to obtain and sustain the highest level of professional expertise.

Surveying the silent majority
Realizing that not all citizens have the time to attend council meetings to voice their opinion on community issues, the West Linn, Oregon (16,000), city council decided to conduct periodic surveys to capture the opinions of the silent majority. The council hired a firm to design the survey questions, analyze the results, and train volunteers to make the survey via phone calls. The volunteers survey three hundred to five hundred residents every six to eight weeks. Results are provided to city officials and published in the city newspaper.

Source: *The Guide to Management Improvement Projects in Local Government,* vol. 15, no. 2 (Washington, DC: ICMA, 1991), no. CCR-10.

The professionalization of community leadership

More than ever, good business management requires hiring the most highly qualified people to fill job vacancies. Today, this is as true for government as it is for business, particularly when it comes to filling vacancies in department directorships and senior supervisory positions.

The tradition of restricting job applications to residents of the community or filling all supervisory positions by promotion from within the organization is no longer considered good practice; it may be illegal (a violation of affirmative action) as well as a violation of sound business procedures. The office of police chief should no longer be considered a reward for long and meritorious service in the department.

Instead, the trend in filling management positions is to search for professionals. Professionalism does not mean long employment in the department. Instead, it means recruiting someone, from inside or outside the organization, who has the best record in terms of specialized educational preparation, frequently at the college or university level; related work experience; active membership in public sector professional organizations; and commitment to continuing professional education.

The trend toward professionalism in local government

The emphasis on professionalism started with city managers, but today it embraces many community government employees, including administrative assistants, planners, department heads, departmental staff members, and operating officials such as engineers, health officials, social workers, police officers, firefighters, code-enforcement officers, and recreation directors. Personnel management is discussed in Chapter 13.

The speed with which the trend toward professionalism has accelerated is startling. The number of professional city/county administrators with a master's degree may be as high as 70 percent;[13] two-thirds of all public works directors have a college degree, and nearly 20 percent have a master's degree; the number of college-educated police officers is growing rapidly, and some communities require a college degree of all police recruits. The master of public administration (MPA) degree is, by a large margin, the professional credential most often sought and offered by professionals in local government administrative and service occupations.

Professional associations

Local governments have always been served by a sizable number of professional associations committed to the improvement of local government services and the professional development of local government employees. These include national organizations, such as those listed in Figure 1–7, as well as state municipal leagues and state-level organizations serving county and township officials. Local governments in Canada are served by the Canadian Association of Municipal Administrators and by the Federation of Canadian Municipalities.

Figure 1–7 Professional organizations serving local governments: a selected list. These and several other organizations are shown each year in *The Municipal Year Book*, published by the International City/County Management Association, with information on programs and services of each organization.

American Library Association
American Planning Association
American Public Health Association
American Public Welfare Association
American Society for Public Administration
American Water Works Association
Building Officials and Code Administrators International
Canadian Association of Municipal Administrators
Federation of Canadian Municipalities
International Association of Assessing Officers
International Association of Chiefs of Police
International Association of Fire Chiefs
International City/County Management Association
International Conference of Building Officials
International Personnel Management Association
National Association of Counties
National Association of Housing and Redevelopment Officials
National Association of Towns and Townships
National Civil Service League
National Council for Urban Economic Development
National Institute of Governmental Purchasing
National Institute of Municipal Law Officers
National League of Cities
National Municipal League
National Recreation and Park Association
Public Technology, Inc.
U.S. Conference of Mayors

Such organizations place primary emphasis upon improvements in the delivery of professional services. They also stress official responsibility and accountability, employee professionalism, and personal responsiveness to citizen needs and concerns. Because such organizations are continually searching for better, more efficient ways of delivering local services, community government workers who are active members become the means by which new ideas are put into practice at the city, county, village, and town level.

Afterword

It is very clear that community governments cannot function in the future as they have functioned in the past. The tried and trusted formula for community problem solving ("How did we resolve this problem the last time?") is now obsolete. The old methods simply will not work. The world today is too different and changing too fast to justify reliance on the old ways.

This does not mean, however, that change is always good, or even that new ways are necessarily better than old ways. The old adage that says "Those who do not study history are bound to repeat the mistakes of the past" is still very valid. The challenge for community leaders, elected and appointed, is to link the past with the future and to avoid the mistakes of the past by determining which old ways have continuing utility and combining them with new ideas and modern technologies in the search for more effective ways of meeting today's and tomorrow's challenges.

It is in this linking process that really good professional administrators can make a unique contribution. It is a part of the job of such professionals to be familiar with past and present practices in other communities, to know which problem-solving strategies are working and which are failing elsewhere. That professional knowledge, combined with elected officials' insights into what will and will not work locally, provides the core of what can be an unbeatable local leadership team. With such a team, a local community puts itself in the best possible position to meet the growing challenge of providing community government. ■

---

1 The survey asked participants which level of government they felt gave them the least for their money. Forty-one percent mentioned the federal government; 26 percent named the state government; only 21 percent pointed to local governments. See *Urban Outlook*, vol. 12, no. 21 (New York: Alexander Research and Communications, 1990), 6.

2 U.S. Advisory Commission on Intergovernmental Relations, *Significant Features of Fiscal Federalism*, vol. 2 (October 1991), 82.

3 The discussion that follows is updated and adapted from Laurence Rutter, *The Essential Community: Local Government in the Year 2000* (Washington, DC: ICMA, 1980). Substantial reliance was also placed on Amy Cohen Paul, ed., *Managing for Tomorrow: Global Changes and Local Futures* (Washington, DC: ICMA, 1990).

4 James R. Griesemer, "Introduction," in *Future Challenges, Future Opportunities: The Final Report of the ICMA FutureVisions Consortium* (Washington, DC: ICMA, 1991), 2.

5 James D. Slack, *AIDS and the Public Work Force: Local Government Preparedness in Managing the Epidemic* (Tuscaloosa: University of Alabama Press, 1991).

6 See, for example, George Frederickson, ed., *Ideal and Practice in Council-Manager Government* (Washington, DC: ICMA, 1989).

7 David Osborne and Ted Gaebler, *Reinventing Government* (New York: Addison-Wesley, 1992).

8 David Rapp, "Federalism Reinvented: The White House Has City Hall to Thank for Much of Its Plan for Streamlining Government," *Governing* 7 (November 1993): 76.

9 Peter F. Drucker, *The Age of Discontinuity* (New York: Harper Torchbooks, 1978), 241-242.

10 See Rutter, *The Essential Community*.

11 Amy Cohen Paul, *Future Challenges, Future Opportunities: The Final Report of the ICMA FutureVisions Consortium* (Washington, DC: ICMA, 1991).

12 Griesemer, *Future Challenges, Future Opportunities*, 1.

13 David N. Ammons and Charldean Newell discovered that 69.3 percent of the managers studied had a master's degree. See their study, *City Executives* (Albany: State University of New York Press, 1989), Table A-12.

2 The Legal Aspects of Community Government

For every power they exercise and for every service they provide—for their very existence—cities, counties, villages, and towns are dependent on law. Such fundamentals as their form of government, minimum standards for the services they provide, and the liability that may result from the unauthorized or improper exercise of their official powers are all prescribed in, and limited by, law. The purpose of this chapter is to describe and discuss major aspects of state and federal laws that govern the functions and activities of community governments.[1]

Sources and limits of authority

The United States Constitution makes no reference to cities, counties, villages, or towns. Community governments are creatures of the state in which they are located, and their authority is derived entirely from state law. Their powers may be enlarged, abridged, or completely withdrawn by the state legislature, except where home-rule provisions in state constitutions vest them with local sovereignty independent of the legislature. The degree of powers possessed by community governments is further defined by state courts.

In most states, courts ordinarily adhere to the so-called Dillon's Rule when construing the powers of community governments. The rule states that these governments can exercise the following powers and no others:

> *First, those granted in express words; second, those necessarily or fairly implied in, or incident to, the powers expressly granted; third, those essential to the accomplishment of the declared objects and purposes of the . . . [community government] . . . not simply convenient, but indispensable.*[2]

Under the rule, any fair, reasonable, or substantial doubt concerning the legitimacy of a power is resolved by the courts against the government and the power is denied. Therefore, a community government cannot perform any act, make any contract, or incur any obligation not authorized by law. Acts beyond the scope of the powers granted are illegal and void.

Municipalities, created to meet the needs of closely settled areas, and counties, established with arbitrary boundaries as arms of the state government, generally derive their powers from three levels of state law. Those are the state constitution, state statutes, and local laws enacted for individual communities.

Most cities and a few counties function under charters, which may or may not be local laws of the legislature. In some states, such charters are approved by the legislature; in others, local voters approve the charter for a particular community government. Charters usually prescribe the form of government under which the municipality or county is organized and its powers and responsibilities. As a 1993 handbook for mayors and council members in Georgia states:

The primary purpose of a municipal charter is to bring a municipal corporation into existence and to grant it specific powers of local government. (A basic power granted to Georgia cities is the police power—the power to protect the health, safety, and welfare of the public.) The charter also provides the municipal corporation with a governing body to exercise its powers and with a form of administrative organization. As the fundamental law of the municipality, the charter is comparable to a constitution at the state or federal level of government.[3]

There are a number of different charters: special- and general-act charters, classified general-act charters, optional general-act charters, and home-rule charters, with the degree of local control increasing in roughly the order listed. Special-act charters are those granted by the legislature to specifically named local governments, while the general-act charter establishes uniform powers and the same form of government for all cities or counties in a state. Classified general-act charters classify local governments, often by population, and grant those within each class certain powers and a specific structure. Optional general-act charters permit a local government to select and operate under one of several plans provided by general law.

In other cases, community governments are organized in accordance with the form of government and the powers specified in a general state statute. All states also use statutes to grant and deny powers to community governments. Sometimes a state statute and a charter provision will conflict on a particular subject. Which one prevails, or whether they can be reconciled in a given situation, generally depends on the extent of autonomy given local governments by state law and the way state courts interpret the law.

The scope of local government powers

Non-home-rule governments The governments can exercise the powers expressly given to them by state law, or powers necessarily related thereto, but no others.

Home-rule charter governments These governments can exercise the powers expressly given to them by their own locally adopted charter, or powers necessarily related thereto, but no others.

Home-rule grant governments These governments can exercise any power of local government except those expressly denied to them by state law.

The National Municipal League, the National League of Cities, and the Advisory Commission on Intergovernmental Relations have all recommended the home-rule grant form of definition for local government powers. To date at least fifteen states have used this scheme, with Illinois' system generally considered to be the most liberal and successful.

Most states now provide home rule as an optional method for organizing and empowering municipal governments, and an increasing number of states extend the home-rule option to counties as well. Under the provisions of home rule, communities are usually given the authority to draft, adopt, and amend their own charters or governmental structures and to exercise local government powers within the limits (which are usually much broader for home-rule governments) imposed by the constitution and general laws of the state. The essence of home rule is recognition of local authority to act without prior specific legislative authorization; that authority is reinforced by the limitation of state power to enact laws regarding matters falling within the home-rule grant. Although home-rule cities and counties ordinarily possess more authority over local affairs than do non-home-rule governments, they are still subject to considerable state control. How much freedom they have is determined largely by the legislature and state courts. Under home-rule charters, communities can exercise the powers expressly given to them by their charter, or powers necessarily related thereto, but no others. In a few states, home rule is provided not through charters, but through general state grants under which the municipality or county can exercise any power of local government not specifically denied to it by general state law.

Forms of government

Several basic forms of community government are found in the United States. For cities and villages, these are the mayor-council, council-manager, and commission forms. In New England, however, town meeting and representative town meeting governments generally are found. Counties operate under the commission (or board), commission-administrator, or commission-county executive form of government.

City and village government

Under the mayor-council form of government, there is ordinarily a legislative body called a city council and a separately elected chief executive known as the mayor. Depending on the amount of administrative

Figure 2–1 Section of the charter for the city of Philomath, Oregon (2,000).

PREAMBLE

WE, THE PEOPLE OF THE CITY OF PHILOMATH, BENTON COUNTY, OREGON, in order to avail ourselves of self-determination in municipal affairs to the fullest extent now or hereafter granted or allowed by the constitutions and laws of the United States and the state of Oregon, by this charter confer upon the city the following powers, subject it to the following restrictions, prescribe for it the following procedures and governmental structure, and repeal all charter provisions of the city enacted prior to the time this charter takes effect.

BE IT ENACTED BY THE PEOPLE OF THE CITY OF PHILOMATH, BENTON COUNTY, OREGON:

Chapter I NAMES AND BOUNDARIES

Section 1.1 Title of Enactment. This enactment may be referred to as the Philomath Charter of 1986.

Section 1.2 Name of City. The municipality of Philomath, Benton County, Oregon, shall continue to be a municipal corporation with the name "City of Philomath."

Section 1.3 Boundaries. The city shall include all territory encompassed by its boundaries as they now exist or hereafter are modified pursuant to law. The city recorder shall keep an accurate, up-to-date description of the boundaries. The copies and descriptions shall be available for public inspection during regular office hours.

Chapter II POWERS

Section 2.1 Powers of the City. The city shall have all powers that the constitutions, statutes, and common law of the United States and of this state expressly or impliedly grant or allow municipalities, as fully as though this charter specifically enumerated each of those powers.

Section 2.2 Construction of Powers. In this charter, no mention of a particular power shall be construed to be exclusive or to restrict the scope of the powers which the city would have if the particular power were not mentioned. The charter shall be liberally construed to the end that the city may have all powers necessary or convenient for the conduct of its municipal affairs, including all powers that cities may assume pursuant to state laws and to the municipal home rule provisions of the state constitution.

power granted the mayor, this form is called either a "strong-mayor" or "weak-mayor" plan. The strong mayor has the authority to prepare—and control the administration of—the budget, appoint and remove a number of department heads, and direct the activities of city departments. The mayor may also have the power to appoint a chief administrative officer to assist in managing the local government. In contrast, the weak-mayor form is characterized by fragmented authority. The mayor has limited powers of appointment: a number of principal offices are filled by direct election or by the council. In addition, the mayor lacks the authority to develop the budget and has little or no administrative control over operations. Although it is difficult to draw a distinct line between the strong- and weak-mayor plans, the latter continues to be more commonly used.

The council-manager form is being adopted by an increasing number of communities and is now used by a majority of cities and villages with populations of 10,000 or more.

Mayor-council government is still found in most American municipalities, but the council-manager form is being adopted by an increasing number of communities and is now used by a majority of cities and villages with populations of 10,000 or more people. Council-manager government vests the policymaking authority in the elected council and the administration of the community in a professional manager who is appointed and removed by the council. The council, which is usually small, not only serves as the legislative body, but also provides political leadership. The mayor is directly elected in most council-manager communities. However chosen, the mayor's formal powers are usually restricted to presiding over council meetings and making appointments to boards and commissions. As part of the council, the mayor usually votes as a regular member and ordinarily has either limited veto power or none at all. In many council-manager communities, the mayor's role as a political leader is expanding.

Municipalities with the commission form of government elect commissioners to serve collectively as the policymaking body and individually as the heads of various administrative departments (e.g., public works and public safety). This form has declined in use over the years, and today it is found in only a few communities.

Prevalent in, and almost exclusive to, the New England states are the town meeting and representative town meeting forms of government. Under the town meeting system, all qualified municipal electors meet at least once a year to establish town policy and choose selectmen to carry out policy. With representative town meeting government, the voters select citizens to represent them at meetings. All citizens are permitted to participate in the meetings, but only the representatives can vote. Professional managers are sometimes chosen to supervise the town's operating departments.

County government

The majority of counties function with the traditional board or commission form of government, which has a central governing body ordinarily called a board of commissioners or supervisors. As a rule, the board selects one of its members as presiding officer, whose additional authority is usually limited to presiding over commission meetings. Frequently, board members or committees oversee or head county departments responsible to the commission. No single administrator supervises county operations. Moreover, the commission shares administrative and policymaking responsibilities with a number of independently elected officials such as the sheriff, district attorney, county clerk, treasurer, tax collector, recorder, assessor, and coroner. In addition, state or county law may establish numerous independent boards and authorities (health, hospital, housing, park, and library) to administer various programs at the county level.

Increasing in use is the commission-administrator form of government. The administrator may be called a county manager, chief administrative officer, or administrative assistant, or may have some other title. The essential difference among these positions is the amount of power granted to the administrator. The county manager has most of the authority of a city manager, and is appointed and removed by the board of commissioners. The chief administrative officer has some but not all of the powers of a manager, and is usually appointed and removed in the same way. The administrative assistant is similar to the chief administrative officer, but ordinarily does not appoint or supervise heads of departments. The independently elected county officials and appointed boards found under the county commission form of government exist in varying numbers under the commission-administrator form.

Gaining greater support in recent years is the commission-county executive form. This form has legislative and executive branches; the chief executive is elected by the voters. The commission operates as the legislative body, much the same as the council in a strong-mayor city. The executive prepares the budget, appoints department heads, and administers county operations, often with the assistance of a professional appointed administrator. Often, there are fewer independently elected officers under this form than under the other two.

Metropolitan and regional government

Especially in metropolitan areas, the need for more equitable and efficient regional service delivery has generated various proposals for improvement, most of which require legal authority for implementation. Many factors have contributed to this need, including inadequate local services or duplication of services, unequal or dwindling tax bases, reduced federal assistance, and transportation and pollution problems.

Proposed solutions range from informal intergovernmental agreements to the formation of special districts and regional governments. They include formal service contracts between governments, grants of extraterritorial powers, and consolidation of services, functions, and even governments. As a general rule, if a community is authorized to provide a particular service to its citizens, it may contract with another local government to provide or be provided with that service. Strengthening and modernizing county government has also been advocated as a solution to metropolitan problems. Such actions would empower counties to provide urban services and to operate with more independence, as stated in the charter or enabling act. Counties would become more than an arm of state government. Modernization also envisions greater use of the commission-administrator and commission-county executive form of government, and more extensive cooperation with other local governments.

Special districts and independent authorities have often been created or authorized to deal with specific metropolitan problems. Ordinarily, these are independent, special-purpose units of government with their own governing bodies, taxing powers, and borrowing authority. They are typically established to provide such services as public utilities, transportation, environmental regulation, and public housing. Many observers feel that the proliferation of such districts further fragments regional government and accentuates regional service problems.

State and federal standards and mandates

Local governments receive their authority from the state, but increasingly the federal government also affects local government activity.

General state standards and mandates

The general laws of each state contain a number of statutes that set standards for, and govern aspects of, the operation and structure of community governments. Some subjects frequently covered by general law are optional forms of government, including the powers and duties of officials; incorporation, annexation, and consolidation procedures; land use control and growth management; local elections; merit and retirement systems; financial operations; and open meetings and records. Failure of a community government to comply with these laws invites problems and may nullify a local ordinance or action.

In the 1980s and early 1990s, state legislatures increasingly passed laws imposing service requirements on community governments. Such laws, called mandates, have been strongly criticized by local officials when the state does not—as is usually the case—provide funds to cover the cost of local compliance with the state's directives. State mandates are common in the areas of education, environmental protection, labor management, transportation, and housing.

Federal standards and mandates

Since the 1960s, Congress and the state legislatures have been imposing service requirements on local governments. Over the years, the types of community activities and practices coming under federal scrutiny have increased significantly. Congress has enacted a number of statutes per-

Figure 2–2 Sources and limits of local government power.

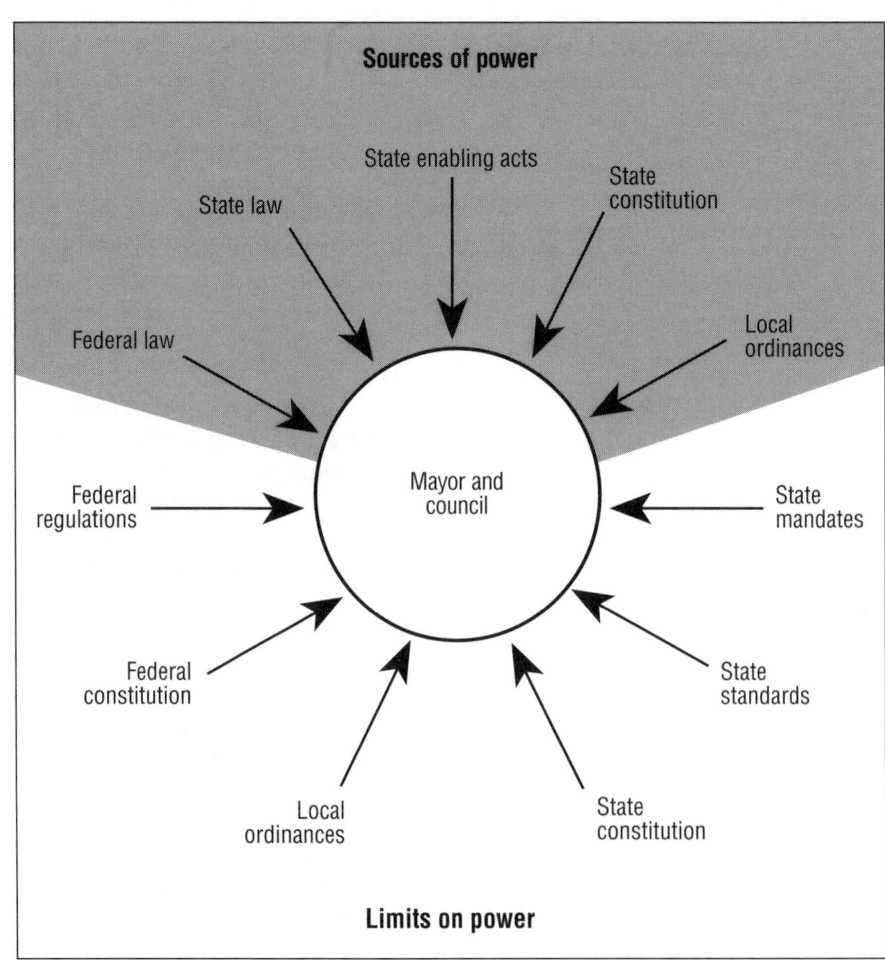

taining to such matters as personnel practices and environmental protection. Also, numerous federal lawsuits alleging the violation of various constitutional rights continue to be brought against community governments and their officials. Subjects on which federal decisions have been rendered include unequal or terminated public services, employee rights, law enforcement practices, jail conditions, obscenity, and zoning. It is therefore critically important that community officials be aware of relevant federal statutes and court rulings and recognize their potential application to proposed or existing community enactments, policies, and practices.

It is critical that community officials be aware of federal statutes and court rulings and recognize their application to community enactments, policies, and practices.

In the area of environmental protection, community water supply systems must meet the requirements of the federal Safe Drinking Water Act, which sets maximum levels for a number of chemical, radioactive, and biological contaminants. Community governments are also subject to the Federal Water Pollution Control Act and its amendments in the Clean Water Act, which require public sewage-treatment plants to have a permit under a national program to eliminate discharge of pollutants into the waterways. Solid waste disposal falls under the federal Solid Waste Disposal Act, amended as the Resource Conservation and Recovery Act in 1976 and 1984. Under that act, in 1984, Congress directed the U.S. Environmental Protection Agency to develop environmentally protective standards for sanitary landfills; these became final in 1991.

A number of federal statutes affect community personnel practices. Of major importance is the 1964 Civil Rights Act, which was amended by the Civil Rights Act of 1991. This act makes it unlawful, for all but the very small communities to which it does not apply, to discriminate against a person with regard to hiring; firing; compensation; or the terms, conditions, or privileges of employment because of the person's race, color, religion, sex, or national origin. It also is unlawful to limit, segregate, or classify employees or job applicants on the basis of race, color, religion, sex, or national origin in a way that deprives anyone of employment opportunities or otherwise adversely affects the status of an employee. With exceptions, the Fair Labor Standards Act establishes a minimum hourly wage for employees and provides for payment of a premium for overtime work. The Equal Pay Act prohibits, with exceptions, sex-based differentials in pay for the performance of jobs that require equal skill, effort, and responsibility, and that are performed under similar working conditions. The Age Discrimination in Employment Act provides that employers may not discharge, fail or refuse to hire, or otherwise discriminate against any individual with respect to compensation, terms, or conditions or privileges of employment because he or she is forty years of age or older.

Two federal acts deal with discrimination against disabled individuals. The Vocational Rehabilitation Act stipulates that an otherwise qualified person who has a disability cannot, solely because of the disability, be excluded from or discriminated against in any program receiving federal financial assistance. Most recently, Congress in 1990 enacted the Americans with Disabilities Act, which prohibits discrimination against qualified individuals with disabilities in virtually all aspects of employment. It also prohibits discrimination against disabled persons in the provision of public services and access to public facilities.

A federal act having a major and continuing influence on community functions and policies is the Civil Rights Act of 1871. Under this law, officials and employees themselves, as well as communities, can be held liable for constitutional violations arising from official actions or omissions. Two other important statutes affecting community government functions are the Sherman and Clayton Antitrust Acts. The courts have held that local governments and officials can be found liable for violating these acts unless communities are authorized by their state to engage in a noncompetitive activity.

Ordinances and resolutions

Within the limits set by state law, local legislative bodies (e.g., city councils, village boards, county commissions) may enact their own "legislation." This legislation is usually passed in the form of ordinances or resolutions. Ordinances and resolutions deal with such subjects as zoning, taxes, sale of alcoholic beverages, peddling, traffic control, solid waste, sewers, snow emergency policies, the budget, capital improvements, personnel, and departmental organization.

Generally, ordinances are viewed as establishing relatively permanent rules or laws for the community, whereas resolutions are not laws but ministerial acts of a special or temporary nature. However, when a community government is empowered to legislate and the authorizing law does not specify the mode of exercising the power, the enactment is ordinarily valid whether passed in the form of an ordinance or resolution. The valid enactment of ordinances or resolutions often requires adherence to specific procedures found in state laws or in ordinances that govern such matters as number of public readings, method of voting, majority necessary for passage, and public hearings. When procedures are dictated by state law, they may be considered mandatory by the courts, and failure to follow them can result in the invalidation of an ordinance or resolution. Unless it is required by law, which is rarely the case, ordinances and resolutions do not have to follow a prescribed form or to be codified. Nevertheless, a standard form and codification can result in more orderly, understandable, and accessible ordinances and resolutions and may reduce or prevent court challenges to them.

In many states, the initiative and the referendum are alternative ways to enact ordinances or laws. An initiative permits a specified number of voters to propose changes in ordinances or laws, which are then accepted or rejected by the electorate. A referendum permits voters to accept or reject proposals put forth by the local legislative body.

Contracts and franchise agreements

Communities have no power to contract or to incur any liability unless specifically authorized by state law to do so. A contract beyond the scope of a local government's power is void. Moreover, certain formalities may have to be observed or certain conditions met when entering into a contract. Examples are (1) that a contract be authorized by the passage of an ordinance; (2) that votes authorizing a contract be recorded; (3) that a contract be in writing; and (4) that a contract involving the expenditure of funds be preceded by an appropriation. If mandatory procedures are not followed or required conditions are not satisfied, a contract can be invalidated. However, a contract usually will not be declared void if mere technical formalities have not been followed, as in the failure of the mayor to sign an ordinance.

When a person makes an illegal or unauthorized contract with a community, the contract is invalid and not binding even if the person has completely performed his or her part of the contract. Such a contract cannot be ratified by the acceptance or use of its benefits by a local government. Thus, it is the responsibility of a person contracting with a community government to determine whether the latter has the authority to enter into the contract.

Figure 2–3 An ordinance of the city of Mesquite, Texas (101,484).

ORDINANCE NO. 2535

AN ORDINANCE OF THE CITY OF MESQUITE, TEXAS CREATING A NEW SECTION 10-8 OF CHAPTER 10 OF THE CITY CODE ENTITLED "CRUISING" AND PROHIBITING CRUISING IN CERTAIN DESIGNATED ZONES; PROVIDING FOR A PENALTY NOT TO EXCEED FIVE HUNDRED ($500.00) DOLLARS FOR EACH OFFENSE; PROVIDING FOR A SEVERANCE CLAUSE; AND DECLARING AN EMERGENCY:

WHEREAS, the City of Mesquite has a compelling interest in controlling traffic congestion, noise, and litter on public and private property; and

WHEREAS, a compelling interest has been demonstrated in controlling interference with the use and enjoyment of property by the citizens of Mesquite; and

WHEREAS, a compelling interest has been demonstrated in maintaining access to public thoroughfares by public safety vehicles;

NOW, THEREFORE, BE IT ORDAINED BY THE CITY COUNCIL OF THE CITY OF MESQUITE, TEXAS:

SECTION 1. That Chapter 10 of the City Code of the City of Mesquite is hereby amended by adding a new Section 10-8 ("Cruising") to read as follows:

Section 1. Definitions

(a) A "traffic control point" as used in this section means any point or points within no cruising zones established by the police department for the purpose of monitoring cruising.

(b) A designated "no cruising zone" as used in this ordinance means any and all streets, alleys, and other public property located within or partially within physical boundaries described by resolution of the City Council, including any streets, alleys and other public property describing the boundaries of the zone.

Section 2. Cruising Prohibited

(a) No person shall operate or permit a motor vehicle under his care, custody, or control to be operated so as to pass a traffic control point three (3) times within any two-hour period between the hours of 8:00 p.m. and 4:00 a.m., on any day of the week, within a designated no cruising zone.

(b) The City Manager shall erect signs giving notice of any no cruising zone and any regulations governing such zone shall not be effective unless such signs have been placed or erected.

(c) No violation shall occur except upon the third passage of a vehicle by the same traffic control point within the aforementioned two-hour period.

(d) No cruising zones shall be designated by resolution of the City Council.

(e) It shall be a defense under this section that the vehicle was being operated for business purposes at the time of the alleged violation. The burden shall be upon the person operating the vehicle or under whose care, custody, or control the vehicle is being operated to prove that the vehicle was being operated for business purposes at the time of the alleged violation.

SECTION 2. That should any paragraph, sentence, subdivision, clause, phrase, section or provision of this ordinance be adjudged or held to be unconstitutional, illegal, or invalid, the same shall not affect the validity of this ordinance as a whole or any part or provision hereof other than the part so decided to be unconstitutional, illegal, or invalid and shall not affect the validity of the remainder of Chapter 10, or any other provision of the Code of the City of Mesquite.

SECTION 3. That any person, firm, or corporation violating any of the provisions or terms of this ordinance shall be deemed to be guilty of a Class C Misdemeanor and upon conviction in the Municipal Court shall be punished by a fine not to exceed Five Hundred Dollars ($500.00) for each offense.

SECTION 4. The fact that the present ordinances of the City of Mesquite do not adequately protect the safety of the inhabitants of the City creates an urgency and emergency and the preservation of the public health, safety and welfare requires that this ordinance shall become effective immediately from and after its passage and the publication of caption.

DULY PASSED AND APPROVED by the City Council of the City of Mesquite, Texas on the 20th day of June, 1988.

George A. Venner, Sr.
Mayor

ATTEST:

Lynne Prugel
City Secretary

APPROVED:

Jonathan Graham
City Attorney

A community can, however, ratify and make binding an invalid contract made in its behalf. The contract must be one that was authorized and is invalid only because it was defectively or irregularly executed, or executed by an officer not empowered to bind the government. The ratification of an invalid contract is subject to the same formalities and conditions that pertain to other community government contracts; communities may not incidentally or casually ratify an invalid contract. Therefore, acts of ratification must clearly and directly exhibit a knowledge of the facts and the intent to accept the contract.

In a similar manner, a community government may find itself liable under an invalid contract. If a community government receives goods or services under a contract into which it could have entered, but which is invalid because of improper execution, the community government cannot deny its liability. It will be liable for at least the value of what it has received. However, a community government can deny liability if the acceptance of work or goods under an invalid contract was induced by fraud or deception.

Public works contracts

Accompanying the power to make public improvements is the authority to enter into public works contracts. Within constitutional limits, the state legislature may regulate the making of such contracts, and in most states statutory requirements and procedures have been enacted. Competitive bidding is one of the most common requirements, and usually community governments must advertise for sealed bids. State statutes cover such concerns as when and how long advertisements for bids must be published and what information bids must contain.

Usually, compliance with the requested bid form is mandatory, and a community may demand that each bidder pay a reasonable sum to cover the cost of the bid proposal form and the contract with its specifications. As a rule, bidders must submit a cash deposit or other security to guarantee their entry into the contract. This bond is forfeited by the winning bidder if he or she fails to enter into the contract. In addition, a contractor invariably is required to give bond for faithful performance of the contract and to indemnify the community government for damages caused by the contractor's failure to complete the project within the specified time. In many cases, other bonds are required, including those for the protection of subcontractors supplying labor, materials, and equipment.

A contract usually must be awarded to the lowest reliable bidder. However, a community ordinarily has the power to reject all bids and readvertise, abandon the project, or perform the work itself.

Franchises

Generally, a franchise is a special privilege, such as the exclusive authority to construct and operate a public utility, conferred by a government on an individual or corporation. Franchises are also granted by virtue of a government's control of streets, highways, or rights-of-way. For example, the government may collect a percentage of the revenue of a cable television or electric power company in return for permitting it to run cables or power lines above or below public roads and streets. The government may also exact a flat yearly fee from a taxicab company for using community streets. The power of communities to enter into franchise agreements is governed by local charter and state law; thus, community governments must turn to those sources for guidance regarding the extent of their authority and how it may be exercised.

Split-bidding

Cadillac, Michigan (10,100), uses a new bidding process to save money on large construction contracts. Large projects are divided into different bids. In one bid the contractor supplies both materials and installation; in the second, the contractor performs the installation only with materials obtained separately by the city in a third bid. This procedure may result in several benefits: the low installation contractor is matched with the low materials supplier; the city does not have to pay sales taxes on materials purchased; the contractor is not able to "pad" the labor bid or hide costs in the materials bid; and the contractor can save on insurance costs because the size of the contract is reduced. The city saved over $500,000 in the first three contracts on which this system was used.

Source: *The Guide to Management Improvement Projects in Local Government,* vol. 17, no. 1 (Washington, DC: ICMA, 1993), no. MGT-1.

Conflict of interest

Public officials may not use their office for private gain. Many states have passed statutes prohibiting such use, but even where no statutes exist, the courts invariably refuse to uphold public contracts that serve an official's self-interest. Violations can result in invalidation of the contract; return to the community of all profits received by the interested official; removal of the official from office; or criminal prosecution in states where such an act is a crime.

In addition to avoiding self-serving contracts, public officials must avoid situations in which their public actions may be affected by, or come into conflict with, their personal interests. If this is impossible, they should disqualify themselves from acting in those situations. A good example is the case of a council member who voted for a zoning variance requested by his employer. The court held that the official should have disqualified himself, and it also overturned the vote, even though there were enough other affirmative votes to approve the variance. Disqualifying personal interests must be immediate, definite, and demonstrable, but they need not be financial or direct. It makes no difference that there is only a potential conflict of interest and no dishonesty or loss of public funds involved, nor is it necessary for the official to benefit personally from the situation. Public officials would also be wise to avoid situations that, although legally permissible, appear to create a conflict of interest. For example, a council member who manages a hotel with facilities that sell alcoholic beverages should not participate in discussions or vote on measures dealing with the sale of alcohol.

Reprinted by permission of Johnny Hart and Creators Syndicate, Inc.

Liability of community officials and governments

Until the mid-1950s, local governments enjoyed broad immunity under state law from tort (civil) liability based on the actions of their officers and employees. By the mid-1980s, however, substantial erosion of this protection had occurred through legislative acts and court decisions that either completely abolished or restricted the doctrine of sovereign immunity, which protected governments from such lawsuits.

In most states, the test of whether the action of a local government or a public official can be the basis of a liability suit is whether the action is discretionary or ministerial. A discretionary (quasi-judicial) act is one that requires the use of personal judgment and involves the power to make decisions and choices. A ministerial act is generally understood to be one performed in a prescribed manner. Examples of discretionary acts that do not generally serve as a basis for governmental liability are decisions by a community to construct a road or bridge in a particular location or to provide police services. In contrast, ministerial acts that can result in liability include the improper construction of a road or bridge or employment of a clearly violent or mentally unstable person as a police officer.

Steps to reduce personal liability risk

1. Arrange for the purchase of public official liability insurance to cover all government employees, including elected officials. Be sure the policy covers exposure to civil rights suits.
2. Formulate all government administrative policies and procedures in writing; have them reviewed by legal counsel as to legality, including constitutionality; make copies easily available to all employees and officials. Be sure policies make adequate provision to protect the civil rights of government officers and employees as well as citizens doing business with the government.
3. Undertake immediate training of all officers and employees regarding the intention of established policies and procedures and the liability inherent in noncompliance or in actions that might be interpreted as violating the civil rights of another.
4. Establish a system for monitoring employees' familiarity and compliance with established policies and procedures.
5. Seek the advice of the government's legal counsel and other appropriate legal advisers when policies and procedures are adopted or revised and when administrative decisions are made in areas of potential risk. Any personnel decision that might adversely affect another person is an area of potential risk.
6. Increase the level of professionalism in the organization and be sure that administrative leaders are up-to-date in their understanding of areas of potential civil rights risk.
7. Increase the use of outside experts in the decision-making process who can provide guidance in keeping policies and procedures updated and in accord with changing professional legal mandates and requirements.

When public officials perform purely ministerial duties required by law, they can be made to pay damages caused by the improper performance of those duties when the injury is caused by mistake or neglect. On the other hand, when officers and employees perform discretionary acts within the scope of their authority, they are usually immune from personal liability to anyone injured by their erroneous acts or omissions unless the latter are done corruptly, maliciously, willfully, or oppressively. The courts have used the words *malicious* and *oppressive* in holding public officials liable for having a citizen's house torn down without notice, directing the filling in of a lot with full knowledge that the action would result in the flooding of another person's land, and revoking a building permit for the sole purpose of driving a competitor out of business.

Although the doctrine of sovereign immunity has been abolished or significantly restricted in all states, in the 1990s there probably is a higher level of protection from liability than there was in the 1980s.

The level of immunity is therefore generally higher for discretionary acts. It is important to note, however, that the distinction between discretionary and ministerial acts is not always discernible, and thus the question of immunity or liability is not clear-cut for the courts.

Even though the discretionary-ministerial test is used in determining liability in most states, courts in a few states continue to rely on the "function test." Under this test, if a community engages in a "governmental function," something—such as the operation of a court system or a public library—that can be performed only by a government, then ordinarily it will not be liable for claims based on its activities. However, if a community government engages in a "proprietary function," an activity that may be performed by a private entity and is more akin to a business enterprise—such as residential garbage collection or the operation of a parking garage—the community may be held liable to the same extent as would a private business. There are inherent difficulties in applying the function test, because aspects of some purely governmental functions can result in liability and a number of governmental functions are performed by private entities. Consequently, court rulings defining governmental and proprietary functions are not always consistent.

Although the doctrine of sovereign immunity has been abolished or significantly restricted in all the states, it is probably safe to say that in the 1990s there is a higher level of protection from liability for communities and their officers and employees than there was in the 1980s. This shift is the result of state legislation granting immunity to local governments and their officials and employees when they are engaged in certain activities so that community governments have some protection from the almost paralyzing effect of widespread liability claims. Part of this move has been the enactment in most states of comprehensive liability laws placing statutory caps on the amount of damages recoverable from local governments and their officials and employees. In addition, many statutes authorize only the payment of compensatory damages, which reflect the actual cost of the injury, and prohibit punitive damages, which are awarded to punish or make an example in order to deter similar conduct in the future.

Many states have also passed laws enabling communities to purchase liability or indemnity insurance covering claims based on negligence, contract rights, or violations of civil, constitutional, or common-law rights. In addition, many states have authorized communities to provide self-insurance, participate in liability insurance pools, and adopt policies for settling claims and defending themselves against damage actions. These laws, however, do not protect public officials and employees from lawsuits that charge them with willful, fraudulent, or malicious acts, or for crimes involving theft of public property.

The community government attorney

Every government needs the continuing services of an attorney. Most smaller community governments retain attorneys who are private practitioners to handle their legal work, but a growing number of mid-sized governments employ one or more attorneys full-time and retain private practitioners for their expertise in particular kinds of cases. In any event, a government must reach a clear understanding with its corporate counsel concerning duties and compensation. As to duties, the attorney should, among other things, prepare ordinances and legal instruments; advise the government's council or commission and departments on official legal matters and inform them of pertinent changes in the law; attend council or commission meetings; represent the government in court and in settling claims; review proposed contracts; and approve title to property the government is planning to purchase.

Because the attorney is not a member of the council or commission, his or her role is limited to handling the legal affairs of the community and providing legal advice to its officials. There is a clear distinction between the role of a council member who happens to be an attorney and that of the community government attorney. Elected officials, regardless of their legal background, should not perform any of the duties of the corporate counsel.

The most common mistake community government officials make is to call their attorney only after they are in trouble. Many legal problems and much expense can be avoided if the attorney's advice is sought during the decision-making process, and if the advice is followed. Moreover, the attorney should be informed of legal problems when they first arise rather than when they have gotten out of hand. The attorney can help prevent or reduce problems by conducting training programs on the legal responsibilities of officers and employees, the limits of their authority, and the legal ramifications of improper or unauthorized actions. Establishing a system for keeping officers and employees abreast of relevant legal developments, particularly with regard to personal and governmental liability, is also useful. The community government attorney is a valuable resource, but will be of limited help if less than full advantage is taken of his or her legal services, which can and should be readily available.

Attorneys and code enforcement

A largely unsung, but vital, role of the community government attorney is code enforcement. It is through local codes, and especially building codes, that communities make the primary provisions for public safety and welfare.

Local governments are assigned the police power of the state to establish and enforce standards for building construction, housing, sanitation, and other activities affecting the safety, health, and welfare of the community. These standards, as reflected in various codes and ordinances, provide the only viable means for ensuring the orderly development of a community, preventing slums, and safeguarding life and property.

To achieve these ends, communities usually pass and then enforce their own building code, housing code, electrical code, and plumbing code. Such codes are usually prepared from national model codes.

The attorney's role in code development and enforcement is critical. The attorney prepares proposed codes for legislative consideration and prepares amendments as needed to update the codes; provides needed legal training to those who will enforce the codes; and prosecutes those charged with violating the codes.

Afterword

The American love of lawsuits is well known and documented, and the propensity of individual citizens to use the courts as a means to win settlements and change government behavior is increasing. Community governments can look forward to more legal challenges and more demands for monetary compensation. All such demands—whether legitimate or not, whether victorious or not—drain away funds badly needed to underwrite the increasing cost of community services.

Thus, knowledge of the law is becoming more important in community government, and community leaders must assume a double burden: they must personally make greater efforts to know and work within the law, and they must exercise greater oversight to be sure that government workers do likewise.

Improved knowledge of the law requires that more energy and effort be devoted to training, both for leaders and for employees. Working within the law requires greater involvement of legal counsel in program planning, in employee training, and in monitoring service delivery. In today's world, investments in preventive law pay bigger and bigger dividends to community governments.

But compliance with the law should not be sought solely for monetary reasons. Community governments should strive for full compliance with the law because it is the right thing to do. The law is an expression of community values. Governments and leaders who do not respect and abide by the law cannot expect community residents to do so. Familiarity with, and respect for, the law and the democratic institutions it represents are essential in providing community government. ■

---

1 Portions of this chapter have been drawn from Charles R. Adrian, *State and Local Governments*, 4th ed. (New York: McGraw-Hill, 1976), 134-136, 172-193; Arthur W. Bromage, *Introduction to Municipal Government and Administration*, 2d ed. (New York: Appleton-Century-Crofts, 1957), 205-210, 239-247; Paul T. Hardy and J. Devereux Weeks, *Personal Liability of Public Officials Under Federal Law*, 4th ed. (Athens: Carl Vinson Institute of Government, University of Georgia, 1988); International City/County Management Association, *The Municipal Yearbook* (Washington, DC: ICMA, 1982, 1988, 1989, 1991, 1992), 178-181 (1982); 3-11, 197-257 (1988); 25-32, 55-62 (1989); 76-80 (1991); and 51-56 (1992); Melvin B. Hill, Jr., *State Laws Governing Local Government Structure and Administration* (Athens: Institute of Government, University of Georgia, 1978), 1-42; Richard H. Leach and Timothy G. O'Rourke, *State and Local Government: The Third Century of Federalism* (Englewood Cliffs, NJ: Prentice-Hall, 1988), 183-205; John C. Pine and Robert C. Bickel, *Tort Liability Today: A Guide for State and Local Governments*, 1st, 2d, and 3d eds. (Washington, DC: Public Risk Management Association and National League of Cities, 1986, 1991, 1992); James H. Svara, *Official Leadership in the City* (New York and Oxford: Oxford University Press, 1990), 44-54; J. Devereux Weeks and Emily Honigberg, eds., *Handbook for Georgia Mayors and Councilmembers*, 2d ed. (Athens: Carl Vinson Institute of Government, University of Georgia, 1984), chs. 4, 5; J. Devereux Weeks and Paul T. Hardy, eds., *Handbook for Georgia County Commissioners*, 3d ed. (Athens: Carl Vinson Institute of Government, University of Georgia, 1992), chs. 4, 5, 8, 10, 17, 18, 24.

2 John F. Dillon, *Commentaries on the Law of Municipal Corporations*, 5th ed. (Boston: Little, Brown and Co., 1911), 449.

3 J. Devereux Weeks and Paul T. Hardy, eds., *Handbook for Georgia Mayors and Councilmembers* (Athens: Carl Vinson Institute of Government, University of Georgia, 1993),59.

3 The Office of the Clerk

The position of clerk is one of the oldest and most common in local government. The office can be traced back as far as ancient Greece, and it was one of the first government positions established by American colonists. Clerks became an integral part of new communities in the United States, serving to record births, deaths, land and financial transactions, and actions taken at town meetings. At the county level, clerks also served local courts.

Today, only the positions of mayor and chairperson of the county governing body are more common than that of clerk, which exists in nearly all community governments, including those of cities, counties, villages, and towns. Although the position is usually filled by election at the county level, in cities and villages the clerk is likely to be appointed.

Although the position is common, the title assigned to it varies widely from one kind of government to another and from state to state. In New Jersey, the terms *municipal clerk*, *city clerk*, *borough clerk*, and *township clerk* are used at the municipal level. In New England, the position is commonly known as *town clerk*. The title *clerk-treasurer* is used in Indiana; *city* and *village clerk* in Illinois; and *clerk-tax collector* in Mississippi. In Texas, the clerk is often known as the *city secretary*; in Utah the title is commonly *city recorder*; and in Ohio the term *clerk of the commissions* is used. At the county level the term *county clerk* is used more often. However, counties also experience a similar variety of titles: these include *clerk to council*, *clerk to commission*, and *shire clerk*.

The duties of the clerk

The duties of the clerk continue to be essential and, in many small communities, as broad as they have been in the past. The functions of the clerk may be likened to the infrastructure of the community: they are vital to the operation and welfare of the local government organization and the community, but most often they remain unnoticed until a problem arises.

There are probably no two clerks with exactly the same duties and responsibilities because of differences in local traditions, state laws, local laws, the size of each locality, and the individual skills and personalities of the clerks. However, there are many responsibilities common to the office.The clerk maintains official records and documents; records and publishes council or board minutes; and serves as the information center for inquiries from other county or city departments, other government units, and citizens. In certain regions of the country, the clerk may keep vital statistics and maintain the financial records of the government. In nearly three-quarters of today's communities, the clerk is the election administration officer. In two-thirds of communities, the clerk is responsible for issuing licenses and permits.

Duties of the clerk
Through various surveys the International Institute of Municipal Clerks (IIMC) found that the following duties are performed by nine of ten clerks, regardless of geographic location or population of the local community: maintaining official records and documents; answering inquiries from other municipal departments and citizens; retaining custody of the city seal; maintaining official ordinance and resolution books; recording council minutes and maintaining the minute book; countersigning official documents; arranging council meetings; administering oaths; and supervising clerical staff.

A significant number of clerks, especially in smaller communities, serve as chief administrative officer, overseeing all operations of local government and implementing the programs and policies determined by the governing body. At the county level, the list of duties may include acting as clerk to the fiscal or superior court; computing property tax extensions and rates; and recording property transactions.

"But first, Miss Ooga will read the minutes of the last meeting."

Most of the functions listed can be grouped into the following broad categories: central services, records management, recorder of deeds, election administration, finance administration, licenses and permits, secretariat to the governing body, general administration, and public information. These subjects will be discussed in order in the remainder of this chapter.

Central services

Central service functions that are commonly the responsibility of the clerk's office are preparation of the governing body's agenda and various computer applications. Some clerks are also responsible for centralized purchasing, personnel administration, and grant administration (these functions are discussed in Chapters 12, 13, and 15 of this book).

Agenda preparation

A central service function commonly performed by the clerk where there is no chief administrative officer is the preparation of the board or council's agenda. The agenda is used to outline the items to be considered at a meeting and usually establishes the order in which they will be considered. Each item on the agenda should contain sufficient information to help the presiding officer know what action is needed and to inform the other members of the body and the public. Effective agenda preparation can help ensure that a meeting runs smoothly and efficiently.

In preparing the agenda, the clerk should consider agenda items proposed by members of the governing body, the public, other departments, and other governments. He or she should also review the actions of the previous meetings to determine whether an item should be placed on the agenda as a result of some earlier action, such as a second or third reading of an ordinance, a tabled motion, or a request for reports.

In many small communities, agendas are often fairly informal and are used by the presiding officer merely as a reminder of the issues to be considered.

Agendas for governing bodies may vary substantially in format. In many small communities, agendas are often fairly informal and are used by the presiding officer merely as a reminder of the issues to be considered. Larger communities may have more formalized rules that establish a precise format, requirements for submitting agenda requests, and mandates for publication or distribution of the agenda at a specified time. Rules of procedure may also place restrictions on what action a governing body may take on issues not listed on the official agenda.

Agendas may be organized with the management of the policymaking process in mind. Items placed at the beginning of the agenda, for example, are more likely to receive extensive discussion than items at the bottom of the agenda. Restrictions placed on the time allowed for discussion, or on the amount of input from citizens during discussion, may also influence the legislative body's treatment of an issue and the ultimate decision.

In addition to preparing the agenda, the clerk is often responsible for posting or publishing notices of governing body meetings in order to comply with state and local laws and regulations. Notices of meetings typically must be made public through prescribed methods at a specified time in advance of the meeting; they must also include information on the business to be considered.

Computer applications

The use of computers by local governments in almost all areas has broadened substantially in recent years. Support of government functions through both word and data processing is an important aspect of the central service role, particularly in small communities where the expense of only one computer can be justified. In such cases, the computer is often placed in the clerk's office.

Software for government applications is becoming more readily available and more affordable. Many local governments use word processing equipment for the storage and retrieval of records and for manipulation of text. The most common applications include general correspondence, minutes, ordinances, resolutions, and agendas.

Computer applications

Westminster, Colorado (66,000), has developed a program to send work orders via computer from the utility billing office to the meter shop. The new system has reduced work order turnaround time by 70 percent, speeded responses to citizen requests, and reduced citizen complaints by 90 percent.

Source: *The Guide to Management Improvement Projects in Local Government*, vol. 15, no. 1 (Washington, DC: ICMA, 1991), no. MGT-8.

However, the application of the computer to governmental functions has gone beyond traditional word processing. Other applications include accounting and financial reports, contracts and agreements, indexing, newsletters, and purchase orders. Many of these applications are available through software designed to perform a specific function or in packaged programs that perform several functions.

The specific type and size of computer system needed in a local government environment depends on the tasks to be performed and the funds available for the acquisition. A local government may tap a number of sources to determine the equipment and software needed. A visit to a similar community already using a computer is a good first step. Consultants—available in the private sector and, in many states, through state universities and municipal leagues—are another good source. In addition, organizations such as the International City/County Management Association, International Institute of Municipal Clerks, and Municipal Finance Officers Association often sponsor meetings and seminars and publish reports concerning computer operations.

Records management

Records management is virtually a universal responsibility of the office of the clerk. The most common areas are maintaining essential government records; maintaining the minutes of council and commission meetings; and maintaining government codes, ordinances, resolutions, and charters. Often these records extend back to the origin of the county or municipality and contain all resolutions or ordinances passed by the governing body.

At the county level, the clerk's office often serves as the depository for all vital records for the county. The office maintains original copies of all birth, death, and marriage documents (generally these are indexed chronologically). From these documents, certified copies can be provided to the public. Guidelines governing the accessibility of these records are set in each state through a local records act.

The clerk may also maintain various historical records. The desire to provide historical highlights for anniversary celebrations, as well as the growing interest in genealogical research, has spurred citizen interest in older records. The preservation and availability of cemetery records, vital statistics, tax rolls, census data, and property transfers have become pressing needs in many communities.

Legal requirements

Certain records are required by law to be kept for specified periods of time. For example, financial records of federal grants often must be made available for audit years after the money has been spent. Moreover, many states impose penalties for destruction or alteration of specified records.

In most states, the county clerk is required by law to file commissions for notary publics, record names adopted by new businesses, issue marriage licenses, and maintain campaign disclosure documents and various kinds of financial statements. The county clerk may also be required to compute the property taxes for the different units of local government, based on the rates allowed by law and the assessed value of residential, commercial, and industrial property within the district. From these rates, individual tax bills are prepared.

Some records are considered confidential, such as tax returns, employee personnel files, or reports of police investigations. Allowing access to confidential records by unauthorized persons is often punishable by law; on the other hand, refusing access to most public government documents, files, and records is also a punishable offense. Most states have strict regulations governing accessibility, and the clerk must be aware of all legislation pertaining to the public's right of access to records. Without a knowledge of what is subject to right of privacy laws and what is subject to freedom of information laws, clerks can expose both themselves and their governments to substantial liability.

Effective management of records

Besides historical and legal considerations, several other factors are causing clerks to pay closer attention to records management. First, some local governments are simply running out of storage room, and funding for additional storage often has a low priority. Second, modern computers and word processors may be improving the efficiency of the organization, but they are also capable of producing reams of paper records at the touch of a button, much of which must be stored. Third, many state legislatures have passed or are passing laws that require local governments to adopt record retention schedules and management programs. Fourth, administrators and staff in many communities are becoming more and more frustrated as the documents they seek become harder to find.

Most states have strict regulations governing accessibility, and the clerk must be aware of all legislation pertaining to the public's right of access to records.

Filing, storing, and microfilming are some of the tools used in records management, but to answer the problem of record storage by buying another file cabinet, expanding the storage area, and microfilming everything typically leads to mismanagement of records. Boasts about how much was thrown away in the latest "cleanout campaign" are little more than an admission that storage areas were poorly utilized by holding unnecessary or superfluous material. As the city clerk of a Florida city once remarked, "If you microfilm trash, all you have is smaller, nonbiodegradable trash."

Records management

Urbandale, Iowa (23,500), developed a records management program to conserve valuable storage and work space and to improve records management efficiency. The program identified which departments are responsible for which records; determined a retention time for each record category; produced a records retention manual; adopted a records ordinance, and established a records management committee. The city plans to microfilm essential records, move retained records off-site, and destroy records no longer needed.

Source: *The Guide to Management Improvement Projects in Local Government*, vol. 17, no. 1 (Washington, DC: ICMA, 1993), no. MGT-3.

An effective records management program usually begins by determining what constitutes a record. Most people understand that documents, letters, and other papers are records, but some are surprised to learn that maps, photographs, magnetic tape, and microfilm can also be records. In fact, local government records can be many materials in many forms—anything produced or received in the official conduct of local government operations.

If the records management program is to be comprehensive, all local government records should be identified and inventoried. The inventory worksheets may contain information for each category of record regarding size, location, series (groups of related records), names, numbers, descriptions, and recommended retention periods. Following a review of the inventory sheets, a more formalized record retention schedule for each category of record is determined. States with laws that require local governments to have a records management program usually require that record retention schedules be approved by a specified state agency.

Records retention

Record retention schedules govern the disposition of records by prescribing how long, where, and in what form the records are to be kept. The schedules are based on a review of the administrative, legal, fiscal, and historical value of the records. Typically, the schedules call for records not required for day-to-day office use to be transferred to a centralized storage area, where they are maintained until destroyed in accordance with the schedules.

Series function and description

The series function and description sections are *crucial* in order for the State Archives staff to understand the series being scheduled so that an appropriate MINIMUM RETENTION is established. Please make every effort to describe the function and description with detail and accuracy.

Series function: Try to build on, not re-copy, the series title. This should be a clear and concise description of why and how the record series is used and created.

For example: "Records information on purchasing items used to monitor expenditures . . ."

Series description: Should contain a short description of the types of information contained in the series. Describe any unique characteristics or qualities of the record series. LOTS OF DETAILS HELP!

For example: Describe the headings of the form; the different types of records in the file (Name, Address, Date); or staff reports, worksheets, maps, or miscellaneous information that explains the information in the series.

Record copy: Is this the only copy of the series? Is this the official copy required for retention? Is the copy necessary to preserve and utilize the information for the agency? State who holds the record if your department does not hold the record copy.

Reproduction: How and where is the information contained in this series reproduced?

Arrangement: How is the series arranged? (Alpha, numeric, chrono, other order)

Present retention: Has the series been scheduled by the State Archivist in the past? If yes, cite the schedule number and the retention period. If no, write "UNSCHEDULED."

Proposed retention: How long should this record series be kept based on Administrative, Fiscal, Legal, and/or Historical needs?

Justification: What is the justification for retaining the series? What is the basis for the proposed retention period?

Oregon Administrative Rule (OAR)
Oregon Revised Statute (ORS)
Audit Period: What is the audit requirement?
Federal Req: What is the federal requirement?
Administrative/Archival: Is the retention based on the needs of the office, or does the series have historical value? Salem Revised Code requirement?

In other words, what is the *value* of a record?

Source: Adapted from *Records Management Manual*, city of Salem, Oregon.

A clerk may not destroy any document without obtaining written consent. In most states the office of the secretary of state administers the local records division and regularly advises the clerk on matters regarding document retention and destruction.

In most states the office of the secretary of state administers the local records division and regularly advises the clerk on matters regarding document retention and destruction.

Many important records are scheduled for permanent retention because of their legal or historical value: charters, minutes, ordinances, vital statistics, and cemetery records are but a few. Very old records tend to deteriorate physically, especially if abused or neglected, and a scientifically controlled environment may be need to halt their deterioration. Many local governments are unable to provide the proper environment because they lack the necessary technical expertise, facilities, or financial resources. In such instances, documents are often placed in the custodial care of state agencies, colleges and universities, regional facilities, libraries, or other institutions experienced in the preservation of documents.

Copies of many records are permanently preserved on microfilm or microfiche. By photographing and greatly reducing an image and preserving it on a roll or rectangle of film, copies are produced that require far less storage space than the originals. The original or copies may be stored at another site, reducing the likelihood of total loss. Records preserved on microfilm or microfiche may be viewed on specialized viewers, or a hard copy may be printed on paper.

The value of records

Knowing the value of a record series assists in determining the appropriate minimum retention for that series.

Administrative value:	Assists in the operation of government for either current or future work. Ensures administrative consistency and continuity.
Legal value:	Contains admissible evidence of legal rights or obligations of the local government, such as legal decisions and opinions, fiscal documents, agreements, leases, titles, contracts, claims, and legal dockets. Preserves documentation as required by law to protect the local government against court action.
Fiscal value:	Accounts for public funds such as budgets, ledgers of accounts receivable and payable, payrolls, and vouchers. Documents availability of funds for operational purposes.
Historical, archival, or research value:	Preserves adequate documentation on significant historical events including the local government's operations, origin, policies, authorities, functions, and organizations, as well as significant administrative decisions. (Records with archival value are assigned permanent—or indefinite—retention periods; records selected for research purposes are critically examined and reevaluated periodically to ensure that the material being accumulated is actually filling a valid research need.)

Source: Adapted from *Records Management Manual*, city of Salem, Oregon.

Implementation of an effective records management program can be a substantial financial undertaking. However, once established, the program is easy to maintain and provides cost-effective use of office space and equipment.

Recorder of deeds

In many states, the county clerk also serves as the recorder of deeds, maintaining the index and records of all real property transactions. All real estate documents, corporation papers, city and village ordinances, separation and discharge papers for military service, and other miscellaneous documents are recorded on microfilm. Once recorded, the original documents are returned to the persons who presented them for recording. Mechanics' liens and notices of tax liens (both federal and state) are filed, and the originals are retained permanently in the clerk's office. Financial statements showing liens on chattel property and termination statements are also filed. In many counties, by order of the county board, the clerk also maintains a tract index of real estate transactions, which indicates the title to each property and any mortgages or liens against it.

Each document is assigned an official document number at the time it is presented for recording. Then it is entered in the proper book and indexed for quick reference and retrieval. These records are generally put on microfilm for permanence and security.

Election administration

Election administration, one of the primary functions of local government, may be the responsibility of the city, village, or town government; the county government; or a combination of both. Even state and federal elections are conducted at the local level by local election officials, including the clerk. Election administration, however, is closely regulated by state and federal laws and court decisions. Strict compliance with this body of law is absolutely necessary.

Election administration

The duties of election administration are becoming more and more detailed each year as new legislation broadens the clerk's responsibilities. Basic election duties that the clerk must fulfill include

Maintenance of a permanent record of registered voters

Issuance and receipt of all candidate petition filings

Issuance of official publications relating to elections

Appointment and training of election judges

Printing and delivery of all necessary election materials

Tabulation of results

Canvassing of final election results.

Registration

To be eligible to vote, an individual must register with the appropriate local authority. In many localities in the United States a single registration is all that is needed, but some communities maintain separate voter registration rolls for local elections. In many parts of the country, people are required to register according to their party affiliation for primary elections.

State and federal laws, as well as court decisions, have had the effect in recent years of making the registration process easier for the prospective voter. The elimination of poll taxes, literacy tests, and lengthy residency requirements has been influential in expanding the voter base. Additional locations for registration have been authorized, and provisions for absentee, or "postcard," registration have been implemented. If an individual wishes to challenge his or her removal from the registration rolls, he or she is normally entitled to a due process hearing. In some areas, bilingual ballots are required. County and municipal clerks generally have major responsibility for voter registration.

Motor voter bill

In May 1993, legislation was passed that has become known as the "Motor Voter" bill. This law directs states to provide voter registration forms in motor vehicle offices. The law also requires states to allow registration by mail (at the time the law was passed only twenty-eight states allowed such registration). Estimates of the number of additional people expected to register as a result of the law have run as high as fifty million.

Source: *New York Times*, May 12, 1993, A16, col. 4.

The voting process

The actual voting process itself may be accomplished in a variety of ways. Paper ballots, voting machines, and vote recorders are the principal methods. Absentee ballots are available for persons unable to attend the polls on election day. Rules and regulations regarding the conduct of the election are designed to ensure ballot secrecy and to prevent fraud. County or municipal clerks typically are responsible for the management of the voting process.

Campaign laws

Local governments are often required to enforce campaign laws. Intimidation of voters at the polls and even the presence of individual candi-

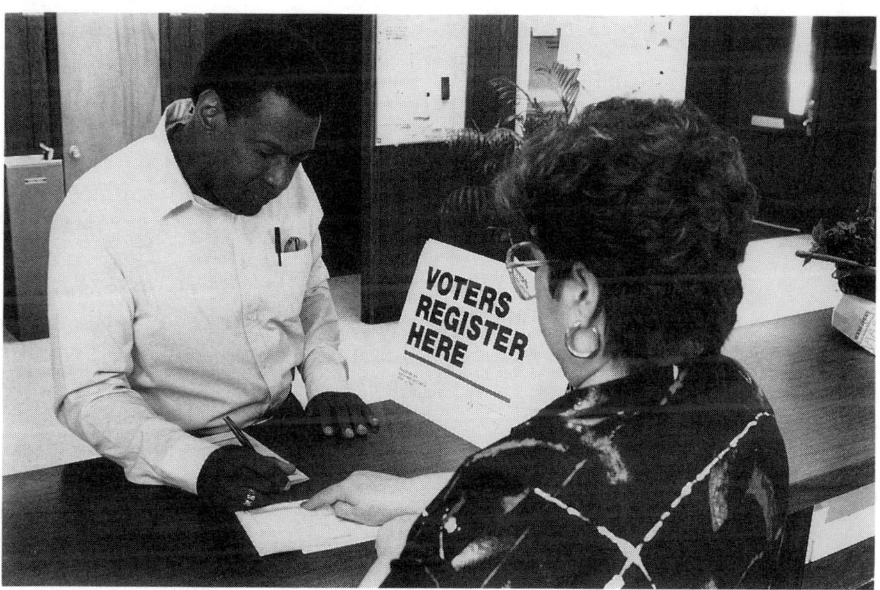

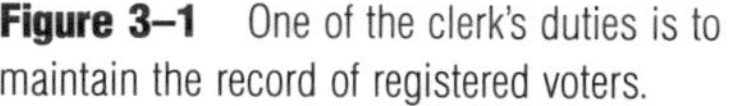
Figure 3–1 One of the clerk's duties is to maintain the record of registered voters.

dates at the polls are expressly prohibited in many localities. Laws requiring candidates to make a personal financial disclosure and to report campaign contributions and expenditures often specify that such filing be done with local authorities—typically the clerk.

Consolidation of election duties

The use of computers in the registration and election process has enhanced the efficiency of the clerk's office.

In many states, recent legislation has brought about a reform of the local election process. Election consolidation has taken election duties away from school secretaries, township clerks, and city clerks and placed the election process under the administration of the county clerk alone. Other reforms provide for a single election administrator, fewer voting hours, trained election judges, and consistent polling places. The reforms have significantly expanded the election responsibilities of the county clerk. Experience indicates that the consolidation of responsibilities in combination with the other reforms has enhanced voter participation and understanding, in part by streamlining and adding a degree of continuity to the process.

Changes in the process

Several other changes in the traditional election process have been implemented or are the subject of experimentation. The use of computers in the registration and election process has enhanced the efficiency of the clerk's office. Manual registration rolls are now being transferred to computers. Vote counting by computer (using punch card ballots) has speeded the tabulation of election results. Other changes being tried or advocated include election-day registration, conducting election entirely by mail, Sunday elections, increasing the number of days on which to vote from one to several, and even voting electronically from one's home.

Curbside voting

To make voting more accessible for disabled citizens, Rockville, Maryland (45,000), offers curbside voting to any person arriving at the polls in a car who is unable to get from the car to the voting room because of a physical condition that would make walking too taxing. The election judges verify the voter's eligibility and bring the ballot and voting device to the car.

Source: *The Guide to Management Improvement Projects in Local Government*, vol. 16, no. 1 (Washington, DC: ICMA, 1992), no. LHS-4.

Finance administration

Finance administration is a major function of local government operations. Although the subject is reviewed in detail in Chapter 12, it is pertinent here because most clerks have responsibility for some aspect of finance administration. In many local governments, particularly small jurisdictions, the clerk is the treasurer or finance officer. It is not unusual for the clerk to do the accounting, billing, bill collecting, and budgeting. Other tasks of finance administration often handled by the office of the clerk include tax collection, bid procedures, issuance of bonds, payroll, cash management, and investments. In larger jurisdictions, the financial responsibility of the clerk is often limited to managing the budget of the clerk's office.

Licenses and permits

The licenses and permits issued by a local government both regulate and produce revenue. Most clerk's offices issue licenses, but usually only in the smaller communities does the clerk have the authority to give out building and zoning permits.

The requirements that must be met by someone requesting a license vary greatly. Generally speaking, the greater the potential for impact on or damage to the community and its citizens, the stricter the licensing requirements. In many places, contractors must document their competency, taxicab drivers have to have good driving records and adequate insurance, and convicted felons are not allowed to receive alcoholic beverage licenses.

When discretion in granting a license is allowed, it is usually the governing authority or an appointed board that decides whether to issue the license; the clerk usually has very limited discretion. If the proper application and fee are submitted, it is generally the duty of the clerk to issue the license.

Generally speaking, the greater the potential for impact on or damage to the community and its citizens, the stricter the licensing requirements.

Typically, however, the clerk is required to make some determination of the facts to ensure compliance with licensing requirements. The clerk may have to verify whether the proposed location of a new business has the proper zoning. The clerk may also have to determine whether certain requirements have been met, such as those for parking spaces, square footage, availability of rest rooms, or insurance coverage. Some licenses require the prior approval of building inspectors, code enforcement officers, fire inspectors, or health officials. If the price of a license is based on the income or gross receipts of a business, the clerk is often empowered to examine the financial records of that business.

Some local governing bodies may try to use the licensing function to prohibit or regulate activities by establishing excessive fees or unreasonable requirements. Courts have usually held such ordinances invalid when challenged. For example, several jurisdictions have been forced to pay high court costs and attorney's fees after unsuccessful attempts to prohibit solicitation by religious groups.

License fees vary greatly throughout the country. Several states have established uniform business licensing provisions that apply to all local government units. Other states leave the decision to the local government or place a limit on the amount that a local government may charge.

Secretariat to the governing body

In addition to recording and maintaining minutes, ordinances, and resolutions of the governing body, the office of the clerk often provides other support services: selling reports, researching current issues, providing messenger and mail service for the governing body, and performing copying and other secretarial services. As secretariat, the clerk's office assists and advises the governing body with respect to such matters as parliamentary procedure and the relationship of proposed actions to state and federal law. In smaller communities, the governing body depends on the clerk to supply information concerning changes in state and federal laws and regulations.

Most local governments have several boards or commissions in addition to the governing body. Staff support may be provided by the clerk's office for planning and zoning commissions, development authorities, and tax review boards.

General administration

As mentioned earlier, the clerk in smaller communities will often serve as the government's administrative officer. This service can become significant when there is not a chief administrator to handle the day-to-day duties of government. The efficient and effective operation of the community then becomes dependent upon a strong working relationship between the governing body and the clerk/administrator. When the clerk serves as the administrator, his or her duties expand to include functions such as preparing the budget and financial reports, handling payroll functions, dealing with state and federal grants, accounting, and human resource management.

Public information

The office of the clerk traditionally serves as a public information center for local government, although larger jurisdictions may have a formally designated public information office (see Chapter 14). Inquiries and complaints in many areas commonly come to the clerk's office, including those that are not the responsibility of the clerk. The clerk may have the information readily available, may obtain the information for the interested party, or may refer the matter to the appropriate office or individual. There are a number of reasons that this role is appropriate for the clerk.

First, the clerk serves as the repository for official records of the jurisdiction and any inquiry regarding the details of an ordinance, an action of the governing body, or the membership of an appointed board or commission is appropriately submitted to the clerk's office. Second, the clerk's office is a logical starting point for persons unfamiliar with a particular government.

Citizen and consumer assistance

Stafford County, Virginia (68,000), established a Citizen and Consumer Assistance Office in 1990 to respond to escalating numbers of citizen requests for information and assistance and to reduce the work overload such requests placed on county employees. Utilizing one part-time employee and a pool of volunteers, the office staffs a busy lobby reception desk and switchboard during working hours. The number of citizen inquiries and complaints handled increased from 221 in March 1991 to 5,153 in March 1992. Participating in the program as volunteers has been particularly popular among senior citizens.

Source: C. M. Williams, Jr., County Administrator, county of Stafford, Virginia, 1993.

In addition, people prefer to deal with individuals whom they know, and there tends to be greater continuity in the clerk's office than in most other government offices. Many clerks have remained in office through a succession of mayors, council members, administrative officers, and department heads. The clerk is usually well known in the community, either personally or by name, and often is the individual who first receives a question or complaint from a concerned citizen.

Professionalism of the clerk's office

It should be apparent at this point that clerks wear many hats. In small communities, the clerk may be the entire government staff. Even in large communities with various departments, the clerk's office typically retains responsibility for a broad range of functions, many of them—such as records management and election administration—requiring a high degree of specialized knowledge and expertise.

Because of the importance of the office and the technical competence required, growing emphasis has been placed on professionalization of the office of the clerk. Clerks are increasingly seeking opportunities for professional development and looking for ways to acquire specialized knowledge and competence, share information, and develop improved methods for discharging their diverse duties.

Membership in professional organizations continues to increase, as does the number of clerks seeking certification and participating in training programs. The principal organizations offering professional services to clerks are the International Institute of Municipal Clerks (IIMC) for municipal clerks and the International Association of Clerks, Recorders, Election Officials, and Treasurers (IACREOT) for county clerks. Founded in 1947, IIMC now counts more than nine thousand members in the

Figure 3–2 Standards for attaining the IIMC Certified Municipal Clerk designation.

CERTIFIED MUNICIPAL CLERK

BASIC REQUIREMENTS

Each applicant must:

1. be a Municipal Clerk or Deputy Clerk,
2. be a member of IIMC for three years,
3. be at least 18 years old,
4. believe in and practice the IIMC Code of Ethics,
5. submit an approved IIMC application form with appropriate documentation and the required fee, and
6. furnish a letter from a fellow clerk as a sponsor.

STANDARDS FOR CERTIFICATION

In addition to meeting the basic requirements, an applicant must attain a total of 100 points — 50 points in each category.

I EDUCATION	POINTS
*Bachelors degree in Public Administration or related field	50
*Satisfactory completion of an IIMC-approved Municipal Clerks' Institute	50
*Associate of Arts degree in Public Administration or related field	25
*Bachelors degree in an unrelated field	25

(Related fields include, but are not limited to: political science, government, business administration, accounting, economics, finance, or one of the social sciences.)

AND

II EXPERIENCE	POINTS	MAX
Experience as full-time, administrative, Municipal Clerk or Deputy Clerk	4 per yr.	40
Experience as part-time or nonadministrative Municipal Clerk or Deputy Clerk	2 per yr.	40
Other full-time administrative position in local government prior to becoming Municipal Clerk or Deputy Clerk	2 per yr.	30
Administrative position in federal, state, or province government	1 per yr.	30
Administrative position in business	1 per yr.	30
Attendance at IIMC Annual Conference	4 each	20
Attendance at State, Provincial, or Regional Clerks' meetings	2 each	10
*Education courses and in-service training relating to your position	1 for each 10-hr. course	10
*Relevant university or college credited course work	½ per credit hr.	25
*Satisfactory completion of home study courses in *Supervisory Management for Municipal Clerks*, offered through Michigan State University or *An Introduction to Records and Information Management*, offered by ARMA International.	5 per course	10

**Appropriate documentation to be filed with application*

United States, Canada, and several other countries. IACREOT, founded in 1971, has some fourteen hundred members throughout the United States and other countries. Both hold annual conferences, publish newsletters, and issue bulletins. In addition, state associations of both city and county clerks exist throughout the country. Often the city clerks and county clerks meet separately, but training programs for the two are frequently combined.

Afterword

The office of the clerk handles a variety of tasks and makes a substantial contribution in local government by managing information and providing continuity to local governing processes. However, as political jurisdictions grow in population and furnish more and more services, there is a corresponding growth in specialization. New city and county departments are created, and they frequently assume a broad range of responsibilities held by the clerk in smaller jurisdictions. In such instances, the responsibilities of the clerk tend to be narrowed to those that support the work of the governing body.

However, thousands of small jurisdictions continue to exist throughout the country. A large number of smaller communities are also just beginning the process of incorporation or of formalizing a government structure. In such jurisdictions, the responsibilities of the clerk continue to broad and varied.

The role of the clerk in the future will be more than the sum of the responsibilities of the office. The future role will be determined by how clerks react to the challenges of new technology, increased citizen demands, changing values in the workforce, the vitality of the political environment, the impact of new laws and court decisions, and budgetary limitations. Important, too, will be the skill with which individual clerks are able to establish and maintain good working relationships with the elected officials and chief administrative officers in the jurisdictions they serve. Clerks who jealously guard the functions of their office or compete with other officials for influence and power may see the functions of their office diminish. Clerks who are cooperative, supportive members of the local governing team will see their influence grow and expand.

As mentioned earlier, clerks are increasingly pursuing opportunities for professional development. They are also striving for recognition in several ways. Many local governing bodies have adopted resolutions proclaiming the observance of Clerk's Week annually in May. State governors have signed similar proclamations, and such resolutions have been introduced in the U.S. Congress. Clerks and clerk organizations have taken an active part in many statewide municipal leagues and county government organizations. Clerks, as individuals and as a group, have expressed their views to state and federal legislators on proposed legislation affecting local government.

What will be the role of the clerk in the future? The answer will most likely be provided by the actions of clerks, individually and collectively. Whether the responsibilities of the office are broad or narrow, if the trends toward professional development and public recognition continue and expand, the role of the clerk will continue to be one of the most important in an effective local government. ■

PART II

Building a Better Community

INTRODUCTION

If the primary function of community government is to improve the quality of life of the community's residents, then clearly a primary task is to build a better community. This is a charge that applies to old, established communities as much as it applies to new and expanding communities. Every community is constantly building, changing, developing, and striving to meet more effectively the needs of its residents. As people move in and out of the community, and as members of the community move from one stage of life to another, the needs of community residents change. Community government must be sensitive to these changes.

Part of building a better community is organizing an efficient system of streets and a convenient mix of residential, recreational, commercial, and industrial land uses; building a pleasant environment in which natural resources are protected; and ensuring that housing is safe, affordable, and adequate to meet citizen needs. The process by which such planning is accomplished is the subject of Chapter 4.

Building a better community means enforcing building codes designed to ensure the quality, safety, and attractiveness of buildings. Different communities locate responsibility for code enforcement in different agencies; it is sometimes part of planning, public works, or fire services, and sometimes in a separate department. Although this book does not devote a separate chapter to the subject, it is introduced in Chapters 2 and 4. (Code enforcement is also covered in Chapter 11, which deals with fire services.)

Building a better community also means meeting the economic needs of citizens. This requires ensuring an adequate supply of employment opportunities, but it also means providing the commercial and professional services needed to support contemporary life. Of importance, too, is building a tax base to finance services. These are the challenges that are a part of economic development, the subject of Chapter 5.

In addition, building a better community means providing the infrastructure upon which the community depends—streets; bridges; sidewalks; parkways; traffic controls; and water, sewage, and garbage disposal facilities. Providing these facilities is part of the community's public works function, which is discussed in Chapter 6.

Building a better community also means providing services and facilities that help people find enjoyment and fulfillment in their leisure time. Communities do this by providing parks, recreation and fitness facilities, community centers, libraries, and an array of specialized educational and recreational programs. The challenge of providing these leisure services is the focus of Chapter 7.

Finally, and perhaps most important, building a better community means taking care of those residents who need special services or facilities, such as physically disabled citizens; those who need economic assistance, such as unemployed residents or low-income mothers with dependent children; those who need medical care; those who have developed debilitating addictions to drugs, alcohol, or gambling; those who need help acquiring language, reading, job, and other basic life skills; those who have been victimized by crime, racial or sexual discrimination, or poverty; and two other groups, the young and the elderly, both of whom have special needs. Delivery and management of the growing array of human services is the topic of Chapter 8.

The task of building a better community requires attention to each of these services. Their delivery, which is a responsibility of both counties and cities, increasingly requires collaboration and cooperation between county and municipal governments.

4 Planning

Where are we now? Where do we want to be in the future? How do we get there? The professional planner asks these questions in a continuous planning process that involves setting goals to address problems and issues; identifying alternative courses of action and gauging the consequences of each alternative; selecting and implementing the alternative that best addresses the goals; and monitoring the chosen course of action to ensure that the goals are met. Put simply, to plan is to apply foresight to action.

That, in theory, is how planning works. However, in practice, the steps of the planning process may be out of sequence, or they may work simultaneously or in small, often uncoordinated increments. All the information needed to evaluate alternatives may not be available, or it may cost more to obtain than the importance of the decision merits. Political factors may eliminate alternatives (such as siting a landfill near a subdivision of expensive homes) before they reach formal consideration. Or the decision maker may decide a goal is unreachable or needs to be changed.

Cities and counties today face a future made even more complex and ambiguous by an often contentious political environment. Local officials turn to planning as a mechanism to step back from the daily preoccupation with "hot button" issues, to obtain the big picture about their community, to reach consensus on an approach, and then to chart a desired course. For them, planning is a method of reaching thoughtful and just decisions that result in a better life for all.[1]

Although planning can have social and economic dimensions, the topic as covered in this chapter concerns primarily land use, the natural environment, community facilities, transportation, and housing. After touching on the historical backdrop of American planning and the forces shaping contemporary planning, the chapter discusses how communities practice planning. It addresses the major components of local planning—the comprehensive plan, the capital improvements program, and zoning and subdivision control. The chapter then turns to a number of current topics in planning, including growth management and neo traditional planning.

American city planning: the historical context

Early planning focused on the imposition of physical order on the urban community, particularly by eliminating slum housing, secondhand stores, taverns, pool parlors, and the like. Beginning in the period from 1910 to 1920, devices such as zoning were employed to control land use, and later, in the 1950s and 1960s, urban renewal programs were created to clear and often rebuild large tracts of blighted areas in central cities. Early planners believed that imposing physical order by eliminating slums, ensuring homogeneous land use, and providing model tenements, broad streets, and large parks would lead to social order, speed the assimilation of the waves of European immigrants into the mainstream of American life, and ensure a middle-class life-style for all.

Planning is likely to be the result of intense bargaining among interest groups, with the planner serving as the broker of ideas.

The fault lines in the "old culture of planning," as it has been termed, began to show in the late 1960s and early 1970s. Indices of change included stepped-up citizen activism, moratoriums on development, growth management initiatives, and mandatory referendums on rezonings. The old culture began to make way for a new culture, the New Pragmatism, which takes a strategic action orientation in response to a turbulent society.

The old culture approached implementation in a leisurely manner. With a time horizon of 20 to 30 years, it was, on occasion, ponderously slow to respond to problems of urban growth and development. By contrast, the new, action-oriented culture attempts to respond to a more dynamic political setting and emphasizes the translation of plans into results in a very short period, often within one to two years.

Under the New Pragmatism, planning is more likely to be the result of intense bargaining among interest groups, with the planner serving as the broker of ideas. As a result, planning is less likely to be done on the sweeping monumental scale of early efforts and more likely to be done in carefully negotiated increments. Although respect for the natural and built physical environment has escalated, planners no longer believe that the physical environment alone shapes values or influences whether an individual becomes a good citizen.[2]

Forces shaping contemporary planning

Contemporary planning has been shaped by many forces, among them greater citizen participation, environmental concerns, expectations for a high quality of life, revisions in state legislation enabling planning, the changing family structure, and state and federal court rulings circumscribing the powers of local government.

Citizen activism

Citizen activism at all levels of government has prompted planners to be more flexible and more sensitive to diverse interests. A new awareness of the environment has increased recognition of the interrelated impacts of development decisions on air, water, land, and flora and fauna. Land is now valued as a *resource* as well as a *commodity*; land's function is no longer solely to make money. Land value is now recognized as stemming from many different uses:

Ecological—to support complex natural communities, such as wetlands

Agricultural—to provide food and natural materials

Aesthetic—to permit enjoyment, for example, of a beautiful view along the seacoast

Developmental—to provide a site, for example, for low- and moderate-income housing.[3]

As urban areas have sprawled outward, citizens have become reluctant to raise taxes to subsidize the new infrastructure (roads, bridges, utility lines, parks) needed to support urban life. Fiscal retrenchment has forced reconsideration of how to pay for the infrastructure and support systems and services required by growth. At the same time, the transformation of the urban and rural landscape into "edge cities," high-intensity nodes of office and commercial development in suburban and exurban areas, has often spelled the loss of the sense of community, that intangible mixture of shared experiences, activities, and values that bonds residents of an area together. Lacking an ingrained sense of community, residents may in turn feel alienated from local government or suspicious of its actions or motives. Furthermore, planners are no longer planning only for a household that is largely middle-class and consists of two parents and their children (children being the principal conduit through which the traditional family participates in community life through schools and recreational and cultural activities). They now plan for households that consist of poor families, elderly couples, single parents and their children, childless couples, or groups of disabled persons.

Creative land use

Skokie, Illinois (59,000), found a creative use for an unimproved and underused piece of land along a canal bank. Working with a citizens group, the village turned the land into the Skokie Sculpture Park, a half-mile stretch of grass and bike paths decorated with trees and shrubs, seating areas, and sculptures. The village landscaped and maintains the area; the citizens group funds the selection and installation of the sculptures.

Source: *The Guide to Management Improvement Projects in Local Government*, vol. 15, no. 4 (Washington, DC: ICMA, 1991), no. LD-16.

Figure 4–1 The best response to citizen activism is a planning process that promotes communication among city and county officials, community leaders, neighborhood representatives, and interested persons from the community at large in an effort to reach agreement on community goals and methods of achieving those goals.

State intervention For cities and counties, there is a new actor to contend with in the planning process: the state, which is increasingly exerting its prerogatives in areas such as the environment. Over the past twenty years, states have taken on review of (and, in some cases, overridden local responsibilities for) functions and decisions once considered to be solely the domain of the local government. Now states may review and certify local plans or regulate development in coastal zones or environmentally sensitive areas such as wetlands.

Court decisions

As a result of recent decisions by the U.S. Supreme Court, property owners can now obtain monetary damages for land use regulations that are shown to constitute a "temporary taking" by denying all economically viable use of the property. Although such claims are often difficult to prove in court, the availability of compensation for a temporary taking—and the Supreme Court's desire to see a connection between the purpose of the regulation and the advancement of a "legitimate state interest"—have made local governments redouble their efforts to ensure more rigorous justifications for regulatory decisions.

Uniqueness of small communities

Finally, planning for smaller cities and counties occupies a special niche in local government. It is distinctly different from big-city or large-county planning because the participants' relationships with one another are ongoing and more intimate. In this setting, the planner must truly be a generalist, often addressing problems that elsewhere might be handled by specialists. Because of limited resources, the planner does not have the luxury of gathering massive amounts of data or spending weeks on the development of lengthy reports.

In such an environment, where they survive from planning commission meeting to planning commission meeting, planners must be especially sensitive to customer service. The planner may need to be patient in listening to an old-timer recount the history of struggles over the current zoning code, willing to accompany a resident to her property to view firsthand a code enforcement problem, or able to deflect the wrath of a developer or homebuilder over delays blamed on the local government. It is here that planning can be at its best in devising pragmatic and creative solutions to the problems of community growth and change.

How communities plan

Planning occurs through a variety of formal or relatively permanent legal structures and informal or temporary arrangements devised to solve a specific set of problems. These exist to organize the work of planning; to fulfill legal requirements, such as holding public hearings on plans and development proposals; and to ensure citizen participation by providing people with opportunities to express their views on planning issues and influence the outcome of public policy decisions.

Planning commissions

The planning commission, the most common institutional structure for planning, was devised to represent a broad cross-section of community interests; interpret community values to professional planners; and act as a buffer between planners, local political interests, and the governing board. Composed of seven to nine members appointed by the chief elected official or legislative body, planning commissions advise the governing body on planning issues. Given strong leadership, planning commissions tend to work well in small to medium-sized communities (generally, those with populations of less than 75,000), particularly where the commissioners have a good working relationship with elected officials.

Elected officials

The early twentieth-century government reform movement that gave rise to modern American city planning—along with the council-manager form of government and the civil service system—minimized the role of elected officials in planning; elected officials, in theory, were to refer controversial issues to semi-autonomous boards such as the planning commission for clear-headed, nonpartisan advice. Only the planning commission had the authority to undertake planning, adopt a plan, and, in many cities, employ a professional planning staff. Shut out of the planning process, elected officials often ignored the commission's advice.

Now elected officials, particularly in high-growth, environmentally aware communities, have begun to assert their right to a role in planning. Because they decide whether to adopt the policies, levy the taxes, and allocate the funds that help determine the community's future, planning becomes little more than an academic exercise without their understanding and support. When elected officials have a role in formulating planning policies, they work harder to implement them. In some communities, one or two elected officials sit on the planning commission as representatives of the legislative body, breaking down the wall of formality that is sometimes erected between the two and strengthening the influence of practical politics on the advice of the commission.

The chief administrative officer

In many small communities without a staff planner, the chief administrative officer, usually the county, city, or village administrator, is the de facto planning officer and thus may facilitate the work of consultants and citizen task forces, and may even administer development regulations. In any case, the administrator must establish an atmosphere conducive to effective planning. Without the support of the chief administrative officer, who is in a position to command and direct the organization's resources, planning will typically founder and fail, regardless of the talents of the people mentioned in the following paragraphs.

The planner

Many smaller communities employ a single planner whose job is to prepare plans and studies, administer regulations, and staff boards and commissions. Today, most planners have graduate or undergraduate degrees in city and regional planning from accredited planning programs. Others may be trained in architecture, landscape architecture, engineering, or related social sciences such as geography and urban studies. Many professional planners are members of the American Institute of Certified Planners (AICP), an affiliate of the American Planning Association that conducts testing and issues professional credentials. Planners certified by AICP have met requirements for education and experience, have passed a rigorous examination, and are subject to AICP's "Code of Ethics and Professional Conduct."

The attributes needed by a professional planner depend on the community for which the planner works. Still, a planner should have a generalist's background and be technically competent. The modern planner, as the introduction to this chapter implies, must be able to function in a politically turbulent environment. Consequently, an undogmatic personality, the ability to listen and accommodate, an appreciation for democracy (and its foibles), and sensitivity to a variety of often conflicting viewpoints are desirable traits.

The planning consultant

Although many communities have a full-time planner, many others find it more feasible to retain a private planning consultant whose services are confined to a specific assignment. A consultant can bring a new perspective or dimension to the local planning process.

The community should first formulate a clear concept of why it wants a consulting service. Typically, the community will distribute a request for proposals spelling out the tasks required and the product expected. When choosing a consultant, officials should carefully explore the credentials and experience of each candidate to ensure a good fit; never engage a consultant on the basis of the least expensive bid alone. A regular reporting system should be established in order to keep the community aware of progress. The reporting system also helps put the community on notice that it must fulfill its commitments—reviewing work in a timely way, scheduling public meetings, providing necessary data, paying the consultant—in order to benefit from the contract.

Value engineering

James City County, Virginia (26,000), uses the expertise of a value engineering firm to evaluate building projects before construction begins. By reviewing every aspect of proposed building designs to evaluate facility reliability, reduce operating costs, assess appropriateness of proposed building materials, and ensure the orderly evaluation of alternatives, the firm is able to save several hundred thousand dollars per building project. The firm is employed to evaluate all construction plans involving estimated costs of $1 million or more.

Source: *The Guide to Management Improvement Projects in Local Government*, vol. 15, no. 3 (Washington, DC: ICMA, 1991), no. MGT-20.

The planning department

In medium-sized and larger governments, planning is accomplished through a planning department staffed by professional planners, clerical personnel, drafters, graphic artists, computer specialists, and planning interns. Usually headed by a professionally trained planner, the planning department comes under the direction of the city or county administrator. Alternatively, the planning department may be a division of a larger department whose functions may include engineering and code enforcement; it may be part of the office of management and budget; or it may be included in the office of community and economic development.

Advocacy planning

Advocacy planning, popularized by the late planner and attorney Paul Davidoff, envisions a style of planning in which a planner, representing a client's interests, presents "specific substantive solutions" to planning problems as alternatives to the official plans of government agencies.[4] Advocacy planning operates outside rather than inside government to influence its actions, although some planners may function as "guerillas" within a local government bureacracy to advocate alternative or unconventional and presumably progressive views not shared by the bureaucracy. For example, a local downtown business group that feels that the local planning department's work is unsatisfactory or that the department is unreceptive to its views might hire an outside firm to do a plan for the central business district. For the same reason, neighborhood and civic groups, developers and homebuilders, or low-income groups, believing that the government has not done enough for affordable housing, may develop their own plans. Davidoff argued that advocacy planning will improve the quality of official plans because of the competitive nature of the advocacy planning process.

Regional planning

In some areas of the country, planning for an entire region, which may embrace a number of municipalities and counties, is conducted by a regional agency—for instance, a council of governments, an economic development district, or a special planning district. Sometimes special

Multi-jurisdiction planning works best when the dominant governmental ethic stresses regional cooperation and problem solving.

regional planning commissions composed of appointed representatives of municipalities and county governments are established to perform planning for more than one city and the unincorporated area of a county. This arrangement is especially appropriate where there are a number of small communities that cannot afford the services of a full-time professional planning staff. This structure is especially popular in Ohio, Kentucky, and Tennessee.

Under such arrangements, the planning staff works for the regional planning commission, which assumes responsibility for planning for its member communities. The agency's activities are funded through assessments of member communities, consulting fees, and government grants.

Regional planning
Twenty municipalities in Greater Vancouver, British Columbia, have combined efforts to develop a common set of municipal specifications for the development of new subdivisions and public works installations. The uniformity has eliminated obsolete code provisions, reduced conflict and confusion in working with public works contractors, and cut costs in the construction of municipal works.

Source: *The Guide to Management Improvement Projects in Local Government*, vol. 15, no. 3 (Washington, DC: ICMA, 1991), no. LD-12.

In addition to regional planning, regional commissions also provide local planning assistance, serve as depositories for census and other important planning data, and undertake regional studies that can serve as important references for local planning efforts. They frequently prepare regional plans for such specific areas as transportation, parks, sanitation, and economic development.

Inevitably, such organizations have their own internal tensions. Small communities may believe that big-city issues dominate the planning commission's agenda. County and city officials may be at odds over municipal expansion plans. At bottom, multi-jurisdiction planning works best when the dominant governmental ethic stresses regional cooperation and problem solving.

The instruments of planning

The basic documents for planning in cities and counties include the comprehensive plan, the zoning ordinance and map, the subdivision regulations, the official map, and the capital budget and capital improvements programs.

Land Development Guidance System
Because traditional zoning regulations were creating obstacles to the kinds of development encouraged by city planning, Fort Collins, Colorado (87,758), created the Land Development Guidance System (LDGS). Designed to allow flexibility in determining land use and intensity; to encourage and reward creative and innovative design; to link development planning to long-range planning; and to foster citizen involvement, LDGS combines land use, site design, and zoning in one decision. It eliminates traditional zoning requirements and establishes performance criteria addressing design, use, intensity, neighborhood compatibility, and location.

Source: *The Guide to Management Improvement Projects in Local Government*, vol. 17, no. 1 (Washington, DC: ICMA, 1993), no. LD-2.

Comprehensive plan

The comprehensive (or master) plan is a local government's statement of goals, objectives, and policies to guide public and private development within its planning jurisdiction.[5] In order to reflect the changing times and values of a community, the comprehensive plan must be current. Thus, it should be modified and brought up to date on a regular basis, typically at five-year intervals, and it should be consulted as new public-service and zoning issues develop. Elements of a typical comprehensive plan are shown in the accompanying sidebar.

Components of a comprehensive plan

An economic study that inventories the amount, type, intensity, and general location of commercial and industrial development, drawing on census information and other public data. It usually examines the study area in the context of trends affecting the region in which the community is located.

A demographic study involving analysis of population by age, education level, income, and employment characteristics that includes a forecast of population changes over the next ten to twenty years.

An assessment of the natural physical environment—geology, soils, climate, vegetation, ground and surface water.

General policy statements about the community's planning objectives.

A land use plan to give guidance in administering the zoning ordinance and in locating future major public and private facilities.

A major thoroughfare plan to be used in the review of subdivision plats and in preparation of street-improvement programs. The plan contains standards for a hierarchy of streets (principal and minor arterials, collectors, local streets). The major thoroughfare plan may be part of a broader transportation plan addressing the need for bikeways, mass transit, and aviation facilities.

A community facilities plan showing the need and potential locations for schools; parks and open spaces; libraries; municipal buildings; water, sewer, and other utility systems; and landfills.

A housing plan that surveys the condition of the housing stock in the community and assesses the housing needs of persons residing or likely to reside there, particularly those of low and moderate income. The plan may be a Comprehensive Housing Assistance Strategy, a requirement for the receipt of federal community development block grant funds.

A plan for the provision of social services based on the data contained in the demographic study.

Other specific plans needed by the community, such as a fiscal plan, a plan for the downtown area, or a historic preservation plan.

A framework identifying programs and projects to be carried out, their cost, and a schedule for implementation.

The first element in any plan should be an elaboration of the community's goals and objectives. This is usually developed through the strategic planning process, in which the members of the governing board, the planning commission, or both determine goals for the community for various future periods (five years, ten years, twenty years ahead) and develop strategies to achieve those goals. Only after goals and strategies are established can planning related to land use and the development of community facilities optimally proceed.

1987 Comprehensive Plan Summary, Oxford, Ohio

Within the Comprehensive Plan for the City of Oxford are goals, objectives and policies. As used in this document, *goals* are generalized statements describing an ideal situation. This plan has the following overall goals:

To provide an environment in which Oxford's citizens can lead happy, independent, rewarding, meaningful and dignified lives.

To promote a beautiful and well-ordered community through the continued and progressive participation of a thoughtful and informed citizenry.

To accommodate growth or change rationally and economically.

To protect the environment and conserve natural resources.

To assure equal opportunity and the removal of barriers to its realization.

To improve the quality, effectiveness and economy of municipal services.

To achieve a high quality of life through a practical blending of the desirable and the attainable.

To provide safe, adequate and diverse housing for Oxford's residents.

Source: Excerpted from *The Comprehensive Plan* (Summary), city of Oxford, Ohio, November 1987.

The typical comprehensive plan groups future land uses into commercial, residential, industrial, and other categories. It shows the network of thoroughfares and all existing and proposed public facilities. More complex plans may establish hierarchies of uses that gradually increase in size or intensity (e.g., neighborhood commercial versus regional shopping centers). Residential land uses may be shown in different densities (dwelling units per net acre). Industrial land uses may be

Figure 4–2 The restaurant on Main Street competes with all kinds of fast-food establishments. These ten fast-food places were grouped in a circle off a highway to meet the demands of the automobile. Reprinted with permission from Grady Clay, *Close-up: How to Read the American City* (Chicago: University of Chicago Press, 1980).

subdivided into light industrial areas for research and warehousing and into heavy industrial districts for production plants. Plans may also show agricultural preserves, which demarcate prime agricultural land, and special resource protection areas such as wetlands.

The state role in comprehensive planning is growing, with state planning statutes containing increasingly detailed descriptions of what to include in plans. For example, the department of community affairs of Florida reviews and certifies local comprehensive plans to ensure that they comply with statutory and administrative criteria for the various plan elements. Other states, such as Washington, Oregon, and Maine, define a similar role for a state agency in overseeing local planning.

Regulating traffic flow

Because land use patterns in Oak Park, Illinois, were established by the 1930s, before the effects of the automobile were fully known, the village has had to content itself with street patterns designed for an earlier age. In order to achieve its goal of preserving the residential character of neighborhoods while ensuring the safe and efficient movement of people and goods through Oak Park, the village pursues three policies:

1. Encourage through-traffic with origins and destinations outside Oak Park to use primary arterial streets.
2. Encourage traffic that originates or terminates in Oak Park to use arterial and collector streets whenever possible.
3. Maintain village streets in good repair. Highest priority for repair should go to those streets in the worst condition and to those that traffic is encouraged to use.

Techniques that encourage use of a street include

Street widening

Channelization of traffic

Provision of left-turn bays and signals

Restrictions on curb parking

Realignment of offset intersections

Timing of traffic signals

Restrictions on additional driveway openings and removal of existing driveways.

Techniques that discourage street use include

Use of diverters and cul-de-sacs

Curb parking

Refraining from making improvements such as those listed above.

Any action proposed to encourage or discourage use of a street is considered within the context of the surrounding neighborhood and street system. Village staff identify the likely effects on nearby streets and the system as a whole prior to public hearings on any proposed action.

Source: Adapted from the Comprehensive Plan of the village of Oak Park, Illinois.

Zoning map and ordinance

The comprehensive plan is translated into regulation through the zoning map and ordinance. The map divides the community into use districts or zones. The zoning ordinance regulates activities within these zones by controlling the type of use; building height; minimum lot area; front-, rear-, and side-yard setbacks; off-street parking; maximum lot coverage; landscaping; signage; and related considerations. When a zoning change is requested, local government officials examine the comprehensive plan to determine whether the proposed change is consistent with the plan.

The comprehensive plan is prospective and general, providing guidance in establishing use districts and setting standards for those districts. In contrast, the zoning map and ordinance are current and specific, detailing the kinds of uses to which the property can be put in the present and what requirements must be satisfied; together, the map and ordinance constitute the law and can be changed only through legislative amendments.

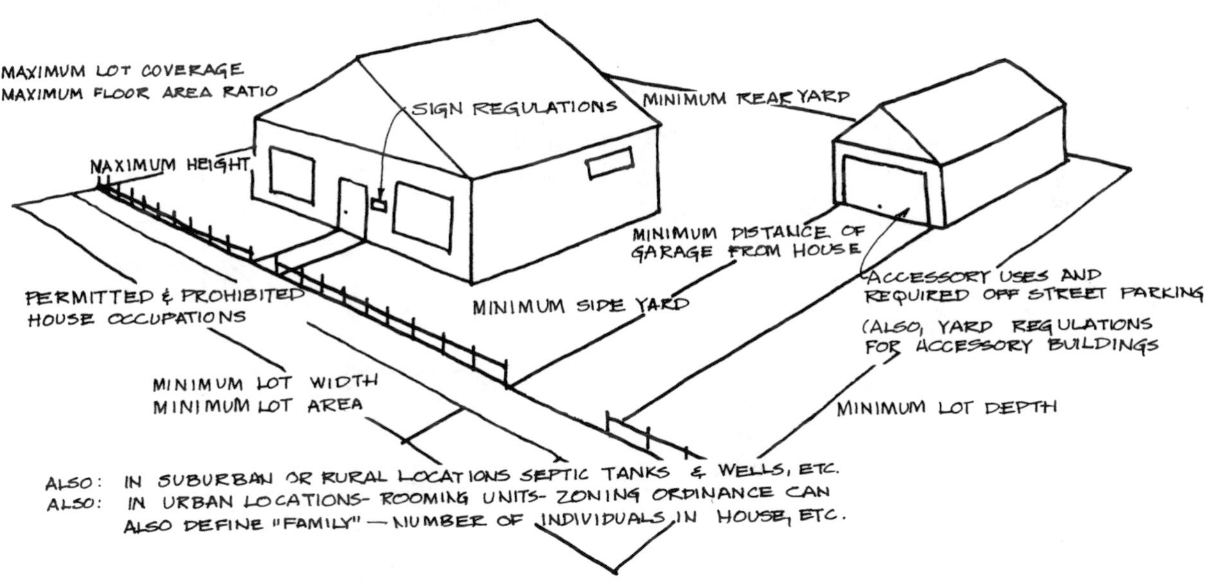

Figure 4–3 Single-family house as perceived by the zoning inspector.

Zoning appeals

Petitions from property owners for site-specific modifications of the zoning regulations are typically referred to a local board of zoning appeals or adjustments. Such bodies are authorized to grant variances—minor departures from the strict and literal interpretation of zoning regulations—for an individual property. Such variances are usually considered when enforcement of the zoning code would cause unnecessary hardship or practical difficulty. An example of a variance might be a reduction of a rear-yard setback requirement when a lot is pie-shaped, leaving insufficient depth. Each such request may need special review in order to determine whether it would be compatible with the surrounding area, whether its impact can be accommodated, or whether the approving body wishes to impose conditions on granting the exception.

Planned unit developments

A planned unit development (PUD) regulation is another technique for altering the application of the zoning ordinance to a large tract of land

Figure 4–4 Section of the zoning map for Oxford, Ohio.

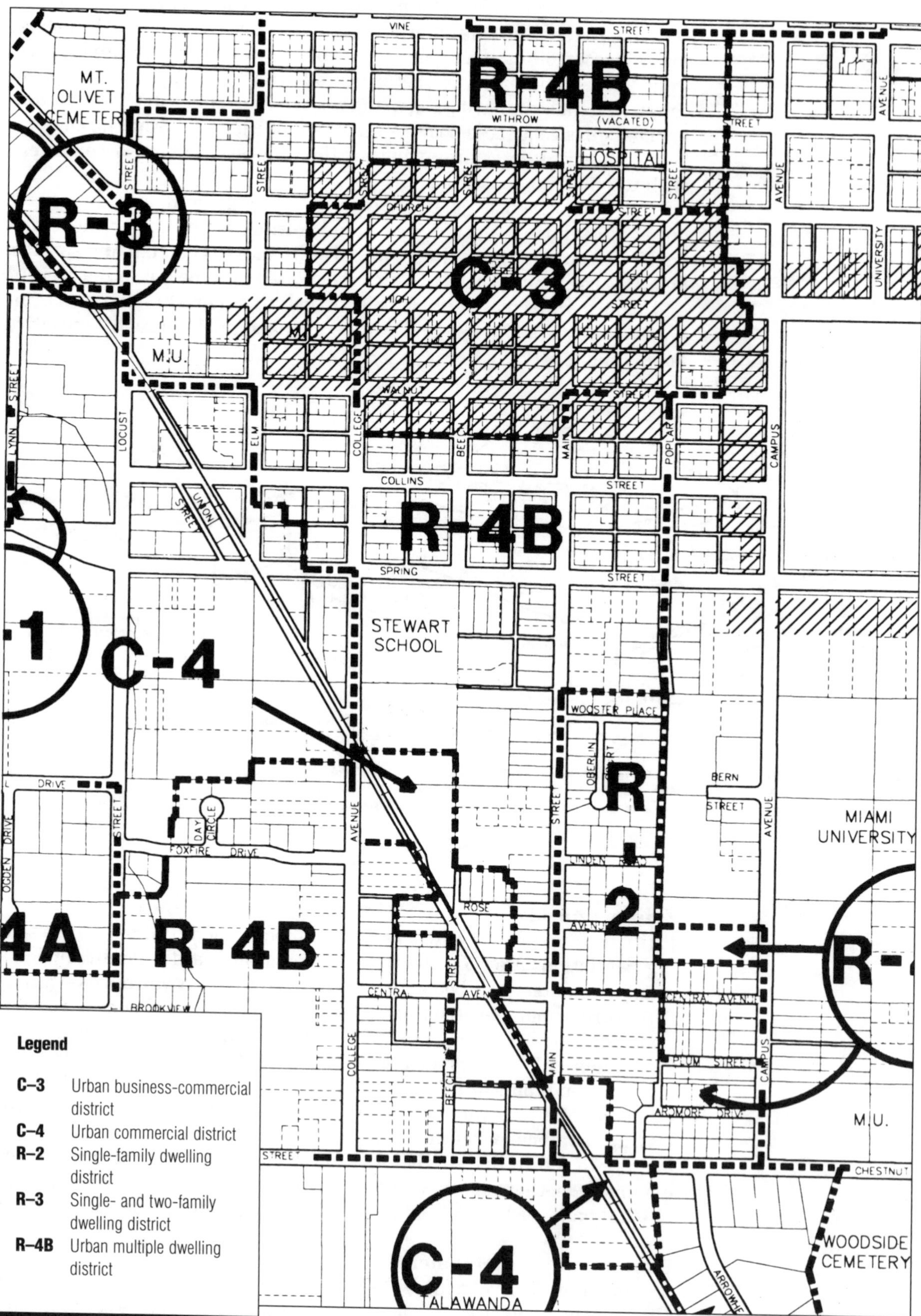

under development. PUD regulations may permit relaxation of the zoning standards for a district, allow mixed uses (single-family and multiple-family housing, residential and commercial development), and provide flexibility in the placement of buildings in exchange for the preparation of an overall plan for the property. Under a PUD, the approved plan establishes standards for the uses of the property and the location of the uses on the site. A PUD can improve site design, preserve amenities such as open space through clustering of buildings, and lower street and utility costs through reduced frontages.

Zoning for open space
Loudoun County, Virginia (66,000), uses its "Hamlet Zoning Ordinance" to encourage developers to make the most of open space. The ordinance allows clusters of five to thirty lots, each as small as one-third acre, in districts that were once zoned for three-acre lots. In return, the developers are required to designate at least 80 percent of the remaining acreage as open space. County residents find the hamlets more visually attractive and enjoy walking and relaxing in the common open areas.

Source: *The Guide to Management Improvement Projects in Local Government*, vol. 15, no. 2 (Washington, DC: ICMA, 1991), no. LD-8.

Exclusionary zoning

Exclusionary zoning is a common problem in some parts of the country. It is enforced through requirements that make the construction of affordable housing difficult if not impossible to achieve by prohibiting it or by imposing additional regulatory costs unjustified by conventional health or safety criteria. Exclusionary techniques include requiring extraordinarily large lot sizes (one- to five-acre minimums) or large lot widths (escalating the cost of streets and water and sewer extensions), prohibiting multi-family dwellings and mobile homes, limiting the number of bedrooms in apartments (to restrict the size of families with children), and refusing to zone adequate land for higher-density single- and multi-family housing.

Subdivision regulations

Most states require that whenever the owner of a tract of land within a city or county divides land into two or more parts for the purpose of creating additional lots for sale or lease—and when the development will involve the creation and dedication to public use of streets, alleys, and other improvements—the owner must prepare a subdivision plat. This plat, or plan of the division of land, must be reviewed, approved, and filed in accordance with the procedures established by state law and local regulations.

Subdivision design should be consistent with general land use and thoroughfare plans (see discussion of the official map, below). Major roads proposed in the thoroughfare plan should be reflected in the plat, and local streets should integrate with the major street system. The plat design should ensure adequate water, sewer, and stormwater facilities and lot design that provides good, well-drained, buildable sites. Once constructed, street pattern, lot design, and public facilities are relatively permanent. Even more than the restrictions imposed by the zoning ordinance, they determine the land use pattern and shape the character of an entire area.

Subdivision inspection

Each community should have an ordinance containing regulations governing subdivisions. In such an ordinance the community sets its standards for site design; for streets, sidewalks, utilities, and storm drainage; and for payments (sometimes called "impact fees") by the developer to help provide schools, parks, arterial streets, and other needed services.

The community's planning and engineering staffs should ensure compliance with the subdivision standards by conducting on-site inspections at two distinct times. First, inspections should be made during the time the preliminary and final subdivision plats are being reviewed and approved. Second, inspections should be carried out during construction of streets, utility lines, and other features of the new development.

Communities lacking the staff expertise to conduct such inspections should contract with private firms that provide such services; it is important that subdivision regulations be strictly enforced.

Official map

The official map is a plat of an area that has been adopted by the local legislative body. Implementing the general recommendations of the major thoroughfare plan, it gives precise locations for existing and planned streets and may also show sites for other public facilities. The official map reserves an area for streets, but does not actually open a street or result in the taking of property for a street. Some official maps are quite detailed, showing a full hierarchy of streets, public drainage basins, proposed future park sites, and related improvements. Others may only show major streets. The official map may control the location of streets in new subdivisions, show street location and existing or prospective street width, and fix the point from which front-yard setbacks for new buildings are measured, relating them to the zoning ordinance.

In a number of states, a proposed subdivision must be disapproved if it does not comply with the official map. Some statutes or local ordinances provide that no building permit may be issued for a building or structure to be put on land set aside on an official map for a street.

Figure 4–5 In eighteenth- and nineteenth-century America, town and country were clearly divided. This photo shows the sharp edge of Scottsdale, Arizona, originally bordered by an Indian reservation. Such division is rare today as town and surrounding countryside become an urban-rural blur of residential development. Reprinted with permission from Grady Clay, *Close-up: How to Read the American City* (Chicago: University of Chicago Press, 1980).

Figure 4–6 Section of the master plan map for Urbandale, Iowa.

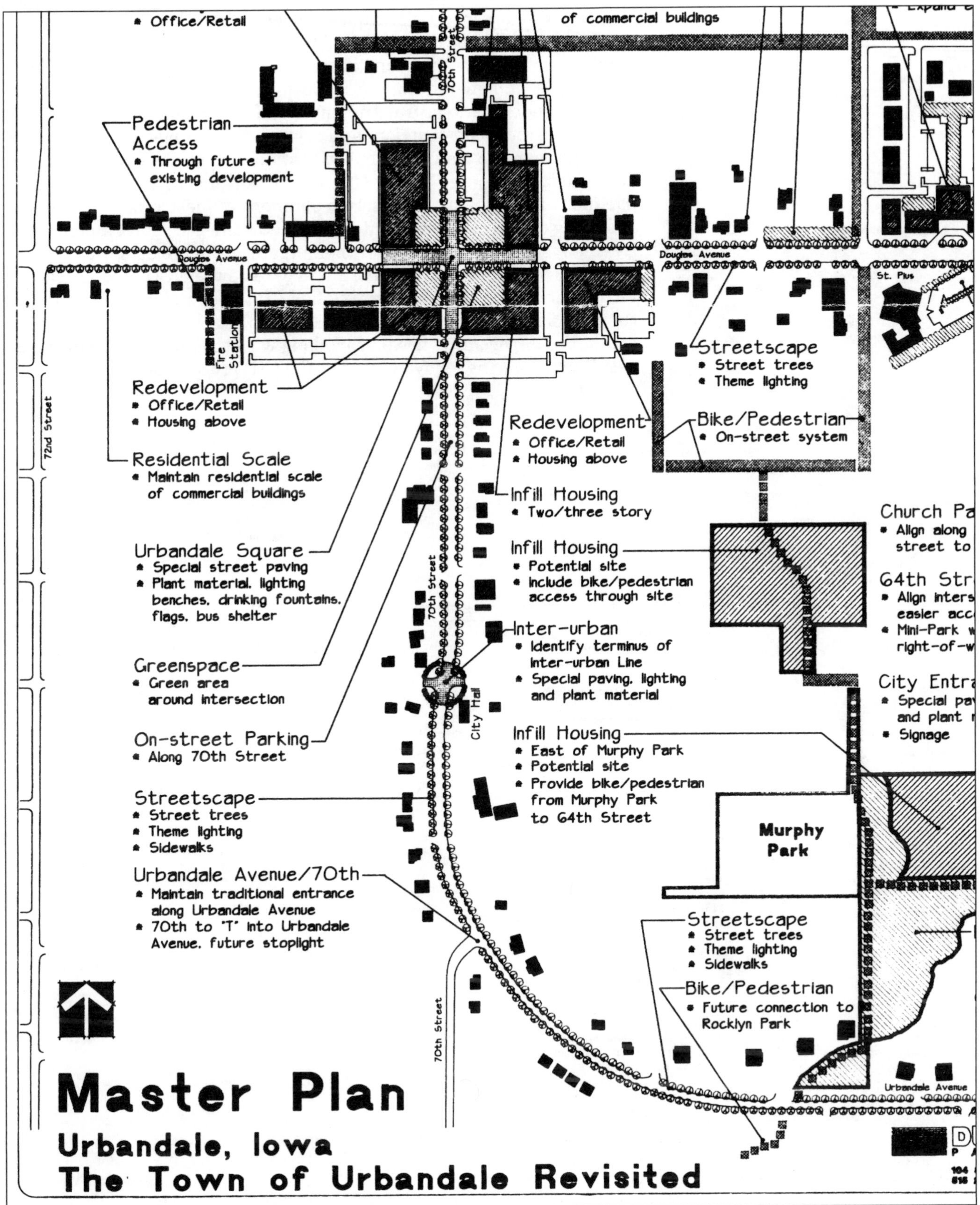

The capital improvements program

Plans for acquiring new public facilities described in the comprehensive plan are made in the capital improvements program (CIP). The CIP is a five- to six-year schedule of capital projects. Included are major, nonrecurring expenditures for municipal buildings, civic centers, fire stations, parks, playgrounds, street construction or reconstruction, sewage plants, water lines, and swimming pools. Costs associated with such improvements include architectural and engineering fees and expenditures for land acquisition, construction, and related furnishings and equipment.

Each year, the planning department (or sometimes the public works department) prepares a new CIP. Often working with the finance department and the chief executive, planners request proposals from all operating departments, evaluate them, determine the government's ability to pay for new projects, and then organize the projects into a schedule. The local planning commission may review the CIP and forward its recommendations to the governing body. If the governing body approves the plan for the first year of the CIP, this is adopted as the capital budget for the forthcoming fiscal year, along with the annual operating budget. Public hearings may be part of the CIP process as well.

Figure 4–7 Portion of the capital budget for Oxford, Ohio.

CAPITAL IMPROVEMENT PROJECTS
PROJECTED RESOURCES AND EXPENDITURES
1992-1996

General Fund/Capital Improvement Fund	1992 Capital Budget	1993	1994	1995	1996
Capital Projects:					
Alley Repair Program	10,000	10,000	10,000	10,000	10,000
Brookville Road Sidewalk	0	30,700	0	0	0
Central Avenue RR Crossing	0	0	0	125,000	0
Fairfield Road Improvement	0	26,000	266,000	0	0
Guard Rail Replacement	10,500	12,000	0	0	0
Hazardous Tree Removal	0	37,260	0	0	0
Hester Road Reconstruction	0	269,900	226,380	0	0
High St. Signalization & Brick Repair	444,000	0	0	0	0
Locust and High Street Signalization	5,000	45,000	0	0	0
Locust RR Signal and Gates	0	125,000	0	0	0
Main and Sycamore Traffic Light	0	20,000	0	0	0
McKee Avenue Improvements	0	0	0	0	78,000
Pumper Truck	0	200,000	0	0	0
Police Computer Upgrade	26,000	0	0	0	0
Pool Repairs	55,000	0	0	0	0
Railroad Crossing Gates	0	0	0	0	430,000
Recreation Van	0	0	0	0	20,000
Rubberized RR Crossings	0	0	0	0	86,500
Sand Volleyball Court & Lighting	0	10,500	0	0	0
Signs for Parks and Rec. Facilities	0	8,000	0	0	0
Street Division Facility Upgrade	0	31,200	31,200	31,200	0
Street Maintenance & Resurfacing Program	50,000	100,000	100,000	100,000	100,000
Stormwater Feasibility Study	30,000	0	0	0	0
Stormwater Improvement Project	0	0	237,400	264,000	0
Tennis and Basketball Court Lighting	0	37,400	0	0	0
Tennis Court Renovation	0	75,000	0	0	0
TRI Center Expansion	0	50,000	50,000	50,000	50,000
U.S. 27/Locust Street Improvements	28,000	300,635	0	0	0
U.S. 27 North Widening	0	0	161,000	1,073,000	0
U.S. 27 South Sidewalk	0	0	180,800	0	0
West Side Connector Study	10,000	0	0	0	0
Withrow Street Reconstruction	260,400	0	0	0	0
TOTAL CAPITAL PROJECTS	928,900	1,388,595	1,262,780	1,653,200	774,500

ix

Current issues

A number of issues continue to shape the practice of planning in cities and counties. Several of these are summarized here.

Growth management

Growth management efforts began in communities that were experiencing rapid rates of growth, particularly in residential development. Feeling themselves overwhelmed by the pace of change and believing their infrastructure would be overtaxed unless proactive steps were taken, these communities began to devise land use and public facilities systems that controlled not only the type and location of development, but also the *rate* at which it could occur.

Development timing
Dominant among these systems were development timing or adequate public facilities ordinances, such as that of Ramapo, New York. These ordinances allowed development to occur only when specified public facilities were shown either to be available to serve the development or provided at the developer's expense ahead of the long-range schedule of capital improvements adopted by the local government. Florida has a concurrency provision in its state planning laws: local governments cannot approve a development permit unless it can be shown that the necessary supporting infrastructure and related community facilities either exist at the time the permit is issued or will exist by the time construction is complete.

Building permit allocations
Communities such as Petaluma, California, have established building permit allocation systems in which only a certain number of building permits are awarded in a city in a given year. Others have established urban service areas—boundaries beyond which water, sewer, and other urban services are not extended and beyond which urban-level development is not allowed.

Impact fee ordinances
These are local ordinances that require a developer to pay a fee to cover the proportional costs, both direct and indirect, for the community facilities (including parks, schools, utilities, local streets, and even major arterial highway development) required to service a proposed development.

Initially, in many parts of the country, the impetus for growth management was the desire to "stop growth at any cost." However, as the movement has matured and benefited from the enactment of supporting state legislation, growth management's major emphasis has been on the importance of ensuring adequate infrastructure before approving development.

Neo-traditional planning

Neo-traditional planning is a rediscovery of the design principles of some early British and American towns. Neo-traditional planning promotes the use of the simple grid street pattern that integrates with the larger road network; public squares and spaces that serve as community focal points; mixed land uses on a pedestrian scale; and alleys, which may also serve as pedestrian paths. Neo-traditional planners try to orient buildings toward common community areas or the street rather than only to the rear yard, as is the case in the conventional American suburb. Neo-traditionalists stress the design of whole new developments that have the ingredients for creating a sense of community and scorn the disconnected, auto-dependent, pedestrian-hostile subdivisions that characterize the outskirts of many American communities.

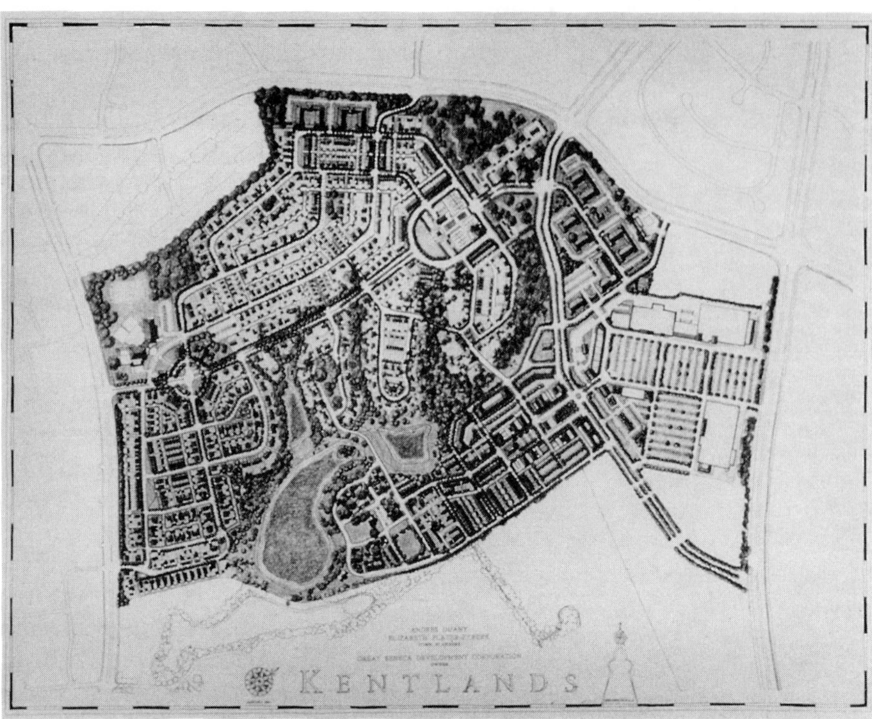

Figure 4–8 Plan of Kentlands, Gaithersburg, Maryland, an example of neo-traditional planning (Andres Duany and Elizabeth Plater-Zyberk, Architects).

Affordable housing

In many communities, finding affordable housing, either for rent or purchase, has become harder. Increasing development costs, scarcity of properly zoned land, the high costs of borrowing, and requirements for adequate supporting community facilities have all contributed to a slow-to-expand housing supply and the shrinking availability of affordable housing.

Affordable housing

The Affordable Housing Program in Panama City, Florida (38,000), has provided 150 new homes over two years at an average price of $40,000. The project involves the use of block grant funds to purchase lots, cooperation with area banks in securing credit, contractor participation in building established home models at discount rates, city reductions in impact and site plan review fees, and city relaxation of land use regulations.

Source: *The Guide to Management Improvement Projects in Local Government*, vol. 16, no. 1 (Washington, DC: ICMA, 1992), no. LD-4.

Comprehensive housing assistance strategy

Planning has responded to the housing shortage in a variety of ways. The federal government, for example, now requires the preparation of a Comprehensive Housing Assistance Strategy (CHAS) as a condition for receiving community development block grant funds and other federal housing-related monies at the state and local level. The CHAS must identify the problems contributing to the lack of affordable housing and actions that may be taken to increase the supply of new and rehabilitated housing for low- and moderate-income persons.

Comprehensive plans

A number of states, such as California, Florida, and New Jersey, now require local comprehensive plans to contain housing provisions that address the long-range need for housing for existing and prospective residents of a community and particularly for low- and moderate-income persons. Using linkage fees, some communities are requiring developers of market-rate housing and office, industrial, and commercial space to contribute funds to build or help rehabilitate affordable housing. Additional state and local government programs intended to expand the supply of affordable housing are presented in the accompanying sidebar.

Programs to provide affordable housing

Fair-share housing planning. New Jersey has established a Council on Affordable Housing (COAH), whose responsibility is to oversee housing planning for the entire state. COAH prepares a fair-share housing allocation plan for housing regions for the entire state that establishes numerical goals for low- and moderate-income housing for these regions. Under the plan, municipalities are expected to take reasonable steps to ensure that land is available for the construction of the number of low- and moderate-income units proposed under the plan. COAH also adopts criteria and guidelines for municipal fair-share goals.

Low-interest loan programs for housing rehabilitation for renter- and owner-occupied dwellings.

Evaluating local zoning codes for regulatory barriers; waiving development or impact fees for affordable housing developments.

Subsidizing, with community development block grant funds or special state grants, site improvements—water and sewer lines and streets—to serve affordable developments.

Streamlining development approvals to minimize construction delays.

Inclusionary zoning in which density bonuses are given for any residential housing development in which a substantial percentage—10 to 20 percent of units or more—are for low- and moderate-income households.

Grants to very low-income households for emergency housing repairs, such as the replacement of a furnace or the installation of additional insulation.

Rehabilitation or construction of single-room occupancy housing, once common in American cities.

Allowing the construction of "granny flats," accessory dwelling units for one or two persons, in connection with existing single-family homes.

Establishing nonprofit housing corporations that actually construct or rehabilitate affordable housing, often with monies from state-administered housing trust funds.

Sources of help

Even though it draws its values and aspirations about current and emerging community issues from the general public, planning is not a job for amateurs. Citizens, local government administrators, and even professional planners frequently need outside help. Important sources of planning assistance for cities and counties include

Regional planning commissions, councils of governments, and state agencies with community assistance programs.

Statewide associations of cities and counties.

State universities with community assistance centers. (These are frequently linked to graduate and undergraduate programs in public administration or in city and regional planning).

National professional groups such as ICMA and the American Planning Association.

Afterword

Planning in the future will bear little resemblance to planning during the last half of this century. The focus will no longer be simply on conventional land use, the desire to promote growth, and attempts to accommodate the automotive society. Instead, planning will become much more complicated: following the lead of neo-traditional planners, it will seek land use patterns that build and reinforce a sense of community; it will be concerned with the adequacy of housing for all income groups; it will be sensitive to environmental as well as economic concerns; and most important, it will focus on controlling growth in order to better achieve diverse community goals.

The processes of planning will also change. As citizens become more active and involved in government (see Chapter 1), they will target the planning process for special attention, seeking proactively to shape community goals and development strategies. Planners will have to become more sensitive to citizen activists, whether those citizens want to change land use patterns or simply complain about their neighbor's building code violations.

The planners of the future, more than ever before, will have to be good listeners, good communicators, and good at the political task of building community consensus. Planners must come to realize that citizen involvement—whether through public hearings, participation on special task forces, or advocacy planning—ultimately leads to better planning. Community plans are improved by the discourse that accompanies the clash of widely diverse views about community goals and how to achieve them. ■

---

[1] Donald G. Hagman, *Urban Planning and Land Development Control Law* (St. Paul, MN: West Publishing, 1971), 1-3.

[2] The discussion in this section is drawn from Stuart Meck, "From High-Minded Reformism to Hard-Boiled Pragmatism: American City Planning Faces the Next Century," *The Planner: The Journal of the Royal Town Planning Institute* (February 16, 1990): 11-15; and Meck, "The Two Cultures of Planning: Toward the New Pragmatism," *Land Use Law and Zoning Digest* (July 1991): 3-9.

[3] Fred Bosselman and David Callies, *The Quiet Revolution in Land Use Control* (Washington, DC: GPO, 1971), 314.

[4] Paul Davidoff, "Advocacy and Pluralism in Planning," in *A Reader in Planning Theory*, ed. Andreas Faludi (Oxford: Pergamon, 1973), 283.

[5] On defining development objectives and comprehensive planning, see generally, William I. Goodman and Eric C. Freud, eds., *Principles and Practice of Urban Planning* (Washington, DC: ICMA, 1968), 327-378. Also see T. J. Kent, Jr., *The Urban General Plan* (Chicago: American Planning Association, 1990).

5 Economic Development

A preoccupation with economic development appears well on its way to replacing baseball as the national pastime of American communities in the twenty-first century. Given the dramatic increase of local interest in job creation, business expansion, and new-income generation, the importance of economic development in the strategic plans of local governments cannot be doubted. As concern over economic development has grown, smaller cities and counties have increased their economic development role, and recent research indicates a continuation of this trend.[1] As competition among communities for prospective business intensifies, the sophistication of economic development programs will also increase.

Both people and jobs are moving farther out, migrating to smaller communities. In his book *Penturbia*, Jack Lessinger describes this move of people and jobs from the suburbs to new and old towns distant from metropolitan areas. As examples of Penturbia, Lessinger points to such places as Whatcom County, Washington (eighty miles north of Seattle); Greene County, New York (one hundred miles north of New York City); and Adams County, Wisconsin (sixty-five miles northwest of Madison). This pattern is also described by G. Scott Thomas in *The Rating Guide to Life in America's Small Cities*, which evaluates the advantages offered to residents and businesses in 219 "micropolitan" areas found across the United States. Communities such as San Luis Obispo, California; Corvallis, Oregon; Fredericksburg, Virginia; Wenatchee, Washington; Hattiesburg, Mississippi; and Ames, Iowa, rank high on Thomas's list of leading small places.[2] These communities are finding increased success in attracting new business operations while maintaining a high quality of life for residents.

A 1991 study by the National League of Cities (NLC), entitled *Small City Economic Development: Roads to Success*, examined economic development in cities with populations of 50,000 or less. The study found that small-town economic development programs are growing in number and sophistication and that smaller communities are doing what they can for themselves to shore up and expand their economic base. A 1991 American Economic Development Council (AEDC) study, as well as the NLC report, suggests that the economic development concerns of smaller communities are becoming increasingly similar to those of this nation's largest central cities.[3]

These concerns are developing particularly in larger urban regions such as Greater Cleveland, Ohio, where several smaller suburban communities are experiencing increased poverty, higher unemployment rates, and decreased tax revenues, prompting inner-ring suburbs such as Euclid, Garfield Heights, Brook Park, and others to mount new economic development programs aimed at restoring the economic health of their communities.

Many counties and smaller cities across the country face problems caused by major plant closings and other economic disruptions. For example, during the late 1970s and early 1980s, communities in Eastern Ohio, such as Martins Ferry, Bellaire, and Steubenville, were shaken by the closing of several major steel, chemical, and coal mining operations. Many smaller New England communities suffered major job and tax-base losses with the relocation of older textile mills. Petersburg, Virginia, an older Southern tobacco town, endured extreme losses when its major employer, Brown and Williamson, shut its doors in 1982.

Officials, developers, and planners must adopt approaches to economic development that enable the community to anticipate and adjust to future changes.

However, the new wave of economic activism by smaller communities has been sparked by opportunities as well as problems. Communities with established economic bases are likely to experience pressures of both growth and decline in the future, as the supply of jobs expands and contracts in response to changes in the economy. Elected officials, economic developers, and planners must adopt more comprehensive approaches to economic development that enable the community to anticipate these phenomena and adjust to future changes.

Many local governments serving smaller cities and counties are faced with severe budget problems stemming from declining tax revenues, reduced intergovernmental support, and a slow national economy. This trend means that, as local governments prepare economic development programs, they must look increasingly at how economic development activities both add to and draw upon the local tax base.

Most definitions of economic development cite job creation, business expansion, new-income generation, and tax-base expansion as expected outcomes of local economic development efforts. Cities and counties seek these benefits in exchange for assisting businesses with facility expansion and location services. ICMA's 1989 survey of local government economic development activities indicates how commonplace this exchange of benefits is.[4] However, local governments' expectations have become more refined over time as communities target higher-quality jobs and business enterprises that are more compatible with community goals, values, and resources. Moreover, communities now seek to build more diverse, stable local economies that more fully support the local population. This chapter discusses these refinements and reviews trends shaping the present and future roles of economic development in counties and smaller cities.

An integrated approach to economic development

The central issue for local governments has shifted from the general decision of whether to get involved in economic development to much more specific choices about what goals to pursue and what programs and strategies to adopt to bring the greatest success in job and wealth creation. This shift indicates that city and county officials are beginning to view economic development as a more integral aspect of the community's overall strategy for community advancement. The AEDC study mentioned earlier confirms this direction and suggests that local practitioners and policymakers are adopting new, more integrated strategies designed to better link overall community well-being with economic development goals.

Strategic planning in small communities

Strategic planning and community consensus-building techniques are being employed by large and small communities alike in an attempt to get community, business, and government leaders involved. In short, strategic planning means a more systematic approach to economic development that recognizes the importance of internal (local) and external (regional, national, global) factors in the economic development

Organizing for economic development
No single pattern of organization for economic development has emerged within community governments. Different approaches seem to work best in different communities. Among the variations, three patterns seem to be more common:

The separate department
Many community governments have established a separate department for economic development. This unit, with its own staff and resources, operates independently—but on an equal organizational footing—with other municipal departments, including planning. Sometimes economic development is linked locally with the federal community development block grant program in a department of economic and community development.

Although common in the past, this form of organization is now used less frequently.

The planning and economic development department
The practice of combining planning and economic development into a single department—or making economic development a separate division within the planning department—is growing in popularity. Although this combination can divert energy from the planning function, it does optimize coordination among closely related activities. DeKalb, Illinois (33,000), recently adopted this form of organization.

Public-private partnerships
City or county collaboration with a private economic development agency provides yet another very common organizational format. Community government departments of economic development or planning often work closely with a private economic development agency. This agency, organized as a not-for-profit corporation, might be established by local businesses, the chamber of commerce, or other community interest group.

It is also common for the community government to provide leadership or resource support for a local economic development corporation rather than staffing its own office of economic revelopment. Lake County, Illinois, for example, provides the professional staff for the local, countywide private economic development corporation.

Private economic development corporations often serve a geographic area larger than a single municipality, but they rarely cross county boundaries. As a result, several community governments in the same area sometimes help support a single, area-wide economic development corporation.

General
Regardless of how the economic development function is organized—and of whether local development efforts are directed and coordinated by a private not-for-profit corporation—the enabling ordinances needed to impose impact fees or waive utility hook-up charges, must be passed by the local general purpose unit of government (e.g., county or municipality).

Source: Michael Peddle, Northern Illinois University, 1993.

process. As part of the strategic planning process, a community identifies critical issues and problems that might have an impact on the community and assesses its strengths, weaknesses, opportunities, and threats in relation to the critical issues. The process thus enriches the "information environment" in which a community's public and private sector stakeholders make decisions about how to use its resources to support job development, generate income, and increase tax collections. Better information contributes to better decision making.

A 1990 survey indicated that seventy-two of the ninety-eight communities surveyed (74 percent) used strategic planning to guide their development activities.

Numerous smaller communities have prepared strategic economic development plans in recent years. For example, Mentor, Ohio (45,000), prepared a strategic economic development plan in 1986-1987 following the closing of three major industrial plants, which eliminated more than 3,000 well-paid jobs from the local economic base. Mentor, like many other smaller communities attracted to strategic planning, saw the need to take account of external issues in its analysis of future development options. The strategic planning process enabled the community to gain a broader prospective of its economic environment.

A 1990 survey of communities in the states of Montana, North Dakota, South Dakota, and Wyoming indicated that seventy-two of the ninety-eight communities surveyed (74 percent) used strategic planning to guide their development activities. The vast majority of the surveyed communities were very small in size.[5] Beulah, North Dakota, and Hutchinson, Kansas, represent two good examples of smaller communities combining strategic planning and consensus-building techniques to produce implementable city economic plans. Both communities allowed diverse groups to participate in the planning process.

Most cities included in ICMA's 1989 survey stated that business retention and expansion and business attraction were the top two priorities being pursued through their economic development programs. Downtown development, small business development, and economic base diversification were other top priorities identified in the survey. Strategic planning can help the city or county to develop effective responses to all of these issues.

Targeting

As an element of strategic planning, targeting can help smaller communities identify those industries and jobs that best match community resources, goals, and values. This matching process serves to increase the long-term success of local economic development efforts. Because many companies focus on the larger regional area when making a decision to locate, it may be worthwhile for smaller communities to work with utility companies and other regional economic development groups in conducting target industry studies. For example, Utah Power and Light Company, which serves a wide range of smaller communities in Utah, conducts for them target industry studies based on different regions of the state. Local communities are actively involved in the implementation of study results and in working with prospective employers to evaluate the advantages of their communities.

Precise targeting of development opportunities is a common characteristic of economic development programs. A 1991 nationwide survey of almost 500 economic development organizations conducted by Growth Strategies Organization in Reston, Virginia, found that 92 percent targeted their business prospects.[6] Targeting is indicative of greater selectivity in the type of growth being encouraged by communities, a sign of the increasing sophistication of local programs.

Attracting and retaining business

Communities that develop a strategic economic development plan often identify as major goals the attraction of new business and the retention and expansion of existing business. After briefly introducing these topics, this section describes some of the activities that local governments in small communities may undertake in their efforts to attract and retain

Strategic planning in Rock Hill, South Carolina

Rock Hill was traditionally a textile center, but in the late 1970s, technological advances brought the closure of thirteen mills, and the community of 43,000 lost all except its residential tax base. In the past six years, however, Rock Hill has brought in forty new high-tech, high-wage industries, many from abroad; renovated all of its schools and playgrounds: and installed public art.

Rock Hill began its quest to become a more livable community by the year 2000, called Empowering the Vision (ETV), early in 1988. The strategic visioning process began with the formation of a steering committee chaired by Mayor Elizabeth Rhea, which was composed of the chief elected and executive officials of each of seven institutions—the city, York County, Rock Hill Economic Development Corporation, Rock Hill School District, Winthrop University, York Technical College, and Rock Hill Chamber of Commerce.

The committee decided to capitalize on the city's proximity to burgeoning Charlotte, North Carolina, twenty-five miles to the north, while maintaining the city's distinct identity. It chose to concentrate on six market niches that make Rock Hill unique. Through the ETV process, Rock Hill would channel its resources into projects offering the greatest opportunity to make a difference—as an education city, a garden city, a business city, a cultural city, a historic city, and a functional city.

The steering committee established a framework for the massive citywide participatory process and appointed six task forces of twenty to thirty community leaders, each of which were charged with formulating plans. A strategic plan marketing office was set up in a vacant former department store downtown. The facility provided meeting space for community groups and an exhibit area where the six committees rotated presentations on the plan.

As Rock Hill is the only Charlotte ring city with a four-year state college, the plan called for Winthrop University to beef up performing arts offerings and graduate programs to help make Rock Hill an education city. Teacher salaries were also raised to one of the highest levels in the state. To make Rock Hill a garden city, entryways to the city were landscaped, and downtown was made to resemble a college campus.

Rock Hill developed a regional shopping center to deter residents from driving to Charlotte, built a conference center and adjacent hotel, and is aggressively marketing its business parks to fulfill its goal of being a business city. A major piece of public art is being installed for each of the next ten years to make Rock Hill a cultural city.

Rock Hill, the historic city, decided to maintain downtown, 90 percent of whose structures are owned by the economic development corporation, as a sense of place, since many other city features are new. The city has improved its wastewater treatment plant, developed affordable housing, installed a new traffic light synchronization system, and undertaken road work to ensure that Rock Hill is a functional city.

The ETV process was successful because plans were kept flexible to respond to economic forces or new opportunities. Rock Hill holds a biennial retreat to update the plan.

Source: Adapted from *Nation's Cities Weekly* (March 29, 1993).

business. These activities include promoting downtown, small business, and workforce development; formulating and implementing a policy on economic development incentives; and marketing.

Business attraction

Many smaller communities have been successful in their efforts to attract new business operations. Such efforts have become increasingly important because companies are more mobile than ever, according to leading site location consultants such as PHH Fantus; CRS Sirrine; and Moran, Stahl, and Boyer. Business attraction efforts are becoming better integrated with other community economic development efforts, greatly improving their effectiveness.

Smaller communities are growing in popularity as locations for a wide range of manufacturing and service industries.

Back-office relocations head the current list of hot recruitment targets for many smaller communities. Smaller communities are competing for the back-office operations—the routinized clerical and administrative functions—of large manufacturing and service corporations, which in many cases have fled high-cost centers such as New York City and Los Angeles and relocated to small cities and counties. Citibank recently relocated its credit card processing operations from New York City to Sioux City, South Dakota. Scranton, Pennsylvania, has attracted back-office operations from Metropolitan Life Insurance, U.S. Fidelity and Guaranty, Warner Communications, and other large corporations.

Competition for manufacturing plants remains very keen, as states and communities work to improve their advantages and increase their attractiveness. Smaller communities are growing in popularity as locations for a wide range of manufacturing and service industries because of such factors as the lower cost of doing business, relative absence of the social and economic problems facing big cities, and availability of high-quality land resources. Small towns such as Bentonville, Arkansas; Orrville, Ohio; Freeport, Maine; and Park City, Utah, have been put on the map by attracting and developing the corporate headquarters of major companies such as Wal-Mart, J.M. Smucker, L.L. Bean, and Mrs. Fields Cookies.[7] And smaller cities and counties are no strangers to the large Japanese auto manufacturers and their suppliers, who have chosen places such as Marysville, Ohio; Georgetown, Kentucky; and Smyrna, Tennessee, as locations for new manufacturing operations.

Existing business retention and expansion

A community's success in attracting new employers depends to a great degree on how successfully the community has taken care of existing businesses, and increased attention is now being given to the needs of those businesses. This added attention is reflected in new and improved services in areas such as workforce development, site location assistance, infrastructure improvements to accommodate existing industry growth, reducing local business operating costs, and streamlining government regulations related to local business operations.

However, smaller communities should not overlook the benefits to be gained in using outside resource groups such as the state government, colleges and universities, and regional planning organizations to organize and undertake retention and expansion activities.

Working with utility companies

Utility companies are valuable allies to local governments in conducting effective business retention and expansion programs. Telephone companies such as New Jersey Bell, Illinois Bell, and Michigan Bell play an important role in helping smaller communities within their service areas to survey and assist existing businesses. A 1991 survey by GTE Telephone

Operations indicates that business retention and expansion is a growing concern to the thousands of smaller communities the company serves across the nation.[8]

Working with state governments
Similarly, states can play an important role in this area, as evidenced by the role played by the Minnesota Department of Trade and Economic Development in the Minnesota Business Retention and Expansion Program. Almost ninety Minnesota communities currently participate in the program, relying upon it to help them retain existing companies. The Ohio Cooperative Extension Service has helped more than fifty smaller Ohio cities and counties to organize effective ongoing business retention and expansion programs. Most of these communities are located in rural or nonmetropolitan locations, but some are suburbs of larger metropolitan areas.

Historic district renovation
To halt the decline of its downtown business district, Itasca, Illinois (7,000), passed an ordinance declaring its main street a historic district and then offered incentives to historic district property owners to participate in the restoration of the area's nineteenth-century facade. A $20,000 grant from a local bank was matched with $20,000 in village funds to provide matching grants of up to $8,000 to building owners who renovated storefronts. Brick sidewalks were laid, light poles were replaced with old-fashioned lantern poles, trees and flowers were planted, and a pond with swans and a Victorian swan house were built in a downtown park. Village revenues are now increasing from tourism and new businesses locating in the historic district.

Source: *The Guide to Management Improvement Projects in Local Government*, vol. 15, no. 2 (Washington, DC: ICMA, 1991), no. LD-6.

Geographic targeting

Most communities strive for a healthy balance of residential, commercial, and industrial development. Toward this end, specific areas within the community are often targeted for development.

Downtown development
Downtown areas are the focal point for development of various types of retail and office space in many smaller communities. Key priorities in downtown development include retail business retention and attraction; street and building beautification and revitalization; consumer attraction; image building; security enhancement; promotion of tourism; and other actions that contribute to downtown viability.

Downtown business in many smaller communities is significantly affected by the development of regional shopping malls and other activities that draw shoppers away from the central business district. Often the only strategy that works in these cases is to re-establish the downtown area as a multi-use center providing for tourism, specialized retail shopping, government and local business offices, and other activities. This approach requires comprehensive planning by local government and private development groups.

Community-wide planning
Effective community-wide strategic planning helps city and county officials coordinate downtown development efforts with neighborhood and

industrial development activities. Five smaller cities (Cranford, New Jersey; Longmont, Colorado; Morris, Minnesota; Roswell, Georgia; and Wharton, Texas) were identified as examples of successful and innovative downtown development efforts in the NLC's 1991 study on small city economic development.[9] The common denominator in all cases was a strategic and comprehensive approach to solving downtown development problems such as consumer attraction, street and storefront beautification, and crime reduction. This broader approach addresses both the internal, or local, factors (such as crime reduction) and the external factors (such as competition from regional shopping malls) that shape development prospects in downtown areas.

Quality economic development
Fairfax, Virginia (20,000), is committed to an aggressive economic development program that focuses on retaining existing businesses. The city sponsored Fairfax Quality Day, a day-long seminar at the town hall for local and regional businesses. The educational program featured management and quality experts from local businesses presenting seminars on the effects of quality on business, implementing quality improvement in small and medium businesses, and quality in public service. The seminar, which was sponsored by fifteen local businesses and organizations and will become an annual event, cost $59 per attendee. Approximately 110 persons attended. The event raised $7,229 in total revenues, including sponsor donations and registration fees. Although expenses exceeded revenue, sponsors donated funds to establish a seed fund for the 1994 meeting. Next year's Quality Day will recognize a business that has demonstrated achievement in using the quality management practices. The seminar helps local businesses improve their ability to succeed and boosts the local economy.

Source: *The Guide to Management Improvement Projects in Local Government*, vol. 17, no. 2 (Washington, DC: ICMA, 1993), no. LD-9.

Small business development

Most local economies are dominated by smaller businesses. A variety of programs have been created to strengthen the competitiveness of smaller companies and increase their contribution to local economic development. Business incubators, small business development centers, local entrepreneurial training programs, community-based seed and venture capital pools, and other resources have been created by local and state economic development organizations to assist smaller companies and entrepreneurs. Many of these programs are realistic possibilities for smaller communities to consider.

Business incubators are facilities used by many communities across the country. Originally these facilities offered low-cost commercial space for new firms; now they provide a variety of managerial and technical support to fledgling businesses. Many incubators have been started in older industrial facilities that have been rehabilitated to accommodate smaller companies.

Many other communities are developing new programs focused on helping smaller companies increase international exports, apply new technology to increase productivity and enhance product quality, and increase access to existing capital markets for both investment and working capital.

Targeting high-growth and technology-based smaller companies is becoming more common as an economic diversification strategy. *Inc.* 500 companies, which include some of the fastest growing companies in the country, are a regular target for prospect development efforts. Strategies to develop and attract smaller companies with direct links to the existing local economic base are becoming more common. These efforts focus on encouraging smaller companies that are suppliers or customers of existing local companies and industries to develop new facilities and jobs within the area.

Free small business seminars

Lakeland, Florida (61,000), provides free seminars for small business owners. Using volunteer speakers from local businesses, the sessions cover a variety of topics including financing, bookkeeping, cash-flow analysis, legal structures, business planning, and marketing. Existing, new, or potential business owners benefit from the knowledge of guest speakers, and class attendance has more than doubled since the program began.

Source: *The Guide to Management Improvement Projects in Local Government*, vol. 15, no. 1 (Washington, DC: ICMA, 1991), no. LD-1.

Workforce development

The quality of the local workforce is an increasingly important factor in business investment and location decisions. The issue is equally important to existing and new industries in evaluating the advantages of a community. To compete for new business opportunities, smaller communities must demonstrate that the local labor market can meet the future growth needs of business.

Working with educational institutions

Local schools, colleges, and universities often need assistance from local governments in planning improvements to their education and training programs that focus on the local labor force. Local government economic development offices, because of their regular contact with business and industry, can provide educational institutions with useful advice on how to plan more effective training programs that meet the needs of local employers and residents. Several communities have used local community colleges extensively to address area labor needs. Reports by the National Council for Urban Economic Development and the Midwest Research Institute identify both urban and rural models for successfully drawing upon community colleges as economic development resources.[10]

Day labor

Confronted with large numbers of immigrant day laborers coming to the community each day in search of work, Brea, California (34,000), established the Brea Job Center for Day Workers to establish an orderly process for matching workers with employers. With a 54-percent job placement rate, the center has expanded to offer job, language, and life-skills training, health screening, immunization, and well-baby care in an effort to offer hope of a better life to immigrant workers.

Source: Tim O'Donnell, Assistant City Manager, Brea, California, 1993.

Working with the private sector

Where private industry councils (PICs) have been formed to provide job-training services to area residents and employers, these programs should be integrated and coordinated with local economic development programs and other training resources such as those found at community colleges and vocational schools. Adams County, Colorado, is a very good example of how employment and training programs can be better linked to local economic development efforts. The Adams County Employment Center and the Adams County Economic Development Corporation coordinate their efforts to help existing industry and attract new companies to this suburban county near Denver by jointly identifying types of jobs to be developed in the future. Their efforts include promoting employment opportunities for recipients of public assistance.

Training and resource inventory

Local job-training programs, high-quality schools, college- and university-based training facilities, and other resources should be the first priority for communities preparing for future economic development. An inventory of nearby training programs and resources can be very useful to corporate human resource managers. The Greater Cleveland Growth Association, serving a seven-county area in Northeast Ohio, prepares such an inventory for use by its members and other businesses interested in training opportunities in the region. The inventory includes training resources found in several smaller communities in the area.

Workforce information

Accurate and current information about the local labor force should be included in marketing materials designed for business investors. These materials should include data on skill availability, wage levels and benefits, commuting patterns, and sources of new labor in order to allow corporate site selectors and their consultants to evaluate the area as a business location. An annual employer survey is a useful approach to collecting these data. Data collection is another area in which utility groups can be helpful to communities. Illinois Power, for example, has developed a standardized survey to help communities in its service area collect employer data on a regular basis.

State employment service bureaus, like the Ohio Bureau of Employment Services, are important labor-market information sources for smaller communities preparing labor profiles of their areas. The Economic Development Program at Cleveland State University has been working with state officials to expand the availability and use of industry and employment data from Ohio's employment security agency files. A research database and network of statewide researchers are being formed to make this information available to local governments and other groups concerned with economic development and employment generation.

Economic development incentives

Communities and states across the country have used various public sector financing and tax incentives to encourage job creation and economic development, and many local government officials now face a "catch-22" situation in which they are criticized whether they use these tools or not. The incentive issue remains a difficult one as local government officials attempt to prepare their cities and counties for future job creation and business expansion.

Many businesses see these incentives as important to expansion and site location decisions, especially in economically distressed areas that

It is important to think beyond the individual project level when setting policies on local economic development finance.

may pose greater than average risks to successful operations. Economic developers and elected officials often believe that in order to be competitive in recruiting business they must offer incentives. Others, however, do not believe that public funds should be used to increase the profits earned by private parties, such as business owners and stockholders. Regardless of the position taken, it is essential that businesses know beforehand a community's policies on these matters. It will save much confusion and misunderstanding in the long run.

Perhaps local officials would find it helpful to think of the incentive issue in the larger context of the community's development goals. How can public and private sector investments be best used to finance development? It is important to think beyond the individual project level when setting policies on local economic development finance. At the same time, the policies established should have a positive impact on individual projects.

Impact of incentives

Academic and professional journals have been flooded with articles in recent years criticizing economic developers, planners, and elected officials for using incentives.[11] Other researchers raise concerns that incentives are unnecessary and waste taxpayers' money; they do not work the way they were intended; and they give to those firms receiving them an unfair advantage over those that do not. These are common issues that local officials must be prepared to deal with.

Suburban industrial park

To stimulate economic development and create new jobs and a tax base for the community, Huber Heights, Ohio (38,700), developed the Center Point 70 Commerce Park, a 300-acre multi-use complex located along a major north-south highway. After receiving a $530,000 grant from the county, the city constructed a new entrance road, installed park signage, and landscaped the complex. The city has secured tenants, including a 1,000-employee regional transportation distribution center. The complex led to a city-school tax abatement agreement that equalizes the tax benefits to the city and schools from any new industrial or large commercial project receiving property tax abatement. The agreement considers the total tax receipts for personal property, real, and income taxes and divides them evenly between the two parties to minimize the impact of property tax abatement on the schools. The new park has become a cornerstone of the city's development plan and promotes its transition from being a bedroom community of Dayton to being a city with a balanced mix of industrial, commercial, and residential uses.

Source: *The Guide to Management Improvement Projects in Local Government*, vol. 17, no. 2 (Washington, DC: ICMA, 1993), LD-13.

Although some studies have produced accurate and useful analyses of the impact of incentive programs, others are biased and fail to grasp adequately the overall context in which development occurs. One of the most useful analyses of government development-financing programs is a book by Timothy J. Bartik entitled *Who Benefits from State and Local Economic Development Programs?* Unlike many earlier researchers, Bartik finds that these programs produce a measurable benefit to local economies by redistributing jobs to high-unemployment areas and improving business productivity. His findings suggest that (1) state and local policies affect local growth; (2) local growth has long-term effects on the labor market; (3) faster growth helps educationally disadvantaged workers; and (4) state and local economic development is not a zero-sum game.[12]

Tax abatement

Although many earlier incentive programs—such as the federal Urban Development Action Grant Program (UDAG), Industrial Revenue Bonds (IRBs), and many state grant and loan programs—have disappeared, the use of locally approved tax abatement has grown significantly in states where abatements are legal. Tax abatement is a procedure used by local government to freeze real property taxes at a pre-development

Figure 5–1
Excerpt from a page of "Urbandale. What's in It for You?," a brochure promoting Urbandale, Iowa, as a business location.

Access Your Markets Easily

Urbandale is literally a crossroads of the nation, because Urbandale is the place where two of the nation's transcontinental highways intersect. Those highways, Interstates 35 (north-south) and 80 (east-west) put Urbandale in a transportation corridor, making access to Chicago, Omaha, St. Louis, Kansas City, Minneapolis-St. Paul, Milwaukee and Denver easy. In fact, a motor freight carrier can reach those destinations in the same day or overnight. By rail, products reach about 25 percent of the nation in a day, and the farthest point in about four days. Ample air cargo service provides rapid shipment to any destination.

Urbandale's location makes it a perfect site for warehousing and distribution, also for final assembly and light industry. Ask the companies who chose Urbandale for these reasons: Keebler Company, Lennox Industries, Casey's General Stores, the U.S. Postal Service, Super Valu Stores, Inc., Pepsi-Cola General Bottlers Inc. and Compressor Controls.

Today access is quick and easy, but even so, long term transportation improvements are planned to make Urbandale's great location even better.

Urbandale's Chamber of Commerce understands that development sites are not simply cornfields with utilities. Companies want developed sites, those with a built-in sense of community. Again, Urbandale responds. Right now there are business sites ranging in size from 1 to 50 acres, and there are an additional 200 acres zoned and available for fast-track development. In fact, that's what attracted Lennox Industries to Urbandale, the fact that in Urbandale they'd have room to grow.

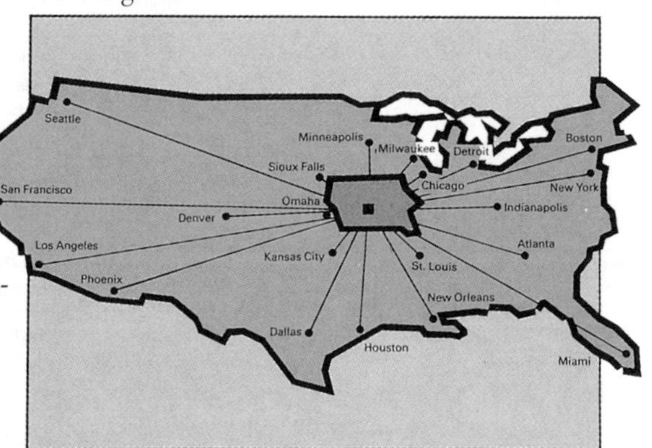

Accommodating Business and Industry

The City of Urbandale, its Chamber of Commerce and the Urbandale Development Association foster the location of business and industry in the community. You'll find us flexible in meeting objectives and timetables. You'll find us working with other agencies to facilitate project development. You'll find us open to new ideas and eager for proven new ways of developing the community. And you'll find us inviting constructive change and investigating new technology.

This isn't just rhetoric either. Urbandale responds. Like when Keebler Company wanted to build a facility in Urbandale's Interstate Acres, we streamlined the construction review process. So, Keebler's project was off the drawing board and under construction in 60 days. We also worked with Keebler on a tax abatement program.

No matter how large or small your business or industry, Urbandale has a site to suit or will help you develop one. That's accommodation. That's Urbandale's commitment to establishing a public-private partnership for the company's and the community's growth and prosperity.

Additional Incentives:

- Right to work law
- Single factor corporate income tax that means no income tax on revenues from sales outside Iowa
- Deduction of 50% of federal corporate income tax from net income to arrive at Iowa taxable income
- Long term federal tax benefits by using the Accelerated Cost Recovery System to accelerate depreciation of machinery and computers

level for a period ranging from five to fifteen years. The community chooses to forgo collection of the additional tax revenues produced by the new investment in order to gain the advantages of new economic development. The advantage to the developer is a reduction in initial and ongoing operating costs, which improves the investment's profitability. After the abatement period, property taxes are assessed at the prevailing rate.

Critics claim that these abatements rob local school districts and local governments of the property tax revenues required to balance their diminishing budgets. Economic developers and elected officials using tax abatement contend that the tax revenues forgone through the abatement are more than recovered through the income and tax stream created by the investment.

A growing concern raised by critics is the use of tax abatement by economically healthy communities, especially suburbs, to encourage the relocation to their community of a plant or office from the central city or a neighboring suburb. They maintain that abatements should be used only in economically distressed areas that need additional help to develop new business and jobs. Those offering abatements maintain that the move is good for the company from a competitive standpoint and also good for the community from a job and tax standpoint.

Community economic development tools

Location and marketing support

Community promotion
Information on the availability of suitable sites for development
Marketing the availability of a sufficient, qualified, and productive labor pool

Development financing

Tax abatement
Funds to finance public projects
Tax-exempt financing to encourage industrial and commercial development
Governmental financing programs
Public, quasi-public, and private development corporations
Tax-increment financing
Special taxing districts

Zoning and permit facilitation

Planned unit development
Mixed use development
Incentive and performance zoning
Permit facilitation and coordination

Land assembly and improvement

Use of eminent domain
Taxing property at full reuse value
Code enforcement
Rehabilitation
Historic preservation and tax credits
Relocation assistance

Project planning

Integration of city plans with private project plans
Analysis of economic base, labor force, and other factors important to projects
Leasing public space and facilities
Lease of city-owned properties to private users
Lease of land and air space

Transportation facilities

Access roads and highways
Airports
Rail access and rights-of-way
Parking facilities
Port facilities and development of navigable waterways

Special public facilities

Parks and recreation facilities
Civic and trade centers

Tax increment financing

As an alternative to tax abatement, some communities have used tax increment financing (TIF) to assist developers with initial development costs. The two are quite different in their impact on the developer and the community, and TIF is finding increased use. Basically, the technique uses the increase in property taxes from the development to help fund certain development costs such as infrastructure. These taxes are placed in a special fund, which is used to retire bonds issued to finance qualified site development costs. Tax increment financing is available to communities in twenty-four states.

State restrictions

State and local government officials in several states are re-examining the policies guiding the use of public financial and tax incentives. Newer approaches seek to limit the use of these programs to projects that clearly alleviate distress in the community and also provide an equitable return on the community's investment in terms of future jobs and taxes. Some groups are pushing for the outright elimination of these programs

Qualities of a successful marketing program

1. Research on the community's strengths and weaknesses in regard to economic development underlies the marketing program.
2. Clear goals and objectives guide community marketing efforts; these goals become the basis for judging the program's success.
3. Marketing activities reflect consistent overall themes or basic messages about the community; too many messages tend to confuse the audience.
4. Market segments, representing target industries or other opportunities to be developed, are carefully defined; marketing activities are geared to these groups.
5. Marketing materials are factual in nature and provide information that is clearly relevant to business decision making; generalities have little impact on business location and investment decisions.
6. Because the economic identity of a smaller community is usually judged in a larger regional context, the advantages of the surrounding area are emphasized in the community's marketing materials.
7. Quality is always more important that quantity. It is far better for a community to develop a few high-quality marketing tools (brochures, community profiles, special events, etc.) than to produce a full complement of marketing materials that are low in quality. The proper mix of marketing activities (public relations, advertising, direct mail, data packages, prospect presentations, special events) must be created.
8. Testimonials from businesses currently located in the community make a stronger impression than claims community officials make about themselves.
9. Creative professional follow-up is undertaken to develop investment leads generated by marketing activities.
10. Marketing activities must be conducted consistently over a long period of time to produce acceptable results; one-shot efforts almost never work.
11. Results are evaluated at least annually to allow for any necessary adjustments to activities in the future, even though economic development activities normally do not produce results in less than a year's time.

by state legislatures or the federal government. For the most part, these actions are seen as unrealistic. If taken, they could place a state or community at a serious competitive disadvantage for future business expansions.

Marketing

Downtown development, infrastructure improvements, support for small businesses, education of the workforce, and economic incentives are all necessary parts of any program to attract and retain business, but marketing is also essential. The local economic development effort must include a comprehensive strategy to promote the community as an attractive location for business. After a realistic assessment has been made of the community's assets and liabilities, local government officials should devise a plan to present the community as a potential site for appropriate businesses and industry. A 1989 economic development marketing study completed by Cleveland State University for AEDC found that public-private partnerships play a key role in this area. Innovative marketing programs were identified in smaller cities such as Gadsden, Alabama; Savannah, Georgia; Spartanburg, South Carolina; and Joliet, Illinois.[13] The accompanying sidebar describes the qualities of a successful marketing program for smaller communities.

Regional approaches and strategies

As communities increase their efforts to attract and retain business, the competition for economic opportunities grows. Communities have thus become aware that the characteristics of different localities and the benefits they offer (for example, an attractive physical environment, a skilled workforce, a good educational system, and economic development incentives) have a major impact on a company's decision concerning where to set up or expand a business. Community officials are also more aware of the interdependence of places: what happens in one area has an impact on others. A plant opening or closing in one city can help or hurt the economic base of a neighboring community, especially within specific regions, where related firms and industries may cluster, or where a business operation in one community draws a significant part of its workforce from nearby communities.

This growing realization of the interdependence of places has led to a trend toward a regional approach to economic development. Smaller cities and counties sharing the same economic region have much in common with one another. These common interests and resources are good reasons for communities to cooperate with one another in increasing economic opportunities. The trend toward regionalism is reflected in an array of new economic development programs and policies. Growth management planning, cooperative approaches to regional development marketing, tax-base sharing, coordinated regional infrastructure planning, and other strategies are receiving greater attention from smaller cities and counties.[14]

Regional development

A number of state governments are encouraging regional cooperation by communities. Ohio recently opened twelve regional economic development offices across the state that help local officials receive state assistance with development projects. Each of Ohio's eighty-eight counties has prepared and submitted plans outlining its top development priorities. Many relate to local infrastructure and environmental cleanup needs. The Ohio regional offices are intended to expedite state assistance and serve as catalysts for regional cooperation. The offices report significant progress toward both goals.

Other states, including Illinois, Virginia, New York, and Indiana, have also implemented strategies for regional economic development. Illinois's Corridors of Opportunity Program provides a geographic and industrial focus for economic development across the state. The industry-targeting component of the program focuses on high-technology, automotive, agribusiness, service-sector, and tourist industries in various regions. The Southern Illinois Corridor, composed of a twenty-county area in the southern part of the state, is heavily focused on development of tourism but also encourages growth in industries such as production of secondary wood products and poultry farming. Most of the corridors encourage smaller communities to join forces in marketing for job creation and business investment.

Virginia established regional planning and development districts in the 1960s. These regions encourage intercommunity cooperation in setting broader priorities related to economic development. A recent report by the Joint Legislative Audit and Review Committee of the Virginia General Assembly found that these districts have reduced the fragmentation of economic development efforts by localities and contributed to more efficient and effective use of limited resources. Predominantly smaller cities and counties are served by these districts.

International economic development alliance

A regional approach toward international economic development has proven successful for four northwest Dallas suburbs—Farmers Branch (26,460), Carrollton (61,960), Addison (7,340), and Coppell (9,820). Working with the Metrocrest Chamber of Commerce, which represents all four suburbs, the group has undertaken an aggressive international economic development program. In 1990, the cities entered into an economic alliance with the Markham Board of Trade and the York Technology Association, representing the town of Markham, Canada, a suburb of Toronto. The alliance has contributed to improved international trade and to the establishment of offices representing Canadian firms and Canadian distribution facilities in the Texas cities.

Source: Richard Escalante, City Manager, Farmers Branch, Texas, 1993.

Tax-base sharing

Interest in regional tax-base sharing arrangements is growing in several states. Although many political and management problems hamper the use of these approaches, several communities are using them or considering their use. For example, the city of Bloomington, the town of Normal, and McLean County, Illinois, developed a plan for sharing costs and tax revenues in connection with a plan that brought a major new automobile assembly plant to the community. Generally, tax-base sharing describes a situation in which two or more local governments share the tax revenues generated by future economic growth. As a policy initiative, this strategy aims to reduce disparities and competition among local governments, encourage long-range development planning, stabilize local tax revenues, and enhance the capacity of local government to meet future service and infrastructure needs.

The Minnesota Fiscal Disparities Program, created in 1971, was the first known program for local tax-base sharing. More recent programs have been created in Wisconsin, Michigan, and other states. Under Ohio law, cities can enter into a contract to establish a joint economic development zone and share the costs and tax revenues resulting from development within the zone. Several cities are now exploring the use of such zones. Sub-state programs have been created in Louisville-Jefferson County, Kentucky; Hackensack, New Jersey; and selected other places.

Public-private partnerships

Public-private partnerships are playing a much larger role in an increasing number of counties and smaller cities. In these partnerships, public and private sector resources come together to promote the development of existing industry and to attract new business. Nearly 30 percent of all communities responding to ICMA's survey had partnerships in place. Another 25 percent of respondents reported that private business groups such as chambers of commerce had taken the lead in their community.[15]

Local government is a key actor in these partnerships. It plays several roles in the local economic development process, such as helping businesses to expand and develop through site location assistance, infrastructure improvements, and various economic incentives and ensuring that development projects are consistent with laws, regulations, and community values.

The form (or organization) of a public-private partnership should always follow function (tasks and goals). Too many communities select an organizational form before defining the job to be done. As a result, many self-inflicted problems arise that limit success. A very common problem is that the organization excludes certain key stakeholder groups from the economic development process. The right people—including representatives of government agencies, businesses, community groups, and the educational establishment—must be involved to get the job done right.

Marketing the local hotel industry

The city of Farmers Branch, Texas (26,460), located near the Dallas/Fort Worth Airport, has formed a public-private partnership with the hotel industry in the city. Through a marketing campaign developed with the assistance of the hotel industry, the city is marketing the use of Farmers Branch hotels across the state of Texas, in surrounding states, and in Mexico. The relationship has proven so successful that the hotel managers asked the city to raise the hotel/motel tax to fund a major Christmas tourism event to attract holiday visitors to the city and the hotels.

Source: Richard Escalante, City Manager, Farmers Branch, Texas, 1993.

Globalization

As the trend toward globalization brings countries closer together, foreign business investment in the United States has grown, and a significant number of international companies make investments each year in smaller communities. Overall, British and Canadian companies have made the largest number of these investments; however, Japanese companies have had the highest increase in the rate of new investments in recent years. States like Ohio, Indiana, Kentucky, and Michigan have experienced rapid growth in this area, particularly in the automotive sector; hundreds of Japanese auto manufacturers and their suppliers have located in these states.

The majority of investments have occurred in smaller cities and counties.[16] Some of them, such as Madisonville, Kentucky (16,800), have aggressively promoted themselves as locations for foreign business.

Madisonville has implemented an attraction program aimed at specific industry targets, zeroing in on Dutch and Canadian companies. The program has been highly effective. Two Canadian firms have located in the community since 1990, and in 1993 the city hosted a Dutch-American golf tournament to attract Dutch business leaders, twenty of whom attended and learned about the advantages the city has to offer for future investment.

Southfield, Michigan, export initiative

In Southfield, Michigan (73,000), a small group of people has taken the initiative to help local firms pursue export markets. Calling itself the Southfield International Trade Program, the group includes a councilperson, the city's economic development director, representatives from the chamber of commerce, a representative from the local technical/business school, and a few other interested people.

When the fledgling organization discussed goals and objectives, it was agreed that the top priority was to find out what Southfield firms were currently doing: what products they were producing, how much they were exporting, what they would like to do, and what training or assistance they needed. The International Trade Program thus took as its first task a survey of local small and medium businesses.

The next step will be to develop packages that can be offered to any member of the Southfield Chamber of Commerce without charge, informing them about programs available to them from various government and private sources and helping them cooperate with other businesses with like needs. The packages will be built around particular industries or types of products or services to encourage piggyback promotions.

The International Trade Program is trying to fill in the gaps for local firms looking for technical assistance in export development. The group is encouraging the local technical/business school, Lawrence Technological University, to upgrade its services so that it can become a small business development center, offering federally funded local help to young companies trying to grow by selling products or services to wider markets.

Source: "Export Development: Local Initiatives," *MIS Report*, vol. 24, no. 4 (April 1992): 9-10.

More communities and states are helping local companies to increase their share of the global marketplace. Export development programs are common in state development agencies and large metropolitan development organizations. Although smaller communities tend not to operate their own export promotion programs because of the lack of economy of scale, development officials in these communities are working with state and regional groups to offer trade development services to interested businesses. Because these services help existing companies to increase their market, they can be considered tools for the retention and expansion of existing business.

Growth management

Although most small communities still rank economic development and growth among their goals, many realize that unchecked economic development can have negative as well as beneficial effects. Possible negative effects are overcrowding, environmental and aesthetic degradation, increased demand for services, and overburdened infrastructure. For many smaller communities, therefore, the concern has shifted from encouraging growth to managing growth.

A recent Urban Land Institute study found master planning, coupled with various other techniques, to be a common strategy for managing growth.

The greatest growth pressures come from housing, retail, and office development. Communities in California, Florida, and the Northern Virginia area experienced extreme development pressure in the 1980s, causing them to become more selective about what type of growth to encourage. States such as Colorado and Oregon have long maintained tight control over development for environmental and aesthetic reasons. Interest in growth management is growing in many other states as well, and not just in those growing most rapidly. Common objectives are to alleviate congestion and crowding caused by high density; to reduce or avoid environmental degradation; and to provide equitable ways to finance infrastructure improvements required by new development projects.

The range of growth management techniques includes tighter enforcement of environmental regulations; development transfer rights; restrictive covenants; subdivision regulations; exactions; various tax and fee systems, including development impact fees; large-lot zoning; conservation zoning; and development moratoriums. The use of these techniques should be defined by the community's overall development plan or strategy. Smaller communities may find it beneficial to examine the experience of communities already using these growth control strategies, such as Fairfax and Loudoun counties in Virginia; Dade and Orange counties in Florida; Prince George's and Montgomery counties in Maryland; and the city of Petaluma, California.

Growth management is also a concern in "new" communities such as Reston, Virginia, and Columbia, Maryland. A recent Urban Land Institute study examined the experiences of fifty-eight new communities across the country. The study found master planning, coupled with various other techniques, to be a common strategy for managing growth in these communities.[17]

Figure 5–2 An effective growth management strategy balances the demands for environmental protection and economic development.

Growth management and economic development

Growth management can enhance economic development by establishing a framework for development, fostering a positive business climate, and reducing the negative consequences of development.

Business executives recognize that an area's business climate consists of far more than the local government's willingness to grant concessions and incentive packages in order to attract new industries and expand existing operations. A free-for-all approach to growth in which anything goes and any industry is considered fair game detracts from the local business climate in the minds of many private sector executives.

On the other hand, a growth management system that sets forth an orderly plan and reasonable criteria for development, while recognizing the importance of preserving the quality of life of residents and corporate clients, sends a positive message to business executives. Certainly, market access, labor costs, raw materials, and transportation availability remain critical components of location and expansion decisions. However, various quality-of-life factors, ranging from the educational system to recreational opportunities to the capacity of the social service system, are becoming increasingly important to businesses seeking to relocate, expand, or develop.

Source: Adapted from Charldean Newell, ed., *The Effective Local Government Manager* (Washington, DC: ICMA, 1993), 152.

Conclusion

It is difficult to offer general advice applicable to the thousands of counties and smaller cities found across the country. Nevertheless, these communities may want to consider the following observations.

America's smaller communities are prime candidates for future growth. This is evident from past and current patterns of commercial and industrial development. Moreover, many of these localities already recognize their potential and are working hard to achieve it. The rich and diverse array of programs and strategies identified by the studies reviewed in this chapter suggest that economic developers, planners, and elected officials serving these communities are open to experimentation and innovation.

Several authors, including David Osborne and Ted Gaebler, have written about the need to reinvent government and make government units more entrepreneurial.[18] Already, many established and emerging smaller communities around the country reflect an entrepreneurial spirit not unlike that of the entrepreneurs who are building America's fastest-growing and most exciting businesses, and the widespread use of public-private partnerships to achieve local government goals is one obvious manifestation of that spirit. Hard work lies ahead for communities that follow this path, but initial developments are encouraging. For example, more communities are devising and implementing strategic plans to guide their economic development efforts. More communities are concerned about the creation of higher-quality jobs that offer residents a respectable living standard. Finally, many communities are focusing increased attention on helping existing businesses to become more competitive through workforce development, improvements in current technologies, and expanded opportunities for international sales. If these preliminary efforts hold true, the new, more entrepreneurial approach to government will have a positive impact on these communities' economies.

Those individuals guiding economic development efforts in smaller communities are more professional and strategic in their approach than earlier generations of economic development practitioners working in the public sector. This improvement is due at least in part to the efforts of national associations such as ICMA, the National Council for Urban Economic Development, AEDA, and others that provide valuable opportunities for local practitioners to increase their knowledge and sharpen their skills.

Current indications point to a greater reliance on regional approaches to economic development to improve local resources and develop new opportunities.

Current indications point to a greater reliance on regional approaches to economic development, which will call upon counties and smaller communities to work more closely with their neighbors to improve local resources and develop new opportunities. New regional development programs, like the one launched by the Ohio governor's office and department of development, offer the promise of more intergovernmental cooperation in economic development. Increased cooperation is especially important in light of shrinking budget support for infrastructure and educational improvements.

Counties and smaller cities must strike a balance between promoting and managing growth in the future. Although this need is especially evident in fast-growth areas, it will be more necessary in slower-growth environments as well. New environmental regulations addressing issues such as wetlands, solid waste disposal, and other problems will represent new challenges for local governments concerned about achieving economic growth in an environmentally conscious time. Limited funds for development-related infrastructure will contribute to more growth management as well.

Smaller community economic development programs must address issues associated with both economic growth and decline in the future. Even growing communities must be ready for possible plant and office closings that dislocate workers and reduce the local tax base. A slower national economy and the impact of broader social, economic, political, and technological events can introduce new pressures for local economic change.

Competition for economic development opportunities is expected to remain keen in the future. Smaller communities fared reasonably well in this competition in the past decade. Future competition will require even better-focused strategies that link community resources and development opportunities. The key in the future will be to sustain growth and achieve long-term community stability. This challenge goes beyond simply keeping existing employers and attracting a sufficient number of new ones. It requires that economic development activities be more closely coordinated with other community priorities such as education, quality of life, and environmental management.

In general, smaller communities have much to be encouraged about in considering their future economic health; nevertheless, hard work lies ahead.

Afterword

Economic development may not replace baseball as the national pastime, but it surely has become the biggest game in town for the governments of small cities and counties. In fact, Kane County, Illinois, used economic development techniques creatively when it purchased a minor league baseball team in a successful effort to make residents aware of the county as a community. Kane County's efforts also demonstrated the importance and value of strategic planning, not only for economic development, but more important, for community development.

The communities that ultimately win at the economic development game will be those that employ strategic planning and economic development as tools to achieve a predetermined set of community goals. When thus employed, economic development contributes to the task of building a better community, and development of the total community is, after all, the ultimate purpose of any economic development activity. ■

---

[1] See Cheryl Farr, "Encouraging Local Economic Development: The State of the Practice," in *Municipal Year Book 1990* (Washington, DC: ICMA); Donald Haider, "Place Wars: New Realities of the 1990's," *Economic Development Quarterly* (May 1992); John P. Pelissero and David Fasenfest, "A Typology of Suburban Economic Development Policy Orientations," *Economic Development Quarterly* (November 1989); *Small City Economic Development: Roads to Success* (Washington, DC: National League of Cities, 1991); and Harry Black, *Achieving Economic Development Success: Tools That Work* (Washington, DC: ICMA, 1991).

[2] See Jack Lessinger, *Penturbia* (Seattle, WA: SocioEconomics, 1991) and G. Scott Thomas, *The Rating Guide to Life in America's Small Cities* (Buffalo, NY: Prometheus, 1990).

[3] See American Economic Development Council, *Economic Development Tomorrow: A Report from the Profession* (Chicago: 1991).

[4] See Cheryl Farr, "Encouraging Local Economic Development."

[5] See Michael Fladeland, "Strategic Planning in Communities in North Central States," *Economic Development Review* (Summer 1991).

[6] See Ross M. Boyle, "Summary of 1991 GSO Survey Responses on Targeting Practices of Local Economic Development Organizations" (Reston, VA: Growth Strategies Organization, 1992).

[7] See David A. Heenan, *The New Corporate Frontier: The Big Move to Small Town, USA* (New York: McGraw-Hill, 1991).

[8] See Nancy Williams, "Community Agenda for the 1990's: A Corporate View," *Economic Development Review* 9 (Summer 1991).

[9] See *Small City Economic Development* (Washington, DC: National League of Cities, 1991).

[10] See CUED, *Community Colleges: An Economic Development Resource* (Washington, DC: December 1989) and Midwest Research Institute, *A Portfolio of Community College Initiatives in Rural Economic Development* (Kansas City, MO: April 1989).

[11] Many articles on this topic have appeared in the last two to three years in *Economic Development Quarterly*.

[12] See Timothy J. Bartik, *Who Benefits from State and Local Economic Development Programs?* (Kalamazoo, MI: W. E. Upjohn Institute for Employment Research, 1991).

[13] In 1989, the Economic Development Program at Cleveland State University conducted a national study of how cities and urban areas marketed themselves for economic development. The findings were published in a monograph by the American Economic Development Council entitled *Marketing Cities in the 1980's and Beyond: New Patterns, New Pressures, and New Promises* (Chicago: 1989).

[14] See David A. Heenan, *The New Corporate Frontier*.

[15] See Cheryl Farr, "Encouraging Local Economic Development."

[16] See Donald T. Iannone, "Policy Implications of Foreign Business Recruitment as an Economic Development Strategy: The Case of Japanese Automotive Investment in the United States," *Economic Development Review* 6 (Fall 1988).

[17] See *Developing Successful New Communities* (Washington, DC: Urban Land Institute, 1991).

[18] See David Osborne and Ted Gaebler, *Reinventing Government: How the Entrepreneurial Spirit is Transforming the Public Sector* (New York: Addison-Wesley, 1992).

Public Works

More than two hundred years ago, Adam Smith wrote that the functions of government should be limited to providing for the national defense, affording the protection of law, and *undertaking indispensable public works*. What are public works? In the book entitled *Management of Local Public Works*, ICMA adapts a definition from the founder of the American Public Works Association, Donald C. Stone:

> *Public works are the physical structures and facilities that are developed or acquired by public agencies to house governmental functions and provide water, power, waste disposal, transportation, and similar services,* and are managed by experienced, intelligent, dedicated professionals to facilitate and ensure continuously better service to the public *[emphasis in original].*[1]

The American Public Works Association (APWA) has identified 145 different functions that are related to public works.[2] These functions can be classified into municipal engineering, equipment services, transportation, water resources, solid wastes, building and grounds, administrative management, and special services. These functions (with the exception of special services) correspond with APWA's professional membership categories.

Municipal engineering includes those functions most closely related to civil engineering. A majority of the local governments responding to an APWA survey indicated that they perform the following municipal engineering functions: new facilities design; construction inspection; surveying; and strength testing of materials such as concrete. Larger public works agencies tend to perform their own engineering services, although smaller jurisdictions typically contract services out to consulting firms. Virtually all jurisdictions contract out major and complex projects.

Equipment services, referred to as fleet management in larger jurisdictions, involves the management of vehicles and other equipment. Sixty-two percent of public works departments maintain their own equipment, and 55 percent also maintain vehicles from other departments. The larger the jurisdiction, the more likely it is to provide equipment services.

Transportation includes major systems such as streets, bridges, sidewalks, airports, and seaports, and services such as traffic control. Transportation is a major responsibility of virtually all public works agencies, although some of the services may be provided by contract. More than half of the respondents to the APWA survey provided street and catch basin cleaning, street and sidewalk maintenance, snow and ice removal, traffic sign installation, street painting and striping, curb and street cut inspections, street construction and design, traffic sign manufacturing, bikeway construction, and bridge maintenance.

The APWA survey indicated that 52 percent of responding department heads prepared their own departmental budgets.

Water resources include water supply, water distribution, stormwater and flood control, wastewater collection, and wastewater treatment. Although many public works departments provide their own stormwater control, wastewater collection and treatment and potable (drinking) water are often provided by other departments, such as single-purpose water or wastewater departments or regional special districts. Quite often, the extent of the local government's responsibility is a function of its size and the proximity and accessibility of the area's major water source.

Solid waste collection is primarily the responsibility of local public works departments. *Solid waste disposal*—landfill operations, incineration, and recycling—tends to be provided by regional agencies or by the private sector.

Building and grounds refers to management of public buildings and other public facilities. This function includes urban forestry as well as some construction and janitorial and maintenance activities.

Organization of public works

There is no standard or recommended organizational structure for fulfilling local government public works functions. There is not even agreement about what should be included under the label public works. Some communities, for example, place functions such as code enforcement, traffic engineering, and parkway maintenance under public works; others place such functions elsewhere (e.g., code enforcement in a building department; traffic engineering in the police department; and parkway maintenance in the parks department). Some communities place all vehicle maintenance in the public works department. Others give each operating department the responsibility for maintaining its own vehicles, or they contract out this service.

Some communities place all public works functions in a single department; others place responsibility for streets and sidewalks in a public works department but have a separate water department; sanitation department (to remove and dispose of solid waste, wastewater, or both); building and grounds department; forestry department (for street trees); and engineering department. There is no evidence to suggest that one or another organizational pattern is better; size of community, range of public works functions, complexity of operations, and idiosyncratic local considerations all combine to shape the organization's structures.

The appointment of a person with a background in civil engineering as director of public works has been common practice for many years. More recently this practice has begun to give way to the employment of public works directors who have training and experience in public administration. Some communities now require their public works director to have a master of public administration (MPA) degree and work experience in a public works department. The need to use the services of consultants with highly specialized engineering knowledge and the increasing complexity of government management suggest that administrative training and experience will be increasingly demanded of public works directors in the future.

Administrative management includes not only operations management and supervision, but also support activities such as agency budget preparation, human relations, and fee collections. Larger public works agencies tend to provide these services themselves, whereas smaller agencies tend to use the support of centralized units in the jurisdiction. The previously mentioned APWA survey indicated that 52 percent of responding department heads prepared their own departmental budgets.

Special services as identified by APWA include such things as dead-animal pickup, cemetery operation, dock maintenance, shore preservation, and beach maintenance.

This chapter does not attempt to describe all the functions listed above. Instead, it stresses the importance of maintaining infrastructure, both physical and human; it looks at the engineering function, focusing in particular on the use of consulting engineering firms by smaller jurisdictions; and it discusses three issues of particular concern to public works directors today: solid waste disposal, water resources management, and transportation management. Finally, the chapter describes some of the general management challenges faced by public works directors.

Public works functions

Streets and highways	Engineering
Street cleaning	Solid-waste collection
Snow removal	Solid-waste disposal
Street lighting	Solid-waste billing
Street striping (marking)	Building inspection
Street signs	Building maintenance
Surveying	Custodial services
Traffic engineering	Construction inspection
Traffic signals	Park maintenance
Traffic signs	Cemetery operation
Water treatment	Radio system
Water distribution	Parking meter system
Water meter reading	Equipment maintenance
Water utility billing	Animal control
Water service	Computer operation
Sewage treatment	Electric power distribution
Sewage collection system	Electric power billing
Sewer utility billing	Gas power distribution
Storm sewer system	Gas billing
Storm water management	Street tree planting and maintenance
Zoning/subdivision control	Airport services

Infrastructure management

Unfortunately, most people take little notice of public works until there is need for repair. Concern over the condition of infrastructure began to emerge in the 1980s when the nation's infrastructure systems were declared to be either in ruins or on fragile foundations.[3] In 1984, Congress established the National Council on Public Works Improvement to prepare a report on the state of the nation's infrastructure. Over five thousand pages of research material were prepared over a two-year period, resulting in the council's "Report Card on the Nation's Public Works" (Figure 6–1). The report demonstrated the unevenness of the infrastructure system and gave the nation an overall "grade" of *C*, considered to be barely passing.

Figure 6–1

REPORT CARD ON THE NATION'S PUBLIC WORKS			
Subject Category	**Grade**	**Successes/Recent Changes**	**Problems/Future Weaknesses**
Highways	*C*+	Federal and state gas tax increases have injected new capital into the system. This, along with increased O&M spending, has improved pavement conditions. However, quality of service in terms of congestion is declining.	Spending for system expansion has fallen short of need in high-growth urban and suburban areas. Many roadways and bridges are aging and require major work. Needs of most rural and smaller systems exceed available resources. Highway Trust Fund has a sizeable cash balance.
Mass Transit	*C*-	Federal capital grants have helped improve quality of service in some areas, but overall productivity of the system has declined significantly. Growth of transit vehicles is double the rate of increase in ridership. Diverting people from cars is increasingly difficult.	Mass transit is overcapitalized in many smaller cities and inadequate in large, older cities. Systems rarely are linked to land-use planning and broader transportation goals. Maintenance has been erratic and inadequate, especially in older cities.
Aviation	*B*-	In general, the aviation system has handled rapid increases in demand safely and effectively. However, service has begun to decline in the face of increasing airport and airspace congestion as a result of strong traffic growth. The air traffic control system is currently undergoing a $16 billion modernization.	Congestion is the system's primary problem. Despite recent increases in authorizations, sizeable cash balance remains unspent in the Airport and Airway Trust Fund. The air traffic control system needs substantial upgrading to maintain safety.
Water Resources	*B*	Water Resources Act of 1986 made cost-sharing mandatory for many types of water projects. This change should improve project selection and reduce overall project costs.	Cost-sharing will improve efficiency but also increase local costs of water projects. Poorer communities may find it difficult to finance projects. Implementation is often excessively slow and cumbersome.
Water Supply	*B*-	While regional performance varies, water supply stands out as an effective, locally-operated program. Strict new standards created by the 1986 Safe Drinking Water Act will require drastic increases in water rates over the next decade.	Many public water systems suffer from pricing below costs, inability to meet purity standards, or source contamination. Storage and distribution systems are deteriorating in some older cities and supplies are limited in some parts of the West and several cities along the East coast.
Wastewater	*C*	Over 75% of U.S. population is served by secondary treatment plants. Shift from federal grants to state revolving loans may improve efficiency of plant construction. Broadened focus on nonpoint source pollution and groundwater contamination may accelerate progress toward cleaner water.	Despite $44 billion federal investment in sewage treatment since 1972, water quality has not improved significantly. This is due in part to uncontrolled sources of pollution, such as run-off from farmland and roadways. Overall productivity of secondary treatment facilities is declining, resulting in an increase in water quality violations.
Solid Waste	*C*-	Testing and monitoring of solid waste facilities are more rigorous as a result of tougher environmental standards. Waste-to-energy technology is growing as alternative to landfills. More aggressive waste reduction, separation, and recycling efforts are beginning at the local level. However, few states have moved boldly on these measures.	Nation faces significant costs of adequate and safe facilities. Limited data suggest trends toward fewer but safer landfills, rapid growth in resource recovery, and little progress toward waste reduction. Public opposition to siting all types of facilities is a major problem.
Hazardous Waste	*D*	Funding for site clean-up has increased five-fold since 1986, but progress has been slower than expected. Only a small fraction of the two tons of waste per capita produced in America each year is being treated safely. Major challenge is still ahead of us.	Nation has forfeited much of its opportunity to reduce waste before it is produced. Waste control legislation promotes "end-of-pipe" rather than source reduction solutions. Congressional mandates and schedules may be overly optimistic, given administrative resources. A massive backlog of poisons and needed cleanup projects faces the nation.

Deferred maintenance

The main contributor to the poor condition of the nation's infrastructure is deferred maintenance. Americans have been very good at building structures but for a number of reasons have not been as enthusiastic about keeping them up.

Federally influenced deferred maintenance

Historically, conditions of intergovernmental grants to local communities have made it seem reasonable—even to good managers—to defer needed maintenance. Until recently, the federal government would not fund maintenance and minor rehabilitation of infrastructure, but it would support new construction or replacement. As a result, too often locally funded maintenance was deferred, allowing a facility to deteriorate to the extent necessary to qualify for federally funded replacement or major rehabilitation. The cumulative impact of such decisions is that taxpayers nationally are paying a higher cost to maintain the integrity of infrastructure systems.

Impact of a federal policy

An example of federally influenced deferred maintenance is provided by federal policy regarding the use of the federal Airport and Airway Trust Fund. The federal government will not finance maintenance through the fund, but it will replace runways that are beyond repair. Rather than spending local money to extend the life of runways, local officials are prompted to allow them to deteriorate to a potentially unsafe condition, then close them down (an inconvenience to citizens) and construct new runways on the same site, using federal dollars.

Hidden from view

The fact that many infrastructure systems are hidden from view is a second cause of deferred maintenance. Systems may be underground, like water and wastewater systems, or they may be underwater like bridge foundations. Until the introduction of improved technologies such as remote-control video machines, it was physically difficult to inspect for wear and damage on such systems.

Financial tradeoffs

A third reason for deferred maintenance is that during times of fiscal austerity, maintenance of existing structures is easily deferred to future years in lieu of cutting other popular local services. In a sense, it is easier to take the risk that the infrastructure will not fail in the current fiscal year than to cut expenditures on direct service delivery. Occasionally local government managers lose this bet, with disastrous consequences.

Consequences of deferred maintenance

The 1983 collapse of the Mianus River Bridge near Greenwich, Connecticut; the destruction of the Cypress Viaduct of the Nimitz Freeway in Oakland, California, during the 1989 earthquake; and the Great Chicago Flood of 1992, which resulted from deferred maintenance on tunnels under the Chicago River, all serve as grim reminders of what can happen when local public officials take chances on deferring public works maintenance.

Lack of political payoff

Yet another reason that maintenance is deferred rests in the lack of a political payoff for maintenance. Politicians like to be associated with growth and development and therefore are quicker to embrace new construction. Maintenance, on the other hand, is just that—maintaining existing systems. There are no ribbon-cuttings associated with the filling of a pothole, and no one is anxious to put his or her name on a rehabilitated sewer line. These are low-profile activities, often considered mundane by political standards.

Repair, rehabilitation, and replacement

Public works managers must pay attention to maintaining infrastructure even if politicians do not. Infrastructure management strategies are organized around what are described as the three *R*s: *repair*, *rehabilitate*, and *replace*.

Repair involves correcting a minor problem. Pothole patching, roof repair, and crack sealing are considered repairs. These activities maintain the integrity of the existing structure. *Rehabilitation* is an intervention made to improve the existing quality of the structure or to restore it to its original condition. Efforts to improve the strength of a structure or to replace major components are considered rehabilitation. If pothole patching is repairing, then a complete asphalt overlay would be considered rehabilitation. *Replacement* involves the demolition of an existing system or facility and the construction of a new and improved one.

Repair and rehabilitation require yearly funding through the annual operating budget; however, these strategies can save money in the long run by extending the useful life of a facility. The downward slope of the curve in Figure 6–2 represents the deterioration of pavement over time, with the typical life of pavement estimated at twenty years. The life span of each pavement will vary depending on design standards; changes in volume, weight, and speed of traffic; weather; and pavement cuts for utilities. The horizontal axis of the graph represents a quality index, in this case on a one-to-five scale.

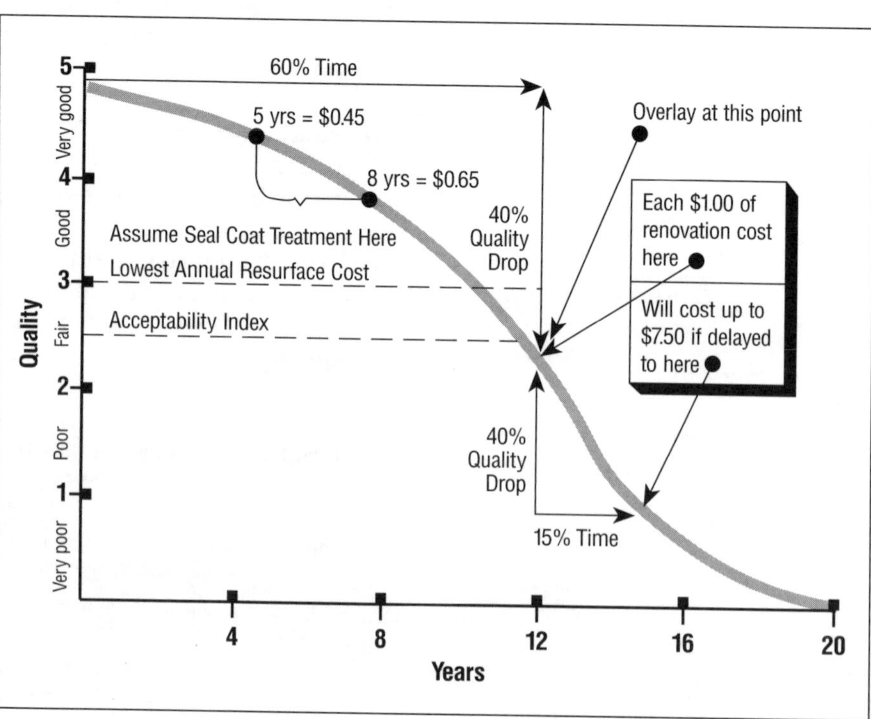

Figure 6–2 Road deterioration over time and relative costs of renovations.

Figure 6–2 correctly indicates that deterioration accelerates over time. There is a 40-percent reduction in quality over the first 60 percent (twelve years) of estimated life. However, there is an equal 40-percent reduction in the next 15 percent (three years) of life. Therefore, using this figure, one can formulate maintenance strategies. The cost to place a single-seal coat treatment on very good (4.5 Percent Serviceability Index [PSI]) pavement at Year 5 would be $0.45 per square yard; to place a double-seal coat treatment on a good (4.0 PSI) pavement may cost $0.65 per square yard. Delaying maintenance until the pavement needs rehabilitating by, for example, placing a hot-mix overlay in Year 12 (2.5 PSI) will require an expenditure of $1.00 per square yard. However, if the maintenance is delayed until Year 15, when the pavement is very poor (2 PSI), the cost will escalate to $7.50 per square yard.

A variety of computer packages are designed to assist not only with pavement management but also with maintenance schedules for other infrastructure systems.

A variety of computer packages are designed to assist not only with pavement management but also with maintenance schedules for other infrastructure systems. Good systems are able to provide information on maintenance history, current conditions, and future performance. These computer packages should also be able to target components for maintenance and present information in a format that is understandable to decision makers. Managers may then direct funds to those projects with the greatest need.

When a system or facility has not been adequately maintained, or when a community's needs change (for example, because of a population increase or the introduction of new technology), replacement becomes necessary. Replacements are planned as part of the capital improvements program and funded through the capital budget. Examples include the construction of new fire stations, wastewater treatment plants, major streets, swimming pools, city halls, and water lines.

Maintaining human infrastructure

The definition of infrastructure at the beginning of this chapter stated that public works are "managed by experienced, intelligent, dedicated professionals to facilitate and ensure continuously better service to the public." This definition could be expanded to include not only those who manage public works systems, but also those who develop the technologies, materials, and processes that make public works more efficient. These individuals constitute the human infrastructure of public works.

Despite acknowledgment that human beings are a vital component of the infrastructure system, there has been no consistent and sustained attention from any level of government concerning a human infrastructure policy. Nor have isolated funding spurts for infrastructure included components for training, research and development, or technology transfer. Unfortunately, when budgets get tight, training and professional development budgets are among the first to be cut by local policymakers.

The recent APWA survey of public works directors referred to previously indicated that formal education is an important ingredient in the successful management of public works. Of the respondents, 55 percent believed that an engineering degree is necessary; 39 percent preferred a management degree; and most agreed that continuing education should focus on managerial training. The traditional engineering curriculum at the college level offers little opportunity for students to take advantage of management, finance, and other public administration electives. The overwhelming support for continuing training in the managerial arts is an indication that engineers have come to appreciate the value of management training in their professional development.

The importance of training and development

The use of new technologies, materials, and managerial methods in public works may be hampered when governing bodies do not understand and appreciate the value of formal education, continuing education, and attendance at conferences and workshops—maintaining the human infrastructure—especially for public works managers.

The capital and operating budgets of public works agencies make them among the largest community agencies. Unlike their counterparts of old, future public works managers will not have the luxury of experimenting with hit-or-miss management techniques, processes, or materials while on the job; the stakes are too high. When dealing with expensive infrastructure systems, maintaining the human infrastructure is the best way to ensure peak productivity.

Top managers are not the only public works professionals who need continuing education. Middle managers and those directly involved in supervising operations can gain from regional workshops and state and national conferences. The two largest conferences for general public works departments and their managers are the APWA International Congress and Exposition and the North American Snow Conference. Although conferences of this kind are beneficial and allow practitioners to share solutions to common problems, local budgets may not permit attendance by all of a department's management personnel. Recognizing this, the APWA has developed workshops, such as "Basic Supervision in Public Works," and video presentations, such as "Small City Fleet Management," for local presentation by nationally known instructors.

Some public works personnel are required to have licenses administered by state agencies. These licenses are intended to assure minimum levels of competence in the operation of such facilities as water, wastewater treatment, and power plants. Professional associations and state agencies provide the training necessary for licensing on various levels. As a rule, the more highly regulated the public works function, the more likely it is to require a license.

Engineering and public works

Local government engineering includes highly sophisticated aspects as well as more technical and skill-related engineering functions. The former includes preparation of major capital improvements and design of such projects as arterial streets and water treatment plants. Engineering technologists, on the other hand, perform functions such as establishing and setting street and sidewalk grades, inspecting construction, and implementing computerized maintenance systems.

Registered professional engineers

All states require that public works engineering designs be approved by a registered professional engineer (PE). In Ohio, for example, the designs for all new construction projects estimated to cost more than $4,000 must be prepared by PEs. To attain registration as a PE, an engineer must graduate from an accredited university engineering or related science program, have four years' post-baccalaureate experience, and pass a rigorous series of state-administered tests.

Because, among other things, of the sheer volume of construction and other capital projects for which the county engineer is responsible, many states require that county engineers be PEs; some require professional surveyors' (PS) registration as well. Most cities do not require the public works director to be a PE; however, not having a PE on staff means that both small and large construction and design projects must be approved by someone outside the organization, although non-PEs can conduct inspections. In many communities, this means contracting out virtually all engineering functions to consulting firms.

Consulting engineers

Regardless of the size of the city or county, every public works agency at some time needs a consulting engineer. Probably the most important reason for hiring a consultant is to acquire the expertise needed for a specific job without having the expert on the agency's regular payroll. In small cities, a PE or a PE firm is required to supervise all design and construction projects—even when local employees are involved in those projects.

Middle-sized agencies with a PE on staff, and even a fully staffed engineering department, require the assistance of consulting engineers to augment staff on very large or complex projects (for example, the total reconstruction of a major commuter bridge) or when the expertise needed is for a one-time project (for example, retrofitting or upgrading a wastewater treatment plant). Regardless of the jurisdiction's size, consultants typically work directly with a staff member—usually the local government's staff engineer, public works director, or chief administrative officer.

Consulting contracts

Most jurisdictions follow "accepted purchasing practices" that do not allow them to contract with a consulting engineer or firm that has not been through some formal selection process. Although bidding is not required in all states, increasingly most large consulting contracts for engineering services are bid out. It is important to note that contracts for engineering services are not awarded on the basis of the lowest bid. Proposals are evaluated according to technical qualifications; cost is not considered during the selection process. The most common method of contracting is to first issue a request for proposals (RFP). RFPs can be used on a project-by-project basis or for ongoing services over a fixed period of time.

In any contract with a consultant, it is important to set forth as clearly as possible the obligations of both the agency and the consultant and to establish the performance standards that must be met, including deadlines. The contract should clearly state the objectives of the agency and the results required. All phases of the work should be considered the consultant's responsibility; however, the jurisdiction should review work in progress to ensure that the consultant complies with the contract. Usually consultants will provide preliminary reports, followed by construction plans and specifications. Finally, they may be asked to observe or supervise construction as it progresses.

Consulting contracts
Engineering consultants should not be selected on the basis of the lowest bid. Many states, including Virginia, require a municipality to evaluate consultants before price is considered. The jurisdiction must select a preferred consultant and then negotiate a contract. If negotiations fail, the jurisdiction can consider the next consultant.

Pre-qualification screening

Evaluating vendors before the RFP is circulated is called "pre-qualification screening"; this procedure is being used increasingly to shorten vendor lists. Criteria for evaluating consulting firms should be established.

Consideration should be given to issues such as the size, breadth, and geographic location of project staff, and past experience in the specialty area. This practice shortens the turn-around time on bids and ensures that unrealistic or irresponsible bids are held to a minimum.

Smaller jurisdictions tend to have more experience with contracts because many of their activities require outside assistance.

Usually, consultants are screened in regard to their capability and interest during an initial interview. Those who meet the basic qualifications are then asked for bids on the work to be performed. It is also important to establish additional provisions for required extra work and to define circumstances under which charges for extra work or change orders will be paid (e.g., state or federal requirements, unforeseen circumstances, and labor disputes).

Pre-bid conference

A pre-bid conference is usually held before large jobs are put up for bids. During the conference the staff typically brief prospective bidders on the scope and specifications of the job and answer their questions, helping reduce problems caused by an uneven understanding of the project and the intent of the RFP. Such conferences result in proposals that are more comparable in both their compliance with specifications and cost.

Contract pricing

Methods of pricing contracts include lump sum, percentage of construction cost, cost plus, and various combinations thereof. The lowest bid is not necessarily the best; typically, this coincidence is the exception rather than the rule. Even though some councils may pressure directors to accept only the lowest bid, cost should never be the main criterion when evaluating proposals to provide professional services such as engineering services.

Consulting in smaller jurisdictions

Smaller jurisdictions tend to have more experience with contracts because many of their activities require outside assistance. Many of these communities keep a consulting firm on retainer in much the same way they may enlist the assistance of an attorney. Typically, the firm is retained to provide a designated number of hours per contract period. The responsibilities of the firm include the supervision of small-project design and construction and attendance as needed at council or board meetings as the technical expert on local engineering issues. In this way the firm becomes familiar with the jurisdiction, its unique political and social environment, and the geotechnical and topological features that have an impact on the design and development of infrastructure systems. Examples of engineering services provided include evaluating easements for stormwater drainage, inspecting services for sidewalk replacement, and preparing capital improvements plans.

Council involvement

Consulting engineering firms that are hired on retainer are often viewed with suspicion by council and board members, particularly if some council members were not involved in awarding the contract; if the engineer makes a determination that has a negative impact on a board member or a prominent constituent; or if the member has questions from other constituents (especially engineers) about a particular proposal. These councilors and some citizens may bring pressure to bid out all engineering decisions, regardless of how routine.

The problem, of course, is that it is expensive and time-consuming to bid out all activities. To avoid having to do this on every occasion, the public works director must make certain that the consulting engineer has no inappropriate influence over government operations.[4] Furthermore, both the public works director and the consulting engineer must be careful not to give the council or the public any *impression* of undue influence.

Although consulting engineers historically made recommendations to the public works director or the chief administrative officer, today there has been a trend toward making recommendations directly to the council, presumably because of an increase in interest and concern for public accountability. All officials, whether appointed or elected, should therefore observe strict ethical guidelines when contracting out.

Solid waste disposal

Because of the growing volume of waste and the growing shortage of disposal sites, the disposal of solid waste is the public works function that now attracts the most public attention. In the 1970s and 1980s concern among public works managers about solid waste (also called "garbage" or "trash") focused on technological innovation and privatization of solid waste *collection*. Specifically, managers pondered whether to provide the service with their own employees or with private firms; whether to provide curbside, backyard, or alley pickup; whether the collection should be performed using one-person, mechanized vehicles or with traditional three- or four-person trucks. Now, the solid waste "crisis" involves the *disposal* of solid waste—not only finding acceptable disposal sites, but also coping with the consequences of past disposal practices.

The magnitude of the problem should not be underestimated. In 1978 there were 14,000 landfills operating in the United States; 70 percent of them had closed by 1993. Moreover, more than half of the remaining 6,000 municipal landfills were due to be closed by the middle of 1994. Obviously, the siting of landfills has become a major problem. Citizens realize that there is a solid waste crisis, but they demand that sitings follow the all-too-familiar NIMBY rule: "Not In My Back Yard."

A number of federal laws deal with various aspects of solid waste disposal; chief among them is the 1976 Resource and Conservation Recovery Act (RCRA). RCRA regulates disposal siting, design, operations design, groundwater monitoring and corrective action, and landfill closures. Most states also passed laws to enforce U.S. Environmental Protection Agency (EPA) guidelines for achieving a 25-percent reduction in the volume of material going to landfills by 1992.

Public works departments therefore face a new challenge: in order to comply with federal and state laws, and to avoid the expense and political difficulty of opening new landfill sites, they must develop an integrated solid waste management strategy, one of whose chief components is a recycling program.

An integrated solid waste management strategy

Most experts agree that any solid waste management strategy should be an integrated policy that incorporates not only the best available technology, but citizen participation as well. A process described as "managing disposal through the 4 *R*s and 2 *B*s" utilizes the hierarchy of solid waste management planning options offered by the EPA: reuse, reduction, recycling, and resource recovery (4 *R*s) and burning and burying (2 *B*s).[5]

Hierarchy of planning options

Using a product again or using it for other than its original intended purpose is considered *reuse*. Reuse is achieved, for example, when washable baby bottles are used rather than disposable bottle liners and when

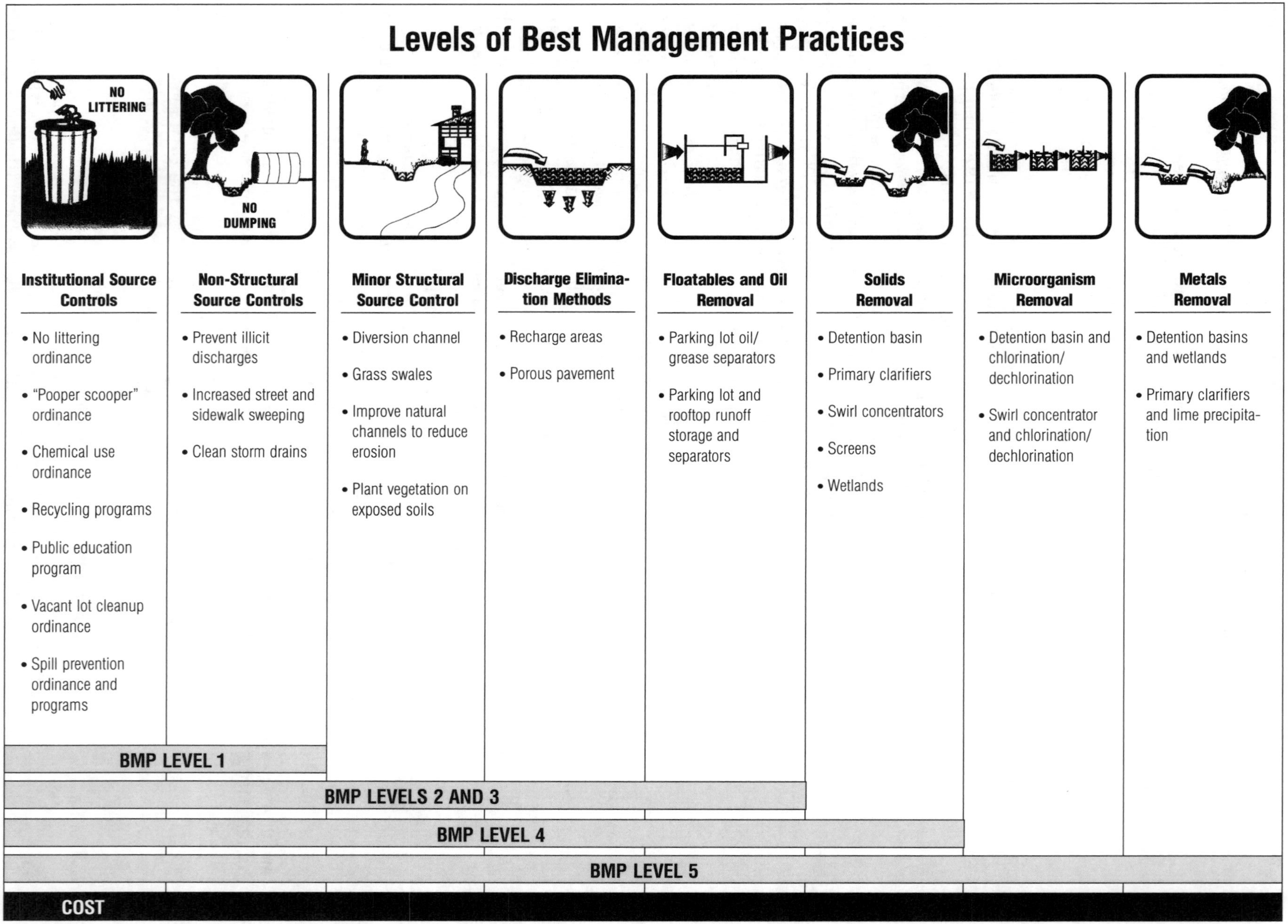
Levels of Best Management Practices
NO LITTERING
NO DUMPING
Institutional Source Controls
• No littering ordinance
• "Pooper scooper" ordinance
• Chemical use ordinance
• Recycling programs
• Public education program
• Vacant lot cleanup ordinance
• Spill prevention ordinance and programs
Non-Structural Source Controls
• Prevent illicit discharges
• Increased street and sidewalk sweeping
• Clean storm drains
Minor Structural Source Control
• Diversion channel
• Grass swales
• Improve natural channels to reduce erosion
• Plant vegetation on exposed soils
Discharge Elimination Methods
• Recharge areas
• Porous pavement
Floatables and Oil Removal
• Parking lot oil/grease separators
• Parking lot and rooftop runoff storage and separators
Solids Removal
• Detention basin
• Primary clarifiers
• Swirl concentrators
• Screens
• Wetlands
Microorganism Removal
• Detention basin and chlorination/dechlorination
• Swirl concentrator and chlorination/dechlorination
Metals Removal
• Detention basins and wetlands
• Primary clarifiers and lime precipitation
BMP LEVEL 1
BMP LEVELS 2 AND 3
BMP LEVEL 4
BMP LEVEL 5
COST

Figure 6–3 Levels of best management practices.

stores pay refunds for the return of beverage containers that can be returned to and reused by the supplier.

Waste *reduction* involves changing people's habits regarding the materials they use and discard into the waste stream. Examples of reduction include the use of biodegradable packaging or the use of cloth diapers instead of disposable diapers, which alone account for up to 2 percent of the nation's waste stream.

The *R* currently receiving the greatest public attention is *recycling*. Through recycling, materials that were intended to be discarded are recovered and reused in some manner. Aluminum cans can be collected, melted, and recast into new cans less expensively than aluminum can be mined; leaves and grass clippings can be used to create compost. Recycling is covered in more detail later in this section.

The use of waste to produce another resource is called *resource recovery*. Some resource recovery facilities burn solid waste in boilers to produce steam after minimal processing to remove large items such as appliances. The steam is then used to generate electricity. Other facilities screen out recyclables and household hazardous wastes and reduce the remaining organic wastes to solid fuel that can be used at specially designed or adapted energy-production sites. EPA predicts that there will be 350 waste-to-energy sites by the beginning of the next century—more than triple the number that existed in 1989.

Composition of the waste stream varies according to socioeconomic status of residents, season, and mix of industrial, retail, institutional, and residential wastes.

The term *burning* refers to incineration. The energy produced by incineration is allowed to dissipate; it is not converted to productive use. Although the process is commonly believed to cause air pollution, properly functioning incinerators operate in an environmentally controlled environment that changes waste into non-polluting gases and incombustible ash. The ash from these facilities must be placed in landfills.

The last strategy in the hierarchy is to *bury* solid wastes. A properly constructed landfill will have a liner, a drainage system, and devices for monitoring liquid and gaseous byproducts. RCRA regulations mandate that communities monitor the leachate and gases for thirty years after a landfill's closure.

The ideal approach when establishing an integrated solid waste disposal strategy is to use landfills only as a last resort. But this means turning local traditions on their heads; in 1990 two-thirds of solid waste was still going to landfills, and the most common disposal strategy continues to be the use of landfills. However, state goals call for reducing the volume of solid waste brought to landfills by 15 to 60 percent, so most local governments have to develop a waste management policy that incorporates other strategies.

Factors influencing success

A number of factors will influence the success of any approach to solid waste disposal management, including waste quantity and composition, availability of markets, citizen interest, and administrative structure and traditions.[6]

Determining waste quantity and composition In order to estimate how much waste can be diverted from the waste stream, some knowledge of the composition of the waste stream is needed. Composition varies by community according to the socioeconomic status of residents, season of the year, and mix of industrial, retail, institutional, and residential wastes generated. Neighborhoods with higher socioeconomic status tend to generate more solid waste than neighborhoods whose citizens do not tend to

Reuse, reduction, and recycling are sometimes called "coproduced" strategies because they rely on citizens to change their life-styles to comport with waste reduction priorities.

dispose of items as freely. Knowledge about the solid waste stream can assist in making collection and recycling strategies more efficient.

Developing a market for recyclables One of the most vexing problems of a recycling program is that of developing markets for recyclables. The last thing a public works manager wants to have is a successful program with nowhere to send materials for reuse. Public works managers therefore need to be inventive and entrepreneurial in developing markets for recyclables. When the newsprint market became glutted, one enterprising public works director shredded his newsprint and sold it for cattle bedding. Another way around the markets is to pool the recyclables of several cities and capitalize on the economies of scale created.

Developing markets for recyclables

With old newspapers, green bottles, and plastics glutting recycling markets, free-market enthusiasts blame governments for accelerating recycling campaigns far beyond industry's need for the materials collected. In the past four years, curbside collection programs have multiplied from 600 communities across the country to nearly 4,000, and prices for recyclables have plunged.

A survey of 258 cities conducted last year for the U.S. Conference of Mayors found that lack of markets poses the biggest barrier to successful recycling. Other obstacles remain, including government tax breaks and subsidies to promote industries that supply virgin raw materials. Below-cost timber sales from national forests, for instance, help keep prices for wood used to make virgin paper artificially low. Environmentalists complain that if the market truly reflected costs, recycled commodities would already be competitive.

But governments do not have to sit back and let the markets sort themselves out. Governments "own" the potentially valuable commodities that they collect, and they also control a good part of the market for the products created from recyclables. Government agencies spend billions of dollars every year on stationery, park benches, auto and truck tires, and other products that can be made at least partly with recycled wastes. Every state and many local governments have begun to take advantage of their buying clout by giving preference to recycled products. It is not simply a matter of buying recycled products to help small entrepreneurs. When governments are major buyers of a product, they can persuade large manufacturers to make the product with recycled material.

And governments may be making a mistake if they overlook the job-creating potential of recycling programs. The Institute for Local Self-Reliance contends that recycling can offer communities an economic advantage: the attraction of new industries. States that "aggressively market the availability of recyclable commodities to industry will be big winners," according to Peter L. Grogan, past president of the National Recycling Coalition.

Source: Adapted from Tom Arrandale, "How to Cut the Recycling Glut," *Governing* 6 (April 1993): 28.

Citizen interest Reuse, reduction, and recycling are sometimes called "coproduced" strategies because they rely on citizens to take responsibility for their contribution to the waste stream and change their life-styles to comport with waste reduction priorities. Coproduced activities require extensive public education about why the waste stream needs to be reduced, how citizens can participate, and what benefits will accrue to the community as a result of their participation. Citizen efforts work best if all segments of the population are involved in the educational process, including students at all grade levels, members of social clubs, leaders of industry, owners of commercial establishments, and officials within government itself.

Citizen involvement through public education is clearly another component of a successful integrated solid waste disposal plan. Citizens are often ready to recycle before a community is organized to begin recycling. In these cases, public works managers should provide an opportunity for those who wish to recycle to do so by offering drop-off sites or other short-term solutions to accommodate the desire to recycle.

Public education on recycling should occur before a recycling plan is adopted. Adequate citizen representation in the planning process ensures that the input of a solid core of citizens is considered in forming the ultimate plan. Cities and counties then can inform the general public of the program via newsletters, articles in community newspapers, local access cable TV spots and shows, radio talk shows, posters, banners, and public events. Information should include the date that recycling will start, the method of collection, and the types of recyclables that will be collected. Many communities distribute informational calendars (printed on recycled paper) to citizens and coloring books about recycling to local students. Methods of public education are limited only by the imagination and ingenuity of staff.

Administrative structures and traditions Administrative structures must be in place before a successful solid waste disposal management program can be implemented. The details of implementation will vary according to local customs and traditions. Traditions will, for example, dictate whether residents are more amenable to curbside or backyard pickup. Managing a successful integrated solid waste program involves using the *4R-2B* strategies in combination as local regulations and customs permit.

Managing a recycling program

Managing a community-wide recycling effort is the most challenging of the coproduction strategies. A number of questions must be answered before such a recycling program is implemented.

Successful recycling

The Recycling and Disposal Facility in Wellesley, Massachusetts (26,000), reduces solid waste disposal costs and offers a useful community exchange center for residents. The center recycles anything that can be reused. It maintains separate collection containers for corrugated paper, newspapers, magazines, brown paper bags, aluminum foil, glass, cans, returnable bottles and cans, used oil, batteries, leaves and grass trimmings, and firewood. It also has book shelves for a book swap; a "Take It or Leave It" section where people can inspect discarded household items and tools for possible reuse; and a bulletin board for community notices. It its first year, it showed a net gain of $146,000 in sales of recycling materials and reduced waste hauling costs.

Source: *The Guide to Management Improvement Projects in Local Government*, vol. 14, no. 3 (Washington, DC: ICMA, 1990), no. MGT-17.

Voluntary or mandatory?

The first question is whether recycling is to be voluntary or mandatory. In voluntary programs, citizens can choose to participate, whereas in mandatory programs governmental officials find themselves in the unfriendly position of having to ensure compliance. Nevertheless, where solid waste disposal problems are most acute, as in the Northeastern states, a mandatory program may be necessary.

Pick up or drop off?

A second question is whether the recyclables will be picked up (from the curb, backyard, or alley) or whether citizens must drop off items at centralized stations. Many communities have found that recycling must be convenient in order to promote greater compliance. Pickup programs are more costly and difficult to administer, but they enjoy broader public participation.

One of the easiest methods of recycling is for a local public works agency to establish one or more collection stations. These sites require fewer workers; however, in communities where participation is enthusiastic, they often become unsightly when recyclables overflow their containers. Many communities use drop-off sites to collect items that are not collected at curbside. Still others choose to offer the drop-off site as an alternative for residents who do not want their neighbors to know their patterns of consumption. Choosing a recycling strategy requires the public works manager to tailor the program to meet community needs and expectations.

Separated or commingled?

Another question is whether the recyclables will be separated by citizens or commingled in a single container or bag. Many companies have devised containers that allow citizens to separate their recyclables, making it easier for sanitation crews to place the recyclables into partitioned bins on recycling trucks. However, there is some evidence to suggest

Figure 6–4 Recycle Towne, the municipal recycling facility in St. Peters, Missouri.

that citizens would be more willing to recycle if items could be commingled in a single container. The crews would then either separate the recyclables at the curb or bring them to a materials recovery facility. There are trade-offs for each method; the choice depends on how much effort citizens are willing to make and how efficient the crews are.

Goals

All public works managers will be involved in some way or another with planning for solid waste disposal and recycling. It is important to remember that the goal of these efforts is to reduce the volume of waste, not to make money. As more and more communities get into the recycling business, markets will become glutted, prices will fall, and revenues from recycling will decline. However, national and state solid waste reduction goals will still have to be met. Thus, part of any good solid waste reduction strategy will be the effort to build new markets for recycled materials; that, in turn, will require encouragement of new industries that use recycled products. Public works departments should consider using, for example, plastic picnic tables, park benches, and parking lot bumpers built from recycled materials.

Water resources management

A source of water, a means of distributing it throughout the community, and a sanitary wastewater system to collect and dispose of liquid waste are among the primary needs of urban local governments. Because these systems are underground and out of sight, citizens tend to take them for granted. But a local government administrator must have a basic working familiarity with water and sewer system services. Neglect of them for other government services with greater public visibility can lead to their serious deterioration. This section describes community governments' responsibilities for the purification and distribution of drinking water, the collection and treatment of wastewater, and stormwater drainage.

Drinking water

There are over 180,000 potable water systems in the United States. One-half of 1 percent of these systems provide drinking water for 43 percent of the nation's population. The proliferation of so many small systems means local control of water but increases problems of resource allocation, quality control, and interjurisdictional coordination.[7]

Historically, the regulation of drinking water quality was a state and local concern; however, the Safe Drinking Water Act of 1974 empowered EPA to protect drinking water and regulate groundwater quality. Most states have assumed the primary role in enforcing national regulations.

Water conservation

Hofheim, Germany (27,000), uses rainwater to flush the toilets of a new municipal public housing project. The city gets an average of twenty-four inches of rain per year, an amount that is more than sufficient to ensure an adequate supply of flushing water from roof-mounted cisterns. Careful cost calculations have determined that the system not only saves water and is good for the environment, but it also costs less than using drinking water.

Source: *The Guide to Management Improvement Projects in Local Government*, vol. 15, no. 3 (Washington, DC: ICMA, 1991), no. PW-20.

Groundwater provides one-half of the nation's water supply; surface water—which includes the Great Lakes, the world's largest renewable supply of fresh water—accounts for the remainder.

Water supplies

Groundwater provides one-half of the nation's water supply; surface water—which includes the Great Lakes, the world's largest renewable supply of fresh water—accounts for the remainder. Although in the aggregate, water supplies are abundant, they are not well distributed geographically. This problem, together with growing water use (the average household use of water varies from 80 to 150 gallons per day per capita), makes shortage of water one of the most severe problems that will face communities in the early years of the twenty-first century. The problem is sufficiently serious that there have been discussions about increasing rates to reflect the true cost of water and encouraging industries and citizens to conserve it.

Intergovernmental cooperatives

As noted, water as a resource is not distributed evenly across the country. In the Southwest and particularly in California, the issue of access to water supplies has provoked intra- and interstate confrontations, prompting the need for increased intergovernmental cooperation and innovation on the part of both elected and appointed officials.

Planning for the water system

The first item of business for the management of a water system is to determine goals. These are best presented as carefully considered, *written* general objectives. Since the efforts of every person employed by the water system will be directed by the objectives and goals, they should be brief, clear, and concise so that everyone can understand them.

Objectives Deliver potable water of approved quality at the established pressures, and in the quantities and at the rates of flow that the customers desire and are willing to pay for; operate the water department so the total cost of the delivered water is less than the median cost experienced by other cities of approximately the same size with similar source and distribution conditions.

Goals Identify the customers. Provide municipal water service during the period 1994 to 2010 to domestic, industrial, and commercial customers within the incorporated limits of the city and in the unincorporated area of the county for one lot depth along both sides of "X" Highway between the city limits and "Z" River.

System Operate the water system 24 hours per day, 365 days per year in an effective and professional manner.

Source Design and implement by stage construction an intake structure and pumping station capable of producing 10 million gallons per day (MGD) in 1994 and 14 MGD in 2004.

Treatment Design and operate the water treatment plan (1) to produce a treated water that meets all health and quality standards of state health departments and the Federal Safe Drinking Water Act and (2) to meet the average and peak demands for water by the distribution system.

Distribution system Deliver water in the quantity and at the rate desired by the customer while maintaining pressure between 40 and 60 pounds per square inch (psi), except that the pressure can drop to 20 psi when supplying water to fight a major fire.

Firefighting capabilities Consider requirements for firefighting facilities during design of water distribution system. Coordinate design with local fire departments and fire underwriters to assure implementation of national standards for fire protection.

Source: Sam M. Cristofano, *Management of Local Public Works* (Washington, DC: ICMA, 1986), 278-279.

For example, Florida legislation enables regions to establish water authorities that identify regional water needs and develop sources of raw water for delivery to participants. The West Coast Regional Water Supply Authority in the Tampa-St. Petersburg area is a three-county consortium established by a special legislative act to develop and deliver raw water at cost. It has a five-member board with representatives from the three counties and the two large cities in the region. The board's successful planning efforts have led to diminished conflict between urban and rural interests.

Another example is the memorandum of understanding that El Paso County, Texas, has with the local irrigation district to work together in a variety of areas including the joint development of a water resources management plan for the county. Innovative processes such as reclaiming wastewater for irrigating crops or watering golf courses has eased the demand for potable water in some areas.

In 1984, 90 percent of all water systems consistently met EPA standards for maximum allowable bacterial counts while 97 percent met turbidity requirements.

Water purity

The nation's water system is quite safe. In 1984, 90 percent of all water systems consistently met EPA standards for maximum allowable bacterial counts while 97 percent met turbidity requirements. The smallest systems, which serve only 8 percent of the population, account for 93 percent of the maximum contamination level violations and 94 percent of the monitoring and reporting violations. Although the regulatory system is not perfect, the vast majority of citizens receive high-quality potable water.

Restructuring to comply with the Safe Drinking Water Act

Changes made to the Safe Drinking Water Act since 1986 are improving health protection. In 1986, EPA required water systems to meet standards for only twenty-two contaminants. Today, systems must comply with standards for more than eighty different substances including microorganisms and chemical by-products of various industrial and agricultural practices.

These new requirements mean new testing and analysis expenses for all systems and increased water treatment costs for many. Small systems will be hardest hit because they have fewer customers to share the costs. For example, additional water testing costs of $5,000 per year would mean $200 per family served by a system with only 25 connections. However, for a larger system of 2,000 connections the same $5,000 expense would amount to only $2.50 per family.

Restructuring is the adoption of management and/or ownership changes that help a drinking water system address new responsibilities and increased costs. Systems can restructure in a variety of ways. For example:

Groups of small systems can buy and share services together.

Systems can contract with a private company or larger water system to receive services such as operation and maintenance, meter reading and billing, and sample collection and analysis.

A small system can merge with or be bought out by a larger one. Systems may be physically connected following this kind of restructuring, but they don't have to be.

Small privately owned systems can restructure into a non-profit cooperative or public service district and become eligible for federal and state grants and loans.

Source: *Helping Small Systems Comply With the Safe Drinking Water Act*, EPA/812-K-92-001 (Washington, DC: EPA, September 1992).

As late as 1991, 90 percent of all water systems used chlorine as a disinfectant in the treatment process. Although new guidelines call for reducing the amount of chlorine used because of the potential for formation of carcinogens, professionals are monitoring the impact of reduced disinfectant use on the growth of bacteria. Multiple treatment phases may be indicated.

Maintenance of water systems

One of the most serious problems created by the shortage of funds for public works is the neglect of water and wastewater systems, and poor maintenance takes a toll on their effectiveness and quality. One study of eight urban water systems found that from 1 to 37 percent of total water consumption could not be accounted for by conventional measures.[8] The Office of Technology Assessment reports that lining the aged pipes of a major city (proper maintenance) could have prevented a leakage rate of almost 40 percent of treated water over several decades—more than enough to make up for shortages during dry spells. With leakage, there is also the possibility of infiltration of untreated ground water into the "safe" treated-water system. The extent of this problem is unknown because testing is done at the treatment plant, not at residents' taps. The Office of Technology Assessment predicts that local governments will have to increase local capital outlays by 50 percent to comply with current standards of the Safe Drinking Water Act alone, especially those restrictions involving concentrations of lead in treated water.

The Office of Technology Assessment predicts that local governments will have to increase local capital outlays by 50 percent to comply with current standards of the Safe Drinking Water Act alone.

A number of management tools are used to enhance the performance of potable water systems: supervisory control and data acquisition (SCADA) systems to control remote equipment, diagnose system failure, and monitor operating efficiency; distributed control systems to control a smaller number of sites in a less dispersed area; geographic information systems to keep track of the location of underground facilities; and computerized programs to estimate life-cycle costs, optimal maintenance programming, and system operating schedules.

Financing water and wastewater systems

Water distribution and wastewater collection systems, as well as water and wastewater treatment facilities, may be financed through service charges, and capital improvements may be underwritten through the sale of general obligation or revenue bonds. Normally, general obligation or revenue bonds are used to finance only such major construction projects as key trunk mains and treatment and disposal plants. Minor extensions of the system normally are made with funds from the operating budget of the water and wastewater division.

General obligation bonds are used when the community has sufficient service charges or other revenue sources. Revenue bonds, on the other hand, can be used when sufficient revenues do not exist, and the government gives its full faith and credit to the bond buyer that the principal and interest will be paid in accordance with the terms of the bonds. Some state laws authorize local governments to issue joint water-wastewater revenue bonds, wherein the income from supplying water and providing sewer service is pledged as assurance to the buyer that adequate earnings are or will be available to amortize the bonds.

Wastewater treatment

There are more than 16,000 wastewater treatment facilities in the United States handling 37 billion gallons of sewage a day. The existence of natural water drainage basins leads to the consolidation of regional service and

Figure 6–5 In the United States, more than 16,000 wastewater treatment facilities handle 37 billion gallons of sewage a day.

wastewater treatment areas, creating economies of scale that give a strong economic advantage to capital-intensive, technologically sophisticated operations that treat flows from natural basins and serve large areas.

In metropolitan areas, wastewater treatment is often provided by a regional authority or district. In most states these regional districts maintain their own bond rating, allowing them to compete in the market more efficiently. Even where such districts exist, local community governments often assume responsibility for the construction and maintenance of the local (collector) wastewater systems that deliver sewage to the districts' facilities.

When smaller communities run their own wastewater treatment systems they encounter a number of problems that are not so acute in regional systems. First, there is no economy of scale. Second, they operate from a smaller revenue base, which not only increases the cost per gallon treated but also reduces the funds available for training and salaries. Many states offer low-cost training programs to alleviate some of this fiscal pressure; however, better-trained personnel often move to regional systems, where salaries are typically higher. When this occurs, small communities have difficulty retaining licensed operators and must again invest in hiring and training new employees.

Cooperative financing

To stop the threat to the environment of residential septic systems along the shores of Diamond Lake in Michigan and to take advantage of economies of scale, the communities of Dowagiac (6,400) and Cassopolis (1,800) joined with four small townships to form the Area Utility Authority. With each township assuming a twenty-year, $5.7 million debt to provide financing, Cassopolis constructed and operates a wastewater collector system for the townships and an interceptor line from Cassopolis to Dowagiac's treatment plant where the sewage is processed. Individually, the townships were too small to secure the needed financing.

Source: *The Guide to Management Improvement Projects in Local Government*, vol. 17, no. 1 (Washington, DC: ICMA, 1993), no. PW-5.

Demand for treatment facilities

Since the late 1960s, the federal government has funded the construction of wastewater treatment plants. However, capital financing from the federal government dropped from $6 billion in 1980 to $2.4 billion in 1988 to $0 in 1991. State and local financing for operations and maintenance increased from $4.6 billion (1980) to $6.8 billion (1987). Still, EPA's latest *Needs Survey* estimates that $60.2 billion, $250 per capita, is needed to build enough secondary treatment facilities to treat adequately the wastewater being generated by the current population (only 82 percent of treatment plants currently have secondary operations).[9] EPA also estimates that it would cost an additional $84 billion in capital investments to bring all local facilities into compliance with the Clean Water Act. Obviously, finding sufficient funding for these facilities will remain a major obstacle to implementation for states, counties, municipalities, and regional authorities.

Biosolid disposal

A growing concern in many communities is the disposal of biosolids (sludge) from wastewater plant operations. For years, innovative programs have existed that have used biosolids as a soil enhancer. Now EPA and state environmental agencies are expressing concern over the presence in this material of microorganisms that cause communicable disease and of toxic heavy metals. EPA has enacted regulations monitoring biosolid use in land applications, surface disposal, and incineration. The regulations are designed to improve the ecological effects of common uses of biosolids, but they also contain language reflecting recent concern about the effect of biosolid toxins on human health. The cost of correcting detrimental conditions poses further financial problems for state and community governments.

Stormwater management

Under NPDES regulations, potential pollutants washed down storm drains now must be eliminated or storm water must be treated with sanitary sewage.

Since the Federal Water Pollution Control Act was passed in 1972, the federal government has monitored the effluent from wastewater treatment plants in lakes, rivers, and streams by issuing National Pollutant Discharge Elimination System (NPDES) permits. These permits regulate "point source" pollution at the *point of discharge* into the lake or stream. 1990 NPDES regulations require monitoring non-point-source pollutants from stormwater discharges in communities with separate sewer systems that serve populations of 100,000 or more. The consensus is that 1993 EPA regulations will require permits for public entities serving populations of more than 50,000. Local governments must now take positive action to ensure that pollutants are not allowed to enter stormwater drainage flows.

From the 1970s until the early 1990s, federal money was used to separate sanitary and storm sewers. In order to save money, storm water was reintroduced in the drainage flow without being treated. Under NPDES regulations, potential pollutants washed down storm drains (e.g., dog litter, street debris, construction materials) now must be eliminated, or storm water must be treated with sanitary sewage. Further, nonseparated systems are being forced to construct combined sewer overflows (CSOs) and interceptor sewer projects to contain overflows of sanitary and storm water for later treatment rather than risk discharge of sanitary sewage into lakes and streams. There is no indication that these federal regulations will be relaxed even though the federal government no longer funds wastewater construction projects such as CSOs.

Smaller community governments should be aware of the NPDES guidelines for reducing pollutants in their stormwater systems in order to protect the health and safety of their citizens and those in neighboring communities. Industrial plants may include large tracts of land that have been surfaced and therefore do not absorb rainwater, so smaller communities with large industrial plants (e.g., automobile factories) should be especially aware of regulations that may affect them because they may have a higher volume of runoff than would normally be expected in a community of their size. Smaller community governments are increasingly becoming involved in the NPDES process as co-permittees in regional stormwater drainage compacts, which are similar to but smaller than special districts.

Stormwater drainage

Public works managers must also be concerned with stormwater drainage in order to eliminate flooding and other forms of water damage, particularly where groundwater levels are high. Curbs, gutters, catch basins, and retention and detention ponds are components of the drainage system, which must be capable of handling stormwater runoff caused by urban development. Stormwater systems divert water to creeks, streams, and rivers or hold it temporarily in detention basins or for longer periods in retention basins.

Drainage is a significant concern in new residential and industrial developments because each new structure or roadway has an impact on natural drainage. Drainage plans must accompany proposals for new development: good plans incorporate information regarding changes in natural drainage caused by new construction. Most communities require developers to submit a drainage plan that not only indicates the type of system planned, but also fixes responsibility for its maintenance. Often this responsibility is given to a subdivision's homeowners' association or is assumed by the jurisdiction. Developers do not like to deal with retention or detention ponds because they consume valuable real estate; however, when incorporated with plans for recreational uses or aesthetically pleasing open spaces, such ponds work well.

Drainage is also an important consideration in constructing roadways because improper drainage may undermine grades and foundations; standing water in a roadway is a more obvious hazard. The ultimate concern, of course, is with flooding. The old method of diverting any drainage to the nearest creek or stream without regard to other inlets or to the composition of the discharge results in flash floods, erosion, and polluted tributaries. The new method—drainage management and flood control—requires an integrated plan to reduce pollution, reduce flooding incidents, and provide plans for handling major storms.

Transportation management

It has been estimated that there are at least 38,000 government entities involved in the provision, operation, and maintenance of highways, roadways, and bridges in the United States, evidence that local transportation management is indeed a complex intergovernmental task. Nevertheless, most of the actual work of building and maintaining the nation's roads and bridges falls to local governments.

The intergovernmental task

Transportation management involves all three levels of government: federal, state, and local. The federal government's role has been to fund construction and some maintenance, to provide for interstate highways and other roadways, and to set safety standards.

State highway and transportation departments administer a wide variety of state and federally funded road and bridge programs, distributing over 60 percent of outlays. They establish state priorities and allocate funds for these programs. States have to conform to federal regulations concerning driving age, speed limits, and truck access to nonfederal highways before they qualify to receive federal funding.

Shared authority

Although the states own and operate farm-to-market, interstate, and major secondary roadways, most roads (about 80 percent) are locally administered. Forty-eight states share state-collected road funds with their local governments. These governments can include counties (for county roads as well as maintenance of state and federal roadways); municipalities (for city streets); township governments (for some rural roads in unincorporated areas); and special regional authorities (for roadways and bridges under regional control).

ISTEA

Passage of the Intermodal Surface Transportation Efficiency Act (ISTEA) of 1991 brought a major shift in the federal government's philosophy about its role in transportation. The purpose of ISTEA (pronounced "ice tea") is to

develop a National Intermodal Transportation System that is economically efficient, environmentally sound, provides the foundation for the Nation to compete in the global economy and will move people and goods in an energy efficient manner.

ISTEA redefined the national highway system by establishing two categories of roads eligible for federal funding (there had been four); redefined the scope of transportation planning to better integrate transportation and environmental goals; and expanded technology transfer and collaborative research. In addition, ISTEA provides for more flexibility in linking mass transit with highway programs to solve transportation problems; in the past, funding was primarily for highways. This new flexibility is welcomed by managers facing traffic congestion, particularly in urban areas.

ISTEA also requires statewide and metropolitan planning for long-range transportation needs as well as transportation improvement programs. This requirement enhances the participation of community governments in transportation planning. Moreover, states must develop, establish, and implement management systems covering highway pavement, bridges, highway safety, traffic congestion, public transportation facilities and equipment, and intermodal transportation facilities and systems. These state systems cannot help but assist counties and cities in their transportation planning and maintenance capacity.

The community task

A community's street system is its lifeblood; it helps move people and goods, facilitating the interaction that is the basis of community life. From the public works perspective, the street system includes the design and the construction of streets as well as the actual curbs and gutters, storm sewers, sidewalks, parkway trees, traffic control signs and signals, driveways, street lights, and related appurtenances that are a part of the street right-of-way.

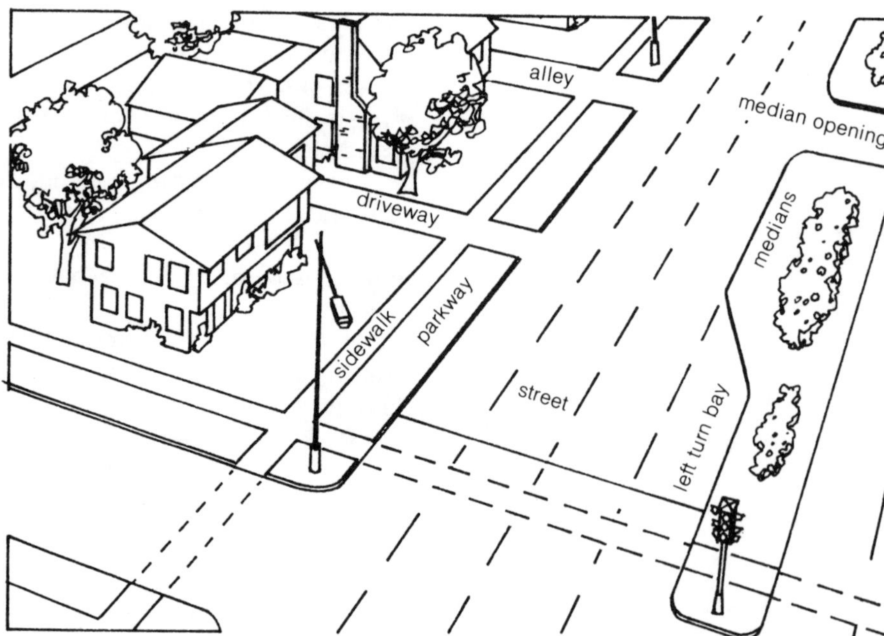

Figure 6–6 Street appurtenances include sidewalks, alleys, medians, and parkways.

Traffic reduction
Peachtree City, Georgia (12,000), found a pragmatic and creative solution to its traffic congestion problem by creating a system of pedestrian paths that connect all subdivision, commercial, and industrial areas of the city. A city ordinance allows residents to travel on the paths in golf carts. Local law allows the carts on local streets, businesses permit the carts to use drive-up facilities, and shopping malls have allotted special parking spaces to the carts. Police patrol the paths on golf carts complete with decals and flashing blue lights. Besides reducing traffic, the golf carts have reduced air pollution and noise pollution.

Source: *The Guide to Management Improvement Projects in Local Government*, vol. 15, no. 2 (Washington, DC: ICMA, 1991), no. MGT-13.

The public works objective is to design, construct, and maintain the street system in a manner that permits full functioning and facilitates the movement of people in all of their pursuits. The function of streets has changed over the years: whereas once it was to provide access to adjacent property, now streets must be designed to move large volumes of traffic within—or through—a given area. Streets also provide the corridors through which utility services—water, sewer, and gas mains; electric, telephone, and cable TV lines—are run. The sidewalks and parkways adjacent to streets provide for safe pedestrian movement, play areas for children, and trees and other plantings to beautify the community.

Design

Equally important, streets and highways play a critical role in determining adjacent land use and thus in setting the patterns of life in the community. Cities with a favorable location (e.g., at a highway intersection or along an interstate roadway) or with good internal traffic flow patterns attract development and prosper; communities lacking these advantages are more likely to experience decline. Residential development, too, is affected by streets. The quality of homes and their value

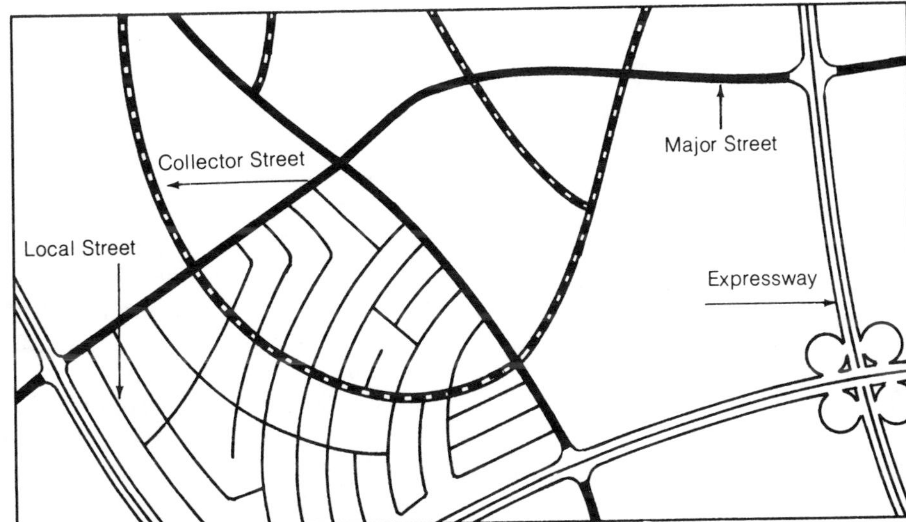

Figure 6–7 Street classifications. Expressways serve high-volume traffic with limited access; major streets (often designated as arterial streets) serve as feeders to expressways and provide for major traffic movements within urban areas that are not served by expressways; collector streets serve internal traffic within an area, such as a subdivision, and connect such areas with arterials; local streets exist only to provide access to adjacent land.

are affected by such considerations as traffic volume, number and location of intersections, ease of access to arterial streets, types of pavement, stormwater drainage, sidewalks, and parkway trees.

Because the street system exerts such a tremendous influence on patterns of land use, the master street plan for a community or a neighborhood is one of the primary elements in comprehensive planning (see Chapter 4). Individual street plans are shaped to a great extent by topography, population density, existing and projected land development, nature of traffic movement, and cost of construction. A properly developed master street plan provides for attractive, accessible commercial areas; helps preserve the integrity of individual neighborhoods, schools, and churches; and reduces traffic problems in future development.

The master street plan should be an officially adopted document that identifies the existing street network and delineates the location of primary arterial and collector streets in undeveloped areas. The plan should provide a framework within which subdivision plats are evaluated, and it should include requirements for dedication of rights-of-way by developers for major future street segments.

Figure 6-8 The One Man Band, a truck with a rig to dispense methocrylate that has improved productivity and perfected the application of an environmentally safe chemical.

Construction

Generally speaking, especially in smaller communities, streets are constructed either by a private firm under contract or by a developer during subdivision development. In either event, the community must enforce construction standards, which should vary for different street types and conditions. It is the responsibility of the public works engineer to develop, periodically update, and enforce these standards.

The job of street construction includes appropriate consideration of construction grades in order to eliminate drainage problems on the road and adjacent properties; the selection of pavement materials, taking into account initial cost, durability, traffic volume and character, climatic conditions, and maintenance costs; stormwater removal through a drainage and storm sewer system; and provisions for sidewalks and parkways

Figure 6–9 Here are some traffic controls we seldom "see." If traffic signs and signals are part of a system (as they should be) the top two photos show reasonably clear and simple information. The information system in the bottom photo, however, is too complex and overloaded.

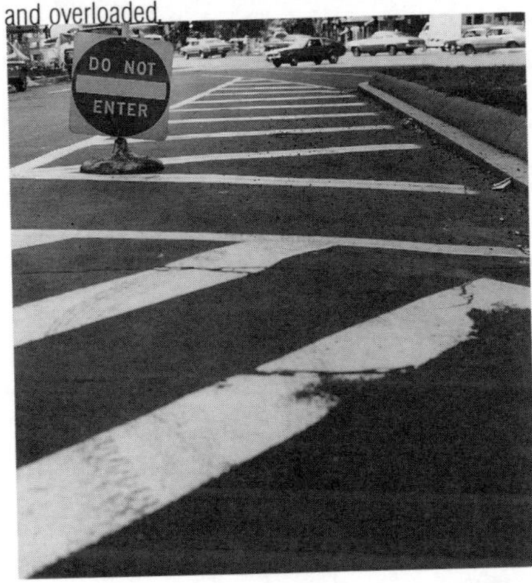

as desired. Prior to construction, it is wise to install the utility lines necessary to meet the needs of present and projected uses of neighboring land for at least twenty years into the future.

Maintenance

The maintenance of streets, sidewalks, alleys, and parkways is a major function of public works departments, in terms of both expense and effort. The cost is best controlled, not by deferred maintenance, but by regularly scheduled repair and rehabilitation performed on the basis of an inventory of individual streets that projects the maintenance needs of each over a period of years. In addition to periodic maintenance, streets should be repaired annually in order to eliminate potholes and extend the useful life of the streets. Finally, streets need to be cleaned at regular intervals. Removing street debris can be effective in lengthening the life of street pavement, minimizing sewer maintenance costs, and improving neighborhood appearance.

Traffic engineering

Traffic engineering involves the study of the movement of vehicles and pedestrians and the design of traffic patterns; the development of improvements in traffic facilities; and the regulation of vehicle use. Studies generally employed by traffic engineers include those on traffic volume, speed, and delay; capacity determination; accident statistics; and regulation inventories. These studies should precede and justify the use of traffic control devices, including signs, signals, pavement markings, and street designations (e.g., speed limits, one-way routes, major traffic routes, and truck routes).

Cooperative contracting

El Cajon, California (85,000), formed a cooperative with four neighboring cities—La Mesa (53,200), Lemon Grove (24,300), Poway (44,500), and Santee (53,000)—to contract jointly with a private firm to handle streetlight and traffic signal maintenance. El Cajon reduced its maintenance and replacement costs 30 to 40 percent through the arrangement.

Source: *The Guide to Management Improvement Projects in Local Government*, vol. 16, no. 1 (Washington, DC: ICMA, 1992), no. PW-2.

Traffic signals and other control devices often affect the capacity of streets and highways more than the street design itself. For example, installation of an unneeded traffic signal may increase rather than decrease the accident rate and restrict capacity of the street unnecessarily. Experience has shown that traffic control devices designed to reduce accidents generally provide better traffic flow as well, and, conversely, traffic control measures designed to increase street capacity tend to reduce accidents.

The construction and maintenance of streets consume a major part of a community's budget, but streets are the arteries through which the lifeblood of the community—its people—move as they go about their daily routines. Streets consume as much as 30 percent of a community's land, but they have a strong impact on the economic health and quality of life of the community.

Public works management in the 1990s and beyond

Leading a public works department may be the most challenging management enterprise in community government. There are a number of reasons for this assertion, which are related to the nature of public works functions, the diversity of employees, and the responsibility for community health and safety.

Management challenges

By virtue of the nature of public works, a director must perform a variety of managerial tasks, each requiring a different style. For traditional public works functions such as street sweeping, the director makes the work rules, and the crews do the work. If they do not, they are subject to disciplinary action. In this scenario, not only does the director have direct control over the activity, but he or she also can instill employee loyalty to ensure that jobs get completed.

This can be contrasted with a contracted function, in which the director tries to control the work of others who are not employed directly by the government. In this situation, the employees may be less concerned with the director's interests than with making a profit. The "people skills" used in the first example may not work in the latter. Good managers are cognizant of the requirements of contrasting situations and either change style or hire someone else to manage those areas in which they have difficulty.

A second challenge for public works directors is managing a diverse workforce. Managing diversity is not the same as adhering to equal employment opportunity or affirmative action requirements, which deal with hiring. Managing diversity means creating an environment for productive work *after* someone is hired. When the term *diversity* is used, it usually refers to diversity in race, gender, sexual orientation, country of origin, or religious persuasion. In public works the term also includes the range of skills and of educational attainment within a department. In a single day a director can deal with PEs, consultants, sales agents, clerical staff, solid waste handlers, unskilled laborers, and so forth. Successful managers will not only be aware of diversity, but will appreciate it and have plans on how best to manage it.

The everyday challenge of public works management is maintaining and enhancing the health and safety of citizens by providing essential services such as potable water, waste treatment, solid waste collection and disposal, inspection services, stormwater management, and a host of other services that protect the environment. These services are considered so fundamental that they, and the people who provide them, are often taken for granted. That being the case, effective public works managers will find ways to enhance the morale of their workers and commend their efforts.

Management tools to increase productivity

It is clear that computers have changed the workplace. The future of public works management will revolve around geographic information systems (GIS), already in use in many departments. GIS is an information management system that can collect, store, and retrieve information based on its spatial location; analyze the related data spatially; select and pass data to application-specific analytic models; and interactively display the selected data both graphically and numerically either before or after interactive analysis. One GIS application often used by public works departments is automated mapping facilities management (AM/FM).

Computers and water conservation
San Juan Capistrano, California (26,000), took its cue for saving money on the water bill from a radio-controlled, computerized golf course sprinkler system. The city installed a computerized sprinkler system on eighteen sites covering fifty-two acres of public land. Now, one person with a computer can regulate the sprinklers by using radio signals. An alarm system senses problems and turns off the affected sprinklers to avoid wasted water. The system eliminated the need for four employees to operate the sprinklers manually and, in its first year, saved the city an estimated nineteen million gallons of water, or enough to pay for the $110,000 system in two years.

Source: *The Guide to Management Improvement Projects in Local Government*, vol. 16, no. 1 (Washington, DC: ICMA, 1992), no. PW-6.

Almost any imaginable public works information can be stored and retrieved using GIS.

Almost any imaginable public works information can be stored and retrieved using GIS. Typically information on parcels, streets, and utility lines is the first to be digitized in public works departments. Any information related to space can be included in the GIS, as well as maintenance schedules and records of service calls, which can also be tracked by location. The most difficult and time-consuming part of GIS is loading the data from maps or other paper files; however, once the base map is constructed, maintenance and updating are all that is required.

Another way to make infrastructure investments more productive is to invest in research and development of more productive materials and processes. For example, composite materials have been used in the aerospace program and in the construction of commercial airplanes for years. Very little in research and development funds in this country has gone to design and test the use of composites in public works construction.

Cutting fuel costs
Sunrise, Florida (64,400), reduced its vehicle maintenance and fuel budgets 33 percent by converting sixteen city-owned vehicles to run on both gasoline and natural gas and by purchasing six pickup trucks that run exclusively on natural gas. Natural gas, which has an octane rating of 130, has no lead compounds to pollute the environment, is in abundant supply, and burns cleaner and costs less per gallon than gasoline. The city also opened a Compressed Natural Gas Refueling Station where it also serves more than 8,000 local customers. It plans to open a second such station, with costs fully funded by state monies, to serve eight local companies that will convert their delivery fleets to operate on natural gas.

Source: *The Guide to Management Improvement Projects in Local Government*, vol. 16, no. 2 (Washington, DC: ICMA, 1992), no. MGT-10.

One promising research initiative is the use of pultruded fiber reinforced plastics in the construction of lightweight bridges. These sturdy structures have obvious applications in emergencies, particularly serious floods. Current building codes call for bridges to contain reinforced steel bars for support—something made unnecessary by the new material. These codes, the vested interests of the concrete and rebar industries, and unions present major barriers to the use of this new material. New industries could emerge, making construction more productive in the long run.

Availability of new technologies does not ensure their application in the field. The most frequently discussed example in public works is that of potholes, which are filled the same way they were filled in the 1950s despite the fact that more durable materials and processes are now available. In the absence of codes forbidding application, the problem is lack of technology transfer.

In an era of fiscal austerity, when responsibility for construction and maintenance of the infrastructure is increasingly taken on by state and local governments, the federal government can assist by funding the kind of research, development, and technology transfer that enable these governments to work more effectively.

Afterword

Managing public works in cities and counties in the 1990s and beyond will be quite different from managing in previous years. The era of community government will bring new modes of citizen participation to fit a more activist citizenry; new and more equitable rules for decision making; and increasing pressure to solve problems regionally as well as locally. It will bring major technological advances: there will be more research and development programs; new technologies and materials; more technology transfer; and even faster advances in computerization—all of which will require smarter, better-trained public works staff. Management, too, will be challenged by fast-tracking of projects, value engineering, and the creation of incentive-disincentive packages for contractors.

Thus, public works—the oldest community service function—shows every evidence of requiring even more professionalism, more creativity, and more competent leadership. With such talent, the field will make a full contribution to the future of the community. ■

---

[1] Sam M. Cristofano and William S. Foster, *Management of Local Public Works* (Washington, DC: ICMA, 1986), 3. Adapted from Donald C. Stone, *Professional Education in Public Works / Environmental Engineering and Administration* (Chicago: American Public Works Association, 1974), 2-3.

[2] The descriptions that follow of APWA functional classifications and the survey referred to therein are found in *Public Works Today: A Profile of Local Service Organizations and Managers* (Chicago: APWA, 1990).

[3] Pat Choate and Susan Walter, *American in Ruins: The Decaying Infrastructure* (Durham, NC: Duke University Press, 1983); National Council on Public Works Improvement, *Fragile Foundations: A Report on America's Public Works* (Washington, DC: U.S. Government Printing Office, 1988).

[4] For an excellent article on the typologies of relationships between communities and their consultants, see Ruth Hoogland Dehoog, "Competition, Negotiation, or Cooperation: Three Models for Service Contracting," *Administration and Society* 22 (November, 1990): 317-340. The article also shows how to establish these relationships and how they can evolve in a way that is mutually beneficial.

[5] Claire L. Felbinger and Robert R. Whitehead, "Management of Solid Wastes Disposal" in *Managing Local Government: Public Administration in Practice*, ed. Bingham et al. (Newbury Park, CA: Sage, 1991), chapter 16.

[6] Marian R. Chertow, *Garbage Solutions: A Public Official's Guide to Recycling and Alternative Solid Waste Management Technologies* (Washington, DC: U.S. Conference of Mayors, 1989), 2.

[7] U.S. Congress, Office of Technology Assessment, *Delivering the Goods: Public Works Technologies, Management, and Finance* (Washington, DC: GPO, 1991), 138.

[8] Patrick Mann and Janice Beecher, *Cost Impact of Safe Drinking Water Act Compliance for Commission-Regulated Water Utilities*, NRRI Report 89-6 (Columbus, OH: National Regulatory Research Institute, January 1989).

[9] Congressional Budget Office, *New Directions for the Nation's Public Works* (Washington, DC: GPO, 1988).

7 Leisure Services

The services that provide cultural and recreational opportunities are unique in local governments. Unlike community services that focus on crises and social ills such as crime, pollution, racism, and unemployment, they bring people together and promote a sense of community. Libraries, cultural activities, and parks and recreational facilities are essential elements of the community that give it life and character.

In an era of financial austerity such public amenities often find themselves competing for shrinking tax dollars. Government officials often feel pressured to justify these services in economic or social terms by designing self-supporting programs and embracing a variety of entrepreneurial techniques and marketing strategies to generate revenue. Yet experience suggests that the public has a different view. It expects and supports leisure services. It passes bond issues to acquire park lands, becomes concerned when youth lack opportunities to participate in organized sports, and reacts strongly when fees are increased or imposed on services it believes should be available to all, such as museums and swimming facilities. Simply put, vital communities have vital leisure service programs.

The development of leisure services began with the urban park movement in New York, Philadelphia, Chicago, and other large cities in the mid-nineteenth century. The demand for libraries and playgrounds came shortly thereafter. They were viewed as critical to the health and welfare of children and necessary for learning, growth, and development. In time, other programs and services such as zoos, public golf courses, museums, and recreation programs for adults were added. Their value was understood. They were helpful in combating juvenile crime, attracting visitors and businesses, and reducing the stresses associated with urban life. These benefits continue today.

Leisure service professionals share similar views. They believe that the development of leisure activities is primarily an individual and family responsibility, but that the provision of facilities is a government responsibility. Furthermore, they hold that leisure services for communities should be planned and administered on the basis of the needs and interests of the people served and resources available. Finally, they argue that such public amenities and facilities are critical to a democratic society because they provide opportunities for people of all walks of life to interact and share common experiences.

Scope of service

Each community decides what its leisure service delivery system should do on the basis of its needs and interests; character, resources, and traditions; environmental features; opportunities available, including those

Figure 7–1 Playground in Davenport, Iowa.

provided by the private sector, nonprofit organizations, and government entities; and relevant state law, local ordinances, and administrative procedures.

There are different views of the proper scope of leisure services. Playgrounds, day camps, and parks are the traditional services provided by park and recreation units, but such units may also provide public gardens, community festivals, and zoos. In some instances, they may also be responsible for the library, cultural arts services, museums, and historic site preservation. Some communities expect local governments to play a supplementary role by offering only those leisure services not provided by someone else. Others would have them offer what they consider to be necessary regardless of the activities of other providers. Some communities operate programs only out of facilities they manage, while others have their leisure services staff seek out and use the resources of others.

Public policy issues abound in determining the scope of service and the wise utilization of resources. The need for gymnasiums and parks for public recreation varies according to the availability of school gyms for nonschool groups and the presence of lands managed by state and regional park authorities or by private land owners who make areas available for public use. The need for public arenas and convention facilities depends on the practices of private developers, hotel and motel operations, and the activities of a convention bureau. Some communities are asked to provide athletic facilities for local sports teams; in other communities this is viewed as the responsibility of the team's sponsor or owner. Some park departments maintain greenways, highway medians, and areas adjacent to public buildings, while other communities assign these responsibilities to a public works unit. In some communities the recreation unit operates play centers for preschool youth; in others, the private and nonprofit sectors perform that service.

Delta, Colorado, recreation complex

With careful planning, even small communities can develop and enjoy major recreational facilities. Delta, Colorado (4,200), has just developed a new, 265-acre park and recreation complex that includes a $3.8-million, 48,000-square-foot building; a 70-acre fishing lake complete with access for disabled users, a fishing pier, a swim beach, and picnic areas; a horse arena; a six-acre commons; five miles of hiking trails; a 500-seat outdoor amphitheater; and a living-history museum.

Source: Chris Miller, Admin. Assistant to City Manager/Tourism Director, Delta, Colorado, 1993.

Community governments use leisure service agencies to achieve a variety of goals and objectives. Recreation is often seen as a means of reducing or preventing juvenile delinquency; recreation professionals are asked to work closely with the police and social services to serve youth at risk. Developing late-evening summer basketball leagues is one such effort. (See accompanying sidebar.) Other communities want their leisure service systems to attract tourists. They encourage developing specialized facilities such as rose gardens and sponsoring attractions such as rose festivals. In Des Plaines, Illinois, the city and the Des Plaines Park District joined forces with the Des Plaines Historical Society to provide the sound financial base and maintenance services needed to keep the society's historic museum operative.

Midnight basketball league
Jackson, Tennessee (52,000), found a way to help keep young jobless youths out of trouble. The city has instituted a midnight basketball league that plays for eight weeks each summer between the hours of 10:00 P.M. and 2:00 A.M. at a refurbished community center. Young men between the ages of seventeen and twenty-one are invited to participate; they sign a contract to play three times a week and practice twice during midnight hours. Strict rules require attendance at a nightly seminar; those who miss the seminar are not allowed to participate in the next game. Scheduled speakers talk about drug use and abuse, safe sex, pregnancy, teamwork, discipline, self-esteem, marketable skills, and grants and training opportunities at colleges and technical and vocational schools.

At the end of the summer, a post-season picnic is held for the players and, with money received from a foundation, the city awards $500 scholarships to five program participants. Recipients are selected on the basis of leadership ability, attitude, work ethic, and teamwork, not on athletic ability. The scholarships may be used for job training at vo-tech schools or applied toward a two-year or four-year college degree program.

Source: *The Guide to Management Improvement Projects in Local Government*, vol. 14, no. 4 (Washington, DC: ICMA, 1990), no. LHS-26.

Organization for leisure services

With such a varied pattern of service responsibilities, it is not surprising to find wide variation in the way small cities and counties organize and deliver leisure services. Perhaps the most common trait in leisure service delivery systems is heavy reliance upon input from citizen boards and commissions (discussed later in this section).

Modes of service delivery

One question facing community governments is that of the relative emphasis on the two modes of leisure service delivery: direct provision and facilitation. Under the direct provision mode, government assumes responsibility for service operations. This mode requires more personnel, general revenue appropriations, and capital development. It also ensures a greater degree of accountability and fixed authority, as well as firsthand knowledge of the public served. Traditional library, park, and recreation services are usually provided directly.

The facilitation mode is more recent. Government assumes the position of broker, with services provided by private and nonprofit organizations. Little league baseball, for example, is usually provided through this mode: a private group organizes and operates the teams, while games are played on community-owned fields.

The facilitation mode involves evaluation and assessment, legal arrangements, and technical assistance. It encourages information sharing and joint planning. It may require the enactment of special legislation to free the service providers from certain liabilities or to encourage their participation. Using this mode does not relieve the government of responsibility for making sure that the services are rendered without discrimination, and government often receives little recognition for its contributions.

Most localities use both modes, but the trend is toward more use of facilitation. Some critics argue that this trend reduces the provision of leisure services for poor residents, who may not be able to provide, for example, the equipment necessary to outfit a little league baseball team.

Organizational patterns

Traditionally, diverse agencies such as park and recreation departments, library commissions, arts councils, and arena authorities provide leisure services. Sometimes, special district governments administer them. As a group, the separate agencies constitute a community leisure service delivery system. One contemporary trend is to combine all agencies into one department of leisure services. Another is to divide the functions, placing the program components in a unit with other human services and the park and recreation division in the unit responsible for public works. Each approach has advantages and disadvantages.

Individual units have well-defined clienteles and a sense of mandate. They have a well-known image and professional identity. There is little ambiguity about role and responsibility; the public knows what to expect when it enters a library, goes to a park, or enrolls in a ceramics class. In addition, individual units can more effectively raise funds and attract volunteers.

Whether agencies are independent or combined in a single department, they should be organized in a manner that ensures communication among them.

However, this approach often fosters competition between units and may encourage a degree of isolation; sometimes it also results in duplication of organizational structures. To eliminate these problems, advocates argue, the various units should be placed under one umbrella agency. But that solution, too, has its shortcomings. Although the budget of a combined department is greater than that of any single unit under the traditional system, its total political and financial support is likely to be less than that enjoyed collectively by the separate individual agencies. The morale of its personnel may be affected with the loss of professional identity, bureaucratic growth may be stimulated, and the public may be confused as to the agency's mission.

Either approach can succeed if the services offered are viable, expected, and effectively presented. The key to success is communication. The local government must keep citizens informed of the services offered by individual agencies (or a combined department) and establish mechanisms for obtaining feedback on these services from the public. In addition, whether the individual agencies are independent or combined in a single department, they should be structured and organized in a manner that ensures communication among them.

Role of citizen groups and boards

Leisure service agencies rely heavily upon the advice of community residents through citizen boards and commissions. Generally such bodies are advisory, but in several states, such as Illinois and Colorado, they have policymaking authority. Board composition is critical. In addition to representing various community interests, board members with technical expertise and insight should be chosen. For example, as a land management agency, a park and recreation department can benefit enormously from the advice of those who know and understand real estate, economic development, and conservation practices. Citizen boards can help analyze resources, determine desirable programs, and recruit volunteers, activity instructors, and neighborhood leaders. In either capacity—policymaking or advisory—the board should be an effective advocate of both the public and the agency.

Leisure service agencies encourage the establishment of support groups such as Friends of the Library, Friends of Parks and Recreation, and Friends of the Cultural Arts. These groups often are well organized, articulate, politically connected, and highly motivated. They tend to be single-purposed. They are able to generate philanthropic support and take pride in their accomplishments. Their role may be caring for a special library collection for the visually impaired or acquiring Native American crafts for an exhibit at the county museum. Such groups add immensely to leisure service systems by adopting parks, purchasing exotic plants, and underwriting specific programs such as a community theater. These efforts require coordination, but they produce significant economic and political benefits.

Perhaps most important, such groups get more people, and especially more community leaders, involved in community service activities.

Operations

As is true with all government activities, the management challenge in leisure services is to provide a high level of services by managing program operations efficiently and effectively within available financial resources. Leisure service operations involves a dynamic combination of people, programs, and physical resources.

Personnel

Effective leadership is a must for successful delivery of leisure services. Lay boards and advisory committees provide one facet of that leadership; professional staff and volunteer workers provide another. Different types of personnel are required depending upon the nature and organization of the system. Specialized positions typically require professional preparation. In some instances, certification is needed, even for volunteers. Organizations with national certification programs include the National Recreation and Park Association (certified leisure professionals), the National Therapeutic Recreation Certification Board (therapeutic recreation), and the National Youth Sports Coaches Association (volunteer youth coaching).

The Jamestown Community Playground Corporation

The Jamestown Community Playground Corporation was created in Jamestown, Rhode Island (5,800), to develop a community playground for preschool and school-age children. The development effort included private fundraising efforts as well as a drive to collect over $20,000 worth of plastic, which was then recycled into plastic lumber. In four days, over three hundred volunteers constructed a 200-foot-square playground made primarily from the recycled plastic lumber.

Source: *The Guide to Management Improvement Projects in Local Government*, vol. 14, no. 1 (Washington, DC: ICMA, 1990), no. LHS-29.

No longer are good intentions, political patronage, or interest in working with children sufficient for employment by leisure service agencies.

The traditions of leisure service agencies are highly compatible with the trend toward downsizing government operations without reducing services. These agencies have always depended heavily upon part-time and volunteer leadership. Whereas professional staff tend to manage operations, demonstrating their skills in organization and program development, it is the part-time and volunteer personnel who provide most of the direct services. They teach classes, coach, check out equipment and books, conduct walking tours, and perform other similar functions. Many systems employ specialists to work with elderly residents and those with disabilities to assist visitors as part of the community's effort to enhance tourism. Program flexibility is achieved by using part-time and temporary personnel. When not prohibited by certification requirements, reliance upon local leaders and residents helps maintain good relationships with neighborhoods, especially those whose ethnic and demographic characteristics differ from those of the professional staff.

No longer are good intentions, political patronage, or interest in working with children sufficient for employment by leisure service agencies. Professional staff are expected to be knowledgeable in management and marketing practices as well as well grounded in the principles of programming and public relations. Park professionals are expected to know about the carrying capacity of resources, facility design, and requirements for effective maintenance. Librarians must be technically grounded as well as skilled in operations and program development. Continuing education, in-service training, and recognition programs are essential for all staff—professional, part-time, and volunteer. Leisure service agencies assist community governments in maintaining good relations with all segments of the community through their personnel practices.

Programs

Programs are the heart of the leisure service delivery system. Programs are everything an agency does to serve the public—from providing guided nature tours to operating an ice rink, from sponsoring a street fair to loaning video tapes through the library.

Program delivery issues are numerous. They involve legal jurisdictions, financial arrangements, service approaches, the number and type of personnel required, and facility operations. The following are examples of common policy questions:

Should libraries be located in neighborhood recreation centers or are mobile library units the best way to serve people?

Should the recreation department organize and conduct adult softball games at its own facilities or should it provide the fields, letting some other agency, such as the YMCA, manage the program?

Should the park department develop and maintain hiking trails or should it solicit volunteer organizations to maintain them, with each volunteer group assigned responsibility for a designated segment?

Should the cultural arts commission sponsor and finance a sculpture class or should it contract the service to an artist and assume only a promotional role?

Figure 7–2 To have a well-balanced program of activities requires full recognition of the preschool group. The need and demand for service to this group has been growing rapidly with changes in family patterns, economic activity, and educational expectations.

Most leisure service agencies consider offering instruction in various leisure activities to be a responsibility. This belief is grounded in the concept of choice—that citizens do not have choices unless they have the skill and knowledge that allow them to pursue alternatives. It is not unusual for a recreation department to offer instruction in ethnic cooking or gardening in addition to the more traditional classes in poetry and needlework. Many programs are self-supporting or held in cooperation with another agency such as a school or college. Some, like a class in wine making, may be taboo because they conflict with local traditions and values, although the interest is there. In that case or in other situations in which the agency perceives a need but believes the activity is beyond its mandate as a direct service provider, it may facilitate instruction through other organizations.

Fitness equipment for disabled citizens
Crestwood, Missouri's (12,000) parks and recreation department installed a special exercycle to allow people with spinal injuries to exercise in a community setting. The local hospital purchased the $19,000 exercycle, and the park department installed it with the existing fitness equipment at the city community center.

Source: *The Guide to Management Improvement Projects in Local Government*, vol. 14, no. 3 (Washington, DC: ICMA, 1990), no. LHS-17.

Physical resources

Facilities vary from place to place. Typically, rural areas do not need neighborhood parks to the same degree that urban areas do; the demand for golf and tennis facilities may be much greater in an affluent, middle-class suburban subdivision than in an industrial blue-collar community. The outdoor recreation patterns in Bend, Oregon, differ from those of Lakeland, Florida. Although national standards aid communities in evaluating their areas and facilities, they should be used only to guide, not to determine action. Leisure service providers must be aware of total community resources as they plan and develop facilities. A master plan is essential.

It is important for communities to make sure they do not overextend their resources. Operational costs require a careful assessment of which programs and services a government should offer and which it should encourage others to provide. Capital developments imply that additional monies will be spent on operations and maintenance. If money to operate and maintain current facilities is tight, then adding more facilities is probably not appropriate unless new sources of funding for operations and maintenance are generated.

Officials should also be aware that developing facilities creates demands for their use. Providing a trail for bikers may stimulate interest in biking but bring the attendant problems of maintenance and management. It may also bring into conflict different publics that previously did not interact. For example, environmentalists may see a bike trail as damaging to the environment, while adjacent property owners may see it as a noise and pollution problem. Others may see it as a leisure opportunity or a positive recreational outlet for young people's energy, which might otherwise be misdirected.

Activity choices and facility use are interactive. Increasing participation in a given activity—for example, tennis—may decrease participation in golf. People devote only a portion of their time to leisure activities,

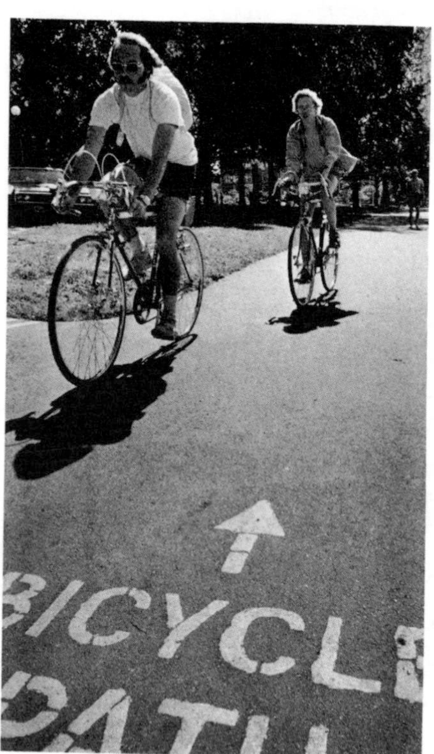

Figure 7–3 Facilities for cyclists are an important consideration in planning parks and recreation areas.

and changes in leisure activities mean changes in facility use. When community governments encourage private entrepreneurs to develop amusement areas such as water parks, they may expect a decline in the use of those facilities that formerly attracted water park users.

Citizens expect leisure areas to be safe, free from crime and other hazards. Proper design and maintenance help reduce vandalism and so does the active involvement of community and neighborhood groups in the operation of these spaces. By empowering users with a sense of rights and obligations and by employing professionally qualified personnel to operate programs and services, many problems are mitigated. Many leisure service agencies find that they must have both a risk management plan and a public partnership plan in order to be successful.

The Corvallis Senior Center

The Corvallis Senior Center began in 1957 as a fifty-member club located in the recreation room in the basement of city hall. Through the commitment of the city and many senior citizens, the center now serves an average of 10,700 people a month in a building that has 11,000 square feet of space. It is owned and operated by the city of Corvallis, with assistance from the Benton County Senior Citizen Council and the Senior Citizen Foundation of Benton County.

It is the center's objective to recognize and promote the ambitions and continued learning of each participant and to offer vital supportive social services for residents who are fifty-five years of age or older. The center also serves as a resource to the community by providing information and training on aging issues and on services that other agencies and organizations offer. It also encourages new images and ideas about aging.

The program administered at the center provides an information and referral service; current information on illnesses that most often affect older age groups; an extensive trip and hiking program; language classes; a play-with-toddlers group; tap dance; and video operas, to name a few offerings. The center produces a monthly newsletter and a quarterly travel brochure, and it has a weekly radio program to advertise upcoming classes and events.

The center recently co-sponsored a free word-processing class for beginners with Crescent Valley High School. Students were paired with senior citizens to co-teach the class with the instructor. It was an excellent opportunity for seniors and students to interact with each other and for the students to get to know older adults in an atmosphere in which the students were the experts. And of course, they all enhanced their computer skills.

The facility is staffed by a director, a part-time travel coordinator, and a part-time custodian; additional administrative and secretarial support is provided through the parks and recreation department. In addition to housing the senior citizen program, the center is rented to the community for private parties, meetings, and events, providing funds that help offset the cost of the program.

As more people live longer and seventy million baby boomers approach retirement age, senior centers and programs that focus on seniors will become an increasingly integral part of community governments.

Karen Emery, Director, Corvallis Senior Center, Corvallis, Oregon, 1993.

Recent trends

Marketing leisure services has become important in recent years. The ability to target specific populations for specific services is valuable when resources are limited. High-risk activities such as mountain climbing, sky diving, and bungee jumping are popular, but they appeal to a small population segment, one generally able to pay for these services. Because safety and liability are major concerns, most leisure service agencies encourage the private sector to provide opportunities for these activities while they concentrate their efforts on programs that carry less risk. A marketing strategy helps ensure that the programs offered are those that the public wants, that the public knows about these programs, and that fee revenues, when appropriate, can be generated.

Biking brochure

To promote bicycling and publicize its five-mile bike path throughout the community, Clawson, Michigan (14,000), designed and distributed a brochure containing biking safety tips and a map of the bike route detailing all museums, schools, city buildings, churches, and community centers on the route. The brochure is distributed at all city facilities, including city hall, the community centers, the library, and public works offices.

Source: *The Guide to Management Improvement Projects in Local Government*, vol. 17, no. 1 (Washington, DC: ICMA, 1993), no. LHS-7.

Although rarely involved in financing local leisure services operations, the federal government influences them through grant programs and regulatory legislation. The three areas most significantly affected are land and facility acquisition, cultural arts programs, and services to disabled citizens. Land and Water Conservation Fund grants in the 1970s

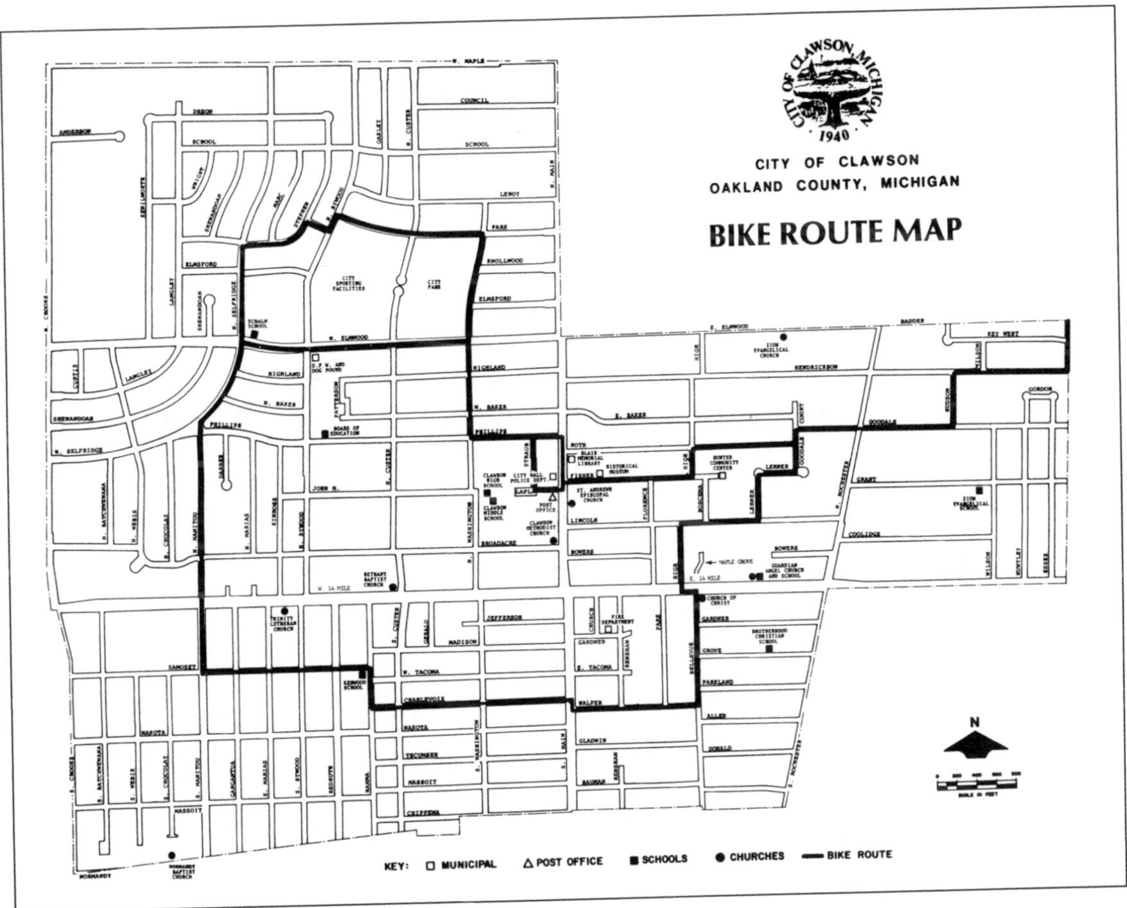

Figure 7–4 Bike route map, city of Clawson, Michigan.

Figure 7–5 Nature trails can be created even in small parks.

and early 1980s funded the acquisition and development of select outdoor recreation areas. The President's Commission on Americans Outdoors made recommendations in 1987 that stimulated interest in greenways and trails and led to legislation that enabled private sector assistance in developing these programs. Expansion of facilities, however, has increased operations and maintenance costs, and some communities find themselves facility rich and program poor. They are expending an increasing percentage of their budgets on maintenance at the expense of program activities. The net result is fewer programs, in general, or an increasing reliance on self-supporting programs, which often narrows the population segment served.

Federal support for the arts and historic preservation during the Nixon and Carter administrations made services available to the public at large that formerly were provided only for the affluent or through private philanthropy. Now some of these services are in jeopardy. Many of the philanthropies have shifted their focus, and the ability to sustain these programs on membership subscriptions is questionable. What will happen to community orchestras, ballets, zoos, and historic buildings? Who will maintain them and how will they be financed? Will they become a program and budget responsibility of local governments, a concern of the local park and recreation department, or a ward of the United Way or will special districts for funding be established to ensure their continuance?

The Americans with Disabilities Act of 1990 and similar legislation have increased the responsibility for providing leisure services for those with disabilities and for eliminating the physical and attitudinal barriers to access. Since the mid-1960s, programs for special populations—elderly, visually impaired, mentally or physically disabled citizens—have become very important. Services to these groups are generally no more expensive than programs for the general population if facilities are constructed sensibly and program design takes into account that there may be a need for a greater number of leaders, both paid and volunteer. However, due to the economic problems that can accompany disability, these programs require more financial support. Fortunately, there are sometimes private, nonprofit organizations, such as the Association for Retarded Citizens, whose support can be solicited.

An innovative playground

Recognizing the need for a new park, Surfside Beach, South Carolina (3,500), built a playground where all children, with and without disabilities, can play side by side. The playground equipment is specifically designed to accommodate children with physical disabilities without separating them from others. Area schools have come to the park for field trips for both disabled and non-disabled students; the park also attracts tourists as well as local children.

Source: *The Guide to Management Improvement Projects in Local Government*, vol. 16, no. 4 (Washington, DC: ICMA, 1992), no. LHS-29.

Among the diverse populations served by community governments, homeless people and new immigrants constitute two groups whose needs have created a new set of policies and concerns for leisure service providers. The facts that many parks have become living quarters for the homeless and that programs may be inaccessible to those for whom

English is a second language are forcing a reassessment of values and approaches. Unfortunately, few organizations assist in empowering these groups, yet their need for programs and services is significant.

Finances

In today's constrained fiscal environment, primary attention must be given to funding sources, innovative uses of cooperation and partnerships with other organizations, and cost-cutting alternatives to deliver services.

Figure 7–6 Park equipment for children can be both innovative and inexpensive.

Recycled plastic for playgrounds
To replace deteriorating wooden playground equipment at a city park, Fairfax, Virginia (20,000), installed a playground structure made from recycled plastic. The new plastic equipment cost 10 percent more than comparable wooden equipment, but the life span of the plastic is triple that of wood. It does not give children splinters, requires no maintenance, and reinforces the city's commitment to protecting the environment.

Source: *The Guide to Management Improvement Projects in Local Government*, vol. 16, no. 2 (Washington, DC: ICMA, 1992), no. PW-16.

Funding sources

As responsibilities of community governments, parks, recreational programs, cultural activities, and libraries rely heavily upon general government revenues to support their operations. Approximately 7 to 10 percent of local government budgets are typically expended on these services, mostly from a combination of general revenues and special taxes from which the proceeds are dedicated by law for use only for recreation, parks, or libraries. Capital development is supported both by general tax revenues and by bond issues, private philanthropy, and state-operated lotteries. More recently, special park and recreation funds have been created, utilizing land transfer fees, impact fees, and other dedicated revenues. According to the National Recreation and Park Association, federal grants provide less than 3 percent of funding for local leisure service systems.

The trend is toward using revenue-producing facilities and programs to support program expansion or contracting with vendors to provide such services as boat rentals, park concessions, concerts, and high-risk activities. In such cases, the leisure service agency responsible for the program may receive a percentage of the gross or an amount set by contract. The proceeds may be controlled by the agency or revert to the general treasury of the community government. When the latter occurs, the entrepreneurial incentive for the agency is diminished.

Community governments must strike a careful balance between leisure service programs that are funded and those that produce revenue.

This fee-for-service approach allows leisure service agencies to provide services without having to increase their reliance on tax dollars, but it also creates inequities. Some citizens simply cannot afford to take advantage of these programs, and thus public leisure activities are no longer available to them.

Viewing leisure services as a public good, community governments employ a wide range of strategies to deal with this problem. Two of the more frequently used are vouchers for lower income groups and public days—free admission to pools, museums, and concerts on given days. Another strategy is to solicit a specific sponsor to underwrite a program, for example, having a civic club provide horse riding for citizens with disabilities.

Entrepreneurial success in generating revenues is motivated by the desire to maintain and expand services, but successes may be seen by some people as evidence that leisure service agencies do not need government appropriations in order to exist or that they can be self-supporting. Experience, however, suggests that this is a short-sighted view. A comprehensive program includes services that are not revenue generating and must therefore receive government funding; in addition, the community government may be criticized by local businesses if it is perceived as competing with them. Bearing in mind the goal of providing leisure services equitably for all residents, community governments must strike a careful balance between leisure service programs that are funded through general government revenues and those that produce revenue.

Interjurisdictional service contracting
Brea, California (33,000), reduced its budgeted cost for community service programs by contracting with the newly incorporated city of Diamond Bar to orchestrate that community's special events, youth and adult sports programs, concerts, and recreational activities. The contract will cover Brea's direct costs as well as a portion of the city's existing administrative and overhead costs for community service programs.

Source: *The Guide to Management Improvement Projects in Local Government,* vol. 16, no. 2 (Washington, DC: ICMA, 1992), no. MGT-11.

Cooperation and partnerships

Cooperative agreements and joint development of areas by two or more governmental units have expanded local recreational services with minimal cost. For example, Arvada, Colorado, leases its tennis center, swimming pool, and community facilities to the North Jeffco Recreation and Park District, which assumes responsibility for operating expenses so that park district residents can enjoy the facilities without additional capital expenditures and the city can lessen its operational expenses. Kinston, North Carolina, contracts with Lenoir County, in which it is located, to provide programs in several adjacent farming communities. To offer a youth baseball and softball program, three neighboring communities in Illinois—Roxana, East Alton, and Wood River—joined forces to share costs of operations. These joint agreements among counties, cities, and special districts enable their residents to participate in programs not otherwise available.

Joint agreements among counties, cities, and special districts enable their residents to participate in programs not otherwise available.

Another pattern involves school districts and community governments acquiring adjacent land to develop jointly. The leisure services department develops its portion with the understanding that it will utilize many of the resources of the school facility for its programs. The school develops its areas with the understanding that the children will use the adjacent recreation and sports facilities rather than having the school develop its own. The community benefits from this arrangement with lower costs, reduced duplication of efforts, and increased leisure opportunities for all.

Another strategy is to develop public-private partnership agreements. Such partnerships have several advantages. For example, when community governments allow private developers to construct specialized facilities such as water parks and ski runs on public lands, the public has additional recreational opportunities without having to expend public funds for capital development. Such agreements typically have developers pay rent or an equivalent payment in kind, an expense much less than the developer would incur if the property had to be purchased. The cost savings may be passed on to participants through lower user fees or by designating certain days as public days. Another example of this type of cooperation can be seen when a power company allows the public to use its watersheds and water areas for recreational purposes. When this is done, the power company is usually given tax credits or relieved of certain liabilities. To the company, the public relations value is considerable, as is the value of the recreational resources to the public.

Cost-cutting

Fiscal constraints that focus attention on raising revenues and providing services through facilitation may also require cost-cutting. Among the more frequently used approaches are deferring or abandoning capital development plans; delaying maintenance; reducing services; and reducing the number of paid staff. A common popular technique is to contract out for certain services such as maintenance, which requires a large investment in equipment.

Cooperative community beautification program

College Station, Texas (52,500), worked with a local community beautification society, Brazos Beautiful, Inc., to sponsor "100 Trees in 100 Days," a program designed to acquire and plant 100 trees in the city's newly developed Wolf Pen Creek Park. The program's goal was to raise $10,000 to provide for an initial planting of 100 trees in the park. Plantings were designed to meet four criteria, for shade, aesthetics, sound absorption (at the perimeter of the park's amphitheater), and species diversification. The effort succeeded in raising funds for 116 trees.

Source: Ron Ragland, City Manager, College Station, Texas, 1993.

Afterword

Leisure service agencies contribute to the health, well-being, and economic viability of their communities by providing facilities for active recreation, by promoting fitness and community pride, and by offering services that attract visitors. One community enjoyed the benefits of this contribution when its park and recreation department sponsored a regional baseball tournament. The department expended $7,000 for tournament promotion, trophies, additional personnel, and utilities, but the three-day tournament attracted a thousand out-of-town guests—parents, players, and friends—who spent $250,000 in the community on lodging, food, and entertainment. Besides improving the community's quality of life, leisure services can provide a significant financial return on the community's investment.

This is an exciting time for leisure service agencies. They are being asked to become more entrepreneurial, more managerial, and more a part of the operations of community governments. They provide opportunities for residents to become involved as volunteers, convert unsightly discards such as landfills and rail rights-of-way into parks and greenways, and generate public support and pride. And because citizens from different social, cultural, economic, and ethnic backgrounds may contribute to formulating policies and come together to participate in programs, leisure service agencies are one of the community government's better democratizing institutions. ■

Human Services

Traditionally, local governments have been responsible for law enforcement, fire protection, emergency services, education, public works, and some public health services. They have also provided services and facilities that appeal to limited segments of the community—for example, libraries, museums, civic centers, and recreational facilities. More recently, they have become responsible for services that are less traditional: the human service programs designed to help poor and disadvantaged people.

Local governments provide some human service programs to confront community problems and social concerns that people are unable to deal with by themselves. Alcoholism, for example, is both a private health and a public safety problem that historically people have been unable to solve alone. The fragmented efforts of well-intentioned churches and charities are usually neither well coordinated nor comprehensive in scope, so local government must provide leadership, coordination, and other needed services.

Still other human services, such as the elimination of architectural barriers to the physically disabled, are provided in response to state and federal mandates. Local governments are often given responsibility for such services, but little or no authority for program design. Programs created by the federal government are typically designed to be free of local and state biases in an attempt to ensure nationally uniform standards.

Recognizing the role of local government in serving the poor and disadvantaged population, the International City Management Association issued a policy statement in 1969 asserting that

> *Local governments' efforts to assure justice and provide service equally to all citizens have failed too often to serve adequately those whose needs are greatest. The poor, the old, the handicapped, the subjects of ethnic and racial discrimination have often been overlooked by local government. That society as a whole has failed them, increases the responsibility of the local government management profession to intensify its efforts now to serve them better. . . .This cannot be done with good intentions alone. Positive programs are necessary. Each professional must devote his position of responsibility in the local government structure to the fundamental objectives of achieving social and economic justice.*[1]

Inevitably, there are differences of opinion regarding the best way to deal with community problems. To reduce delinquency, some people may want to increase the number of police, others to start a drug education program, and still others to provide youth with opportunities for employment or recreation. Although education and employment options may be less expensive and more effective than hiring police, administrators may have a difficult time convincing elected officials, and subsequently the community, that adding human service programs instead of hiring additional officers may be a more effective response.

However, problems such as violence, poverty, unemployment, substance abuse, and AIDS, which were once found mainly in large cities, are spreading to smaller communities in the suburbs and rural areas. Many communities are realizing that in order to avoid major, expensive, and disruptive problems later, it makes sense to invest in preventive human services such as health education, child care, and counseling now.

Attitudes toward human services

Federal and state mandates and regulations, court orders, laws, an adversarial environment, and the growing magnitude of social ills—combined with limited resources—have created an array of obstacles for the government leader who attempts to deal with the human service needs of a community. Successfully overcoming these and other obstacles requires that the administrative leadership learn to work in concert both with elected officials and members of the community. Often this may require efforts to modify the attitudes toward human services of elected officials, members of the community, and possibly the administrative staff.

Elected officials

Professional staff may find that some elected officials believe that social problems should not be government's problems; they believe that social problems are best handled by the family, churches, other nonprofit organizations, or professional counselors. In some officials, this attitude may be the result of bias against poor and disadvantaged people. Yet others, especially those faced with limited resources, may simply want to focus on the more tangible needs of the community: new streets, parking lots, or more police protection. Whatever belief is held, administrative leaders may have to convince elected officials of the need to do something about the social problems confronting the community.

Deliberate speed should be the rule in efforts to change attitudes toward human services. The administrator who tries to make changes before laying the groundwork and building public support may soon be looking for another job. The process requires effective two-way communication with elected officials.

The administrator should provide elected officials with objective information on (1) community needs; (2) resources, if any, currently being expended in the community to cope with those needs; (3) shortcomings of the status quo; and (4) alternative courses of action. Rather than coming across as altruistic or paternalistic, which may cause elected officials to attribute administrative concern to "softheartedness" or a patronizing attitude, the administrator should come across as an effective communicator of an identified community need.

Community attitudes

In seeking support from the community, government leaders may encounter resistance. Many residents are, at best, ambivalent about human services as long as they receive the traditional services they expect from their local government (i.e., police, public works, roads, planning, and parks). Some may feel that dealing with social problems is not the responsibility of local government. Others may be interested in helping, but they may be more concerned about the impact of needed assistance on an already escalating tax burden.

Further compounding the problem may be an attitude of distrust that often exists among the people the community is trying to help. This distrust may emerge from differences in language and culture, or, as often happens, it may emerge from the failure of past efforts. African Americans, Asian Americans, Native Americans, and Hispanic Americans have often been promised help, but they have just as often been disappointed by a lack of follow through or by misguided programs. Such recurring disappointment may breed distrust of any outsider who offers help.

The government leader must work to gain the support of the community. Like those of elected officials, the negative attitudes of the community can often be overcome through better communication. Although there is often mistrust or dislike for programs placed in the context of "welfare," support is often found when issues or problems are isolated or individual programs are examined. The leader's role then becomes that of communicating the very specific nature of the problems confronting a number of residents, driving home the human aspect of human service programs.

Administrator attitudes

Administrators can easily be preoccupied with the more obvious and more demanding problems facing a community. Issues of infrastructure decay, rising crime rates, declining revenues, and the need for economic development are only a few of the pressing problems facing the administrator. In such circumstances it becomes quite easy to become more concerned with the "big picture" issues at the expense of the issues confronting a smaller, less vocal segment of the community.

Administrators must make a committed and sustained effort to human services if those services are to have a chance of succeeding. They must be careful not to be so preoccupied with the big picture that they fail to show visible concern for the segment of the community most in need. Certainly the administrator alone cannot be expected to correct the social ills of the community, but the administrator can be expected to take a leadership role in encouraging and helping community and elected officials to do so.

Human service programs and concerns

The concerns with which communities are increasingly expected to deal are seemingly endless. Although there is no universally accepted list of local government programs that fall under the heading of human services, a representative group of such programs would include those concerned with

Youth
Elderly citizens
Racial prejudice
Housing
Transportation
Employment
Child care
Mentally disabled citizens
Physically disabled citizens
Health and public health
Alcohol and drug abuse
Consumer protection
Crisis management
Redevelopment
Poverty
Tenant rights.

Youth

If a community does not deal with youth problems through its social programs, eventually it will deal with worse problems through its law enforcement department. The traditional youth problems of vandalism, truancy, and alcohol and drug involvement seem to be continually increasing. Adding to these traditional problems are increasing levels of teenage pregnancy; sexually transmitted diseases, including AIDS; gang violence; and the overall devaluation of human life.

Employment programs have proven to be one of the most effective ways of assisting youth to avoid or overcome these problems. A school district may provide job training programs; other efforts include recreational programs, tutorial programs, halfway houses for runaways, and counseling for drug abuse or pregnancy. Some communities operate therapeutic group homes to treat young people who otherwise would be placed in training schools. They may also operate group homes and receiving homes for foster children, and some identify children's needs in their strategic planning efforts.

The need for collaboration

The current social welfare system divides the problems of children and families into rigid and distinct categories that fail to reflect their interrelated causes and solutions. Services designed to correspond to discrete problems are administered by literally dozens of agencies and programs, each with its own particular focus, source of funding, guidelines, and accountability requirements. Even though a child and his or her family may need a mix of health, education, child welfare, or other services, separate and often conflicting eligibility standards and rules governing the expenditure of funds militate against comprehensive service delivery. Although each provider may offer quality services, no single provider is likely to assist each individual, much less his or her family, to identify a tailored set of comprehensive services, ensure that they are received, and evaluate their outcome.

Schools alone are not responsible for solving all of the problems that keep young people from succeeding there. Bringing together the assortment of services so urgently needed by the third of our young people who are most at risk requires a joint effort by all child- and youth-serving sectors. Increasingly, practitioners, policymakers, parents, and taxpayers agree that finding ways to keep children in school and learning is not somebody else's problem. It is a shared responsibility.

Agencies concerned with mental health, employment and training, child development, recreation, and health and welfare, as well as education, have a vital interest in promoting school success. Unless young people struggling to avoid or overcome multiple problems receive adequate prevention, support, and early treatment, they are unlikely to develop the basic skills they need to survive in the job market. Virtually without exception, this failure will worsen their non-academic problems and increase the demand placed on human services for more costly treatment and long-term financial subsidies.

By combining a wealth of expertise and a variety of perspectives, interagency partnerships have the opportunity to reorient systems away from the narrow dimensions of single agency mandates toward the broad-based needs of children and families.

Source: Adapted from Atelia I. Melaville with Martin J. Blank, *What It Takes: Structuring Interagency Partnerships to Connect Children and Families with Comprehensive Services* (Washington, DC: Education and Human Services Consortium, 1991).

In order to be most effective, a community's youth programs should be structured to ensure active cooperation among different agencies in the community: local government departments, nonprofit organizations, and other jurisdictions. A disjointed criminal justice system, in particular, will serve as a barrier to effective youth programs. Working in isolation, police and probation departments may regard each other with suspicion, resentment, and even hostility. Bringing such agencies together to work cooperatively can yield substantial results.

Community forums can be a useful method of involving all sectors of the community in attempts to address concerns and problems related to youth. In March 1993, for example, Catawba County, North Carolina, held a Children's Summit to which it invited business, government, and service-agency leaders in order to focus attention on the large number of problems affecting children. The summit succeeded in drawing attention to these problems, and it produced a long list of recommendations to the board of commissioners, including a call for the appointment of a Children's Advocacy Council.

In addition, elected officials may wish to appoint a youth commission, a mayor's council on youth opportunity, or youth representatives to regular boards and commissions in order to give youth a voice. If representatives are given a valid mission and their role is clearly defined, representation can produce beneficial results.

Elderly citizens

Common needs of elderly citizens include transportation, housing, health care, nutrition, recreation, employment, and financial resources; these needs are typically greater among the elderly than among the population as a whole. Reduced fares and fare-box subsidies are examples of programs that can ease the transportation problems they face. Housing programs, meals-on-wheels, consumer protection, guardianship services, counseling, recreation programs, and the elimination of barriers to the physically disabled are additional examples of programs that can benefit the elderly.

Many governments appoint a council on aging to give senior citizens a voice and to evaluate programs. Other communities use existing organizational structures to facilitate similar functions. Financial help and advice on implementing programs for the elderly are available through the federal government's Older Americans Act, Social Service Block Grants, Medicare, and Medicaid.

Residential alternatives for elderly citizens

Catawba County, North Carolina (114,000), gives elderly and disabled individuals the option of remaining in their own homes or entering a nursing or rest home. A social worker and nurse assess the feasibility of the citizen remaining in his or her own home and determine the in-home services required to enable him or her to remain there. After the assessment, the agency either provides the services needed in the home or contracts for their provision.

Medicaid reimburses the eligible population for the provision of the services as long as they do not exceed the actual cost of nursing home care. During the ten years since it began, the program has avoided over $1 million in Medicaid payments. It is not only a cost-effective program, it satisfies many citizens' desire to remain at home.

Source: J. Thomas Lundy, County Manager, Catawba County, North Carolina, 1993.

Racial prejudice

Undoubtedly, racism is one of the greatest and most pervasive barriers to progress in the social sector. Many opponents of social programs believe that these programs are devised solely to benefit racial minorities. Although they are not based on fact, such attitudes affect the behavior of many. Thus, all aspects of local government must operate in concert to overcome such misperceptions and to eliminate racism in all its guises.

As the population of North America becomes increasingly diverse in the 1990s, all local government officials must demonstrate cultural sensitivity and awareness. Training in cultural diversity will help administrators and department heads to examine their own attitudes and to recognize and deal with racial prejudice among employees. Employee behavior that can be seen as racially prejudiced or insulting cannot be tolerated. Employee training and stringent administration of nondiscrimination regulations are two of the best ways to deal with racism.

The ECHO Program

Warren County, New Jersey (91,500), instituted the Elder Cottage Housing Opportunity (ECHO) Program to assist older people to remain in the community as long as possible with dignity and independence and to delay the need for institutional care of the frail elderly as long as possible. Under the program, residential property owners are permitted to place small homes on their lots to house elderly relatives. Such homes enable elderly individuals to enjoy the privacy of their own home while being close to their families, who can assist them as needed. The homes are removed from the property when they are no longer required.

To allay local fears that the homes would not be removed and would increase population density, the county contracted with a supplier to provide it with cottages that it purchases and rents to participating families. The rent charged pays for insurance and maintenance costs and helps build a reserve fund for the cottage's removal. When the family no longer needs the cottage, the county guarantees its removal within ninety days and stores it until it is needed by another family.

Source: Anne Schneider, Executive Director of the Office on Aging, Warren County, New Jersey, 1993.

Housing

Decent housing for all has been a stated objective in the United States for over half a century. To achieve this objective, administrators should identify and utilize federal and state programs that best fit the community's needs. These programs range from government-owned and -operated housing projects to conservation and rehabilitation programs. Local governments can also enlist the assistance of nonprofit organizations such as Habitat for Humanity to help provide suitable housing.

Communities that wish to provide more housing should review their zoning ordinances and subdivision regulations and, if appropriate, make changes that will facilitate the development of land for housing. Flexible housing regulations that permit planned unit development, cluster housing, zero lot line development, and transfer of development rights will encourage developers to build housing for families with low and moderate incomes. Communities may also wish to review their building regulations. Although most regulations relating to safety and quality must be retained, it may be possible to adjust regulations that unnecessarily increase housing prices.

It is important to remember that citizens cannot make choices about housing if they are not informed. Local governments, chambers of commerce, developers, and builders should distribute information to educate the public about available housing options.

Transportation

Although some areas require area-wide mass transit, most communities can benefit from a more modest approach. Some operate bus lines; others subsidize private firms that might otherwise go out of business. Reduced-fare programs are popular with senior citizens and youth, and a few communities have tried free bus service. Some communities without bus service have volunteer transportation programs that enable elderly and disabled residents to go shopping and to get to medical appointments. It is increasingly important for small communities, especially those in rural areas, to consider transportation as a necessary component in human service delivery.

Employment

If a community's unemployment problems are severe, the chief administrator, working with the elected body, must make proactive efforts to increase employment opportunities. Such efforts, described in more detail in Chapter 5, may involve consulting an advisory committee of labor and government officials to stimulate ideas for job creation; using private sector training and placement services; or providing leadership in attracting and keeping businesses in the community. With jobs and regular paychecks, people can begin to deal with their needs in terms of their own priorities, not those of a government program.

Figure 8–1 The Brea Job Center, established by the city of Brea in 1990, provides educational opportunities as well as a meeting place for employers and casual laborers. Under a 1994 agreement with the city, the North Orange County Regional Occupational Program assumed management of the center.

The Amherst Job Bank

Amherst, New Hampshire (10,000), created the Amherst Job Bank to help unemployed citizens. Administered by a town employee, the job bank serves as a matching service between townspeople looking for work and local employers. Out-of-work citizens, including high school students and senior citizens, list themselves with the bank, and the list is circulated to employers. Jobs performed include window washing, lawn mowing, house painting, office assistance, and babysitting. Listed employers have included other citizens, law offices, local businesses, and apple growers. The job bank worked with 120 prospective employers and employees in its first four months.

Source: *The Guide to Management Improvement Projects in Local Government*, vol. 15, no. 4 (Washington, DC: ICMA, 1991), no. LHS-31.

Child care

In many families, both parents work outside the home, creating a need for child care. Adding to this need is the growing number of single parent families. In the past, local government's role in child care was viewed negatively. Because of such problems as noise and traffic congestion, communities found child-care centers less than desirable and enacted zoning ordinances against them. Today, communities are rewriting zoning ordinances to allow centers, and some are operating centers on their own. Under federal prompting, centers are changing, offering educational and cultural activities as well as custodial care.

Figure 8–2 Checklist for implementation of a community day-care center.

Implementation checklist

1. Determine need for center. Conduct a child-care needs assessment, which might include a survey of existing child-care facilities; census data on numbers of preschool children by neighborhood; neighborhood concentrations of preschool children; income levels by neighborhood; patterns of neighborhood movement; demand for services exceeding supply; and other considerations.
2. Develop program proposal. Include a statement of need, program outline, target neighborhood, size of center, number of children served, preliminary budget, and scope of services.
3. Determine steps necessary to secure local government approval. Depending on various factors, including funding source, a determination of the requirement for public hearings and citizen input may be needed.
4. Determine funding. Day-care centers for a target population meeting specific economic criteria are eligible for state and federal funding, when available.
5. Secure funding. Submit a detailed program proposal to funding source.
6. Establish bookkeeping and financial management procedures. This task can be completed once funding has been awarded.
7. Select site. Once a target neighborhood has been identified, determine a specific site on the basis of existing state and local health, fire, and zoning regulations for day-care centers, as well as the specific design of the proposed center. If renovations or modifications are required on site, decide on cost, time frame, architectural plans, contractor, and so forth.
8. Secure license for center. The state health department (or similar agency) issues the day-care center license, contingent on fulfillment of specific facility, staffing, program content, health service, and food service requirements.
9. Develop staff. Establish criteria for staff selection. Advertise for, interview, and hire staff.
10. Develop curriculum. With regard for federal and state guidelines, develop a curriculum designed to meet the educational, social, and emotional needs of the children served. Curriculum development also involves purchase of learning tools, toys, equipment, and other items.
11. Link up with appropriate supportive services. Include services such as health screening, nutrition, staff training and development, and so forth.
12. Include and encourage parental and community involvement. Involve those affected in as many phases of program planning and implementation as possible. Form an advisory council.
13. Admit children and begin program.

Mentally disabled citizens

Two aspects of mental health service provision have moved to the forefront. The first is the community mental health center. These centers help citizens cope with a wide range of problems, from transient personal difficulties such as divorce and unemployment to long-term problems such as mental illness, alcoholism, drug dependence, or developmental disabilities. The centers may be run by the local government, by nonprofit agencies, by hospitals, or by a combination of service providers.

The second aspect is deinstitutionalization. The number of mentally ill and developmentally disabled people housed and treated in large, usually state-run, institutions has been reduced. More of these people have been returned to the community, where they live and receive needed treatment on an outpatient basis. Deinstitutionalization has had a great impact on local government by putting tens of thousands of formerly institutionalized people into communities.

Housing, medical management, recreation, employment, and social contact are common needs for this population. Communities must assume responsibility for their well-being and must be prepared to deal with community sentiment of the "anywhere but here" variety in regard to siting group homes. Public education and cooperation among police departments, human service agencies, and hospitals are vital; cooperation among governments is also important. The county government, for example, may be responsible for locating a mental health group home, but the site chosen may be within the city limits; the city's zoning regulations must therefore be followed. Governments need to cooperate to ensure that a complete array of needed services is provided, rather than focus solely on city-provided or county-provided services.

Because deinstitutionalization appears to be an established, continuing policy, community leaders would do well to plan for long-range solutions to the challenges it presents.

Physically disabled citizens

Federal laws requiring equal access to public facilities have had a profound impact on local government. The Americans with Disabilities Act

Figure 8–3 Checklist for implementation of a program to remove barriers to disabled citizens.

Implementation checklist

1. Are your public works, planning, and building and safety staffs familiar with the latest building code and other regulations dealing with the removal of architectural barriers to disabled individuals?
2. Is someone on your staff knowledgeable about local programs for the disabled and able to respond to public inquiries?
3. Do you have a citizen advisory board that counsels staff and elected officials on the needs of disabled individuals?
4. Are disabled persons appointed to citizen advisory boards that consider personnel, architectural, or planning matters?
5. Does your transit system make provisions for transporting disabled citizens?
6. Do city parking lots have spaces reserved for disabled persons?
7. Does your recreation program include activities for disabled residents?
8. Are all city programs, including meetings of elected officials, located in buildings that are accessible to those with limited mobility?
9. Does your city provide public information and education regarding the needs of disabled individuals? Do you have an "awareness day" or other activities to demonstrate support for the disabled?
10. Does your community have housing units specially designed or equipped for disabled inhabitants?
11. Does your affirmative action plan include disabled individuals?
12. Do you send recruitment materials to agencies providing services to the disabled?
13. Do you hire disabled persons in proportion to their numbers in the community?

of 1990 has set a rigid timetable for adapting buildings to make them accessible, ensuring employment opportunities, and providing access to transportation for disabled individuals. Local officials will have high visibility and accountability as they deal with the requirements of the act, for example, by providing facilities such as wheelchair ramps, specially designed restrooms, lower drinking fountains and public telephones, and elevator buttons with braille coding.

Health and public health

Health issues have grown increasingly important in the delivery of human services. Local government is playing a larger role in determining the response to a growing list of significant health concerns. Traditional areas of concern include prevention and control of communicable diseases through education; chronic disease prevention and control; injury prevention; environmental health; and infant, child, and adolescent health.

Integrated service provision

Confronted with a disproportionate share of Los Angeles County's AIDS caseload, West Hollywood, California (36,500), provides a continuum of care through integration and coordination of a number of city-created or city-funded services, including medical care, counseling, transportation, and housing. The city works closely with the West Hollywood Homeless Organization to provide both emergency and transitional housing as well as health screening, case management, job training and placement, mental health and addiction recovery services, and meals. The city also supported the development of a twenty-two-unit apartment building designed to meet the needs of low-income, disabled persons. Preference goes to people with AIDS.

Source: Lloyd Long, Director of Human Services, West Hollywood, California, 1993.

Communicable diseases

Historically, local health departments have monitored the spread of communicable diseases and established primary intervention programs. In recent years these diseases have increased substantially, with HIV infection and AIDS reaching epidemic proportions. Fear of those infected has resulted in discrimination in housing, employment, education, and health care. In short, the AIDS epidemic has placed a major financial burden on health care systems throughout the country and is subjecting many communities to new and powerful pressures.

Prevention through health education

Community health programs are assuming increased leadership in efforts to prevent disease through education. The role of local health programs in providing immunization for such vaccine-preventable diseases as measles and polio is on the rise, too. The goal of immunization programs is the total elimination of these diseases in the community, a goal recently achieved worldwide with smallpox.

Prevention and control of chronic disease

The prevention and control of chronic diseases such as cancer, high blood pressure, and heart and lung diseases are also important concerns. With the increased understanding of their causes, public health workers have designed programs to reduce risk factors associated with these diseases. Eventually, prevention, screening, and early treatment will have significant effects on their prevalence. For example, many communities are emphasizing the importance of decreasing tobacco use and improving diets to prevent cancer. Local governments have taken leadership roles in offering smoking cessation programs and in restricting the use of tobacco in government buildings. The promotion of adequate exercise and nutrition—even dietary counseling—are activities also found in local public health programs. Finally, because drunk driving and alcohol-related diseases are public health problems directly related to heavy alcohol consumption, many community programs promote the responsible use of alcohol.

Injury prevention

Injury prevention is another part of the public health agenda. Communities involve themselves in injury prevention through education, regulation, and legislation. A local prevention effort may involve education regarding protective technology such as seat belts, helmets, and protective clothing. Because traffic control, pedestrian habits, smoke alarms, and other factors may have an effect on rates of injury, police and fire departments often participate in injury prevention activities.

Environmental health problems

Public and government concern about environmental health problems is increasing. These problems are caused by human exposure to a variety of dangerous contaminants; contaminated drinking water is a hazard of particular concern. Contamination can occur in many ways, including accidents, poor sewage treatment, agricultural practices, and inadequate care in disposing of toxic substances. Abandoned dumps and underground fuel storage tanks are also serious concerns.

The needs of the large numbers of children being raised in poverty must be addressed if proper growth and development are to occur.

The health problems related to air and water contamination created by landfills are a major concern, as is exposure to toxic substances such as pesticides (on farmland or suburban lawns) and solvents in the workplace. In other communities, lead-based paints, asbestos, and even radioactive wastes are concerns. Environmental sanitation and health are therefore key areas for local government action. Programs designed to ensure the safety of citizens have become extremely important.

Infant, child, and adolescent health programs

Efforts to ensure adequate nutrition and a healthy start for young infants are increasing in many communities. In particular, the nutrition and health needs of the large numbers of children being raised in poverty must be addressed if proper growth and development are to occur.

The Monroe Maternity Center

To provide a safe, inexpensive alternative to delivering babies in distant hospitals, rural Monroe County, Tennessee (30,500), helps fund the Monroe Maternity Center. Certified midwives provide nutrition counseling and childbirth education, deliver babies, provide prenatal and postpartum care, and pay three visits to babies and mothers at home. The center delivered 116 babies in 1991 with an average stay of six to twelve hours in the center for uncomplicated deliveries. The county oversees the center with a county-appointed board of directors, owns part of the building, and provides maintenance, facilities insurance, and backup funding when needed.

Source: *The Guide to Management Improvement Projects in Local Government*, vol. 16, no. 1 (Washington, DC: ICMA, 1992), no. LHS-2.

Adolescent health is also of growing concern. Dissemination of adequate health care information on sexual behavior, the prevention of sexually transmitted diseases, birth control, pregnancy and birth, and parenting skills is extremely important. So, too, are education and treatment programs for mental health and substance abuse problems.

National estimates show that over 12 percent of all children under the age of eighteen need treatment for mental health problems.

For some communities, access to mental health services for adolescents is especially important. The dramatic physical and emotional changes that occur during adolescence make young people especially vulnerable to emotional and behavioral disorders. National estimates show that over 12 percent of all children under the age of eighteen need treatment for mental health problems. Also of concern is teen suicide. In the past twenty years the rate of suicide among adolescents from ten to nineteen years of age has doubled and is now the second-leading cause of death for teenagers. Communities need to be aware of community-based and family-centered programs that can combat these problems.

It is important to remember that health problems are especially prevalent in specific groups. These include people who have little access to health services because of poverty or isolation, pregnant women, babies and small children, and elderly citizens. These groups need the advocacy of a community public health program to attain and maintain good health.

Alcohol and drug abuse

Communities continue to feel the impact of alcohol abuse. Treatment for alcohol-related conditions takes an increasing percentage of health care funds, and alcohol is the single most frequently found human factor in fatal automobile accidents.

Although drug programs abound, few are unqualified successes, and enforcement of anti-drug laws receives far more federal support than education or treatment of the problem. Still, there are programs that do achieve success. For instance, former addicts have been successful in prevention efforts with youth. Halfway houses and crisis centers are also effective.

Former addicts on parole usually need help finding employment, which can help them establish the sense of personal worth essential to helping them keep "clean." Besides encouraging private sector employers to consider giving jobs to former addicts, government can look at its own hiring practices.

High school youth council

Los Alamos County, New Mexico (18,000), has experienced a 30-percent decline in juvenile vandalism and a 42-percent reduction in juvenile arrests for driving while intoxicated since forming a youth board composed of high school students who organize drug-free social activities for their peers. These students teach younger students to avoid using drugs through example and through presentations and skits. The county supplies buildings and park facilities, provides a base office and clerical support, furnishes equipment, and provides half of the program's $18,000 budget. The board, elected by high school students, raises the balance of the money, runs the program, and reports to the elected officials regarding the program.

Source: *The Guide to Management Improvement Projects in Local Government*, vol. 15, no. 3 (Washington, DC: ICMA, 1991), no. LHS-20.

Consumer protection

Although consumer protection is probably better handled by counties, larger cities, and higher levels of government, it can be pursued with just one or two investigators. Alternatives include contracting with a consumer protection council for watchdog services or entering into a cooperative program with other local governments. The office of the county attorney (usually called the district or state attorney) should be a good source of aid.

Crisis management In communities that experience turmoil and dissension, particularly those with racial or ethnic problems, the chief administrator needs a personal sensitivity to and knowledge of community groups and events. It is equally important to have the information and ability necessary to interpret situations fairly for everyone involved. If no staff member can keep in touch with troublesome events and analyze their meaning, then the administrator needs to secure information firsthand. The administrator should work closely with the police but should be aware that there are often other ways to solve problems.

Redevelopment Redevelopment involves the physical rebuilding of blighted areas. Redevelopment programs should be closely tied to social planning; the relocation problems of residents and small businesses should receive special attention. Although there have been well-publicized failures, there have also been important successes. Laws on redevelopment vary from state to state, so a good starting point is the state code.

Home ownership for low-income families

To help provide affordable housing to low-income families and to rehabilitate deteriorating homes, Englewood, Colorado (30,000), held a lottery under the Urban Homesteading Program to sell six homes for one dollar each. Families selected to purchase a home were required to perform extensive renovation and live in and maintain the home for five years. Although the federal homesteading program ended in the 1991 fiscal year, Englewood will continue a low-income ownership program with already remodeled homes.

Source: *The Guide to Management Improvement Projects in Local Government*, vol. 16, no. 2 (Washington, DC: ICMA, 1992), no. LD-11.

Poverty The word *poverty* describes a condition in which people have insufficient funds to meet basic needs. However, people living in poverty are likely to need more than money. Whether their poverty stems from subtle discrimination, being a school dropout or a displaced homemaker, or another cause, those in poverty often feel exploited and powerless and have a sense of failure and dependency. Unable to share in most social and material benefits, they feel alienated from the community. Many local governments are now actively implementing the Welfare Reform legislation of 1988 by providing education, job training, day care, and transportation to enable welfare recipients to become self-supporting.

Tenant rights Low-income and undereducated people can be victims of unscrupulous landlords or of people who, in good faith, acquire investment property and find that the costs of maintenance or rehabilitation exceed their rental income. Local governments can provide educational programs concerning legal rights covering such subjects as rent increases, evictions, leases, repairs, and common illegal practices. Government can also teach tenants what to look for before renting and provide home-management training. Whenever possible, tenants and landlords should be encouraged to resolve disputes voluntarily. Absentee landlords are a special problem, however, and efforts to hold owners responsible for the condition and safety of buildings is often the responsibility of local governments. If the community operates a public housing authority, local government employees must be sensitive to the problems of tenants.

Local government's responsibility

Primary responsibility for developing policies and programs to attack human problems has been assumed by the federal and state governments, but that does not mean that there is no role for local government. As noted in Chapter 1, local government is the government of last resort; it is the government that deals one-on-one with individual citizens on a daily basis, and it is the government that ultimately must cope with the human problems or distress unresolved by federal or state programs.

Furthermore, although the federal and state governments have primary responsibility for policy, in most instances it is local governments that bear the major burden of administering human service programs. Perhaps in no other area do the three levels of government—federal, state, and local—work so closely together in delivering services. (Intergovernmental collaboration is described more fully in Chapter 15.)

Community government's role in human services can be broken into three categories: (1) taking responsibility to see that local human service needs are met; (2) using the office of the city or county manager or chief administrative officer to provide the necessary leadership and oversight for the community's human service effort; and (3) being aware of the impact of routine government operations upon human service concerns and consciously using those operations to minimize community problems. Each of these is discussed in the subsections below.

Strategies for providing human services

A community government can act as obtainer, catalyst, coordinator, or provider of human services, or it may play all four roles simultaneously. The essential requirement is to ensure that needs are met.

Not-for-profit agencies

Not-for-profit agencies are private, nongovernmental corporations organized to provide a particular public service, usually with a special emphasis on serving those who cannot afford the service. Their boards of directors are composed of civic-minded individuals who serve, usually without pay, as a community service. Such corporations employ professional staff who are paid fixed salaries. Any year-end revenue balances are reinvested in service programs.

Many human service programs are provided by such agencies. Funding is derived from government and foundation grants, private fund-raising, and fees for services delivered to those who can afford to pay.

Many county governments, for example, will levy taxes for community mental health programs and then give the tax proceeds, in the form of grants, to private, not-for-profit mental health centers. In this way, the counties ensure the availability of community mental health services without assuming the responsibility for administering a mental health agency. Many community-owned hospitals are also organized and operated as not-for-profit agencies.

Obtainer

A community does not have to provide services directly; instead, it may obtain someone else to do so. The community may purchase services from a private organization, a not-for-profit agency, or a charitable organization. It may, for example, contract with a local restaurant to provide a daily meal program for the elderly; secure volunteers to deliver meals-on-wheels to people who are confined to their homes because of illness or disability; pay a family service agency to provide counseling programs for dysfunctional families; or subsidize cab rides for the handicapped.

Mental health programs, drug counseling, and various youth programs are often managed on a regional basis.

Still another way of obtaining services is to join with other agencies; mental health programs, drug counseling, and various youth programs are often managed on a regional basis. Major programs (e.g., housing and transportation) may have to be provided on this basis if they are to be effective on a metropolitan scale.

Sometimes a government can ensure the availability of a service in the community by persuading a service provider from another area to open a branch office in the community, even if only for a few days a month. Often, with prompting, a volunteer group of citizens might take on a particular venture.

Catalyst

Another approach is to act as a catalyst by encouraging existing governments, private organizations, or not-for-profit agencies to supply services in a facility provided by the community government. Some communities have built or rented space to be shared by a variety of agencies that offer human services. Such space does not have to be expensive. Old houses, acquired as part of a site for a future public facility, often serve this purpose well.

The Ben Gordon Community Mental Health Center

DeKalb County, Illinois (74,000), provides community mental health services in the county by providing a local, not-for-profit agency, the Ben Gordon Community Mental Health Center, with a building to house its offices and treatment facilities. The center sends counselors to distant communities in the county if office space is made available to them in those locations. The center's funds come from federal, state, and local grants, including an annual grant from the county's mental health tax levy; from private fund-raising; and from fees charged for its services on an ability-to-pay basis.

Source: James Graves, President, Ben Gordon Community Mental Health Center, DeKalb, Illinois, 1993.

Coordinator

There may be a multitude of public and private programs already operating effectively in or near the community. In such circumstances, the community government's role may be that of coordinator. This involves ongoing needs assessment, planning, and evaluating of existing programs to ensure that needed services are available. Most important, it means developing the level of interagency communication and cooperation needed to ensure a balanced, adequate program of service provision.

In such circumstances, the coordinator also performs a vital referral function. Although a helping agency exists to assist those in need, the person in need may be unaware of its availability or of his or her eligibility to use its services. Many community government workers have frequent contact with people who need help. Such workers can be trained to identify these people and refer them to appropriate agencies for help. Police officers, switchboard operators, and recreation staff are especially high on the list of those who can be trained as referral agents.

Provider

Sometimes, direct government provision of the service is the best or only available strategy, when, for instance, no other government or charitable agency offers the service or special circumstances demand community action. In designing a new service delivery system, other communities that have provided or are providing the service should be consulted; their experience can be invaluable in developing a new system.

The administrator's roles

The administrator may play any of several roles in providing human service programs and often plays several simultaneously. The roles played depend heavily on the duties that elected officials assign or allow the administrator to have. Elected officials may exercise little oversight or require the administrator to work in close concert with them. The roles often played by an administrator include those of leader, goal setter, power broker, ambassador, advocate, and ombudsman.

Leader

If the elected officials or the administrator is not dedicated to the concept of human services, it is unlikely that much will be done—or done effectively. Conversely, a dedicated administrator can convey a sense of both commitment and the importance of the action to the elected officials, the community, and staff. Although an administrator alone can do little to improve the quality of life for those in need, he or she can act as a leader in the process. The administrator can provide the direction necessary to move from a human service need to a human service program and finally to a human service solution.

Goal setter

The administrator can also play an important role in helping elected officials set goals. The administrator's function is not to tell the elected council the best course of action but to suggest goals and alternatives that allow them to achieve what they believe is needed. It is the job of the administrator to document needs, assess public interest, identify desirable goals, determine alternatives, and make policy recommendations to elected officials. The effort put forth by the administrator in properly communicating needs, suggesting effective goals, and selecting viable alternatives can dictate the success or failure of the human service program.

Power broker

The skillful administrator can maneuver within policy guidelines and arbitrate in the public interest.

Although it is not a popular concept, an administrator is often required to play the role of power broker, especially in communities where many private and not-for-profit agencies share the task of providing human services. The more economically and ethnically diverse the community, the more divided it will be, and the more conflict will mark government activities.

To be caught amid competing interests is a dangerous position, but the skillful administrator, with the understanding and support of the elected officials, can maneuver within policy guidelines and arbitrate in the public interest, always seeking to use government influence to coordinate the efforts of diverse social service agencies toward the goal of ensuring adequate human services for the entire community. Such maneuvering and arbitrating are part of the fundamental political role, in the best sense of the word *political*—making policy choices based on the careful consideration of alternatives.

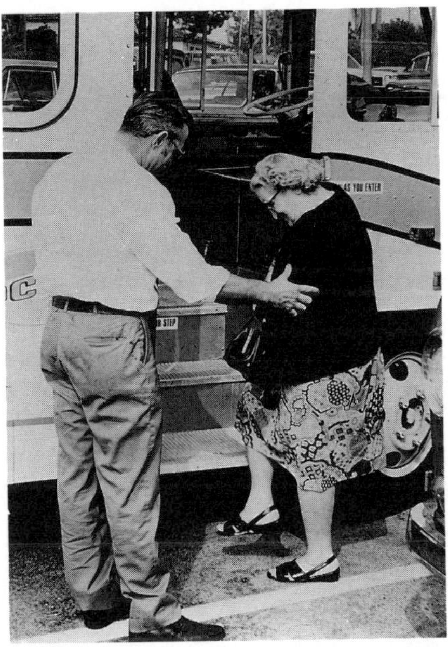

Figure 8–4 The thoughtfulness of individuals can do much to enhance the overall human service efforts of a local government.

Ambassador

Although the role of ambassador may sometimes be filled by the mayor, county board chairperson, or elected county executive, the role often falls upon the administrator. In such cases, the administrator must work to create links to other government and social service agencies in working out solutions to the problems of the community. The administrator must act as liaison in dealing with other government units, whether city, county, state, or federal. The increasing importance of intergovernmental and intersectoral relationships in the effective management of the community is discussed in greater detail in Chapter 15.

Advocate

As an advocate, the administrator pleads the case of those in need—poor, young, and old people and members of racial and ethnic minorities. Typically members of these groups are those least able to represent themselves adequately in the government process. Advocacy involves making officeholders and other administrators aware of problems and encouraging them to take action. This role grows in importance in communities that lack an individual, department, or committee assigned to represent these groups.

Ombudsman

As ombudsman, the administrator ensures that his or her own organization is fair and responsive to the needs of poor and disadvantaged citizens. This role involves presenting the interests of the community before other levels of government and, occasionally, before large corporations.

Meeting human needs through existing government operations

An opportunity to improve human services often presents itself through the regular operations of government programs. For communities that want to do something but have few funds with which to begin or operate human service programs, using operations policies to minimize human problems in the community is especially attractive. Government policies that can be designed to serve human service needs include particularly those concerned with hiring and training, establishing fees, investing funds, using regulatory powers, and generally setting the tone of the organization.

Hiring

Residents lacking employment skills can be hired, trained on the job, and later brought into regular, full-time employment. The local government can participate in job training programs supported by the state or federal government. However, even without state or federally funded programs, hiring and development goals can be set for poor or disadvantaged residents of the community. The success of such programs will require a commitment, not only on the part of the administrator but also on that of elected officials and the staff of the organization. Working with nontraditional employees will require department heads who are conscious of others and committed, or such employment programs probably will not work.

Training

Training can do a great deal to ease the integration of nontraditional employees into the workforce. A training program can assist newly hired workers gain a better understanding of the organization, their function, and the part their function plays in the organization's mission.

Diversity training

An ongoing training program in cultural diversity helps sensitize all local government employees to people from different racial, ethnic, or cultural backgrounds. Such training, given regularly, will not only help employees understand new, and especially nontraditional, employees, but it will also help them to relate better to residents of the community who come from different backgrounds.

Diversity training is especially important for those who are seen as authority figures.

It is important to remember that diversity training should be ongoing with all employees; attitudes and values are not changed in a single session, nor are old prejudices easily erased. Diversity training is especially important for police officers and emergency service employees, human service workers, park and recreation personnel, and those who are seen as authority figures. Such training does not guarantee the absence of conflict, but it can reduce the likelihood of a thoughtless remark or a careless action offending someone and possibly triggering an unfortunate incident.

Establishing fees

Tailoring tax policy to promote certain public policies is probably as old as imposing taxes. Such tailoring can be used to promote human welfare by easing the tax burden on those less able to pay. Some communities have reduced utility rates for the elderly and low-income citizens. Others have offered reduced bus fares or have deferred or reduced property taxes for such citizens. In other communities, community-run swimming pools that charge admission offer free passes to children from low-income families.

Figure 8–5 A meals-on-wheels program helps meet the social as well as nutritional needs of elderly citizens.

Communities that do not have sufficient revenues to sustain existing human services or develop new programs can obtain needed funds by charging user fees, either for the new programs, for some existing programs, or both. For example, elderly residents who pay part of the costs of services such as transportation or meals-on-wheels can provide an important source of revenue to help support these and other valuable services. Care must be used in designing programs that are dependent on user fees, however, as not all those who need the program may be able to afford the fee. Those with little or no ability to pay can be offered discounted or free services.

However, programs to reduce taxes or fees can fail if they make recipients feel self-conscious about receiving special treatment. Communities must also be conscious of whatever legal requirements may be pertinent.

Investing funds

Judicious use of temporarily idle funds can also promote human service goals. Besides investing such funds to increase revenues, local governments may use idle or excess funds as leverage in convincing local banks to make housing loans available to certain parts of the community. The excess or idle funds can also be deposited in minority-owned banks to stimulate their growth and economic activities.

Regulatory powers

The community can also use its regulatory powers to promote human service goals. Ordinances requiring open housing, for instance, have been a major tool in promoting neighborhood integration. Though there are some administrative costs involved in such efforts, it is unlikely the costs would be prohibitive in a small community.

Departmental policies

Minority communities are often particularly sensitive to law enforcement procedures. A well-trained police force, emphasizing good rapport with all parts of the community, can prevent small problems from getting bigger. A sensitivity to different cultures and to the use of resources other than law enforcement to solve problems may not guarantee a peaceful community, but it will go a long way toward achieving social progress. Good police work can prevent or at least minimize social problems; bad police work aggravates them.

Meeting transportation needs

Recognizing that transportation problems prevent many social service clients from obtaining permanent full-time employment, James City County, Virginia (33,000), donates surplus county vehicles to the Community Action Agency which, in turn, donates them to low-income residents who need transportation.

Source: *The Guide to Management Improvement Projects in Local Government*, vol. 14, no. 3 (Washington, DC: ICMA, 1993), no. LHS-22.

Fire department policy can also play a role in human services. In one Texas community, before the last pumper leaves the scene, firefighters advise the family of Red Cross and other programs that are available to provide them with assistance. Later the fire marshal contacts relevant agencies to advise them of the burnout and give them information about the family. This process helps to ensure that the family will have their needs met quickly, thereby lessening, to the extent possible, the impact of the trauma they have experienced.

Community-oriented policing project

The police department in Southern Pines, North Carolina (9,000), confronted with major drug-related crime in an apartment complex, instituted a community- and problem-oriented policing policy. The department employed a community service officer to serve as public contact, secured a grant to hire and equip two patrol officers to work in high-crime areas and receive special training in the community-oriented policing philosophy, and established a community center in a converted apartment in the complex. The center provides space for a police satellite office, making the police more accessible. It also offers a place for community functions and established social programs for children and adults based on the expressed needs of the residents.

Support for the project came from local residents; local businesses, churches, and the United Way, which provided supplementary funding; and the apartment ownership, which supplied the apartment. The result has been a 70-percent drop in calls for police service in the area together with a heightened sense of togetherness among the residents of the apartment complex.

Source: Kyle Sonnenberg, Town Manager, Southern Pines, North Carolina, 1993.

Leadership

The sensitivity of the community's political and administrative leaders is critical to providing good human services because the leaders set the tone for the whole organization. If staff perceive that a sensitivity to diversity is not important at the top, it is not likely to permeate very far down into the organization. Similarly, if staff and citizens know that decision makers are serious about listening, they are more likely to be sensitive to the views of others. One important way that top administrative officers can set a good example is to take steps to ensure that appropriate community groups, and especially minority groups, are consulted about pending policy and administrative decisions that affect them.

Management concerns in the delivery of human services

All community governments provide a broad range of services and play many roles in the human service field. Each role or service poses critical management challenges regarding citizen participation, planning, organizational options, staffing, finances, and program evaluation.

Citizen participation

Some regard citizen participation as an empty phrase or a passing fad, and some elected officials and administrators may not really want citizen participation. However, achieving success in most human service areas is difficult, if not impossible, without effective citizen participation. Public meetings and annual reports, the traditional means for communicating with citizens, do not begin to go far enough, especially in the field of human services. Administrators should consider using the communication forms and techniques described in Chapter 14; in addition, they should bear in mind that human service administration provides unique opportunities and poses special challenges.

Some communities have umbrella human service bodies that oversee many programs: for example, youth commissions, senior citizen councils, and disability advisory committees. If such groups are staffed by human service workers who are involved in the community, local government administrators gain an invaluable, two-way conduit for communication with key community leaders.

Ideally, community government leaders communicate personally with various interest groups; knowing how to communicate effectively is an important part of this process. If a group speaks a different language or has little experience in dealing with government, its members may be comfortable only with talking through another member who acts as intermediary.

Another way of encouraging participation and developing rapport with interest group leaders is to provide leadership training for them. One manager described this process as "releasing the energies in the people" and reported how thrilling it was to watch individuals who once had little hope for progress begin to learn to deal with their problems.

STRIDE

In Albany, Oregon (34,000), citizens, government, business, and local interest groups joined together to form STRIDE, a coalition to promote change in the community. During a planning meeting that lasted two and a half days, STRIDE participants, including one hundred community representatives, established a community action plan for future improvements in housing, education, government, and employment. Work groups were formed to address issues and to draft work plans. The groups deal with basic needs for employment, food, clothing, and shelter; youth; drug abuse; families; and career opportunities. A Community Planning and Prioritization committee oversees all groups, orchestrates the long-term plan, and marshals community commitment.

Source: *The Guide to Management Improvement Projects in Local Government*, vol. 16, no. 3 (Washington, DC: ICMA, 1992), no. MGT-15.

Some may find it hard to believe that going to a government office can be a terrifying experience, but for many people that is often the case. Thus, it is helpful for local government officials and citizens to meet in familiar settings such as local schools, senior centers, a sheltered workshop, or a counseling center. Government leaders who hold meetings in such settings are typically pleased at the response.

Planning Two areas of knowledge are vital to the planning process: knowing who needs help but is not getting it, and knowing what human services *are* being provided in the community. Determining needs and inventorying resources are often done simultaneously as the first steps in planning human services. Subsequent steps may include a social base study, which is roughly equivalent to the economic base study that is normally part of a general land use plan, and a social impact statement. Involvement of elected officials in the planning process is also vital.

Determining needs

If people think they might get help, they will acknowledge the need for it, but if they do not expect help, they will not.

Numerous potential problems—too many to explore in detail here—await those trying to decide who needs what in human services, because needs can be defined in many different ways.

If someone says, "I need help," the person has an *expressed need*. Others have needs but do not say so. These are *perceived needs*, because the administrator believes that they may exist. If in providing a service an administrator must choose between two people with different needs, the administrator will draw conclusions about their *relative needs*. Evidence shows that needs grow or shrink depending on the availability of help. In other words, if people think they might get help, they will acknowledge the need for it, but if they do not expect help, they will not. Needs, then, are somewhat elastic.

Determining needs can be a process that includes receiving or soliciting citizen input; assigning citizen task forces; observing needs identified by citizen groups, interest groups, and the media; and monitoring changing demographic and socioeconomic trends in the community. Need determination must also include close attention to state and federal requirements for what services must be provided, at what level, and to whom—including explicit minimum qualifications for clientele participation.

The Health Care and Referral Clinic

A community needs assessment in Bartholomew County, Indiana (63,700), indicated a need for health care for the medically indigent. The county established the Health Care and Referral Clinic to provide routine medical care to citizens without a source of health care. Clinic patients are screened by registered nurses and, when necessary, referred to volunteer physicians. The clinic reduces the volume of nonemergency patients to emergency rooms and treats citizens' illnesses before they reach the crisis stage.

Source: *The Guide to Management Improvement Projects in Local Government*, vol. 16, no. 4 (Washington, DC: ICMA, 1992), no. LHS-31.

Several methods are available to quantify needs—each useful, some time-consuming, others expensive, none foolproof. One method is to assess existing programs. The data collected from the assessment often show trends, reveal user profiles, and demonstrate the capacity of existing programs to provide services and meet needs.

Another method is to carry out formal surveys. Though this method is usually expensive and time-consuming, there are shortcuts that do not affect the survey's ability to provide valuable information. These include using the telephone and abbreviated question lists, and using volunteers or university students.

Whereas a good needs assessment is a valuable management tool, a poor one is probably worthless.

When focusing on highly controversial needs, such as community housing for the mentally disabled, the expert opinions of community workers are sometimes useful; they are often voiced at the public hearing. Although it remains questionable whether the testimony at such hearings represents the community as a whole, the hearings do provide an opportunity to gather information from diverse sources. Hearings are especially effective if the community is alerted well beforehand of the opportunity to be heard.

Another method of assessing needs is the focus group. This technique involves gathering information from planned discussions among the people from whom information is desired. A group of community human service workers, for example, might be asked to spend a half-day in a focus group. The group is then given a predetermined number of questions to answer through group discussion. A convener, who knows what information is desired, can lead the discussions in order to keep them on track and elicit the desired information. Discussions are recorded and information is later taken from them. Focus groups can be made up of representatives from the different categories of persons to be served (e.g., youth, single mothers, senior citizens, disabled individuals, unemployed workers); of human service clientele; or of professional human service workers.

Other methods and combinations of methods also enable government leaders to focus on needs. Whereas a good needs assessment is a valuable management tool, a poor one is probably worthless. Although a needs assessment does not guarantee that the political process will respond to meet identified needs, a well-planned process of assessing needs can help mobilize support for the political decisions that follow.

Resource inventory

Once areas of need in the community are identified, the next step is to inventory existing public and private resources. The best place to start is with the local United Crusade, United Givers, United Way, or other such organizations. They may already have completed studies on social indicators affecting the entire region and surveyed the agencies available to help. Such an inventory can serve as a quick appraisal and immediately identify some of the worst problems and the best resources. Using information already compiled avoids needless duplication of effort.

If an inventory is to be conducted, it should also include the government itself. Public resources include the federal Departments of Labor, Housing and Urban Development (HUD), and Health and Human Services (HHS); state departments of economic development, human resources, and planning; county welfare and health departments; and, in many cases, school districts.

Charitable and not-for-profit agencies are another resource. Some types of public and charitable operations are workshops for disabled workers, residential treatment centers for children, adoption agencies, family counseling agencies, the Salvation Army, coordinating councils, urban coalitions, the Urban League, emergency relief organizations, Big Brothers and Big Sisters, halfway houses, hot lines, job counseling services, legal aid groups, rehabilitation centers, associations for disabled citizens, homemakers' services, and visiting nurses associations.

Churches also offer a large variety of social programs, either through local congregations or through centralized special-purpose organizations. Several business organizations operate in the job training sector and offer consulting services to nonprofit agencies.

A thorough inventory will often reveal many areas of overlapping objectives and activities. Such information may alert community leaders to the need for better coordination, and thus enable them to provide better services.

Elements of planning

Optimally, those concerned with planning human services should develop a plan that is integral to the community's general plan. The plan should also be flexible, frequently updated, and integrated with those of other governments, neighboring communities, and community action agencies. Minimally, the plan should push community leaders to think through social problems and their possible solutions.

Because the composition of the community's social structure can change rapidly, a social base study should be part of this plan. The study need not be overwhelming; it can be an extension of the needs assessment that is then combined with long-range goals.

The study should contain specific types of quantifiable information, such as the number of people unemployed, individuals and families below the poverty level, and the number of people over the age of sixty-five. The goals, too, should be quantifiable, and realistic.

Too much red tape and too many bad procedures have been created in the name of good planning, but the concept of an impact study still has great validity.

A social impact statement is another element of planning for human services. For some time, communities have prepared environmental impact reports on proposed public and private projects within their boundaries. Too much red tape and too many bad procedures have been created in the name of good environmental planning, but the concept of an impact study still has great validity. In the end, a community's impact study should not be three separate statements (environmental, economic, and social). It should be one statement that analyzes and integrates all three facets, without artificial distinctions between social and physical programs. Such comprehensive impact studies are new, and they may not be done as well as they should be, but if communities are to become more humane and livable in the future, this method holds great promise.

Elaborate general plans with well-rehearsed social impact statements are not absolutely necessary to deal with social needs. If a major industry closes down within a month and puts 20 percent of the community's labor force out of work, there is not enough time to compose elaborate statements or plans. However, communities that look ahead and approach their social programming on a systematic basis can do much to prevent future crises.

Involvement of elected officials

The administrator should try to involve elected officials in the planning process. As stated earlier, the negative attitudes of elected officials can handicap the provision of community human services. It is important that government take the lead in discussing and resolving human service issues. Making officials aware of the process helps them to decide how far the administrator can go toward resolution. For particularly difficult social problems, the appointment of an ad hoc task force to make recommendations may be much less threatening and more effective than appointing a permanent human service commission.

Involvement of the community

In addition to involving elected officials in the planning process, the administrator should also try to involve members of the public and leaders of the various groups in the community. Local government officials will be more successful in planning effective human service programs if they listen to the wider community's ideas and concerns.

Organization

There are four principal organizational alternatives to consider when organizing to provide a new human service function: (1)attaching the function to the administrator's office, (2) creating a new organizational unit, (3) adopting a multi-agency approach, or (4) creating a strategic alliance with a proxy provider. No single alternative is necessarily right in every situation.

Administrator's office

If the community is small, there are advantages to assigning human service personnel to the chief administrator's office. Such a move tells elected officials, the community, and the staff that the administrator takes human service problems seriously and is not going to let them get buried in an existing department. This approach may be particularly beneficial if the services deal with minorities or others who feel they were previously neglected or treated unfairly. Such an assignment maximizes opportunities for communication between the people to be served and the local government. It is also easier for the central staff to compile needed information about other interrelated programs and to monitor information from diverse sources so that it is easier to identify emerging problems and give local officials early warning, before problems get out of hand.

If a community cannot afford staff to deal with particular human service needs, or if the problems do not warrant additional personnel, another approach is to form an interdepartmental task force, such as a social concerns committee. This approach enables the administrator to take the lead in educating management personnel about the social problems of the community, the resources available, and how staff may relate to them.

Integrated approach to rehabilitation

Gaithersburg, Maryland (32,000), owns and operates transitional housing for homeless addicts and alcoholics in recovery. In order to keep single parents in the program and reunite them with their children, the city places them in apartments; has them sign a contract requiring them to undertake specific activities including attendance at a minimum of three Alcoholics Anonymous or Narcotics Anonymous meetings per week; uses a case manager to counsel them and monitor their progress; and requires them to attend classes and workshops to improve their living skills. The city gets program referrals from the department of social services, the county addiction rehabilitation program, and local shelters.

Source: *The Guide to Management Improvement Projects in Local Government*, vol. 14, no. 4 (Washington, DC: ICMA, 1993), no. LHS-27.

New organizational unit

The community government may want to establish a separate department of human services. Many county governments have now established human service departments to deal with the social needs of the community. By having a separate department, the community will be able to enjoy many of the benefits listed in the previous option without taking away from the other functions of the administrative staff. Although more costly than the previous option, it does facilitate the employment of experienced human service staff. Assigning such individuals directly to the provision of human services will more than likely improve the efficiency and effectiveness of human service programs.

Multi-agency approach

It may prove beneficial for a community to consider a proxy provider of a human service.

A particular situation may call for a multi-agency response, such as an ongoing attack on the problem by a team of staff members from agencies affected by the problem. Such a multi-agency group helps to overcome fragmentation. When the team is made up of the top members of the participating organizations, coordination and cooperation usually flow downward through all the affected units. An example of such a multi-agency response is a community effort to combat youth gang activity. Representatives of law enforcement agencies, the schools, and youth service agencies might establish a task force to address the problem.

Proxy provider

As revenues become tighter, available staff time decreases, and service demands increase, it may prove beneficial for a community to consider a proxy provider of a human service. (This option was discussed earlier, in the section on strategies for providing human services.) Proxy providers are private or nonprofit organizations that provide a service on a fee basis.

Some communities have turned to the use of vouchers with which human service clients can secure services from their choice of private or not-for-profit providers. This method is often used, for example, for the provision of day-care services. Many communities subsidize organizations so that they will provide homeless shelters or food programs. Other communities depend upon volunteers to help them provide the service themselves. Whatever the service needed, a local government should consider the option of having a proxy provider for it.

Summary

Except for very small and very poor communities, it is fair to say that some kind of organizational unit for developing human services is necessary. Such a unit represents the community government's commitment to dealing with human needs, a commitment that is neither a luxury nor a temporary measure for dealing with an isolated set of needs.

Staff qualities

Persons with a background in administration or community organizations may best fill staff positions in human service programs. Candidates may also be required to hold a degree in a relevant subject, such as public health, social work, or public administration. If one of the community's problems is communication between the government and those needing services, someone with fieldwork experience who is capable of winning the confidence of the community is preferred.

Frequently, inviting service recipients to participate in the selection process is helpful. Although relating to specific groups is important, the person employed must also be able to relate to the community as a whole. If not, the administrator may have to spend an inordinate amount of time smoothing ruffled feathers. Having potential candidates meet with clientele ahead of time can often prevent community relation problems down the road.

When the program involves managing the day-to-day delivery of services, administrative talents are needed. If the program depends on county, state, or federal funding, human service staff must also be able to write grant proposals. Most important, however, staff members must know how to learn about and deal with the local community.

The coordinator's primary stock-in-trade is the confidence he or she is able to engender.

A community organizer may be useful in implementing certain human service programs, especially when a neighborhood or group needs to assess and deal with its own needs. The organizer can also help develop local leadership. Police personnel have found community organizers helpful because of their "street sense" and their network of contacts.

The human service coordinator must be just that—a coordinator, able to coordinate the work of various agencies in the human service field. As already noted, some of the local government's human service contribution can be made through regulatory programs, but enforcement should not be the sole function of any human service staff member. Much more can be accomplished through facilitating. Moreover, the community wastes talent and perhaps misses opportunities if the member is restricted to an enforcement role.

The coordinator's primary stock-in-trade is the confidence he or she is able to engender in various client groups. If perceived as a law enforcement official, the coordinator will lose the ability to function in this important role. Thus, some administrators prefer to use the coordinator as mediator, facilitator, or broker between conflicting groups.

Finance

Human services is an area of government in which there is never enough money in the budget; moreover, spending obligations go up in tough economic times, when government revenues are apt to decline. During these periods, the family that needs counseling, the unemployed worker who needs a job, and the individual who needs a warm meal or a doctor's help cannot wait for better times. The years when community governments could rely heavily on state or federal grants to meet these needs—or to tackle a transportation or housing assistance program—are past. Furthermore, it is highly unlikely that much new state or federal government money will be available for social programs in the near future.

Today, sustaining even traditional community services, let alone launching a new human service effort, requires difficult budgetary decisions. However, it is during bad economic times that the need and demand for human service programs becomes greatest. An administrator may be required to become more creative, and sometimes entrepreneurial, in his or her approach to funding human service programs.

Reassigning staff

Some programs can be provided simply by reassigning current staff. As discussed above in the section of this chapter devoted to meeting human needs through existing government operations, many human service initiatives require little or no additional funding. If the program is vital, a way to reorganize staff and staffing priorities can and should be found.

Marshalling community resources

Other activities can be implemented by marshalling existing community resources. To do a responsible job in the social sector, the community government need not offer a single program directly. If another agency can be persuaded to add drug counseling and alcohol treatment to its list of services, a major problem may be solved. If a school district can be persuaded to establish a child-care center or if the human service coordinator can organize a group of volunteers to run such a program, the mission can be completed.

Coordinated human services in the schools
To combat the effects of many kinds of social problems evident in children in the public schools, Catawba County, North Carolina (114,000), has organized human service teams to work directly with the children in school settings. Each team consists of a social worker from the department of social services, a nurse from the public health department, and a psychologist from the mental health department. The teams are assigned specific schools with the purpose of responding to social problems that interfere with the education process. These teams often function as a bridge between the schools and families as well as provide ready access to other services. From the child's perspective the teams function as providers, advocates, and brokers of services.

Source: J. Thomas Lundy, County Manager, Catawba County, North Carolina, 1993.

Reallocating funds

Finally, holding the line, cutting back, or reducing the incremental funding for existing services will usually free up resources for reallocation. The administrator who asks really tough questions about the budget and is willing to work to change long-held views may find a surprising amount of money for new social programs.

Budgeting for human services

Having determined possible sources of funding, the administrator should develop a separate budget for human service programs, taking into account proposed government expenditures as well as the spending of other public and private agencies in the community. The human service budget should be part of the overall budget document, thereby institutionalizing the services.

Evaluation

After going through all the steps—assessing needs; taking stock of resources; and planning, organizing, and implementing programs—it is important to evaluate efforts. Evaluating social sector programs is often difficult, but it is not impossible. There are several different approaches.

Goal attainment

Determining the level of goal attainment requires a clear understanding of the goals and objectives of a program and a strategy to measure them. For example, if the goal is to improve the nutrition of elderly residents who live alone, and if the number of hot meals they eat is directly related to good nutrition, a goal of delivering five hot meals a week to every elderly person living alone might be set. Simple recordkeeping can provide the information needed to determine when that goal is met.

Cost effectiveness

Methods of determining cost effectiveness attach a dollar cost to some benefit, such as an hour of training provided, a referral made, or a hot meal delivered. Knowing the dollar cost per benefit may affect decisions about whether to maintain, increase, or cut back a program. For example, if the cost of delivering one hot meal a day to an elderly person is five dollars, it may be deemed too expensive even if it achieves the goal.

Program support
Still another approach is to measure public or consumer support for a program through surveys or other methods. It is not unusual for a program to remain popular and strongly supported even if it fails to meet its goals and exhibits poor cost effectiveness.

Goals of the evaluation
In these three approaches to evaluation (and there are others), much depends on the questions being asked. Given the complexity of human service programs and the difficulty of measuring their various dimensions, it is important to know who is going to use the evaluation information and for what purposes. Too often, evaluation information is interesting, but not timely or relevant. Some programs have failed because poor program design or faulty implementation did not show up in early evaluations. A problem cannot be corrected if it cannot be seen, and it may not be correctable if discovered too late.

Monitoring human service activities is often difficult because of their nature, inadequate means of measuring results, and uncertainty about what the results should be. In addition, evaluation is too often performed by persons or agencies with vested interests in the programs.

Afterword

The role communities may take in providing human services will ultimately be determined by elected officials. This reality, however, does not excuse local administrators—the chief administrative officer, department heads, and even middle managers—from concern for those in the community who need special help. The quality of life in the community cannot be sustained, regardless of the quality of public works, public safety, and leisure services, if the needs of those with special problems and challenges are not met. The possibility that elected officials are reluctant to address such needs, for cost or other reasons, only increases the responsibility of the professional administrator to alert elected officials and the community to unmet human needs, potential social problems, and alternative strategies for dealing with them.

Human service programs may often involve enormous difficulties and complexities, but it is essential for the social health of the community that local governments provide or oversee them. In terms of simple expediency, if not moral obligation, administrators should choose the path of anticipation and prevention rather than the more expensive, more traumatic, and less satisfactory method of trying to react to a situation after it has reached serious or crisis proportions.

Administrators should communicate the importance of meaningful human services to their governing bodies; superficial support will result only in disillusionment as the expectations of those in need are raised, then disappointed. Communities involved in human service programs need to commit themselves to long-range planning and follow-through just as they do with public safety, public health, and other ongoing programs. Only then will the community reap the rewards of a successful effort. ■

---

[1] International City Management Association, Executive Board policy statement, 1969.

PART III

Protecting the Public

INTRODUCTION

Public safety is a major responsibility of community governments. A narrow view of public safety includes only police and fire services. A somewhat broader view also includes services dealing with emergencies, particularly medical emergencies and disasters. The following three chapters on public safety services reflect the broader view.

The community government services discussed in the three public safety chapters provide resources to cope with direct threats to the public. Public safety officials stand ready twenty-four hours a day, seven days a week, to do whatever is necessary to protect the citizenry.

Public safety personnel, organizations, and activities share common characteristics despite major differences. Personnel are highly committed and specially trained to carry out their responsibilities. They are mobile and use dedicated communications systems. Organizations pay great attention to coordination of activities through designation of formal command responsibilities. All public safety activities are expensive because of the level of response capability that must be maintained.

Organizational arrangements for the delivery of public safety services vary. The chapters in this book are divided into emergency management, police, and fire and emergency medical services (EMS) to reflect the most common organizational divisions found in practice. Some of the variations on these patterns are also discussed.

Although disaster response and other emergency services are often provided by regional units that cross jurisdictional boundaries, local community governments still have the primary responsibility for disaster planning and emergency preparedness in their communities. Chapter 9 discusses the need for communities to have an integrated, comprehensive emergency management plan and describes the four main components of comprehensive emergency management: preparedness, mitigation, response, and recovery.

For the most part, police services are handled by a single organization, for example, a sheriff's office or a municipal police department. But, as Chapter 10 makes clear, police and fire departments may be combined within one public safety unit or a consolidated police and fire services unit. However they are structured, many police agencies are changing their organizational models and approaches to management in response to increasing demand for service, shrinking budgets, and mounting pressures for law enforcement offices to be sensitive to community concerns. Chapter 10 discusses interlocal agreements for service provision; community policing and community relations; personnel recruitment, development, and training; and innovations in technology and methods of patrol.

Fire departments are most commonly found within municipalities, but county fire departments are growing in number. Chapter 11 discusses the policy choices communities make as they decide how to provide fire services and the management issues that arise in the delivery of these services. The chapter deals with the many aspects of fire prevention and suppression—including public education, code enforcement, personnel, and equipment.

Because most fire departments today play a role that goes beyond dealing with fires, the chapter also discusses hazardous materials, rescue, and emergency medical services. (EMS can be provided by a separate unit, but they are most often located within fire departments.)

As the following three chapters show, communities deliver their public safety services in different ways. But all community governments have the same responsibility for protecting the public.

Emergency Management

Government efforts to cope with potential and actual disasters—with violent storms, earthquakes, explosions, terrorist acts, airplane and train crashes, toxic waste spills, riots, or any of the other common causes of community disruption—are termed *emergency management*. The concept covers both emergencies and disasters, although the distinction between them is substantial. Emergencies are occurrences that can be handled adequately with community resources (e.g., a fire, localized flooding, an auto accident); disasters are occurrences of sufficient magnitude to disrupt a community so that outside assistance is required (e.g., a major flood or an earthquake). These events may be natural, or they may be the result of human acts—accidental or intentional. Although communities try to prevent or control emergencies and disasters, they cannot stop extreme natural forces. However, much can be done to limit their damage. Preparing for disasters is most effective when emergency management is an integral part of everyday local government operations.

The most opportune time to plan for disasters and emergencies is long before they happen, because often they give little advance notice:

> *October 17, 1989, began like any other day in Santa Cruz, California, but at 5:04 P.M. the earth shook for about fifteen seconds. In a moment the city was transformed from its normal state to a disaster area, and the course of local history was changed.*
>
> *The downtown was in ruins. People were trapped in buildings that were damaged or virtually destroyed. The phone system was out of service. The electricity was out.*[1]

Because the need for emergency preparedness may be neither self-evident nor readily financed by elected officials, it is imperative that local government administrators take the initiative to establish an emergency management program as an ongoing community function. This chapter discusses the need for integrated emergency management, describes the activities involved, and briefly addresses related issues.

Elements of emergency management

Comprehensive emergency management is an integrated effort to prevent—or minimize the seriousness of—emergencies and disasters and to plan and coordinate the community's response to them should they occur. It requires establishing partnerships among professional emergency management personnel and across jurisdictional boundaries to prevent, respond to, and recover from disasters. Coordination is a key factor in establishing a comprehensive emergency management program.

Some emergency planning is conducted in most municipalities and counties, but it is performed by people in diverse positions. Larger cities and counties may have an emergency management unit. In smaller communities, overall responsibility for emergency planning may lie with the local government manager, a full-time or part-time emergency preparedness coordinator, or within the fire or police department.

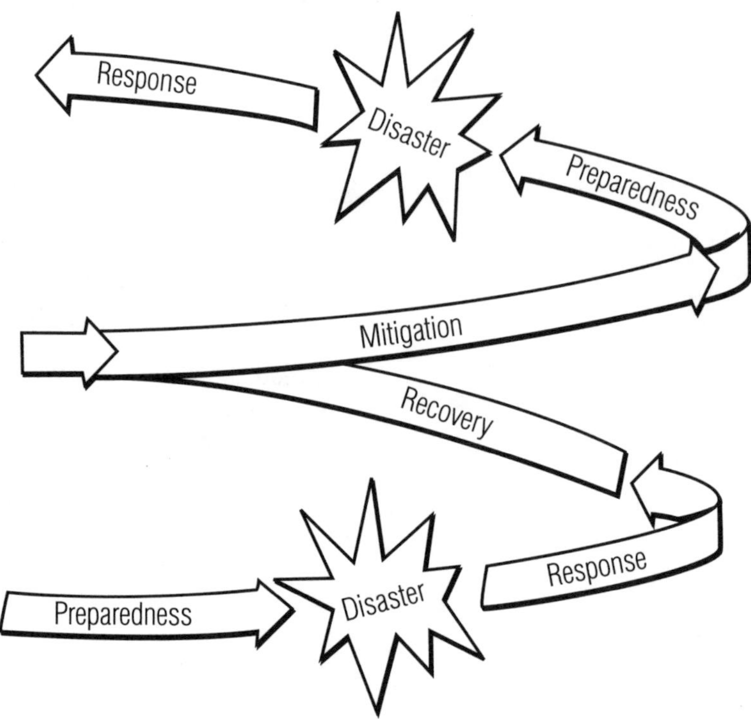

Figure 9–1 Emergency management phases.

Community Disaster Response Program

Devastated by the disastrous Loma Prieta earthquake of October 17, 1989, Watsonville, California (35,000), developed the Community Disaster Response Program to enable the public and private sectors to work more closely together to prepare for, and recover from, future natural and technological emergencies. Put together by a South County Disaster Response Team made up of representatives from the local Red Cross, the World Service Workers of America, Pajaro Rescue Mission, the Pajaro Valley Ministerial Association, Pacific Bell, the county Human Resources Agency, the Volunteer Center, Second Harvest Food Bank, Watsonville Community Hospital, the Pajaro Valley Chamber of Commerce, the Watsonville Fire Department, and the Watsonville City Clerk's Office, the plan's distinguishing feature is its network of local government agencies, community organizations, and businesses.

Some of the problems faced by the city in 1989 resulted from failure to anticipate the needs of the city's Spanish-speaking residents. The city did not have information available in Spanish about emergency services, food served by some of the agencies was not culturally appropriate, and Latino families were afraid to go into established shelters. To prevent a recurrence of such problems, the new plan provides for the recruitment of Spanish-speaking workers and makes a special effort to develop links with the Latino community.

Source: Steven M. Salomon, City Manager, Watsonville, California, 1993.

Regardless of who has overall responsibility, there are four distinct facets of comprehensive emergency management: preparedness, mitigation, response, and recovery. Although in practice they overlap, each has its own aims and also serves as a building block for the others.

All of these areas demand high levels of coordination. Preparedness is improved by mutual-aid agreements and other forms of interjurisdictional planning. Mitigation is more effective when the entire community has been involved in hazard assessment. Response is stronger when key governmental units and private organizations cooperate. Recovery is faster when tasks and responsibilities are allocated across the widest possible range of agencies and individuals.

Coordination channels resources in order to use them for the overall benefit of the community; it is essential in a viable emergency management program. The more complex a community's organization—that is, the more special districts, overlapping jurisdictions, or organizations with highly specialized responsibilities—the more important it is to ensure coordination; however, coordination is important to emergency managers in every community, regardless of the degree of organizational complexity. The coordination of groups within and between communities can be difficult and time-consuming, but efforts to establish and continually improve coordination save lives and reduce losses from disaster.

Preparedness

Planning for preparedness is undertaken before a disaster occurs in order to build emergency management capacity. It has three elements: the development of emergency operation plans; practice at putting the plans into effect; and public education. It is a serious mistake to assume that preparedness is assured because a written document has been produced. Plans must be kept up-to-date in order to meet changing conditions and requirements, and personnel must know and be trained to perform their jobs under highly stressful conditions.

Preparedness planning seeks to anticipate problems and project possible solutions. Damage to the physical and social environment can be reduced if potential problems and solutions have been identified, studied, and evaluated in advance.

Emergency operation plan

Unless emergencies occur repeatedly in a community, a modest degree of preparedness is all that can be reasonably expected; it is impossible to plan for every contingency. Consequently, a focus on fundamental principles is important. It is tempting to write highly detailed plans, but the temptation should be resisted: details quickly become outdated. An emergency operation plan (EOP) must be as streamlined as possible, including only essential elements.

Elements of a basic emergency operation plan (EOP)

1. Introduction
2. Purpose
3. Situation and assumptions
4. Concept of operations
5. Organization and assignment of responsibilities
6. Administration and logistics
7. Plan development and maintenance
8. Authorities and references
9. Definition of terms

In general, each community should develop a comprehensive written EOP anticipating all hazards that pose a significant threat to the community. Most plans follow a common format based on Federal Emergency Management Agency (FEMA) guidelines. Recommended components of the written EOP are the basic plan; functional annexes in support of the basic plan; and hazard-specific appendices in support of each functional annex.

Figure 9–2 Components of an emergency operations plan.

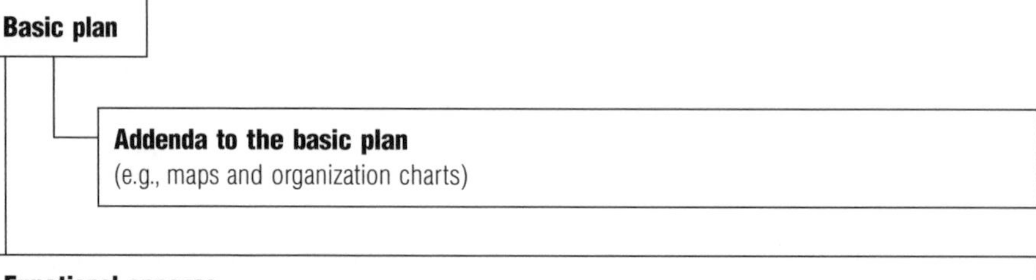

Functional annexes
(e.g., direction and control, communications, warning, emergency public information, evacuation, reception and care, in-place protective shelter, health and medical, law enforcement, public works, fire and rescue, radiological protection, human services, and resource management)

Addenda to the functional annexes
(generic functional work aids, such as maps, charts, tables, checklists, resource inventories, and sample forms)

Hazard-specific appendixes
(e.g., earthquake, flood, hurricane, nuclear attack, nuclear facility accident, depending on jurisdiction's hazards analysis and judgment concerning sufficiency of coverage in the functional annexes, given determined vulnerability and risk)

Addenda to the hazard-specific appendixes
(hazard-specific work aids, such as maps, charts, tables, checklists, and summaries of critical information).

Source: Ronny J. Coleman and John A. Granito, *Managing Fire Services* (Washington, DC: ICMA, 1988), 334.

The basic plan covers considerations such as chain of command during disaster response. The nine elements usually contained in the basic plan are set forth in the sidebar on page 179.

Annexes are elements of the EOP that focus on operations. An annex is used to define a function and assign responsibility for carrying out that function. Standard titles for functional annexes are shown in the sidebar on page 181.

Appendices provide additional details to each annex. For example, Annex C, "Shelter and Mass Care," normally would specify what buildings are to be used as emergency shelters, who is to operate each shelter, and under what circumstances each shelter is to be used. Appendices to Annex C would cover emergency shelter use in different kinds of disasters. Different shelters might be used, for example, to house homeless victims of a flood on a local river or persons evacuated from their homes due to a toxic waste accident on a local rail line. A separate appendix might be provided for each kind of disaster.

The EOP is divided into a basic plan, annexes, and appendices in order to give the plan flexibility. The need for particular annexes depends on local requirements and needs.

Standard functional annexes

A. Warning
B. Communications
C. Shelter and mass care
D. Radiological protection
E. Evacuation
F. Fire
G. Law enforcement
H. Health and medical
I. Emergency public information
J. Damage assessment
K. Public works
L. Utilities
M. Resource management
N. EOC direction and control
O. Human services
P. Hazard mitigation
Q. Hazardous materials
R. Rescue
S. Transportation
T. Training
U. Legal

Hazard analysis

The first step in developing an EOP is to perform a hazard analysis, which identifies potential causes of disasters in the community and determines the level of risk each poses. For example, a hazard analysis should consider the frequency of flooding along local rivers; currently designated truck routing—or lack thereof—for hazardous materials; the location, age, and condition of pipelines; and the classroom location and contents of school chemistry labs.

Hazard analysis is most effective when community groups are involved in the planning process.

Hazard analysis is most effective when community groups are involved in the planning process. The chamber of commerce, industry, and other groups can help identify technological and environmental threats. The chemical industry is especially supportive of emergency preparedness, and the Chemical Manufacturers Association has instituted the Community Awareness and Emergency Response (CAER) Program. Under this program, businesses that manufacture or transport chemicals assist local governments in emergency preparedness and response planning. Information concerning naturally occurring events (e.g., hurricanes, tornadoes, and earthquakes) is available from a number of government and private sources.[2]

Advance Flood Preparedness Schedule

Made vulnerable to flooding by its location, Frankfort, Kentucky (26,000), worked with the Army Corps of Engineers to develop an Advance Flood Preparedness Schedule of Operation. The plan was developed on the premise that floods occur in a fixed course and according to rates and volumes that can be anticipated. Measuring and warning devices on the city dam and information from the National Weather Service provide early-warning information that enables the city to take into account volume and duration of rainfall, drainage area size and configuration, past flood elevations, and types and numbers of structures potentially affected. The plan provides a detailed blueprint for timing and implementing actions to prevent and mitigate loss of life and property.

Source: *The Guide to Management Improvement Projects in Local Government*, vol. 14, no. 3 (Washington, DC: ICMA, 1993), no. PS-19.

Special needs

A number of citizens (e.g., those who are physically disabled, hearing-impaired, or mentally disabled) have special needs and require assistance during an evacuation. It is essential to take these needs into account when developing an EOP.

The Americans with Disabilities Act (ADA) has identified key elements that should be included in an EOP. For example, the shelter plan should provide for disabled individuals' special need for structures and appliances that are accessible to them during their stay at the shelter. Warning and information systems should address the requirements of persons with impaired sight or hearing, those who cannot move freely, and those who are medically dependent. Moreover, all warnings, information, and educational materials should be issued in any languages understood by a substantial portion of the population, in addition to English.

Some states require local emergency management offices to maintain lists of those individuals requiring assistance who voluntarily register their names. However, many people with special requirements prefer to keep their circumstances private and seek assistance only when an emergency occurs. If the emergency manager has not prepared for this eventuality, last-minute calls may overwhelm the communication system and prevent these residents from obtaining the assistance they require.

Emergency exercises and training

Ordinarily, disasters are rare events; it is likely that the community's emergency operation plan has never been implemented. To ensure that government officials and employees, as well as private agencies, know their roles, an emergency response training program is needed.

There are two ways to help ensure that local government and other personnel know what to do when the EOP is implemented. First, when a unit responds to an ordinary emergency such as a fire or a downed power line, the applicable annex should be activated (Annex F, "Fire"; Annex K, "Utilities"). Each annex is an operating plan that outlines the specific actions to be taken in a particular situation. This approach makes the EOP, or at least annexes of it, part of normal operations. Second, an emergency exercise is the primary way for participants to learn their roles and for the emergency manager to test and evaluate the components of the plan. Exercises may include a mock response to simulated events such as tornado damage at a public school, an airplane crash at the airport, or an explosion at a local industrial site. An evaluation of the exercise provides the emergency manager with the information necessary to determine how well the EOP will work in an actual emergency as well as to identify and correct problems.

To ensure that government officials and employees know their roles, an emergency response training program is needed.

Third, local government job descriptions and personnel policies should reflect each employee's added responsibilities during an emergency or disaster. References need not be expansive or complicated. The following is an example from Georgetown, Texas, where emergency management responsibilities are included in every job description:

> ***Director of Planning and Development Services***–*Serves in extension of current duties as required for emergency management, particularly in the areas of mitigation, transportation, damage assessment, and recovery.*

In addition, city personnel policy states that in the event of a natural or technological emergency or disaster, every employee has a role to perform and must be familiar with the city's emergency response plan. Moreover, normal working hours may be suspended and employees required to work as necessary.

The training effort should take advantage of programs and courses available through federal and state agencies; FEMA and state agencies publish schedules showing subjects, locations, and dates of training. The effort should also include locally based training, and it should involve both the general population and emergency response agencies.

Public education

It is important to increase the public's awareness of possible disasters and of what should be done before, during, and after these events. When disaster strikes, citizens are expected to take certain actions or to follow the instruction of emergency management personnel. A public education program must therefore be a part of any comprehensive emergency management plan. A good program not only disseminates educational material on individual and family preparedness, but it also takes the opportunity to learn from disasters that occur elsewhere in order to broaden local education efforts.

Successful education efforts include a component that targets children. Children are often the best means of conveying emergency management information to adults living in the children's households—especially adults who do not read or speak the language in which the information is presented.

Figure 9–3 Sanibel, Florida, uses its *Calendar and Annual Report* to inform the community about hurricane preparedness.

Sanibel Emergency Management & Hurricane Preparedness

As most Sanibel residents are aware, June 1 through November 30 is hurricane season in Southwest Florida. In 1992 there were four named storms, of which only Hurricane Andrew affected Sanibel. Once again, we are cognizant of just how lucky we have been.

Our citizens made the voluntary evacuation prior to Hurricane Andrew a success. Between 80% and 90% of our residents and visitors evacuated with minimal problems. The Sanibel Police Department expended a total of 675 man-hours protecting the Island during this crisis, and no burglaries or other crimes associated with the evacuation were reported.

ZONE CAPTAINS
Sanibel Island is divided into five zones, each of which has a volunteer zone captain and one or more alternate zone captains. These volunteers are responsible for attempting to contact each resident in their zone to inform them of emergency instructions in the event of a major natural or man-made disaster. This is just another way the City tries to keep Island residents informed of potentially dangerous situations.

Additional volunteers are always welcome to assist in each zone. If you would like to volunteer, please call the Sanibel Emergency Management Plan (SEMP) Office at 472-3111. Each year our Island papers publish a zone map with names of captains, however, you can call the Sanibel Police Department at 472-3111 to obtain the name of your current zone captain.

FRIENDS IN SERVICE HERE (FISH)
FISH is a group of dedicated volunteers who provide the needed support and transportation for our elderly or infirm residents. Prior to Hurricane Andrew, FISH transported 97 residents to safe shelter off the Island. If you need more information concerning FISH, or know of someone who needs their services, call 472-0404.

BE PREPARED
In light of Sanibel's near miss with Hurricane Andrew, it is obvious that being prepared for a "direct hit" is a prerequisite to avoid a possible life or death situation. One of the best ways to prepare for a storm is to stock your home with necessary items before the start of the hurricane season. You should have enough of the following supplies on hand to last your family, including pets, for two weeks:

can fruits	pet food	cannned vegetables
can juices	medicine	flashlights/batteries
can meats	tea/coffee	first aid kit
bottled water	candles	grill/camp stove
can soup	batteries	full auto gas tank
dried fruits	cooking fuel	portable FM radio
baby formula	powdered milk	

Hurricane Andrew gave Island residents both a scare and a good test of our hurricane plan.

AFTER THE STORM
If it becomes necessary for public safety purposes to restrict re-entry to Sanibel following a serious storm strike, Island residents will only need their driver's license or voter's registration card showing a Sanibel or Captiva address to gain access to the islands. Non-resident property owners or employees of Island businesses will be required to present hurricane identification cards at the Sanibel Causeway toll booth to gain access to Sanibel and Captiva after a major storm strikes. These identification cards are available from the Sanibel Police Department free of charge. Please DO NOT wait for an emergency to obtain your card.

Re-entry to Sanibel after a storm will depend on several factors, all of which are in the interest of your safety, which include road clearing, removal of downed powerlines, search and rescue missions, and general road and weather conditions. If serious structural damage has occurred, limited access through use of proper identification may be enforced.

PLEASE KEEP INFORMED
The Sanibel Emergency Management Plan (SEMP) utilizes a system of "alert radios" to provide homeowners and businesses with an informational downlink from the Sanibel Police Department. These radios are used to pass on storm advisories, evacuation information, weather advisories, and other information from City Hall. The radios operate on AC or battery power, and are available through the Sanibel Police Department for $60.00.

1993 ATLANTIC STORMS

Arlene	Bret	Cindy	Dennis	Emily
Floyd	Gert	Harvey	Irene	Jose
Katrina	Lenny	Maria	Nate	Ophelia
Philippe	Rita	Stan	Tammy	Vince
Wilma				

Figure 9–4 Brea, California, educates its citizens about earthquake preparedness through the city's official monthly newsletter, *The Brea Line.*

Every Month is Earthquake Preparedness Month

Earthquake preparedness is everybody's business. Emergencies can occur anytime, anywhere. Planning ahead and making provisions for your family's needs can make a big difference in your ability to cope with emergencies.

Before the Earthquake

- Check your home for potential hazards such as defective electrical wiring and leaky gas connections.
- Bolt/strap down your water heater and gas appliances.
- Know where and how to shut off electricity, gas and water at main switches and valves.
- Place large and heavy objects on lower shelves.
- Securely fasten shelves to walls. Brace or anchor high or top-heavy objects.
- Glass, china and other breakables should be stored in low or closed cabinets.
- Have on hand some basic emergency supplies such as a flashlight and battery operated radio, a supply of drinking water (minimum one gallon per person per day) and non-perishable food to last approximately 72 hours. Future issues of the Brea Line will discuss in depth those items you should purchase and store.

During the Earthquake

- First and foremost, stay calm. Think through the consequences of any action you take.
- If you are inside, stay inside as most injuries occur as people run outside. Take cover under a heavy desk or table, in a supported doorway, or along an inside wall. Stay away from glass and windows.
- If you are outside, move away from buildings, trees and utility wires.
- If driving, stop as quickly as safety permits, but stay in the vehicle. A car may jiggle violently on its springs, but it is a good place to stay until the shaking stops. Avoid under and overpasses.
- If you are in a high-rise building, get under a desk or similar heavy furniture. Do not dash for exits, since stairways may be broken and jammed with people. Never use elevators.

After the Earthquake

- Be prepared for aftershocks.
- Turn on the radio and listen for important information on the Emergency Broadcast System.
- Check for injuries and provide first aid.
- Check gas, water and sewage lines for damage. Turn off appropriate utilities.
- Check for structural damage - chimneys and foundations.
- Clean up dangerous spills.
- Don't use telephone except for an emergency.
- Wear heavy shoes.

Remember: Planning for the disaster and practicing what you will do when it happens is the key to family safety. Future issues of the Brea Line will feature important emergency preparedness tips and will suggest supplies to purchase and have on hand. For more information, please call the Brea Fire Department at (714) 990-7622.

Safety tips

To educate its callers, the Southern Manatee Fire and Rescue District of Bradenton, Florida (52,330), plays safety messages over the phone to callers on hold. The tape, which repeats every four minutes, consists of music integrated with five safety tips and listings of services. Callers' reactions have been favorable, with some requesting to be placed on hold.

Source: *The Guide to Management Improvement Projects in Local Government,* vol. 16, no. 2 (Washington, DC: ICMA, 1992), no. PS-12.

Mitigation

Although nothing can stop a hurricane, a tornado, or an earthquake, it is possible to reduce their effects. Mitigation is action taken to eliminate or reduce the degree of long-term risk to human life and property. For example, a community can build dikes to restrain flood waters or enact building codes that require structures to be earthquake resistant.

However, mitigation efforts may be unpopular. People tend to think that disasters will not occur (or recur), and they may be unwilling to spend public or private money on mitigation. In addition, developers may be unwilling to support measures that deny them the opportunity to develop commercially attractive, although vulnerable, sites—for example, land adjacent to a flood-prone river. Nevertheless, for the safety and well-being of their community, local government officials should take an active role in promoting mitigation.

Mitigation measures may be adopted during preparedness planning for a potential disaster or during recovery from a past disaster.

During preparedness planning

As hazards are identified during the first stage in the development of an emergency operation plan, various options for dealing with those hazards emerge that make it possible either to prevent disasters or to mitigate their harmful effects. Before undertaking a major public education campaign on mitigation, a community government must decide which option, or combination of options, to use. If citizens are involved in this decision, they will be more likely to support the proposed mitigation measures. Government officials should therefore ensure public participation through public networking, consultation, and debate.

Possible mitigation measures include preparing land-use and management plans for hazardous areas (e.g., prohibiting development in the flood plain or residential development adjacent to an industrial complex); reducing hazards by relocating buildings away from hazardous areas; strengthening building codes; and educating decision makers and the community about risks.

During recovery

Once a disaster has occurred, public officials may be subjected to a number of conflicting pressures. Local business and other community leaders may want to restore "business as usual" as quickly as possible. At the same time, public support for mitigation—which must be carefully planned and takes a significant amount of time to implement—may be much higher than usual. Disasters present an opportunity for dramatic change, for better or for worse. It is important that public officials not be swept along by the seemingly overwhelming pressure to return to normal life as quickly as possible but that they take advantage of public support to implement mitigation measures.

If changes are to be made, they must be made quickly. As each day passes and the memory of the disaster becomes less vivid, support for corrective action weakens. Therefore, redevelopment plans that include mitigation measures must be ready *before* disaster strikes.

Return to normalcy versus mitigation

In a Florida community, the mayor resigned just after a disaster, and the council hurriedly selected an acting mayor who was immediately confronted by three land developers who wanted to get the community back on its feet again. They requested permission to begin cleaning debris and staking out lots for waterfront condos and beach houses. Although several members of the council were not sure about the haste of the whole affair, their concerns were shouted down in the din of ensuing council meetings. When the council finally did pass zoning regulations, one year after the hurricane, the action came as a symbolic and meaningless gesture. Over 4,000 new condos were in place, 2,500 were under construction, and 4,500 were on the drawing board.

Source: Adapted from Thomas E. Drabek and Gerard J. Hoetmer, *Emergency Management: Principles and Practice for Local Government* (Washington, DC: ICMA, 1991), 97.

Response

Response takes place immediately before, during, or directly after a disaster. The purpose of response is to minimize personal injury and property damage through functions such as warning, evacuation, search and rescue, and provision of shelter and medical services. The disaster response effort is directed from the emergency operations center (EOC).

Emergency operations center

The EOC is the area from which previously designated officials direct the response phase of the emergency operations plan. Small local governments usually locate their EOCs in temporary housing at the time of a disaster, for example in a fire station. The functions of the EOC are to

Assess the disaster threat and coordinate organizational resources to counter it

Make the broad policy decisions that guide the overall community response to the disaster (for example, the decision to evacuate)

Manage operations

Gather information

Issue information to the public and the media

Host visitors (for example, state and federal officials or representatives from neighboring communities).

In addition to the police, fire, and public works departments, a number of other agencies and organizations generally have representatives at the EOC. For example, if emergency medical services are not represented as part of the fire department, their representatives are present. Officials from utility companies and from the Red Cross or Salvation Army are normally present. Depending on the nature of the disaster, there may also be representatives from organizations such as the National Weather Service, FEMA, the U.S. Forest Service, or the U.S. Geological Survey.

The local government manager must take the leadership role in coping with disaster, relying on the emergency manager and department heads for advice.

The EOC is staffed by officials with responsibilities for specific functions. Typically, every EOC has officers for communications and for public information. Many EOCs also have officers for damage assessment and for operations and resources planning.

The local government manager must take the leadership role in coping with disaster, relying on the emergency manager and department heads for advice on decisions. Elected officials, especially the mayor or county board president, should be consulted when decisions are made, but they can be most effective as liaisons with the press and the public. They typically lack the experience needed to manage and coordinate the community's response teams.

To appreciate the environment of an EOC, its four predominant characteristics must be understood: (1) pressure to take action; (2) limited and uncertain information; (3) shifting priorities; and (4) overlapping lines of authority and responsibility. Perhaps the most pervasive and formidable characteristic is pressure. The air is thick with pressure to take action in order to prevent or alleviate human suffering and physical destruction. This pressure is intensified by shortage of time: during disasters, decisions often must be made quickly if they are to have any effect at all.

Warning systems

One of the most serious problems in disasters is not public panic, but unwillingness to believe and react to obvious signs of danger. For this reason, an essential responsibility of public officials is to get an effective warning to the public in a timely way. An all-hazard alerting system is an important part of emergency management planning. It should include notification of key public officials, mechanisms for warning the community at large, and provisions for special populations such as disabled or non-English-speaking people. The applicable questions for public health officials are as follows:

Are weather and other indicators of potential emergencies monitored continuously?

Would key emergency personnel be notified rapidly of a disaster or a potential disaster? What if a key individual were out of town?

Who is responsible for alerting the general public about an actual or potential emergency?

Has the role of the media in alerting the public been coordinated with media representatives?

Has the general public been educated about the meaning of the alerting signals and about corresponding actions to take?

Are there special provisions for alerting particular groups such as disabled, institutionalized, or non-English-speaking people?

Telephone notification network

Commerce, California (12,000 residents, 58,000 daytime workers), installed a telephone notification network to alert citizens to imminent danger. The network automatically calls 3,200 residences and 1,700 businesses within one hour and forty minutes. The system dials fifty numbers at a time and redials twice after receiving a busy signal. A recorded message in both English and Spanish notifies households and businesses of such emergencies as earthquakes, toxic spills, and fires, and gives evacuation instructions and necessary precautions. The emergency preparedness team can specify which neighborhoods, streets, blocks, or zip codes will receive the messages. The network is operated out of a bureau in New York, because an out-of-state location allows quicker notification during local emergencies, when long distance calls are more likely to connect than local calls.

Source: *The Guide to Management Improvement Projects in Local Government*, vol. 16, no. 2 (Washington, DC: ICMA, 1992), no. PS-8.

To overcome the public's reluctance to act, disaster warnings must be specific about the danger; be specific about what to do; be specific about who is being warned; be issued through all possible mediums; and be related to previous education efforts. Research indicates that people are not upset by warnings if they are clear and specify the danger and the proper response.

Figure 9–5 St. Peters, Missouri, survived the floods of 1993 by converting a railroad embankment into a permanent rock levee. More than 13,000 tons of rock were used to widen the embankment's base from fifteen to forty feet. In some sections, the railroad tracks were raised nearly four feet (*above*).

Figure 9–6 Volunteers in St. Peters filled 35,000 sandbags (*above right*).

Figure 9–7 The St. Peters water operations continued to function during the floods (*right*).

Evacuation

When a disaster is imminent or in progress, local officials must decide whether to evacuate citizens. The potential risk to evacuees is a primary concern. The EOC commander must scrutinize the evacuees' destination as well as their route and should assess alternative protective measures (such as shelter within the community) before advising that evacuation be initiated.

Police departments usually serve as the lead organizations in the evacuation process. The lead agency must carefully coordinate the timing and conduct of the evacuation with the organizations providing shelter and with those who barricade or mark exit routes (usually public works personnel).

The part of the emergency plan that deals with evacuation establishes procedures for choosing evacuation routes and maintaining the flow of vehicles. It should also address the needs of residents who do not own vehicles; those who own pets; disabled persons; and institutions such as schools, hospitals, nursing homes, and jails.

Community emergency response courses

To prepare the community to respond in the event of a disaster, Santa Monica, California (96,000), established a special division within its fire department to provide courses to residents on emergency response. It provides five different courses, including an eighteen-hour course on disaster response and assistance for city employees, hospitals, businesses, and community organizations; a six-hour course on disaster preparedness for schools; a four-hour course on urban search and rescue awareness for emergency service providers; and a four-hour course on urban search and rescue awareness for the community.

Source: *The Guide to Management Improvement Projects in Local Government*, vol. 16, no. 2 (Washington, DC: ICMA, 1992), no. PRM-8.

Emergency medical systems

Disasters place extensive and often unexpected demands on medical systems. There may be large numbers of patients, a shortage of trained staff, and damage to medical facilities and equipment. Facilities may become congested with victims who have only minor injuries, compounding the difficulty of identifying and caring for those who need immediate treatment. The medical response plan should include, among other things, triage, traffic control, and alternative means of communication. Emergency medical services are discussed in Chapter 11.

Incident command systems

During any emergency that involves response personnel, whether it is large or small, only one person can be in command at a specific site. This person, the incident commander, must assess the situation and available resources, determine an appropriate action plan, monitor the plan's effectiveness, and continually modify the plan to meet the realities of the situation.[3] The on-site incident command point is the command post. In the event of multiple or large incidents, several command posts and incident commanders may be needed. A command post can be a vehicle, tent, or open-air table. Requests for supplies, equipment, or additional personnel should be routed by each incident commander from the command post to appropriate officials located in the EOC. Equipment, personnel, and other resources that are available but not yet needed are kept in the staging area. The EOC has overall responsibility for the incident (i.e., public communication, media relations, resource requests to outside agencies, and perhaps resource allocation).

Dissemination of public information

Another problem created by disasters is the enormous demand for information. Those outside the area want to know what has happened to relatives and friends. Victims want to know what services are available. The public often looks to a leading elected official who acts as spokesperson during regularly scheduled press briefings. Under no circumstances should any spokesperson meet the press unprepared. Anticipating questions and formulating responses ahead of time is an effort that repays itself many times over.

The designated spokesperson must remember that honesty is essential. Statements that normally would be routine and unimportant may assume new significance during a crisis. Unfounded speculation should be avoided. The simplest and safest response to a question for which there is no answer is the frank admission that the answer is not known. If a written press statement is issued, make sure that it is reasonably neat and that there are a sufficient number of copies.

The incident command system

Many jurisdictions employ some variation of an incident command system (ICS) during emergency operations. The incident command center was originally developed as a complex command and control model designed to handle firefighting activity at a major incident in an efficient and organized manner. The system can be defined as a set of personnel, policies, procedures, and equipment working together within a common organizational structure to perform specific missions—usually the management of available resources in an emergency.

Most local government ICS operations are flexible and designed to respond on different levels, depending on the scale of an emergency. In the Santa Cruz system, three levels of operation are identified. For example, the fire department's response to a trash fire would be considered a Level 1 response. The officer on the first unit to arrive (a pumper truck) would be the incident commander and would size up the situation to decide whether more assistance was required.

If the reported trash fire had developed into a major conflagration, the officer would ask for additional resources via the dispatcher, thus moving from a Level 1 to a Level 2 emergency. Level 2 is in essence a greater emergency for which more, or more specialized, resources are required but which is, nevertheless, within the capabilities of the responding department. A situation requiring a citywide response is designated as Level 3 (i.e., disaster). At Level 3, assistance and resources from outside the local government's jurisdiction are required.

Source: Adapted from Richard C. Wilson, *The Loma Prieta Quake: What One City Learned* (Washington, DC: ICMA, 1991), 21, 25.

Response services

Food and clothing, mass shelter, and counseling are crucial services often provided by organizations such as the American Red Cross and the Salvation Army. Special efforts are required to coordinate provision of these services to elderly, disabled, and non-English-speaking residents.

Local police, fire, and water departments and providers of electricity, gas, and telephone services are critical in the initial response to disaster. Police officers and firefighters serve in an extension of their regular duties, with particular emphasis on rescue and on-scene control. Firefighters require special training to handle incidents involving hazardous materials; this training must be coordinated with the overall emergency management plan. Water departments help restore or maintain the water supply and prevent its contamination. Widespread power failures require skills, tools, and experience beyond those normally provided by power company personnel. Because power sources are essential to protecting and saving lives and property, coordination between power companies and government agencies takes precedence over all other activities.

Private sector assistance also comes from the construction and chemical industries. Heavy-duty construction equipment, which can be provided by the construction industry, is essential to clearing roads or removing debris. The chemical industry provides assistance through national information centers, hotlines, and networks of hazardous materials response teams.[4]

Volunteers

Volunteers can be a tremendous asset to the local government during a disaster. Local officials should take advantage of existing skills and talents within the community by identifying and actively recruiting pharmacists, veterinarians, amateur radio operators, clergy, and others who can be trained for specific roles prior to a disaster. However, to be effective, the volunteers must be familiar with citywide emergency plans and understand their place in the response phase.[5]

Volunteer preparedness training
Agoura Hills, California (20,000) has trained a group of two hundred volunteers to help handle the aftermath of a disaster, especially an earthquake. Volunteers attend six two-hour sessions on earthquake preparedness; fire suppression; avoiding danger and exposure to hazardous materials; urban search and rescue techniques; first aid training; and disaster psychology for dealing with behaviors that may impair volunteer efforts. Team members are also trained to reduce earthquake hazards in their own homes, to prepare their families for a quake, to assist neighbors in the event of a quake, and to report potential problems such as gas leaks.

Source: *The Guide to Management Improvement Projects in Local Government*, vol. 15, no. 4 (Washington, DC: ICMA, 1991), no. PRM-26.

Inevitably, regardless of the opportunities for preplanned volunteer training, altruistic tendencies prompt many community members to offer their services spontaneously when disaster strikes. This phenomenon presents itself at every disaster, and emergency managers must be prepared to handle it effectively. A good plan must anticipate legal requirements for registration, screening, and training of spontaneous volunteers. It must provide for the care of these volunteers during their service to the community and take responsibility for dealing with any after-effects they may experience (e.g., provide psychological counseling).

Long-term recovery
It is difficult, if not impossible, to make rational decisions related to long-term recovery in the immediate aftermath of a disaster.

However, some disaster response measures may contribute to long-term recovery if the organization has prepared long-term recovery plans in advance. For example, if officials plan in advance how to strengthen building codes and land-use planning regulations after a disaster, the effects of subsequent disasters will be minimized. Or, if a pre-existing recovery plan specifies how Main Street should be rebuilt after a disaster, time will be saved and arguments avoided after the event.

Source: Adapted from Richard C. Wilson, *The Loma Prieta Quake: What One City Learned* (Washington, DC: ICMA, 1991), 55.

Recovery

Recovery begins immediately with efforts to restore essential services to the stricken area, and it continues until the community returns to normal. Immediate activities include damage assessment, clean-up, and restoration of food supplies, shelter, and utilities. An accessible location should be identified for a disaster application center (DAC) where disaster assistance services are provided. Sites where debris may be burned or disposed of must be identified and made to comply with EPA guidelines.

Recovery activities also include rebuilding the community and implementing mitigation programs. Traditionally, recovery procedures have focused on technical, economic, and administrative recovery; however, there must also be a focus on victims. Once basic safety has been restored, victims who have lost their homes, loved ones, or livelihoods may experience overwhelming psychological reactions. To compound the problem, these reactions often occur when resources that were mobilized for the disaster are being withdrawn. A recovery plan that addresses both physical and psychological human needs is likely to be much more successful than a disaster plan that focuses exclusively on technical, economic, or administrative recovery.[6]

Planning for disaster recovery

As soon as possible after a disaster, local officials must decide what they want to do and who is to participate in planning and implementing the recovery. Local officials must understand the importance of the intergovernmental process, undertake action to ensure intergovernmental cooperation early in the postdisaster period, and make sure that cooperative efforts are implemented by both executive and administrative staff.

If the top elected or appointed officials have foresight and a vision of the community's future, it will be easier for the community to recover from a disaster. Strong, capable leadership increases the likelihood of obtaining the resources necessary to repair damage in the community. Skill and pre-disaster public management experience, in addition to well-established pre-disaster interorganizational relationships, are essential to recovery.

Local administrative and technical mechanisms in place before the disaster usually contribute significantly to expeditious recovery. Administrative mechanisms that become important in the aftermath of a disaster are land-use controls, building codes, inspection and enforcement procedures (e.g., for building permits), mutual-aid pacts for public safety and public works activities, and contract agreements (e.g., for debris removal). Technical mechanisms include maps and detailed assessments of known hazards or zones (e.g., floodplains, seismic zones, and landslide areas). A community with a good recordkeeping system in place will be better able to track disaster-related expenditures.

Ideally, disaster recovery processes should improve the community and make it a better, safer place for citizens. If leaders look at heavily damaged areas as redevelopment sites, the community will have a wider array of reconstruction options. Long-term recovery from a disaster may continue for years until the entire disaster area is completely redeveloped, either as it was in the past, or for entirely new purposes that are less disaster-sensitive. For example, businesses can be relocated and a commercial area turned into open space or park land. In other words, disaster recovery should include a review of ways to avoid future emergencies and capitalize on opportunities to mitigate the effects of disasters that occur.

Source: Adapted from "Planning for Disaster Recovery," *MIS Report*, vol. 25, no. 7 (July 1993).

Disaster assistance services

After every major disaster, donations of goods from across the country overwhelm emergency workers. A predetermined plan for handling offers of goods and services can turn them into true assets by facilitating the process of matching the goods and services offered with those who need them.

If social service agencies are willing to participate in the donation management program, items should be distributed among the agencies according to the types of items each agency handles on a regular basis. For example, donated food should go to the local food bank. Donated clothing and household goods should go to an appropriate agency (e.g., Goodwill Industries, the Salvation Army, or the Ministerial Association).

When a disaster strikes, local authorities and individuals request help from private relief organizations and their state government. These entities give all possible assistance. If requests for assistance go beyond the state's capabilities, the state governor may ask the president of the United States to declare the location a major disaster area. The Stafford Disaster Relief and Emergency Assistance Act provides the greatest single source of federal disaster assistance, the President's Disaster Relief Fund. In the event of a presidential declaration of a major disaster, this act orders FEMA to coordinate federal disaster relief activities undertaken by such agencies as the Small Business Administration, Farmers Home Administration, the National Flood Insurance Program, Veterans Administration (home mortgage modifications), and the Internal Revenue Service.

If requests for assistance go beyond the state's capabilities, the state governor may ask the president of the United States to declare the location a major disaster area.

Community governments may also request technical assistance from FEMA in determining which federal agencies or volunteer organizations have disaster relief programs that could be of assistance.[7]

Appreciation

During a disaster, people want to help. After a disaster, people want to be thanked for their help. It is important to hold a volunteer reception event several months after the disaster. Certificates noting dates of participation and type of help provided should be given to all pre-trained and spontaneous volunteers. Businesses that provided special support by donating materials or labor should be included in the recognition event. Agencies such as the American Red Cross and the Salvation Army should also be recognized for any help they rendered during the disaster.

Legal issues

The emergency manager must ensure that a legal framework is in place, particularly with respect to lines of authority, that allows authorities to make necessary decisions during disasters and to act on them.

In general, tort suits over alleged flaws in disaster response procedures have been dismissed. In many states, statutory protection is comprehensive. Even without statutory protection, each aspect of response is still likely to be immune from suit, either as a "governmental function" or as a "discretionary action" (see Chapter 2). Both legislatures and the courts have recognized that fear of legal suits may create paralysis, during both planning and decision making during a crisis. Therefore, considerable protection has been accorded to any well-intended effort.

At the operational level, emergency management often involves making life-and-death decisions under extreme time constraints and in the face of uncertainty and personal risk. Courts are reluctant to question the judgment of individuals who must act under such circumstances. This reluctance translates into a tendency to find that the acts in question were discretionary. Only the most flagrant or obvious deviations from procedure or good practice have been found to be negligent.

In addition to the ordinances outlining decision making and responsibilities, it is also important to have fill-in-the-blank ordinances available for immediate approval by the governing body during the response and recovery phases. Price controls, contractor bonds and licensing, establishment of curfews, and disposal ordinances can be implemented quickly through the use of fill-in-the-blank ordinances. Ordinances to regulate building contractors, for example, help protect victims from fraudulent practices of those who try to take advantage of them.[8]

Afterword

Long gone is the era when emergency planning was designed only to provide bomb shelters in the event of nuclear attack. Long gone, too, is the day when emergency planning was considered a relatively insignificant concern among the more pressing problems facing local governments. The task of emergency preparation has become a major responsibility because the likelihood that a disaster will occur is increasing daily, even in smaller communities.

The traditional list of disasters—wars, earthquakes, floods, storms, fires—is being lengthened by social and technological changes. Today disaster can occur if a nuclear power plant, even one several hundred miles distant, experiences an accident; if a truck carrying dangerous chemicals is involved in an accident while traveling through town; if emergency communications systems fail at a critical moment; if old chemicals stored in the high school chemistry lab are improperly moved; if an airplane crashes into a local neighborhood; or if gangs disrupt a local high school pep rally.

The loss of human life and property caused by such occurrences can be enormous. Worse, such losses can be magnified several times over by good-faith, but improper, efforts to help the victims. No public official—elected or appointed—would want to face responsibility for human injuries and deaths caused by poorly planned or misdirected rescue and relief efforts.

There simply is no substitute for adequate emergency planning and regular emergency response drills. Such efforts require the same daily attention and action as police and fire response. The likelihood of disaster response being needed is much less, but the potential loss in lives and property is much greater than that threatened by daily activities. No responsible community official can neglect emergency planning and training if he or she is serious about protecting the public. ■

---

1. Richard C. Wilson, *The Loma Prieta Quake: What One City Learned* (Washington, DC: ICMA, 1991).
2. Thomas Drabek and Gerard J. Hoetmer, eds., *Emergency Management Principles and Practice for Local Government* (Washington, DC: ICMA, 1991), 80.
3. Mayor Nudell and Norman Antokol, eds., *The Handbook for Effective Emergency and Crisis Management* (Lexington Books, 1988), 71.
4. Drabek, *Emergency Management Principles and Practice*, 70-71.
5. Francis E. Winslow, "Caring For Workers and Spontaneous Volunteers: A Local Government Perspective," *The Second Annual International Emergency Management Conference Proceedings*, March 17-19, 1992, San Francisco, California (Needham, MA: The Interface Group, 1992), 84.
6. Patrick Prince and Ann T. Phelps, "'Disaster-Proofing' Your People: Caring for the Psychological Needs of Employees," *The Second Annual International Emergency Management Conference Proceedings*, March 17-19, 1992, San Francisco, California (Needham, MA: The Interface Group, 1992), 204.
7. *Digest of Federal Disaster Assistance Programs*, DR & R-21 (Washington, DC: Federal Emergency Management Agency, 1989).
8. Ken Lerner, "Governmental Negligence Liability Exposure in Disaster Management," *The Urban Lawyer* 23 (Summer 1991).

10 Police Services

As local law enforcement agencies (police and sheriff's departments) approach the twenty-first century, they find themselves confronted by complex paradoxes demanding innovative solutions. The demand for police services is increasing at a time when law enforcement budgets are shrinking or at best remain stagnant. Rising rates of crime are creating a growing demand for more arrests, yet overcrowded jails are causing the court-ordered early release of convicted criminals in forty-one states.[1] The number and degree of violent crimes are growing at a time when law enforcement officers are under pressure to respond more "humanely" and with less force.

The focus of this chapter is on the directions that police agencies are taking as they attempt to solve the paradoxes that confront them. In their attempts, many agencies have begun to reevaluate their form and function. Communities expect the mission of policing to encompass an acute sensitivity to community desires and a willingness to serve the public in a variety of ways. From the agency's perspective, insufficient revenues and increasing demands have created an environment in which ways of providing new and new ways of providing old services must be explored. To be successful, administrators must be innovative and willing to adapt to a changing society.

Role of police and sheriff's departments

References in this chapter to police agencies and services apply with equal validity to both city or town police and county sheriff's departments. Deciding what an individual agency's function will be requires an understanding of community expectations and a commitment to be sensitive and responsive to those expectations. The roles most commonly associated with these agencies include law enforcement, preservation of the peace, crime prevention, traffic control, and the protection of civil rights and liberties.

The existence of similar roles does not imply that police and sheriff's departments are the same; differences do exist, but more often in areas of responsibility than in approach. The county sheriff, for instance, has responsibilities related to the courts and for longer-term custodial systems (jails) that are not typically part of the municipal police function. However, even with these differences, the similarities in functions, roles, concerns, and methodologies are sufficient to allow a discussion that is pertinent to both types of agency.

Delivering police services

Shrinking revenue bases, along with other problems facing law enforcement agencies, have led to a search for more effective organizational structures, service delivery systems, policing strategies, and innovative service methodologies. Organization and service delivery systems are described in this section of the chapter; strategies and methodologies are discussed in later sections.

Departmental organization

To accomplish their assigned role, police and sheriff's departments historically have operated as distinct departments within their respective governments. These departments are organized in various ways; typical organizational structures are shown in Figures 10–1 and 10–2.

Departmental consolidation

Many communities have considered the option of consolidating their public safety agencies in order to generate cost saving, decrease future costs, and improve efficiency and productivity. The following five levels of departmental consolidation are being used in the United States:[2]

Full consolidation has been used to combine police and fire departments administratively and functionally into public safety departments. Typically called public safety officers, the members of the newly formed department perform both law enforcement and firefighting functions.

The police and fire departments remain separate under *partial consolidation,* but some officers (for example, ten of fifty) are trained to perform both law enforcement and firefighting functions. Those trained to perform both functions fall under the supervision of the department for which they are executing the duties at any given time.

Under *selected consolidation,* public safety officers, who are trained to perform both law enforcement and firefighting functions, serve only selected areas of the community. This type of consolidation is typically used only in newly annexed areas. Using traditional service provision

Figure 10–1 Organization of the Piqua police department, Piqua, Ohio.

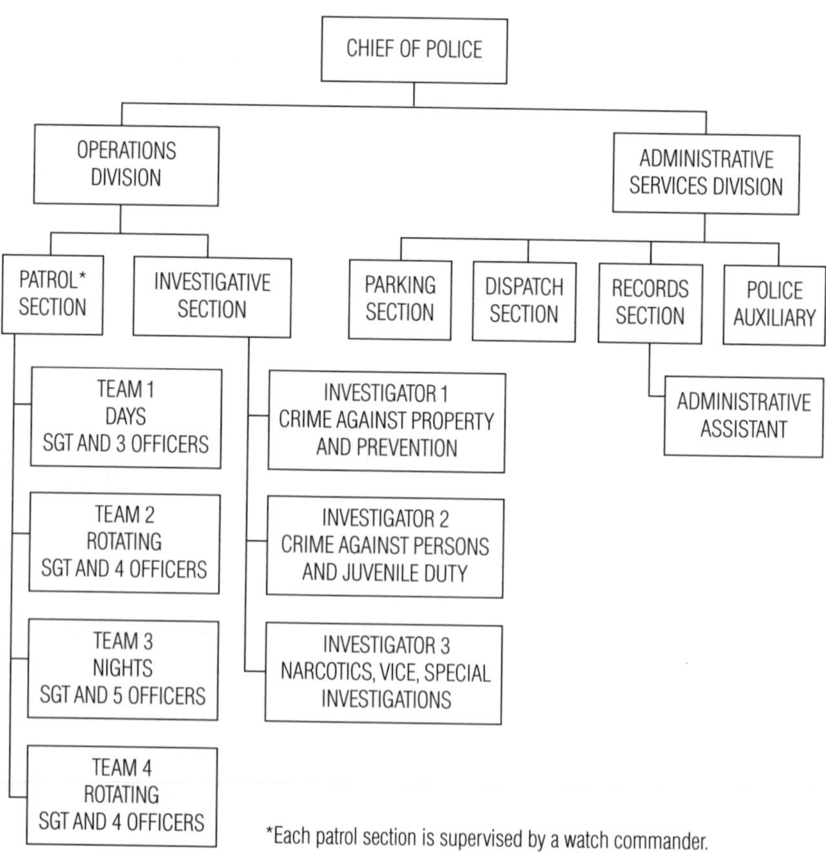

for such areas may require, for example, five more police officers and five more firefighters, whereas the same area may only require seven cross-trained personnel. Because the newer areas have not become accustomed to traditional fire and police protection, they are typically more receptive to consolidated service provision.

Under *functional consolidation,* police officers may perform specific tasks usually assigned to firefighters and firefighters may perform tasks normally assigned to police officers. The tasks are usually of a supportive nature, such as recordkeeping and equipment maintenance.

Nominal consolidation is more administrative than functional in nature. A public service director maintains administrative authority over both the police and fire departments, but the departments remain separate units.

Contracts for police services

Limited revenue bases and increasing demands have led some communities, especially smaller ones, to consider contractual arrangements for police services across geographic boundaries.

City-county contracts

Smaller municipalities sometimes contract with their county sheriff's department to provide police services within the municipal boundaries. Usually such contracts call for a higher level of service (e.g., more frequent patrols) than that routinely made available to the unincorporated areas of the county. Sometimes municipalities enter into such contracts when they do not have sufficient resources to hire their own police officers; sometimes they do so to take advantage of economies of scale and improved coordination in public safety work.

Figure 10–2 Organization of the sheriff's office, Greene County, Ohio.

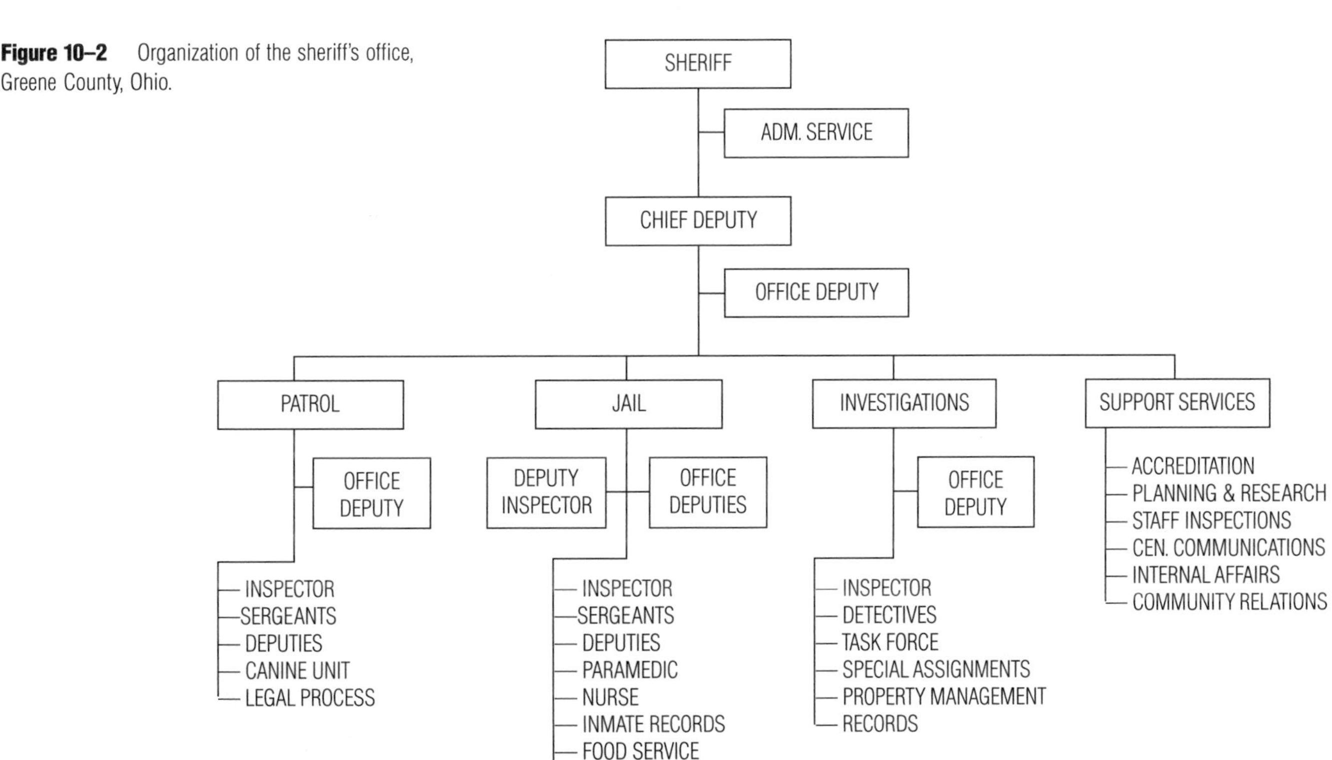

Intermunicipal contracts

Sometimes a municipality will contract with an adjacent municipality for the provision of police services within its boundaries. As is the case with city-county contracts, such arrangements provide economic and service delivery advantages and allow the contracting municipality to establish its desired level of service. These contracts, however, do limit the contracting agency's control over police operations.

Other forms of service provision

Communities use many forms of interlocal agreement, intergovernmental cooperation, some volunteers, and other innovative methods to provide police services. The National Advisory Commission on Criminal Justice Standards and Goals has recommended that "at a minimum, police agencies that employ fewer than ten sworn employees should consolidate for improved efficiency and effectiveness."[3]

Interlocal agreements

Interlocal agreements (or joint agreements) are being used with increasing frequency to improve coordination, secure special expertise, and take advantage of economies of scale in order to provide services or secure a particular service that a community could not otherwise afford. The agreement may be between two or more units in close geographic proximity to each other.

Interlocal agreements are used, for example, to pool expertise and resources in order to obtain special tactical units for hostage situations, sophisticated investigative and forensic expertise, and assistance in "hot pursuit"; to exchange intelligence information; and to exchange personnel for undercover work.

Interlocal agreements are also being used in the provision of jail services. To compensate for decreasing revenues, increasing costs, and overcrowded jails, many communities look to their neighbors to provide jail space. These agreements are frequently between a municipality and its county or between a county and other counties and municipalities in the same region.

Contracting for police services

To increase its police services, Arabi, Georgia (433), contracted with the Crisp County, Georgia (21,100), sheriff's department. The sheriff's department added Arabi as another zone on its patrol route and rotates four or five officers into the zone twenty-four hours a day. The contract also includes use of county jail facilities. Arabi receives more extensive police patrol with better-trained officers than it could afford by operating its own department. Crisp County receives $28,000 and one police car per year from Arabi. It also contracts its police services to the regional hospital for another $50,000 per year.

Source: *The Guide to Management Improvement Projects in Local Government,* vol. 15, no. 3 (Washington, DC: ICMA, 1992), no. MGT-18.

The central police dispatch, or 911, system is an excellent example of how interlocal agreements have allowed communities to lower their costs and increase their efficiency. In Muskegon County, Michigan, eight communities have entered into a joint agreement to provide a centralized police dispatching service. The joint agreement provides a more efficient and effective service than any of the communities could provide independently.

Because 911 systems typically include fire and emergency ambulance services as well as police services, they provide communities and indeed whole geographic regions with better-coordinated public safety systems and greatly improved response to emergencies—and they usually do so at reduced costs.

Intergovernmental cooperation

The delivery of good police services requires a level of cooperation that goes well beyond interlocal agreements.

The delivery of good police services requires a level of cooperation that goes well beyond interlocal agreements. Even without formal agreements, police and sheriff's departments cooperate routinely with law enforcement agencies in adjacent communities. Local law enforcement agencies also cooperate routinely with state and federal law enforcement agencies. State and federal agencies, for example, usually provide laboratory and other forensic services to assist local criminal investigations. The growing problems of drug abuse and gang crime are being fought locally, in part, with specialized task forces made up of federal, state, and local officers.

Law enforcement officers also collaborate closely with a variety of human service agencies, such as schools, youth bureaus, family service agencies, and community mental health centers. Some of this collaboration, such as making educational presentations in schools and participating in youth programs, is designed to prevent crime; some of it, such as work with mental health centers, is intended to provide alternatives to going to jail that may better help individuals correct personal behavioral problems.

Volunteers

Although they are not known for widespread use of volunteers, police agencies, especially smaller agencies, have found ways in which volunteers can help increase efficiency, lower costs, and make up for lost revenues. Volunteers are helping with clerical duties, traffic control, parking enforcement, public fingerprinting, bicycle registration, delivering court documents and evidence, and crime prevention and patrol programs. They are not used for routine police patrol or other direct law enforcement functions, and they are not authorized to use police badges or weapons.

RSVP

To maintain police effectiveness in the midst of budget cuts, the San Clemente, California (42,200), police department enlists the help of retired citizen volunteers with no experience in law enforcement. The Retired Senior Volunteer Program (RSVP) consists of twenty-one volunteers who work in pairs and drive specially marked patrol cars. Vacationing citizens may ask the patrol to check their homes while they are away. RSVP volunteers also check on elderly citizens who live alone if daily phone calls from police dispatchers are not answered and visit these senior citizens once a week for at least fifteen minutes. Since 1985, the senior volunteers have donated the equivalent of more than $665,000 in volunteer time by performing more than 17,000 home checks and 2,200 visits to elderly residents. Parking citations issued by the volunteers have generated more than $249,000 in revenue.

Source: *The Guide to Management Improvement Projects in Local Government,* vol. 16, no. 1 (Washington, DC: ICMA, 1992), no. PS-1.

Policing styles and strategies

In addition to reexamining their structure, many police agencies are also reconsidering the styles and strategies they use to deliver services. Although most agencies continue to operate within either legalistic or service-based policing models, a number of communities have adopted a model that has come to be called "community policing."

Legalistic and service-based models

Figure 10–3 shows the distinctive characteristics of the legalistic and service-based models. The characteristics of most police agencies will conform to one model or the other, although quite often there will be some overlap.

Community policing model

In response to the changing culture that confronts them, many communities have adopted the community policing model, the typical characteristics of which are outlined in Figure 10–4. Similar to the service-based model in some respects, the community policing model embodies a management philosophy that advocates a participatory process of police administration.

Figure 10–3 Legalistic and service models of police organizations.

Legalistic model

1. Highly specialized with great division of labor and a centralized style of command.
2. Stresses rules, policies, and procedures, and obedience thereto.
3. Primary operational thrust is reactive—suppression and apprehension.
4. Impersonal attitude toward public and its problems.
5. Selection of personnel based *solely* on achievement and criteria: tests, education, and past accomplishments.
6. Stresses influence of authority to accomplish tasks.
7. Narrowing of role of employees.
8. Exemplary conduct of employees based on threat, external control, and enforcement of rules.

Service model

1. Generalized approach with less division of labor and a decentralized style of command.
2. Stresses individual discretion and trust of individual decision making.
3. Primary operational thrust is proactive—prevention and deterrence.
4. Personally involved with public and its problems.
5. Selection of personnel based on tests, achievement, and ascriptive criteria with voluntary recognition of need to recruit minorities and different types of people.
6. Stresses influence of persuasion with subtle use of authority to accomplish tasks.
7. Expansion of role of employees.
8. Exemplary conduct of employees based on training, self-control, and individual responsibility.

Figure 10–4 Characteristics of the community policing model.

1. Officers are generalists rather than specialists.
2. Individual responsibility for and autonomy in solving problems at the community level are stressed.
3. Primary operational thrust is to enhance quality of community life; officers are to be peace officers rather than law enforcement officers involved solely in crime control.
4. Officers are interactive information managers, exchanging information with the community and working in partnership with those living and working on the officers' beats.
5. Members of the community are to be involved in identifying policing concerns and issues.
6. There is accountability to the community for achievement of priorities identified by the community.
7. Organizational structure is flattened, emphasizing the importance placed on decision making at the line officer level.

In this process, members of the community participate in the management of the police department and are involved in decisions concerning, for example, the types of patrol used and the selection of police officers. In the administration of the department, emphasis is placed on values rather than on rules, and the department is evaluated according to citizen satisfaction, not by rates of arrest and the number of calls for service.

Figure 10–5 Bicycle patrols can be effective in community policing.

The community policing model places more emphasis on the officer on the beat and the officer's interaction with those working or residing on that beat. Although foot patrols are often employed in community policing, it is possible to implement a community policing program without them. Many communities now use bicycle or motor scooter patrols.

Officers are assigned to specific beats and work with the citizens who work or reside on their beat to identify problems and concerns and assess possible solutions. Emphasis is placed on *preventing* problems and crimes through the combined efforts of those involved. The beat officer is encouraged to seek solutions to problems by working directly with other, related, local government agencies and by interacting daily with business operators, community agencies, and neighborhood families.

In order for community policing to be successful, considerable decision-making power must be delegated to the beat officer. The solutions developed by the beat officer are evaluated only *after* they have been implemented, and they are evaluated according to their outcome—that is, how well they worked.

Community policing is thus a philosophy of service delivery that, once implemented, changes the traditional role of the police in the community. It introduces officers as change agents and facilitators of social service programs and broadens the police function to include conflict resolution, problem solving, and social service referral.

Managing the police agency

Many police agencies are also opting to alter their approach to management as a method of coping with such concerns as decreasing budgets, increasing levels of crime, demand for more services, overcrowded jails, and police morale in the face of public distrust. Today's police administrator has a variety of managerial styles and tools available that can be used in working with any police agency.

Community policing in Southern Pines

Plagued by the crack cocaine epidemic in some of its neighborhoods and moved to action by the drug-related murder of one of its police officers, Southern Pines, North Carolina (9,213), implemented community-oriented/problem-oriented policing in 1991. The town hired a community services officer to serve as public contact person and facilitator for internal and external programs associated with the new approach to policing. Two new officers were hired and trained with this approach in mind.

The police officers met with neighborhood residents, established a community center in a donated apartment where police and residents could meet and work together on joint efforts aimed at children and adults at risk, and formed task forces with residents to sponsor programs.

Funding for the effort was obtained from private donations. The program led to a drastic reduction in drug arrests and a 70-percent drop in calls for service from the high-risk neighborhoods.

Source: Kyle Sonnenberg, Town Manager, Southern Pines, North Carolina, 1993.

Administration

Historically, police agencies have embraced either the military or scientific-management method of administration. Each of these methods is based on an authoritarian management style that allows little latitude for decision making by the line officer. With the goal of efficiency, management opts for strict control of officers and their activities. These models were developed during a period when the typical police employee was unskilled and undereducated, society more readily accepted a rigid managerial structure, and a strong administrator was needed to combat corruption and political influence.

Recent years, however, have seen the entrance of many well-educated officers into policing, the development of sophisticated and diversified training programs, and the recruitment of management personnel from outside the department. The line officer in today's agency is better educated, more technically competent, less likely to accept the rigidity of the authoritarian model, and more likely to want and seek out greater responsibility.[4] Recognizing that the quality of leadership has a direct bearing on employee morale, job performance, and public trust, many police agencies have adopted more flexible styles of management such as strategic management and employee empowerment.

Policing policies

Many police agencies have created comprehensive, well-defined policies to ensure effective operation. However, others continue to operate without any articulated policy statement, relying on ad hoc decision making and managerial intuition. The absence of a formal structure created through policy can create a situation in which management and staff lack a clear understanding of the objectives of the agency. To be fully motivated to accomplish the objectives and to perform at the highest level possible, organization members need to be given standards for performance and the discipline to help them meet those standards.

Planning and evaluation

Police agencies traditionally have displayed a resistance to change, creating a situation in which administrators react to events that are beyond control rather than steer a charted course. If the agency is to respond successfully to the changes in its environment, planning becomes crucial. Developing intermediate and long-range plans can help administrators cope with problems that otherwise may grow beyond their control. For example, monitoring changes in socioeconomic patterns within a community can help an administrator foresee trends that may require alterations in the service patterns of the agency, allowing the agency the opportunity to be proactive rather than reactive in dealing with those changes.

Program evaluation is an extremely important part of planning, and it must be ongoing in order to meet changing demands.

Program evaluation is an extremely important part of planning, and it must be an ongoing process in order to meet changing demands. Although the methods of evaluation used by departments vary, the process typically includes specifying measurable objectives, developing an evaluation design or plan, choosing data collection methods, and analyzing the data. Evaluation can be a vital tool in monitoring departmental goals and objectives, demonstrating efficiency and effectiveness, justifying the need for additional revenues, and making difficult and far-reaching decisions.

Accreditation of law enforcement agencies

The Commission on Accreditation for Law Enforcement Agencies, Inc., provides comprehensive standards that serve as points of reference by which a police agency can measure and improve its performance.

The development of standards and a process for achieving accreditation began in 1979 as a cooperative undertaking by four associations of law enforcement leaders: the International Association of Chiefs of Police, the National Organization of Black Law Enforcement Executives, the National Sheriff's Association, and the Police Executive Research Forum. The program itself became operational in 1983.

Standards cover four major areas: (1) policies and procedures; (2) administration, including personnel-related questions such as recruitment, selection, and promotion; (3) operations, such as investigation, traffic, juvenile operations, public information, and community relations; and (4) support services, such as communications, records, and property management.

To become accredited, a department begins by filing an application. Next it completes a profile questionnaire to ascertain which standards apply to it. A self-assessment follows to make sure it meets the required standards. Then an on-site accreditation team visits the department and prepares a report for the commission, which decides whether to award accreditation or require further action.

Accreditation is for five years. During that time, a department submits annual reports verifying that it remains in compliance with the required standards. Before the five-year anniversary, a department that wishes to remain accredited goes through the formal process again, typically meeting additional standards each time.

Source: Commission on Accreditation for Law Enforcement Agencies, Inc., 4242B Chain Bridge Road, Fairfax, Virginia 22030.

Productivity improvement

In identifying areas in which productivity can be improved, administrators must consider productivity problems, measures of productivity, and productivity targets. Those aspects of police work that are routine and repetitive hold the most promise for improvement and should be scrutinized. Statements regarding productivity improvement should be put in writing and clear objectives specified. This process requires commitment and support from all levels of the administrative structure.

Caution should be used to ensure that efficiency is not achieved through the sacrifice of effectiveness or responsiveness. *Efficiency* refers to the relationship between inputs and outputs; *effectiveness* refers to the impact of the program or policy on the citizen; and *responsiveness* to the way in which the citizen perceives the service provided. Effectiveness and responsiveness are more difficult to measure than efficiency, so an agency may gravitate toward judging itself on efficiency because it is easier to measure. If an agency concentrates too much on efficiency—or on efficiency measures that only approximate effectiveness or responsiveness—effectiveness and responsiveness both can suffer.

Management concerns

The styles and strategies used by the police agency should be designed with some consideration of the problems and concerns that the agency will face in the coming years. Beyond service and budgetary problems, there are employee-related concerns that have the potential to affect the success of the agency. These include community relations, the ethics and integrity of police officers, stress and burnout, career plateauing, labor relations, and diversification.

Community relations

Traditionally, community relations programs have remained outside the mainstream of police activities. Too often, police agencies have established police-community relations units only in response to a community crisis. These programs are often little more than facades, with no true commitment by the department; it only appears that something is being done.

Law enforcement agencies can use a community relations program to help create a favorable public image and to generate support for themselves and their services. In developing a program, administrators should assess public attitudes toward the agency; talk with the leaders of civic, business, and service organizations; and attend public hearings. Information from each of these sources can provide invaluable insight into community concerns. Finally, a community relations program will not succeed unless both the leadership and individual police officers are genuinely committed to it.

"Have a Cup on Us" campaign

After a survey disclosed that only 48 percent of the community's residents were using seat belts, Newton, Iowa (15,000), instituted the "Have a Cup on Us" campaign to encourage seat belt use, educate the community, and promote a positive relationship between the police department and the community. Police officers stopped motorists who were observed wearing seat belts and exhibiting safe driving skills and presented them with a "Buckle Up America" coffee cup and an insert describing the program. They commended them on their driving skills and offered them a free cup of coffee from participating area merchants when presenting the cup. The three-month campaign promoted both positive community reaction and an 11-percent increase in seat belt use.

Source: Kim B. Wadding, Deputy Police Chief, Newton, Iowa, 1993.

Community relations are being enhanced through a variety of programs, including community education, public participation, and alternative patrol programs.

Community education

Community education programs can include a variety of activities such as the "Officer Friendly" program in which police officers visit schools and civic groups to discuss police activities and answer questions. A similar program is the D.A.R.E. (Drug Abuse Resistance Education) program in which officers teach a curriculum to youth aimed at providing them with the skills necessary to resist peer pressure to experiment with drugs.

Crime prevention newsletter

Palm Beach, Florida (16,000), produces a monthly crime prevention newsletter that informs the business community of crime concerns and trends and provides material and ideas that can help reduce crime in the community. The newsletter is delivered to downtown businesses by the police officers who patrol the district, thus increasing positive contact and communication between the officers and the community.

Source: *The Guide to Management Improvement Projects in Local Government,* vol. 15, no. 3 (Washington, DC: ICMA, 1991), no. PS-19.

Public participation

Several agencies have involved themselves in programs that involve the public directly in police activities. As mentioned earlier, one such method is the use of community volunteers, which not only serves to increase the ability of the agency to perform certain functions, but allows citizens to get a closer look at the workings of the agency. Other examples of public participation programs are the Neighborhood Watch program and resident patrols—residents of an area who form their own patrols and report suspicious activities to the police. Beyond crime reporting, these programs can be used to identify local concerns and develop community-based solutions.

Alternative patrol programs

To increase their effectiveness and foster good community relations, many law enforcement agencies are using new methods of patrol. These are discussed later in this chapter, in the section on innovative methods of service delivery.

Ethics and integrity

Police agencies are under greater public scrutiny than ever before. The nature of police work has always given rise to special problems related to the officer's ability to maintain an acceptable level of integrity. Police work offers multiple temptations for corruption, use of excessive force, alcohol and drug abuse, and misuse of the law. Although the occurrence of any of these behaviors may be minimal in proportion to the total number of those involved in policing, media scrutiny can turn one occurrence into an event that is extremely damaging to the entire department.

A survey of police officials in Florida suggests that they believed that properly designed policies, procedures, and training programs can all positively affect the integrity of an agency and the ethics of the individuals within the agency.[5] Such an approach must include a commitment by the administration; the creation of written policies; a well-developed, multifaceted hiring process; properly chosen and trained field training officers; and a continuous in-service training program.

Employee relations

Police officers have become very sensitive about low pay, long and irregular hours, and less-than-desirable working conditions and equipment. Unions and other bargaining units have become a well-established means of representing the concerns of many officers, and collective bargaining has become important in negotiating a broad spectrum of conflicts between management and employees.

Police officers join unions most frequently because of management failure to deal with their concerns. Administrators must recognize and deal effectively with unions and must learn to deal with employee grievances fairly and impartially. Figure 10–7 provides a list of guidelines developed by the National Advisory Commission on Criminal Justice Standards and Goals for police administrators to use in their efforts to maintain positive relations with employees.

Figure 10–6 The code of ethics of the International Association of Chiefs of Police (IACP).

Law Enforcement Code of Ethics

As a law enforcement officer, my fundamental duty is to serve the community; to safeguard lives and property; to protect the innocent against deception, the weak against oppression or intimidation and the peaceful against violence or disorder; and to respect the constitutional rights of all to liberty, equality and justice. I will keep my private life unsullied as an example to all and will behave in a manner that does not bring discredit to me or to my agency. I will maintain courageous calm in the face of danger, scorn or ridicule; develop self-restraint; and be constantly mindful of the welfare of others. Honest in thought and deed both in my personal and official life, I will be exemplary in obeying the law and the regulations of my department. Whatever I see or hear of a confidential nature or that is confided to me in my official capacity will be kept ever secret unless revelation is necessary in the performance of my duty.

I will never act officiously or permit personal feelings, prejudices, political beliefs, aspirations, animosities or friendships to influence my decisions. With no compromise for crime and with relentless prosecution of criminals, I will enforce the law courteously and appropriately without fear or favor, malice or ill will, never employing unnecessary force or violence and never accepting gratuities.

I recognize the badge of my office as a symbol of public faith, and I accept it as a public trust to be held so long as I am true to the ethics of police service. I will never engage in acts of corruption or bribery, nor will I condone such acts by other police officers. I will cooperate with all legally authorized agencies and their representatives in the pursuit of justice.

I know that I alone am responsible for my own standard of professional performance and will take every reasonable opportunity to enhance and improve my level of knowledge and competence.

I will constantly strive to achieve these objectives and ideals, dedicating myself before God to my chosen profession . . . law enforcement.

THE INTERNATIONAL ASSOCIATION OF CHIEFS OF POLICE

Guidelines of the National Advisory Commission on Criminal Justice Standards and Goals for positive employee relations

1. The administrator should seek reasonable benefits for all police employees.
2. An internal two-way communication network between management and the department should be established.
3. Police employees should be sought for advisory information.
4. A grievance procedure should be available for all employees.
5. Specialists should be available to assist in employee relations programs, training, and negotiations.
6. Recognition of the right of employees to engage in political and other activities.
7. Recognition of the right of employees to join or not join associations and unions.

Source: Adapted from Paul M. Whisenand and Fred Ferguson, *The Managing of Police Organizations*, 3rd ed., 241, by permission of Prentice Hall, Englewood Cliffs, New Jersey.

Diversification programs

An additional employee relations issue rests in the way management approaches diversification. Although women and minorities have engaged in police work for decades, many departments still have not achieved complete diversification. An agency that reflects, at all levels, the makeup of the entire community is much more likely to have support from the community.

The local administrator must be sensitive to the problems of women and minorities in the police agency. In their struggle for acceptance as officers, women have encountered such obstacles as discrimination in promotions, job assignments, seniority practices, physical requirements, and maternity policy. They have also been subjected to sexual harassment. The discrimination against women may be rooted in a basic resistance to social change that has perpetuated old arguments and beliefs about a woman's ability to perform fully as a police officer. Beyond this, a very basic resentment has grown as male officers note the increased competition from women for jobs and promotions. Yet it appears that women have made considerable progress within the police services, as witnessed by the increasing numbers of women entering the field in recent years.

Members of racial and ethnic minority groups have experienced the same kinds of obstacle. Minorities, too, are gradually succeeding in changing rigid notions about their abilities to perform effectively as police officers. However, the issue of minority recruitment remains a source of real concern for local administrators. In their obligation to be more responsive to the community, agencies must actively recruit minority members. Communities must show sensitivity to the concerns of minorities within their boundaries and strive to reflect the ethnic makeup of the entire community.

Stress and burnout

Studies regarding the problems of stress and burnout suggest that psychological strain may take more of a toll on the individual officer than physical strain. This finding is not too surprising considering the sources of stress: conflicting values surrounding the job; a high level of responsibility to the community; boredom resulting from days of routine inactivity alternating with the tension of responding to unpredictable crises; frustrating encounters with the court system; and a negative public image. When pressures become too much to handle, burnout occurs.

The effects of stress and burnout reach into the personal as well as professional life of the police officer, affecting his or her physical, intellectual, emotional, and social well-being.[6] The effects may be manifested in alcohol or drug abuse, using excessive amounts of sick leave, or strained relationships. Among the first symptoms is physical fatigue; other symptoms may be a negative attitude toward the job, cynicism, anger, and frustration.

Management must be sensitive to the human side of stress problems and recognize stress and burnout as not only a threat to productivity, but a threat to the individual officer. Officers experiencing stress or burnout may need professional counseling. To head off stress or burnout, specialized training strategies can be useful and easily incorporated into in-service training.

Career plateauing

Career plateauing occurs when officers have the sense that their professional challenges have been met. It may take the form of content plateauing, which occurs when career goals have been met, or structural plateauing, which occurs when officers reach a point in the organizational hierarchy where there appears to be no potential for promotion.[7] Officers experiencing this condition may lose their motivation for work.

Plateauing is not as psychologically or physically debilitating as stress or burnout. Self-worth and self-esteem can remain high for such officers even though their jobs may leave them bored and frustrated. A training and development program that helps officers to realign their career goals and objectives, creates new challenges, or provides new career opportunities can help to overcome the problems created by plateauing.

Training and development

The concerns discussed above, the highly technical and sensitive nature of police work, and the critical importance of the human factor in police operations require an agency to have a solid training and development program. In the 1980s and early 1990s, many police departments had to reduce their training programs because of budget cuts, but administrators should recognize that, even in times of scarce resources, training is essential.

Although training needs will vary from department to department, in each case the complete process requires a serious commitment from management. A formal training policy should be established; training needs assessed; a budget developed; qualified trainers obtained; training schedules developed; and evaluation standards established.

Training philosophy

Police training programs historically have adopted a classic military training model, relying heavily upon the induction of stress in the process. Trainers intentionally place trainees in stressful situations in an attempt to generate response to pressure. The philosophy behind stress training is that it accurately stimulates what line officers will encounter in their work. However, there has been some movement away from stress training in the last two decades. Studies have shown that stress training can undermine self-esteem, create lower levels of motivation, hinder performance, and make recruits more reluctant to make independent decisions.[8]

Non-stress training programs are designed to provide a training environment that builds higher levels of self-esteem, motivation, performance, and service. Such programs concentrate more on the socialization of the officer in the policing subculture.[9] Beyond the traditional topics (e.g.., firearms training and defensive tactics), officers are provided with human relations and communication skills in order to provide better service to the community. Such training has been shown to provide higher levels of job satisfaction, job proficiency, and community acceptance.

Levels of training

Training normally occurs at several levels within the police department and is recognized as an ongoing part of the officer's job throughout his or her career. The most common training levels include

Recruit training The most common type of training, recruit training typically involves such things as classroom training in police rules and regulations, firearms, defensive tactics, and first aid. Less commonly offered, but growing as a component of recruit training programs, is training centered around communication and human relations skills. Recruit training may dictate and shape the officer's career in policing as it is during this period that officers make their transition into the police subculture, often using their instructors as role models.

Field training Often an extension of recruit training, field training includes intensive, controlled activities that involve the transference of experience-based knowledge from veterans to recruits. Such training can be used to expose recruits to staged domestic fights, burglaries, armed robberies, and so forth, all portrayed in as realistic a setting as possible. Recruits' reactions are analyzed and they are given feedback on how they dealt with the situation.

In-service training This type of training varies from department to department. Effective programs are administered on a formal basis and may be done with regular police assignments. Generally, forty hours per year is the minimum recommended instruction per officer.

Specialized training Training should be offered to relevant personnel in such areas as fingerprinting, polygraph operation, and recordkeeping. The training is often offered in conjunction with federal or state agencies, universities, or police academies.

Supervisory training Less common, but no less important, are training programs for newly appointed supervisors. Such training should stress responsibilities, communication, and leadership skills.

Management training The executive level is not exempt from the need for training. Management training should be designed to keep the manager up to date on general procedures and issues and attuned to the needs of the department.

Personnel development

Although closely related to training, personnel development should be broader in scope, seeking to maximize the potential human resources of a department. Traditionally, personnel development programs have concentrated on developing officers for career advancement. However, a combination of restricted revenues and limited potential for advancement has caused many police agencies to reevaluate the goals of their development programs. Today, many agencies also concentrate on providing innovative ways of giving officers greater opportunity to use their abilities and to meet their needs for personal growth and job satisfaction.

Proficiency Incentive Program
To improve overall effectiveness and productivity in its police department, Bend, Oregon (19,500), instituted the Proficiency Incentive Program (PIP), a three-tiered voluntary program that ties salary premiums to ascending levels of fitness, education, and community service. Participating officers work at one of three levels based upon their Oregon police officer certification level and sign contracts declaring how their annual requirements will be met. The program has encouraged officers to keep more physically fit, to continue their education, and to participate in the community in such nontraditional ways as doing home repairs for elderly residents, coaching youth athletics, delivering meals to invalids, and teaching remedial learning classes.

Source: *The Guide to Management Improvement Projects in Local Government,* vol. 14, no. 1 (Washington, DC: ICMA, 1990), no. PS-1.

Employee involvement

A key element in any development program should be increasing the involvement of police officers in responsibilities for planning and management. The increased involvement of officers in decision making promotes self-esteem and a greater commitment to the success of programs and policies that they have helped plan.

Career advancement

Rather than requiring officers to spend long, frustrating periods waiting on a promotion list or forcing officers to apply for positions they do not want just to get pay raises, many agencies have adopted alternative career advancement structures, such as dual-career-ladder programs. In the dual-ladder system, an officer has the option of developing his or her career horizontally within the same position through advancement in technical grades, with corresponding pay increases. The system provides a means of advancement for officers who have no desire for higher rank or who are frustrated with limited opportunities for promotion.

Assessment centers

A tool with great potential in the area of personnel development is the assessment center. Assessment centers are designed to simulate work situations in various administrative positions. Officers are introduced to a variety of experiences designed to measure decision-making ability, communication skills, and other required skills. The assessment center gives the individual officer a useful educational experience as well as a tool for personal evaluation and goal reassessment. Use of these centers helps the agency to make promotion decisions and match the right job with the right individual.

Innovative methods of service delivery

To cope with changing demands and a tightening revenue base and to improve efficiency and effectiveness, many police agencies are also developing and implementing new policing methods. As a result, innovative programs, techniques, and tools have emerged in agencies across the country. The following are examples of developments resulting from progressive, creative approaches to policing.

Patrol programs

One area receiving a good deal of attention is the method of patrol chosen by an agency. A number of alternative patrol programs were tested and developed in the 1980s.

Location-oriented patrol (LOP) and *perpetrator-oriented patrol* (POP) emphasize criminal apprehension, especially for the crimes of robbery and burglary. LOP involves intensified, low-profile surveillance over selected high-risk geographic areas. POP maintains surveillance over individuals believed likely to commit crimes.

K-9 patrol

Recognizing that small communities have a difficult time funding and sustaining community policing models, Hopewell, Virginia (23,000), established a specialized operational unit consisting of two police officers and a sergeant paired with two standard K-9 dogs and a certified drug dog as the cornerstone of its community oriented policing program. Following a community education program to assure residents that the dogs were not a threat, the K-9 partnership was launched through foot patrols aimed both at developing better rapport with neighborhood residents and reducing drug sales.

The program has had a number of benefits: the dogs attract citizen interest and support, the officers feel more secure on patrol, and the dogs have served as a deterrent to crime. Drug dealers have moved out of targeted neighborhoods, and drug arrests have increased substantially. Most important, the police officers are now more receptive to citizens and to solving neighborhood problems, and citizens see officers as friends.

Source: Ellen S. Posivach, Assistant City Manager, Hopewell, Virginia, 1993.

Directed deterrent patrol (DDP) was developed in an effort to maximize the deterrent effect of the patrol officer. A planning team targets crimes to attack with improved patrol methods, and after analyzing data for trends related to the selected crimes, it develops a methodology to direct patrol units to targeted areas at targeted times.

Under *split-force patrol* (SFP), one part of the patrol force is assigned to answer calls for service, to investigate crime, and to perform other specified duties. Another part of the patrol force is used strictly for preventive patrol. The preventive patrol may be given specific patrol assignments in areas that have been identified as high-crime areas or as having a specific crime problem (e.g., increased burglaries or car thefts). Use of the split-force patrol requires careful planning.

Differential police response (DPR) is a patrol strategy that assigns a level of priority to calls for service. Its successful use requires community education in order for citizens to understand and accept that less urgent situations may have a longer response time.

Bike patrol

To bring the police department closer to the people, police officers in Plymouth, New Hampshire (5,000, plus 4,000 students), patrol on bikes. Five of the town's ten officers routinely bike around heavily traveled pedestrian areas for four-hour shifts during daylight hours. Bike patrols are also scheduled around the university calendar and community events. Bike patrols increase police mobility, facilitate enforcement of parking regulations, and help officers curtail illegal drinking by college students.

Source: *The Guide to Management Improvement Projects in Local Government,* vol. 15, no. 4 (Washington, DC: ICMA, 1991), no. PS-22.

Jail services

Perhaps the police function that will require the greatest innovation in the next decade is that of incarceration. The problems confronting police agencies in the provision of jail services are numerous, especially because 97 percent of jails are now rated as overcrowded and three-quarters of the government agencies running them are under court order to improve conditions.[10] (This section applies primarily to county sheriff's offices; municipal police departments typically have only holding cells and are not responsible for incarceration facilities.)

Alternative housing

Some communities have turned to the use of alternative housing to cope with overcrowded jails, including surplus army tents, converted motels, dormitories, converted ferry boats and troop ships, and double celling. Such alternatives allow communities to avoid court-imposed financial penalties and early release orders as well as the large capital expenditures required to build new or expanded jails.

Electronically monitored house arrest programs

As another alternative to building new jails, many communities have adopted electronic monitoring programs.[11] The programs make use of a small transmitter that is strapped to the offender's ankle. The transmitter transmits a continuous signal to a receiver connected to the offender's telephone. If the offender goes out of the transmitter's broadcast range or attempts to remove the transmitter, the home-based receiver relays a telephone message to the central monitoring station. At the central monitoring station (which may be at the police station, sheriff's office, or another location), a computer is programmed with the offender's schedule for such activities as work, counseling, specific shopping periods, and religious services. If the offender leaves for other than scheduled purposes, a violation is recorded and officials are notified.

Some estimates claim that as many as 70 percent of the people in jails could be managed outside jail through intermediate programs.

The cost of the program ranges from one to eight dollars a day; some communities charge the offender the cost of participation. The program is currently used most often for traffic offenders, primarily those convicted of driving while intoxicated. However, the program has also been used for those convicted of other crimes. In such cases, eligibility for program participation is based on the individual rather than the crime.

Innovations in jail construction

Communities are also using new technologies to reduce the cost and time required to construct new or expand existing jail facilities. Among these new technologies are precast concrete cells, mobile trailers, modular buildings, and preconstructed cellular steel cells.[12]

Intermediate programs

To cope with overcrowding and to avoid the early release of prisoners, police agencies in some communities are beginning to adopt intermediate programs.[13] Using detoxification programs for alcoholics, mental health clinics for mentally ill individuals, and pretrial release programs for impoverished people who cannot afford bail, communities can greatly reduce the number of people in their jails. Some estimates claim that as many as 70 percent of the people in jails could be managed outside jail through intermediate programs.

Proxy services

Many communities are using or exploring the use of a proxy in the provision of jail services. Using a proxy to provide jail services may take one of several forms: paying another community to house prisoners, providing regional jails, or contracting with the private sector for the provision of jail services.

New technologies

New technologies offer police agencies tremendous opportunities to improve productivity and compensate for lost revenues. The cost of technological innovations varies widely; some will be available only to well-funded organizations, others to the even the smallest of departments.[14]

Computer-aided dispatch (CAD) systems provide dispatchers with continuous information concerning the status and location of patrol vehicles as well as information on addresses, officer assignments, and location characteristics. Updated systems can also provide information on previous calls, warrants, arrest histories, and gun licenses.

Although original 911 systems provided users with an easy-to-remember number to call in emergencies, certain groups of individuals (e.g., elderly callers, children, visitors to the area, and threatened people) were found to have trouble supplying address information to the dispatcher. When a connection is made through an *E-911 system,* the caller's telephone sends out a tone pulse representing the seven-digit number of the telephone. The tone pulse is sent to the telephone company's database, and an address verification is given to the dispatcher.

Mobile teleprinters are being used increasingly to supplement voice communications to vehicles. Receiving printed communications in the vehicle provides more information, particularly when heavy police radio traffic limits communication. Printed communications also tend to be more reliable, are available to the officer for easy reference, and may be sent while the vehicle is unattended.

Designed to assist the dispatcher and speed up response time, the *automatic vehicle monitoring system* (AVM) provides the dispatcher with immediate information regarding the availability of patrol vehicles within a particular location.

The *mobile data terminal* (MDT) can transmit and receive data directly in the mobile unit, allowing the officer to access state and national computers for warrants and check on driver's licenses or license plates directly and more quickly, bypassing the dispatcher and clearing the air for other purposes.

If equipped with a modem, *laptop computers* can perform the same functions as the MDT, are less expensive, and also allow the officer to fill out reports in the field and transmit them later to the mainframe computer.

Police officers can use *cellular phones* to contact victims or witnesses for information while on route to answer a call, typically decreasing the time required to respond efficiently and clearing radio air for other purposes.

Hand-held computers allow an officer to enter his or her report directly into a computer from the field. For example, an officer investigating an accident would enter all the required information into the computer as it is gathered. The hand-held computer then feeds the information back to a mainframe computer through a satellite feed attached to the officer's vehicle.

Using *digital dictation equipment,* officers dictate reports by telephone rather than write them out. Typically, an officer returns to the station to fill out crime reports for each investigation. By using a push-button phone, the officer can phone in the report to a computer; later, a transcriber accesses the computer report and types it into the system.

Surveillance cameras may be mounted on vehicles to record the activities of officers, offenders, and witnesses. When accompanied by a field mike, the camera creates a record of both the activities and statements of those involved for future court use.

Surveillance cameras

By using electronic recording devices, the police department in Hazelwood, Missouri (15,000), is protecting itself from arrest-related lawsuits. The city realized that the majority of complaints filed against police personnel centered around the booking process and usually came down to the complainant's word against the officer's.

The department bought $20,000 worth of video equipment to provide surveillance of the police department parking lot, prisoner unloading zone, cell area, booking area, and passageways used to move prisoners from one area to another. The cameras record processing of prisoners until they are placed in the cell area or released. Only the chief of police and administrative staff who have the chief's permission view the tapes, which are generally kept on file for two weeks.

Source: *The Guide to Management Improvement Projects in Local Government,* vol. 14, no. 1 (Washington, DC: ICMA, 1990), no. PS-4.

Through an *automated fingerprint identification system,* fingerprints are entered into a computer and matched with prints already logged in the database. What once took a long time manually examining fingerprint books may now take only minutes. Although it is still in the developmental stage, communities such as Pierce County in Washington have successfully gotten a match on 17 percent to 20 percent of their attempts.

In *DNA print analysis,* a physical sample from an accused person is taken and compared with a physical sample taken from the crime scene. If the genetic makeup of the DNA sample from each is identical, identification is almost 100 percent accurate. This type of analysis has been found to be more accurate than fingerprinting.

Using a *computerized sketching program,* a witness answers a number of questions posed on a computer screen. When the interview is finished, the computer generates a sketch of the suspect, which can then be modified according to the witness's instructions.

Operation Stop and Check

To prevent car theft, the Lower Burrell, New Jersey (12,250), police department implemented Operation Stop and Check. More than one hundred participating residents receive two stickers to place on the rear bumper and rear driver's side window of their car. Participants sign a release form and provide information on authorized drivers and the hours the car will most likely be driven. Police officers may stop any vehicle with the stickers without cause between the hours of midnight and 5:00 A.M. Officers verify the driver's identity by accessing data stored on a palm-held computer. If the driver is not authorized on the release form, he or she will be detained until the car owner is notified. The program has effectively stopped the theft of cars with the stickers.

Source: *The Guide to Management Improvement Projects in Local Government,* vol. 16, no. 2 (Washington, DC: ICMA, 1992), no. PS-15.

Afterword

Today's police administrator has a much broader role to play than his or her predecessor. Whereas the police chief or sheriff of the past may have been essentially a coordinator of police services, today he or she plays multiple roles. Tight budgets, rising crime rates, changing service demands, political pressures, increasing citizen awareness and involvement, media scrutiny, and the growing threat of burnout are among the concerns that are forcing administrators to adopt a multifaceted approach to management, as are other factors related to modern crime prevention: the importance of community education and community participation in crime prevention activities; the diverse sociological tactics that are a part of the community policing model; the rapidly changing technology involved in law enforcement work; and threats posed to police integrity by changing social mores. All these considerations require a modern police administrator to be broadly educated, professionally astute, and up to date in order to achieve optimal effectiveness.

In order to be efficient, effective, and responsive within this environment, today's police administrator must become involved in such activities as program evaluation and development, planning, policymaking, and staff development. The administrator must replace his or her traditional police management techniques with communication and negotiating skills and must adopt an entrepreneurial attitude toward developing new methodologies in service delivery. Moreover, the police chief or sheriff must reconsider the very structure of the agency and its roles.

Today more than ever before, the sheriff or police chief must be an expert in applied social science as well as in law enforcement methods to be fully effective in protecting the public. ■

---

1 Joe Morris, "A Municipal Hot Potato," *American City and County* (February 1990): 28.

2 Robert L. Sobba, "Public Service Consolidation: The Answer to Your Community's Needs," *FBI Law Enforcement Bulletin* (February 1991): 6-10.

3 National Institute of Law Enforcement and Criminal Justice, *Central Police Dispatch* (Washington, DC: U.S. Department of Justice, 1975).

4 William Geller, ed., *Local Government Police Management,* 3d ed. (Washington, DC: ICMA, 1991).

5 Susan Braunstein, "Building a More Ethical Police Department," *The Police Chief* (January 1992): 30-34.

6 James M. Childers, "Plateauing in Law Enforcement," *FBI Law Enforcement Bulletin* (June 1991): 16-18.

7 Ibid.

8 Gary M. Post, "Police Recruits: Training Tomorrow's Workforce," *FBI Law Enforcement Bulletin* (March 1992): 19-23.

9 Ibid.

10 Donald Nader, "New Jail Options Offer More Flexibility," *American City and County* (March 1989): 44-46.

11 Fred Scaglione, "Jails Without Walls," *American City and County* (January 1989): 32-40.

12 See Nader, "New Jail Options," for an extended discussion of each of these methods of construction.

13 Barbara Quinn, "Jail Overcrowding: A Systems Problem," *American City and County* (June 1988): 76-85.

14 See Jennifer Carlile, "High Tech Alternatives for Public Safety," *American City and County* (June 1989): 42-56, and Lois Pilant, "Modernizing Your Communications Unit," *The Police Chief* (June 1992): 39-52, for discussions on several of the technical developments and innovations discussed in this section.

11 Fire and Emergency Medical Services

In the popular imagination, fearless firefighters slide down station poles, race to fires, chop down doors, and dash into burning buildings to save lives. While heroic actions do take place in the best tradition of firefighting, those responsible for fire protection have become more concerned over the years with the technical and administrative aspects of fire and other emergency services. Fire prevention, safe evacuation of burning buildings, quick fire extinction, and good coordination with emergency medical facilities are preferable to dramatic heroics.

Good fire departments work as hard to prevent fires as to extinguish them. Fire problems occur because many useful substances are combustible, flammable, or explosive. Often the most dangerous substances, such as gas, are among the most useful. When such substances are placed in proximity to heat, flames, or controlled explosions (such as those in a home furnace) unintended fires may result, harming people and property.

Fire departments were originally created to suppress fires, but the tasks assigned to them have grown over time because of their success in reducing and coping with fire dangers, their traditional role in ensuring public safety, and tight budgets. As fire prevention efforts succeeded, fire department personnel applied themselves to new problems to keep fire departments from shrinking.

Many fire departments now also provide hazardous materials protection, rescue services, and emergency medical services (EMS). Involvement with hazardous materials evolved from concern about properties they may have when they burn (e.g., burning plastics emit poisonous fumes) or concern about the potential for fires at locations where highly flammable, explosive, or poisonous materials are stored. Because of fire departments' ability to provide equipment and personnel and their life-saving tradition, rescue work came naturally to them. From rescuing people in burning buildings, fire personnel came to rescue people trapped in other dangerous conditions. Emergency medical services extend the life-saving tradition. From giving first-aid at fire scenes, fire department personnel extended their medical services to other situations, particularly vehicle accidents and cardiac failures. These additional services are discussed in this chapter because they are usually assigned to fire departments.

Fire prevention

Fire prevention includes all measures that lessen the possibility and severity of fires by reducing fire hazards, making buildings fire resistant, and facilitating the quick and safe evacuation of people from burning structures. Community governments prevent harm from fires by developing and enforcing codes, inspecting buildings, and educating the public.

Attention to fire prevention developed slowly despite the early example of Norfolk, Virginia, where wooden chimneys were banned in 1730. Although some departments always inspected buildings, as in New York City, others were slow to add prevention activities. For example, Norfolk, which organized a volunteer fire company in 1731, did not create a fire prevention bureau until 1920.

Although specialized fire prevention units are sometimes created within fire departments, all fire department personnel take responsibility for prevention. A large part of the work requires coordination with planning, building, zoning, code enforcement, health, police, and other departments; with operators of schools, hospitals, factories, and commercial buildings; and with the general public.

Fire prevention codes

Most communities of five thousand or more residents have a fire prevention code, often adapted from one of the model codes. The National Fire Protection Association (NFPA) model code is well known. National codes are based on a wide range of experience and provide authoritative interpretation and explanation of standards for building construction, electrical wiring, and heat sources; hazardous materials and processes; and public assemblies, fire exits, and fire protection and suppression equipment.

Costs of fire and fire protection

Fire suppression: direct to government

Dollar expenses for firefighters, including direct salary and fringe benefits (purchase of group health insurance, life insurance, FICA, and pensions)

Debt service payments on fire vehicles, communication equipment, and firehouse construction

Annual operation and maintenance expenditures on vehicles, firehouses, and communication equipment, including heat, electricity, gasoline, and labor

Replacement of firefighting tools and equipment, including hoses, axes, and so forth

Maintenance of fire clothing and uniforms

Expenditures for construction, operation, and maintenance of the water supply allocated to fire protection

Salaries and materials used in the fire services for housekeeping functions such as accounting, purchasing, payroll preparation, and planning, or salaries for people in other agencies who perform those functions for the fire protection service

Expenses for police services at fires, ambulance services, hospital emergency room charges, and so forth

Demolition of buildings destroyed by fire.

Fire prevention: direct to government

Salaries and indirect expenses for building inspectors, tank truck inspectors, and so forth (regardless of which agency pays them), vehicles, and other operating expenses

Arson investigation expenses (may include percentage of state fire marshal's services, also police expenses for arrests, county attorneys, judges, prisons, and parole)

Community and public relations expenses

Housekeeping functions described above.

Costs borne directly by citizens (excluding taxes that are included above)

Losses due to fire (uninsured property losses from fire, smoke, or water damage)

Insurance payments

Relocation expenses

Salaries for days lost through injuries and medical costs

Fire prevention costs including code compliance, smoke detector installation and maintenance, standpipe and siamese fixtures, hoses, and extinguishers

Payments to private fire alarm companies.

Nonmonetary losses borne by everyone

Pain, suffering, loss of functions as a result of being injured in fire

Deaths.

Building codes

Because communities enact fire prevention provisions as part of a community building code, fire departments need to coordinate development and revision efforts with the community government department primarily responsible for building code enforcement. Building codes concerning new construction materials and methods require constant monitoring. Particularly important are those provisions dealing with electrical wiring, heat sources, and fire-resistant construction features. Some states prevent communities from enacting their own codes by mandating a state building code.

"Fix-It Tickets"

To remedy code and ordinance violations, code enforcement officers in Provo, Utah (87,000), write "Fix-It Tickets." On the ticket, violators are given a specific deadline for correcting the violation; if the violation is not corrected within that time, the case is referred to the courts. The program has substantially reduced the number of code violations going to court.

Source: *The Guide to Management Improvement Projects in Local Government,* vol. 17, no. 2 (Washington, DC: ICMA, 1993), no. LD-14.

Hazardous materials and processes

Smoke detectors are the simplest, most cost-effective, and most important life-saving fire safety device.

Fire prevention codes also cover hazardous materials. In addition to the obvious hazards associated with explosive and flammable materials, many other materials pose great fire dangers (e.g., grain elevator dust). Hazardous materials that are not a fire risk range from the obvious to the obscure: for example, acids, biocides, radioactive wastes, and heavy metals.

Codes regulate hazardous materials and processes, prohibiting some of them and establishing license, permit, and inspection procedures for others. Requiring the registration of hazardous materials, restricting their use, and acquiring and disseminating information on how to deal with their potential dangers are the first steps in protecting the public from them.

Other provisions

Other code provisions deal with exits, public assemblies, and on-site detection and suppression equipment. Fire exit provisions require that it be relatively easy to escape from burning buildings. Public assembly provisions aim at ensuring that large groups of people can be safely evacuated in the event of fire. On-site fire detection and suppression equipment can be required; more elaborate arrangements are required where there are more people or greater fire hazards.

Codes often require smoke detectors and automatic on-site sprinkler systems in buildings used for particular purposes (e.g., theaters, schools, and hospitals). Smoke detectors are the simplest, most cost-effective, and most important life-saving fire safety device. They save lives, whereas on-site sprinkler systems reduce fire losses to property. Other, more sophisticated, detectors can signal fire suppression units. Fire extinguishers and hoses may also be required.

Code enforcement

Effective fire prevention depends on code enforcement, which requires effort by the fire department and cooperation from other departments.

Fire departments therefore need to keep other departments apprised of fire prevention code provisions and enforcement problems. Personnel from any department can spot fire and hazardous material code violations, and they should be trained to do so. Departments with responsibility for enforcing other codes should aggressively support fire code enforcement. They enhance fire safety when they require fire code compliance before issuing building and zoning permits or health department and liquor licenses. They should issue citations for code violations and inform the fire department of them.

When a code violation is discovered, usually through an inspection, an order to correct the violation is issued to the building owner or occupant. For a first violation, a warning is usually given. After a suitable period for correcting the violation, another inspection is conducted; failure to correct the violation incurs some penalty. Penalties may include fines, denial of the right to use the affected structure, and possibly a jail sentence.

Some inspectors enforce codes reluctantly because they want to maintain the good will of building managers, who may resist complying with directives. Administrators can help by reviewing the enforcement process with inspectors, reinforcing its importance. Sometimes reviews can lead to simplified procedures and better management support as well as more vigorous enforcement.

Departments use fire inspections principally to enforce codes, but they can use them to serve other purposes as well. Inspections bring the subject of fire prevention to the attention of building managers and occupants, especially when inspectors inform building managers of the practical value of fire safety measures such as fire drills and smoke detectors. Inspections also provide an opportunity for communicating important information; for example, during inspections, building managers, including homeowners, can be given checklists of hazards. In addition, inspections conducted by fire suppression personnel serve the important purpose of familiarizing fire personnel with building layouts and construction characteristics.

Public education

Fire prevention education teaches the public how to guard against fire hazards and react appropriately if a fire occurs. The "Learn Not to Burn" curriculum of the National Fire Protection Association, which teaches twenty-six fire safety behaviors, has been particularly effective (see accompanying sidebar).

Fire prevention efforts, especially those associated with smoke detectors, have been an unsung success story. Successful efforts reduce the need for fire suppression and allow departments to attend to other responsibilities. Although the fact may not always be remembered, *the less urgent activity of fire prevention is ultimately more effective than the most urgent fire suppression activity.*

Preventive measures and public education programs can also be used in emergency medicine, hazardous materials, and rescue services. Training, such as in first aid and CPR, offers the most promise in the medical area. Enacting and vigorously enforcing codes are the most beneficial preventive efforts in dealing with hazardous materials and processes. Education probably reduces water and wilderness rescues most effectively, whereas rock climbing and motor vehicle accident rescues may be minimized most effectively through rigorous law enforcement.

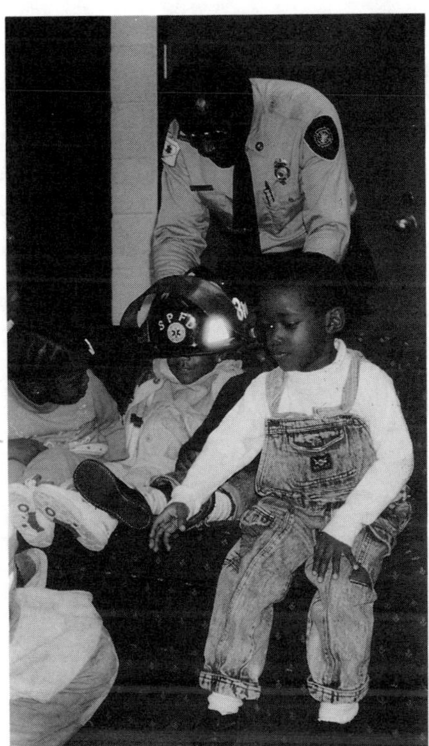

Figure 11–1 The Southern Pines, North Carolina, fire department includes these young children in its efforts to educate the public on fire safety.

Learn Not to Burn Programs

The National Fire Protection Association (NFPA) started its Learn Not to Burn programs in 1973 as the result of a national survey to determine how to reach the public most effectively with fire safety information. This survey of schoolchildren as well as adults in residential, commercial, and professional settings showed that all respondents had an instinctive awareness of fire as a powerful and potentially dangerous force. In many cases, strong underlying fear and concern were expressed. Nevertheless, many people were not prepared to deal with fire.

This lack of action in spite of a strong negative emotional response appeared to be caused by respondents' feeling that they were unable to deal with complex systems or technology and by their dislike of dealing with threatening information. The investigation found that education programs based on fear of fire have little educational benefit and may have a negative influence. This observation led the NFPA to focus its approach on the positive presentation of fire safety behaviors—telling people what they should do rather than what they should not do. Public service announcements were aired to make people aware of life-saving behaviors such as "Stop, Drop and Roll" if your clothes catch fire and "Crawl Low Under Smoke" if you must escape through smoke.

The success of the media campaign led to the development of a comprehensive fire safety curriculum to be used in kindergarten through Grade 8. Since 1975, NFPA has maintained a database of life-saving incident reports called "saves"—case histories of actual fire or burn incidents in which knowledge gained from the media campaign or the curriculum has directly contributed to saving a life or preventing more serious injury. "Save" anecdotes have grown to a total of 103 incidents involving 259 individuals.

Adapted from material from the "Learn Not to Burn" program, National Fire Protection Association, One Batterymarch Park, Quincey, Massachusetts 02296-9101.

Fire suppression and emergency response

Fire departments must always be ready to respond to emergencies: a quick response can make the difference between a routine success and a major catastrophe. Preparation for emergency calls requires the following elements: information, performance evaluation, personnel, training, equipment, and regular reviews of readiness. Although the emphasis in this section is on fire suppression calls, the following comments apply generally to calls for other types of service as well.

Information

Emergency response requires information about predictable problems, response techniques, and station locations. Relevant information should be observed, recorded, and analyzed systematically.

Problems

Each jurisdiction has specific problems; the information most obviously needed deals with the kinds of problem that might be encountered (e.g., the kinds of fire that occur, the most significant fire hazards, and the kinds of hazardous materials present in the community). The precise mix of problems in a community plays a part in determining the location of stations, the choice of equipment, and personnel decisions, especially those concerning staffing levels and the content of and schedules for staff training. The staffing level—the number of staff on duty—is especially critical for fire suppression because differences in staffing levels affect the extent to which fires can be extinguished by initial response teams.

Figure 11–2 Public safety agencies can work together to educate the public. McGruff the Crime Dog and Sparky the Fire Dog shake hands during their appearance at a community festival.

Response techniques

Specific knowledge needed for emergency response includes techniques of fire suppression, methods for handling the specific hazardous materials in the community, rescue procedures for likely situations, and appropriate initial treatment in medical emergencies. Efforts to enhance human safety involve putting fires out and reducing the impact of fires upon building occupants by ventilating buildings to lessen fumes; opening, keeping open, and cooling building exits; and searching for building occupants. The accompanying sidebar, a list of fire suppression activities at a working fire (a fire that is growing and threatening lives and property), shows information needed to plan for techniques, equipment, and personnel.

Fire suppression activities at a working fire.
(The order in which these activities are undertaken may vary depending on the circumstances.)

1. Advance initial attack lines to the most critical positions to confine the fire or protect exits being used by fleeing occupants.
2. Raise ladders for rescue, attack, and ventilation crews.
3. Rescue occupants unable to escape on their own.
4. Advance backup attack lines and lay lines to supply sprinkler and standpipe systems and heavy-stream appliances.
5. Operate pumping apparatus to supply water to the initial attack lines, to sprinkler systems, to later advanced backup lines, and to heavy-stream appliances.
6. Provide forcible entry to the fire building and to immediately threatened buildings in order to accomplish initial ventilation, to enable the initial attack and rescue operations to proceed, and to open ceilings, floors, and walls to search for hidden fire.
7. Handle first aid for injured rescuees and firefighters; perform salvage operations to prevent needless water and smoke damage; and provide emergency lighting service.

Station locations

Locating fire stations is important in fire service planning. The Fire Station Location Package by Public Technology, Inc. is a well-regarded tool. It uses information on response time rather than distances to compare fire station location alternatives. Unfortunately, there are tradeoffs between optimizing response time and minimizing costs. Each jurisdiction has to decide what response time is the best it can afford.

Performance evaluation

Reviews of departmental performance are also essential for planning the activities involved in fire suppression. Systematic review of fire department performance using the kinds of information listed in the accompanying sidebar can be very useful.

Departments should regularly and systematically record and review their work by organizing data to provide insights into fire-related problems, departmental performance, and prevention. Certain relationships may be apparent, such as location and response time, whereas others require further analysis (e.g., why one area has a high rate of fires).

Information needed for performance review

Type of service (fire, rescue, hazardous material, or medical)

Location

Time of day

Response (equipment and personnel)

Response time

Cause of emergency

Losses: personal injuries, death, and property

Causes of losses

Special problems or circumstances.

The information obtained through the evaluation process is useful primarily for decision making. The patterns and relationships observed generally provide more useful information than single cases or totals. Unique events, such as a single large arson fire, distort statistics. Fire department activities should be organized primarily to respond to common problems.

In addition to using information on departmental performance to prepare for fire suppression, departments use it to plan their fire prevention strategies. Current information on fire inspections and fire occurrences can lead to changes in inspection patterns, code provisions, and code enforcement.

Personnel

Emergency services are predominately an exercise in sending people to deal with emergencies. The basic concern sounds simple—a sufficient number of competent people must be available—but the number of people who must be available at any given time is difficult to determine and the total number needed to sustain this level of staffing is easily underestimated. The twenty-four-hour-a-day work schedule requires at least four full-time people to staff each position. To always have one driver available requires that one person be available 168 hours each week, which breaks down to four people working 42 hours every week or three people working 56 hours a week. (Most communities now have a work week that averages 53 hours; the 1985 Amendments to the Fair Labor Standards Act require that firefighters be paid overtime for hours worked in excess of an average of 53 a week, i.e., for more than a maximum of 212 hours in a twenty-eight-day work period.)

The 1985 Amendments to the Fair Labor Standards Act require that firefighters be paid overtime for hours worked in excess of an average of 53 a week.

An additional person must be available for duty when a regularly assigned person is sick, on vacation, or involved in off-site training programs. Each vehicle takes two or more people to operate properly; administration and other assignments take personnel time. Furthermore, the use of part-time or volunteer personnel increases the number of people who must be trained and available to staff each position.

Personnel work

Having people available means that considerable time must be spent recruiting, testing, selecting, and providing appropriate incentives. In addition to the physical and mental abilities and interests on which potential personnel are evaluated, fire and emergency staff must develop through training competencies in technical knowledge and skill development. Training takes time as well as planning and management effort.

Employee types

Departments chose one or more of three types of employee: full-time paid employees, part-time paid employees (auxiliaries), and volunteers. These three types differ in availability and scheduling, pay and benefits, levels of qualification and training, and difficulties for managers.

Full-time paid personnel are easiest to schedule, but most costly. Scheduling is more difficult when more people are involved and when they are not paid to be available. Auxiliaries are used to supplement both full-time and volunteer personnel, especially for firefighting. Volunteers and auxiliaries present greater challenges to managers because there are more of them and they have other concerns that need to be taken into account. The major advantage of volunteers lies in their low cost. Many communities use combinations of full-time, auxiliary, and volunteer personnel.

Being a volunteer for the Urbandale Fire Department offers one reward few other jobs can match.
Few jobs offer you the opportunity to save a life. But as a volunteer firefighter and emergency medical technician (EMT), you could be called upon to do it at a moment's notice.
The men and women of the Urbandale Fire Department are dedicated to protecting the lives and property of the citizens of Urbandale and surrounding communities.
If you have the desire to be part of this important and challenging job, come down to the fire station and talk to any firefighter or EMT. No experience is necessary; just an interest and willingness to learn. And for your efforts, you may receive the best reward any job can give.
Urbandale Fire Department
278–3924

Figure 11–3 Recruitment poster for the Urbandale, Iowa, fire department.

Three kinds of personnel

Full-time: These are professionals who devote their careers to the fire service. Typically, they work a forty- to fifty-six-hour work week, devoting time to training, fire prevention, and equipment maintenance as well as fire suppression duties and other emergency response duties.

Volunteers: These are part-time personnel primarily used on an on-call basis. Fire service work, most commonly firefighting, is viewed as a community service activity. Typically, volunteers are either not paid or are paid a nominal sum on a per-call or per-year basis.

Auxiliaries: These are part-time fire service employees who serve and are paid on a part-time basis. Auxiliaries frequently are employed full-time by other departments of the community government and leave those duties when called to respond to emergency calls.

Incentives

The incentives of public service, public recognition, excitement, and camaraderie attract many people to the fire service. Pay and other benefits are also attractive. Pay for volunteers and auxiliaries may be on a per-month, per-call, time-at-fires, on-call, or training-time basis. Auxiliaries and volunteers may also receive life, health, and dental insurance benefits and participate in pension plans.

Qualifications

Required qualifications and level of training go up from volunteers to auxiliaries to full-time personnel. Although minimum levels must be met for certification, it is easier to require paid personnel to meet particular standards and engage in training.

Availability of volunteers

Experts suggest that it takes three volunteer firefighters on the departmental roster to ensure that one volunteer firefighter will respond to any given alarm. Thus, to be assured of ten respondents to any alarm, a department needs thirty active volunteers. This ratio can be reduced by arrangements that ensure volunteer availability. For example, some fire departments require their volunteer firefighters to take mandatory duty hours in the fire station.

Training

Emergency calls require rapid, effective responses. Time wasted in getting organized and deciding upon a course of action when immediate action is required worsens the problem. Responses should be instinctive, honed through comprehensive, intensive, time-consuming, continuous, and frequently expensive training programs.

Emergency training involves acquisition of knowledge and skill development through drills. Basic knowledge provides the foundation; drills develop the instinctive responses required. Drills with equipment, actual structures, and live fires are indispensable. Some training may include observation of actual emergency responses.

Subjects covered in a fire-suppression training program include orientation, communication, street and hydrant location, emergency vehicle riding and driving, fire preplanning (visiting a site to determine how best to fight a possible fire at that site—for example, where to position trucks, hoses, and ladders), rescue procedures, equipment, tools, first aid, overhauling (making sure no fire remains), and salvage. Drills include vehicle runs; ladder placement; building ventilation; rescues; hookup, line laying, and water application; foam application; and fire preplanning.

Equipment

Firefighting equipment has been improved greatly since the days when colonists shouted "Fire!," gathered on foot, formed lines, and passed leather buckets of water hand to hand from a well to a blazing building. Shouts and leather buckets have been replaced by alarm and communication systems, water distribution systems, fire apparatus and other equipment, and maps showing property locations and access routes. Equipment in fire suppression and other emergency service areas continues to evolve. Some equipment serves more than one service area.

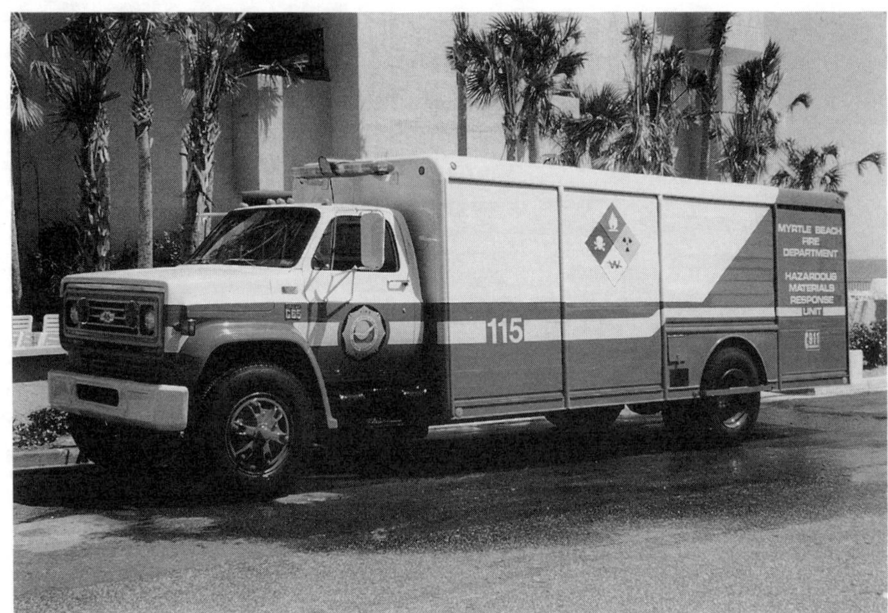

Figure 11–4 A do-it-yourself haz-mat truck created by the members of the haz-mat team in Myrtle Beach, South Carolina. The cost of the used truck and renovations made to comply with Title III regulations was approximately $14,000; a similarly equipped new truck would have cost between $50,000 and $70,000.

Communications

Communication systems link alarms, dispatch centers, vehicles, and onsite equipment. Alarm systems range from human detection of emergencies and ordinary communication channels to automatic systems that detect fire conditions and sound alarms. Dispatch centers receive alarms, dispatch vehicles, and maintain contact with emergency sites. Permanent locations can use dedicated telephone lines, but communications between a dispatch center and vehicles are conducted on dedicated radio frequencies. Firefighters use communication equipment at fire scenes to maintain contact among themselves and with the dispatch center, as well as to operate equipment by remote control.

Water

Water distribution systems supply the basic extinguishing agent for most fires. Water distribution lines and hydrants spare firefighters from having to find a source of water before they can fight fires effectively. In most communities, one of the chief goals of water delivery services is to provide an adequate volume for fire emergencies.

Portable pneumatic rescue pack

Because existing equipment was often ineffective in extricating accident victims from wrecked automobiles, the Cocoa Beach, Florida (14,300), fire department developed its own portable pneumatic rescue pack. The self-contained, dual cylinder, air-powered cutting tool is mounted on a backpack. A leather nail apron is attached and holds chisels, sockets, and air guns. Two firefighters assembled the pack for under $90. Use of the pack speeds rescue time because all necessary equipment is within easy reach, eliminating trips back and forth to the rescue vehicle.

Source: *The Guide to Management Improvement Projects in Local Government,* vol. 16, no. 3 (Washington, DC: ICMA, 1992), no. LHS-22.

Fire apparatus

Alarm systems, communication systems, and water supply systems are stationary; all other equipment is found on response vehicles. Fire apparatus refers to combinations of equipment and motor vehicles carrying the equipment. Fire apparatus vehicles vary widely. The basic unit, found in various sizes, is a "triple combination" pumper with a pump, hoses and nozzles, and a tank carrying water or another extinguishing agent. Increasing in popularity are "quints," which also carry ground ladders and an aerial device. Aerial devices include ladders, platforms, ladders with platforms, and aerial nozzles. Additional equipment includes specialized hand tools (axes), specialty equipment (for rescue, ventilation, and salvage), and personal safety equipment (protective clothing and breathing apparatus).

This description lists the basics but does not cover all possible variations in equipment specifications or combinations or more specialized equipment. Some jurisdictions use water-tank or single-pumper vehicles that pump water from a water supply to a triple combination pumper. Minipumper and crash-fire rescue units are common specialty units. Minipumpers are small versions of the triple combination pumper and

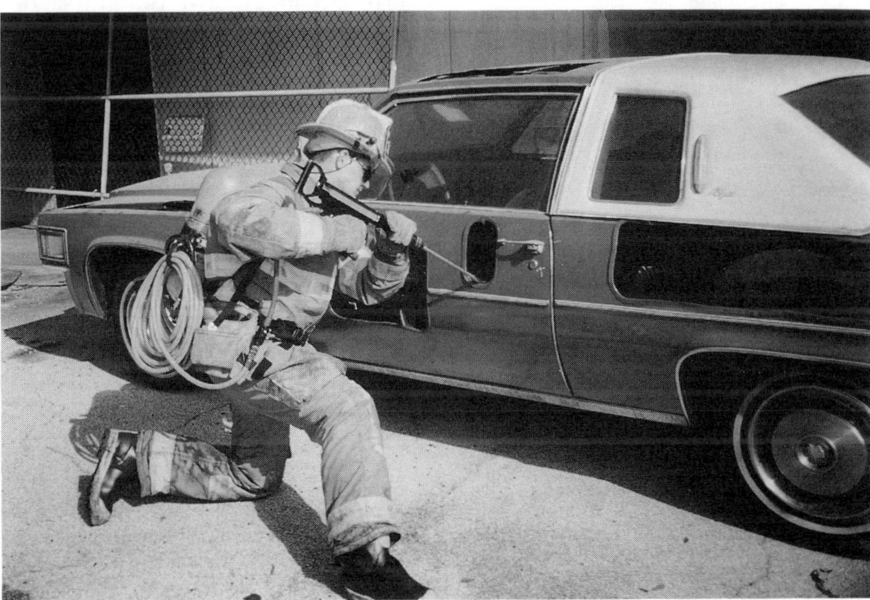

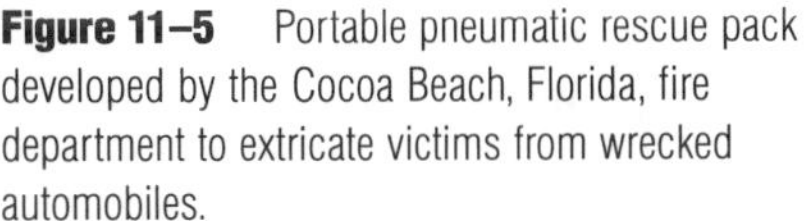
Figure 11–5 Portable pneumatic rescue pack developed by the Cocoa Beach, Florida, fire department to extricate victims from wrecked automobiles.

are sometimes used for first responses to brush, grass, trash, and car fires. Crash-fire rescue units at airports carry foam to prevent or extinguish aviation-fuel fires.

Double-duty fire truck

The fire and rescue department of Fairfax, Virginia (20,000), can arrive at the scene of an accident with all the equipment it needs in a unique fire truck that offers the functions of both a traditional fire engine and a rescue squad vehicle. The truck carries a fire pump capable of pumping 1,250 gallons a minute, 1,600 feet of supply hose, 1,000 feet of fire attack line, 500 gallons of water, nozzles, adapters, and self-contained breathing apparatus as well as a complete complement of tools and equipment found on a full-service rescue squad vehicle, such as medical supplies, the Hurst "jaws of life," and hydraulic equipment.

Source: *The Guide to Management Improvement Projects in Local Government,* vol. 16, no. 4 (Washington, DC: ICMA, 1992), no. PS-28.

Departments' equipment needs vary depending on service problems and organizational and personnel arrangements. For instance, some volunteer companies use minipumpers as a first-response unit because they can be operated by two people and therefore allow quicker initial responses. On the other hand, minipumpers are not always adequate in completely extinguishing structural fires and therefore should not be the sole response vehicle.

Maps

Good maps, showing property locations and access by roads, are indispensable. It is hard for fire personnel to do much good if they cannot locate the emergency.

Readiness reviews

Fire departments maintain the highest possible level of readiness through regular reviews that include a variety of efforts to ensure appropriate preparation. These include reviews of community problems and the adequacy of fire department performance. Regular reviews are preferable, so that the emergency problems of the jurisdiction as a whole can be seen in perspective.

The emphasis in managerial reviews of readiness is always upon potential changes. Fire problems change as new buildings are constructed, uses of buildings change, and new fire hazards develop. Fire departments must adapt to such changes. For instance, a newly developed subdivision may require another fire station, a redistribution of equipment, and more personnel; high-rise buildings may require aerial equipment. Managers can track such changes by regularly reviewing the records of the planning department, as well as by observing events in the community.

Line personnel test and maintain departmental equipment and carry out review activities under the supervision of managers. Tests and inspections should always be made when major items are delivered. Readiness review also covers employees, including their physical fitness and knowledge of procedures.

Emergency medical services (EMS)

If fire departments were named for the type of service call they most often receive, many would be called emergency medical services departments. EMS typically has several different and overlapping aspects: recognition of medical emergencies; response, dispatch, and communication; personnel; medical care; and transportation of personnel and patients. Collectively, they are called prehospital services; the expectation is that EMS care will result in hospitalization.

Recognition of medical emergencies

With doctors' house calls relegated to history, laypersons now diagnose medical emergencies. EMS is facilitated when the public is educated to recognize and cope with medical emergencies. Dissemination of information about the signs of heart attack and stroke, and training in first aid and CPR, exemplify such efforts.

Response, dispatch, and communication

Response and dispatch, often through 911 systems, involve screening calls to verify that an emergency exists prior to dispatch and may include provision of medical advice prior to the arrival of medically trained personnel. Dispatchers can prevent harmful procedures and give detailed directions that may save lives. Also, where choices are available in service responses, dispatchers decide the response level required.

Communication systems vary. The minimum is a fixed dispatch site that can respond to telephone calls, dispatch staffed vehicles, and communicate with vehicles. Additional links include those with hospitals and specialized personnel.

Pre-arrival medical instructions

Sarasota, Florida (52,000), speeded up the response time for medical emergencies by giving its emergency telecommunicators a forty-hour training course enabling them to provide "pre-arrival" medical instructions to callers. Telecommunicators have been taught the techniques used to relieve victims suffering from various conditions and are given flip cards that contain all of the pertinent information that should be explained to callers. The system can be applied to a number of different medical emergencies, including trauma, bleeding, cardiac arrest, unconsciousness, seizures, childbirth, and obstructed airways. Telecommunicators assist about twenty callers each month with such information.

Source: *The Guide to Management Improvement Projects in Local Government,* vol. 15, no. 2 (Washington, DC: ICMA, 1993), no. LHS-17.

Personnel

Personnel matters especially relevant to EMS include training, staffing levels, and work assignments.

Training

The three general levels of medical training for public safety personnel are first aid or first responder, basic life support, and advanced life support. The number of personnel trained at each level determines the amount of medical response available at each level. First aid training is typically required of all public safety personnel.

Basic life-support training qualifies a person as an emergency medical technician-ambulance (EMT-A). This is the minimum level of training required of personnel who provide EMS; the training requires a minimum of 81 hours and usually exceeds 100 hours. The training focuses on maintaining breathing, administering CPR, and treating trauma.

Advanced life-support training qualifies a person as an emergency medical technician-paramedic (EMT-P), often called just paramedic. This qualification requires 800 hours of training, which covers many more

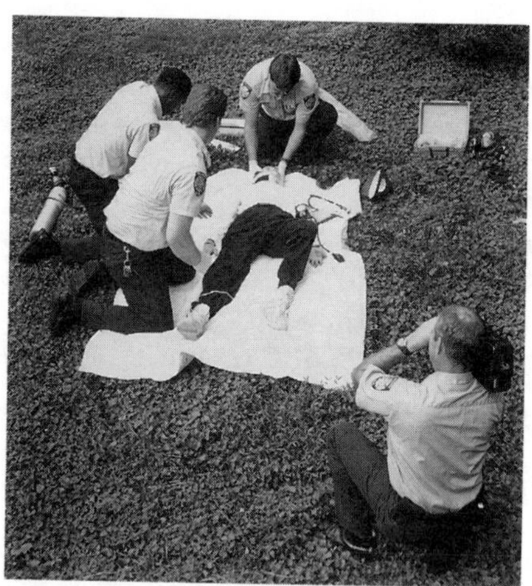

Figure 11–6 Firefighters practice emergency medical techniques during in-service training exercises that are being videotaped for later review.

types of medical difficulties and involves more invasive medical practices such as drug administration. Advanced life-support activities can be carried out only under the supervision of a doctor and therefore require communication with a community hospital.

In some states, intermediate levels of training between basic and advanced life support are recognized. For example, training in defibrillation, which involves electrically stimulating patients' hearts, may qualify a person as a EMT-D or EMT-I, with the *D* standing for defibrillation and the *I* standing for intermediate or intermediate/defibrillation.

Staffing levels and work assignments

The number of EMTs needed to staff an EMS operation depends on the number of EMS sites and vehicles kept ready to respond, the actual or anticipated number of calls, and the variety of work assignments given to EMTs. When EMTs also have fire suppression responsibilities, a department needs more EMTs to maintain a specific response capability. On the other hand, although it may be less expensive to use staff exclusively as EMTs, this option lessens the integration of the EMS mission with the fire department's mission, and of the EMTs themselves into fire departments. It also limits EMTs' career options.

Multilingual communication

Because of language barriers, Delray Beach, Florida (44,000), EMS personnel occasionally had a hard time explaining to citizens the importance of being examined by a doctor after receiving emergency care. To remedy the problem, a form that explains the importance of receiving further medical attention was printed in English, Spanish, and Creole. Each person treated by the EMS reads the form, signs it, and is given a copy.

Source: *The Guide to Management Improvement Projects in Local Government,* vol. 15, no. 2 (Washington, DC: ICMA, 1991), no. PS-18.

Medical care

The medical care provided by emergency medical services is dictated by the emergency aspect of the situation. Medical care starts with an assessment of the situation, which may be complicated by rescue considerations, and of the condition of the victim. Generally, the first thing that emergency medical care providers strive to do is to avoid doing harm. In medical emergencies, a decision must be made very quickly to act or to transport a patient to more qualified medical personnel.

Basic life support measures are noninvasive, essentially done on the surface of the patient's body. These services include keeping airways open for breathing, assisting breathing, treating shock, immobilizing broken bones, moving patients, and assisting in childbirth.

Advanced life support measures include the basic services and also include invasive procedures that go beyond the surface of a patient's body. The more invasive procedures include applying artificial airways, aids to breathing, defibrillation, and intravenous therapy and supplying drugs and other medications. Advanced measures are regulated by state law and require medical control by a doctor affiliated with a hospital. Advanced measures involve the practice of medicine on the street, so to speak, but the medicine is practiced by highly trained technicians under strict supervision.

Transportation

Transportation options are to use either fire apparatus or specialized EMS vehicles. Fire apparatus can get more EMTs to the scene rapidly because of their greater numbers and locations, but they carry relatively little medical equipment and do not transport patients. Specialized EMS vehicles carry much more equipment and may be used to transport patients, but they are fewer in number and may respond less rapidly.

Patient transportation is not a necessary component of fire department EMS services. If EMS vehicles do not transport patients in emergency situations, some sort of a relationship with one or more ambulance services is necessary.

If emergency ambulance service is provided, a further decision must be made about whether to provide ambulance coach service. Coach service means transporting medical patients between locations, such as hospitals, nursing homes, and residences, on a non-emergency basis. Fees from coach service provide a supplemental source of revenue to cover ambulance costs. When ambulances transport non-emergency patients, more ambulances and personnel are necessary to maintain a given level of emergency response capability.

The decision to provide EMS

The decision to provide EMS is a policy decision that should be made by the community government, but once a decision to provide the service is made, the community government will have less control over EMS operations than over other government services. EMS is fundamentally a medical service; the criteria for operational decisions are medical ones. The final arbiters of medical decisions are doctors and not fire chiefs, managers, or governing bodies.

Further, once provided, it is very hard to limit EMS services; EMS service demands are likely to exceed initial estimates. It is also very difficult and politically unpopular to cut EMS service levels or budgets, even during times of severe budgetary stress.

Rescue and hazardous material services

Although rescue and hazardous material services usually operate using the same fire department personnel, vehicles, and communication systems, these services raise special concerns in the areas of information, equipment, and training. The information for both ranges from general to highly specialized. For example, general information used by most departments includes how to deal with poisonous gases and how to extricate people from wrecked automobiles. Specialized topics include accidents in factories using unusual chemicals, nuclear power plant accidents, and glacier rescue. Information for hazardous materials is either very general (in regard to basic procedures) or specific (in regard to particular circumstances and their potential risks).

Equipment for handling hazardous material ranges from protective gear, including breathing apparatus, to earth-moving equipment for building dams to control hazardous liquids, to binoculars for identifying materials at a distance. Rescue equipment includes ropes, winches, and hydraulic cutting tools and spreaders.

The low volume of calls for rescue and hazardous materials responses makes training a special concern because it is very easy to neglect; maintaining training may be difficult.

Locating an emergency water supply

Because of frequent hazardous materials transportation on the four-mile stretch of interstate highway going through Brentwood, Tennessee (16,400), and because there were no fire hydrants along the route, the city's fire department developed a mapping system indicating the location of water sources and secured permission from the state to place blue reflective markers on the roadway to direct public safety crews to the nearest water supply. In a highway emergency, one truck would go to the scene and a second truck to the nearest water supply. The new system enables the fire department to deal with any major incident and shortens the response time.

The city has also passed an ordinance making the shipper or end user financially responsible to reimburse the city for its costs of investigation, mitigation, and cleanup of accidental discharges of hazardous materials.

Source: *The Guide to Management Improvement Projects in Local Government,* vol. 17, no. 2 (Washington, DC: ICMA, 1993), no. MGT-9.

Policy issues

Initially, firefighters were volunteers who formed a social organization at the center of community life to suppress fires. Fire departments subsequently evolved as communities made policy choices in response to changing conditions and circumstances. Communities still confront policy choices as changes in society place more demands on fire departments. At some point, all communities have confronted or will confront the leading policy issues of whether to add fire prevention, EMS, hazardous materials, and rescue services to the task of fire suppression. In addition, they have to confront the related policy issues of how to organize and staff existing and new services.

Organization for provision and production

Communities decide how to organize for the provision and production of new and existing services. Provision refers to funding services; production refers to delivering them. The cost of fire suppression and related services can be borne by city or county governments, by fire protection special districts, by nonprofit agencies, or by private individuals and businesses. Private and nonprofit organizations operate on a subscription or fee basis, although nonprofit organizations may solicit donations, raise funds, and secure additional resources in other ways. Nonprofit organizations established to provide volunteer fire services may consider joining a community government to secure funding and to minimize liability exposure. In some cases, community governments underwrite part of the cost of fire services provided by special districts or private service providers.

Organizing the production of services means assigning responsibility for fire and other emergency services to a particular organization. Usually, but not necessarily, this responsibility is assigned to one or more departments within the city or county government. Some communities rely on volunteer fire departments organized as independent, not-for-profit organizations; some communities contract with other communities (such as a city with a county or a city with an adjacent city) or with external parties to produce the services. The external parties may be private companies or nonprofit organizations other than the local volunteer fire department.

Smaller communities just starting to provide fire and other emergency services may find that other governments can provide those services at less cost. Private companies generally have been able to produce fire protection services at still lower costs than government departments. Rural/Metro Corporation pioneered private sector fire protection services in 1951 in Scottsdale, Arizona. Many private companies, following the example of Rural/Metro, use innovative personnel practices (most personnel are part-time, on loan from government units), manufacture some of their equipment, and take advantage of technological advances. Historically, private ambulance firms provided emergency medical services, but many withdrew from the market because of the cost of complying with increased government regulations.

Personnel choices

Communities confront difficult personnel choices when producing fire and emergency services. Lower costs and greater community involvement make the use of volunteers desirable. Increasingly, however, more service demands (growth in population, housing, and commercial and industrial buildings leads to more fire calls); more complicated response problems (which require higher levels of personnel training); and less volunteer availability make exclusive reliance on volunteers more difficult. More service demands mean not only more calls, but also more effort devoted to fire prevention, training, and administrative tasks. Even existing services are continually made more complicated by preventive work and new technologies.

Communities find it increasingly difficult to secure volunteers, especially during daytime hours. The number of volunteers has decreased as people have become more transient, less interested in fire departments as social institutions, and more frequently employed outside their community of residence. Volunteer service also appears more dangerous than it once did because of the threats posed by AIDS, radioactive materials, and taller buildings.

If reliance on volunteers is impractical, communities must decide whether to pay volunteers to increase their numbers, find other part-time personnel, use full-time personnel, or use a combination of volunteer, part-time, and full-time personnel. Some communities rely on volunteers for evening, weekend, and holiday hours, but use employees from other community government departments to respond to fire and other emergency calls during the business day.

Management issues

Emergency service managers face a variety of management issues that vitally affect the quality of service. Some issues are general; these—management development, innovation management, master planning, and personnel management—are discussed in this section. Those management issues unique to volunteer departments—relationships with the community and personnel matters—are discussed in the next section.

Management development

Modern fire department leaders need to develop their managerial abilities; the long tradition of separating many managerial functions from the fire department has ended. The old admonition, "Chief, you just worry about putting out fires and we'll worry about everything else," no longer applies. In today's environment, new services and chronic fiscal stress require increasingly sophisticated management within the fire service itself.

Improved management is achieved by designating appropriate fire department positions as management positions, selecting and promoting officers to these positions on the basis of managerial ability, and providing them with continuing management education and training.

Increasingly, the modern fire department manager (chief, captain, and lieutenant) has a graduate degree in administration to complement line experience in the fire service.

Fire department managers can also develop their managerial capacity by aggressively seeking out information on trends, issues, and technologies that relate to the fire service. Being a manager in community government requires constant effort to gather the information needed to provide the best possible service to the community.

Innovation management

Fire departments have a proud history and strong public support, both of which can lessen the inclination to innovate. Yet, in a world of constant change, innovation is a key to continued service quality. Innovations come in many forms: in new services and personnel practices, both of which are discussed elsewhere in this chapter, and in technology, organization, and intergovernmental cooperation. These, and the process of managing innovation, are discussed below.

Technology

History provides graphic examples of resistance to change in fire departments. Fire personnel resisted horse-drawn engines, motorized engines, and even windshields, but in general they have become receptive to new technology in recent years. Resistance to technological advances now comes primarily from community governments that are reluctant to spend money on equipment. It is necessary for fire department leaders to show that new technology is effective and efficient.

Organization

Fire departments tend to resist organizational innovations most strongly. These include using alternative service providers; contracting for services with private companies or surrounding jurisdictions; combining police and fire services into public safety departments; partially or completely consolidating fire protection services among adjacent or overlapping jurisdictions; and creating specialized new organizational subdivisions.

Intergovernmental cooperation

Intergovernmental cooperation offers opportunities to improve services without a major increase in expense. The most widely used method is the mutual-aid pact. Through these pacts, neighboring cities and counties pledge to assist one another when they are faced with emergencies for which their emergency response capability is insufficient. Through such agreements, all parties increase their capacity without significant new expenditures.

Other examples of interlocal cooperation are joint training facilities and exercises, joint dispatch facilities, joint purchasing, and information sharing. One promising new innovation involves the shift of some fire prevention activities from the municipal to the county level.

Managing innovation

Innovation starts with recognition of the advantages of change, the barriers to change, and the positive forces supporting change. The advantages of change include better emergency services and lower costs. The barriers include resistance to change, whether expressed through lack of cooperation or political action, and the reluctance of chief executives and political officials to support change or allow new expenditures. Positive forces include persons, information, and arguments that serve to overcome resistance to change. Managed innovation proceeds as follows:

1. Need for change is recognized.
2. Alternatives are identified, explored, and evaluated.
3. One alternative is selected, and the need for and benefits of the change are presented to those whose cooperation is necessary for implementation.
4. Implementation of innovation—including explanations, demonstrations, training, tests, and the evaluation process—is planned with those affected.

Resistance to change is almost universal. Making careful choices not only enhances the prospects for a successful change but also increases the possibility for future innovations. Success in implementing innovations helps melt resistance and activates positive forces for future innovations. Securing early involvement of those likely to be affected by change is often crucial.

Master planning

Master planning for fire and other emergency services requires the entire community to decide what it wants in terms of services, related costs, and levels of risk. Because public safety is involved, the community or its elected representatives need to decide explicitly on the necessary level of services and related risks. Master planning for fire protection, like other planning, involves information analysis; a study of alternatives; community involvement; and choosing, implementing, and reviewing a plan. The governing body is the final authority in approving fire protection and other service plans. Implementation of master plans requires the same kind of attention that managing any other innovation does, and master plans should be reviewed and revised periodically to ensure that they continue to meet community needs.

In dealing with master planning, reliance should *not* be placed on a community's Insurance Service Organization (ISO) Fire Suppression Rating. Some fire departments point to the community's ISO rating as a tangible measurement of the fire department's quality and as a justification for spending more money. The ISO itself, in its Public Protection Classification brochure, strongly asserts:

> *Comments, surveys and criteria are intended* only *for use in determining a property insurance classification. They are* not *intended for purposes of life safety or property loss prevention* [emphasis in original].

Personnel management

In addition to the personnel issues discussed elsewhere, fire departments often face major policy questions involving personnel changes, working hours, and labor relations.

Personnel changes

When policymakers decide to make changes by adding personnel to handle new tasks such as EMS and fire prevention or to supplement existing personnel with other types of personnel such as auxiliaries, volunteers, or full-time personnel, department managers have to explain the situation to their current personnel and encourage them to maintain their effectiveness. Personnel changes are significant. They are a common concern that requires managerial attention in order to avoid negative impacts on performance.

Working hours

Departments with full-time firefighters frequently confront questions relating to the length of shifts. Some departments use shifts based on twenty-four-hour periods; others use shifts from eight to fourteen hours in length. The advantage of shorter shifts is greater productivity. The disadvantage is resistance from personnel who find twenty-four-hour shifts to their liking because it allows them more free time and greater opportunities for part-time employment.

Labor relations

Fire department personnel spend long hours in each other's company and face danger together, which bonds them into a close-knit group. Together, they often resist change and may collectively resist management directives. Perhaps as a result, full-time fire department personnel have become the most highly unionized and militant community government employees. This fact has serious implications for matters involving union recognition, collective bargaining, and contract implementation, which are discussed in Chapter 13, "Personnel Management."

In many places, fire department managers—and sometimes the fire chief—are union members. Departmental cohesiveness has favored this arrangement, but the need for managers to participate in formal labor relations and collective bargaining makes management membership in unions undesirable.

As cohesive groups, fire department personnel are often a potent force in community politics when fire department matters are at issue. People become emotional over public safety issues in any case, and a unified group can mobilize political forces in a fashion matched only by law enforcement groups. Because of this, community managers have learned that many technical decisions may become political issues.

Volunteer departments

The quality of volunteer fire departments over the years and the economies they afford still constitute strong arguments in their favor. The volunteer fire department—an American institution—survives and contributes significantly to public safety. Still, volunteer departments must accept changes. These changes include a more broadly defined mission, more attention to personnel concerns, and an adjustment in their relation to community governments.

A broader mission

Historically, some volunteer departments saw their role exclusively as "fighting fires." As a result, fire prevention, inspections, and code enforcement have been neglected by some departments. Some critics have suggested that pay on a per-call basis makes firefighting more attractive than fire prevention. To take on a broader view of their mission, volunteer departments must work on all aspects of fire safety and also consider providing EMS, rescue, and hazardous material services.

Personnel concerns

Successful organizations, whether volunteer or not, require personnel rules and regulations that function effectively. In a volunteer fire department, where discipline is critical, this principle applies to an even greater degree. Personnel policies ensure that recruitment, appointment, dismissal, probation, and grievance procedures are clear to all volunteers. Such policies also ensure that volunteer firefighters are screened and selected based on job-related qualifications and not on social or political considerations.

Recruitment
Recruitment of volunteers is enhanced by incentives and by programs that increase community awareness of, and support for, the volunteer department. Incentives that should be in a personnel policy include retirement benefits, insurance, compensation, and service awards. Incentive programs should emphasize service and career potential rather than monetary gain. Researchers agree that the primary motivations for voluntary service are

A sense of duty—to provide service and help others

An opportunity to gain experience and learn a new skill

Social satisfaction from interaction with other volunteers

Social or community commitment.

Recruitment efforts should highlight the opportunities to fulfill such needs through the volunteer fire service.In addition to psychological motivations, concrete incentives may be needed to ensure the sustained service of volunteers. Some of the more effective concrete incentives include

Monetary compensation, including retirement benefits

Training and staff development

Formal awards and recognition

Insurance coverage, especially while on duty

Letters of recommendation for future employment

Reimbursement for out-of-pocket expenses

A structured career ladder that allows volunteers to accept increasing responsibility commensurate with their abilities

An active part in planning and goal setting for the department.

Training
Training is especially critical for volunteers. Appropriate training is essential to ensure the safety of the volunteers as well as their successful performance. Because they may be busy with primary commitments elsewhere and can easily put it off, training must be mandatory for fire department volunteers. Personnel policies should establish clear guidelines for such training and specify the consequences for failure to adhere to training requirements.

Relation to community government

Some volunteer fire departments are independent organizations, either special districts or nonprofit organizations, with few ties to community governments. Yet volunteer fire departments operate most effectively when they are an integral part of the community government. The organization of the volunteer department should be set by ordinance, with the fire chief being appointed as a member of the chief administrator's staff so that the fire chief and chief administrator can build a working relationship that ensures good administrative practices.

Like full-time fire departments, volunteer departments must be fully cooperating components of the community's service delivery team.

The volunteer department that selects its own chief and perpetuates itself by choosing new members as the old ones retire is likely to develop into a closed organization that is difficult for community officials to control, that may not give sufficient attention to training and other needs, and that may resist cooperation with other departments in code enforcement and fire prevention. The volunteer organization that does not operate under ordinance has difficulty in some states in obtaining workers compensation. It is important, therefore, for the volunteer department to be established by ordinance, for its leadership to be appointed by community leaders, and for it to work closely with other community agencies.

A well-designed and functioning administrative system is essential for any community service department, including a volunteer fire department. The chief administrator and the fire chief should work together to identify service priorities, set performance standards, determine reporting requirements, establish evaluation procedures, and integrate fire department needs into capital budgeting, annual budgeting, and purchasing procedures. Arrangements must be made to provide support through centralized purchasing, computer dispatching, recordkeeping, grants planning and administration, and personnel management. Like full-time fire departments, volunteer departments must be fully cooperating components of the community's service delivery team.

Afterword

The major challenges for fire departments today are not found at the scene of fires. Rather, they are found in fire prevention, in preparation for fire suppression, and in building the capacity to respond to a growing range of emergencies, especially medical emergencies. Today, more lives are saved and more property loss is avoided by the quality of the training and preparation that goes into fire and emergency response services than by the heroic behavior of officers responding to calls for help.

This means that the role of management, and the importance of trained, professional managers in the fire services, is continuing to grow in importance. Managers are responsible for and must provide the advance planning and the training that mean the difference between success and failure in helping victims and protecting property. The fact that such services are usually delivered under extreme pressure and that no two calls for help are precisely alike only makes it more important that responding officers be well prepared, in advance, to respond properly when they find themselves in the middle of a crisis.

Work conducted under extreme pressure, often with human safety at risk, makes training and sensitive management crucial to meeting the goal of protecting the public. ■

PART IV

Managing Government

INTRODUCTION

As demands for service increase, as public resistance to taxes mounts, and as the process of governing becomes more and more complex, the business of providing community government, building a better community, and protecting the public requires more and more attention to the task of managing government.

Managing government is the business of getting maximum benefit from each taxpayer dollar spent. It is the business of hiring the best and the brightest staff that the community can afford—even when it means investing more money in personnel in the short run so that greater staff expertise will be available to serve the public in the long run.

Managing government also means fostering good communication between the government and community residents. The government cannot effectively deliver services that the community does not support, and the community will not support service programs with which it is unfamiliar or about which it is misinformed. Good communication between government and the public is thus a cornerstone of good government.

In the contemporary era, good government also means working with other community governments. As Chapter 1 pointed out, many different local government units—counties, cities, townships, school districts, and other special districts—share responsibility for service delivery in each community. Only by working together can governments in such a system optimize the community's well-being. Yet intergovernmental activity does not just happen; it must be made to happen, and that requires knowledge and skill as well as good will.

Today, managing government is as challenging as managing big business. Indeed, government is big business. In many communities, government is the biggest business in town. It is the largest employer; it has the largest annual cash flow; it has the most diverse range of activities and responsibilities; it has the greatest effect on the daily lives of local residents. Not surprisingly, then, it takes just as much specialized knowledge, experience, and managerial talent to make government efficient and effective as it does to make business profitable.

This part of the book focuses on management because good management is so important to good government. Chapter 12 deals with the management of the community's money; it discusses budgeting and financial management. Chapter 13 describes the tasks involved in recruiting, selecting, developing, motivating, and directing the best possible workforce for the community government. Chapter 14 examines the challenge of communicating with the public. Chapter 15 discusses relations among the levels of government—federal, state, and local.

Familiarity with these chapters will not, by themselves, prepare a person to be an informed, skilled community government manager. These chapters serve instead as an indicator of the magnitude of the managerial challenge, a brief survey of what is needed and expected in each of these managerial areas, and a further elaboration on the subject first introduced in Chapter 1: the need for professionalism in local government management.

This part of the book is dedicated to addressing the common demand that "government be run like a business." Just as successful businesses, and especially big businesses, are managed by professionals, so too should community government, itself a big business, be managed with the same kind of specialized managerial talent.

12 Budgeting and Financial Management

"Do more with less," the community government anthem of the nineties, has the most impact in the area of budgeting and financial management. Financial support from federal and state governments erodes while those governments continue to impose more mandates requiring more spending by community governments. Community governments find themselves forced to reconcile scarce resources with strong citizen demands for services. Many citizens, despite high service expectations, oppose new revenue measures.

Sound budgeting and financial management form the basis for community governments' responses to these pressures. Budgeting is the process of deciding how to raise and spend money; financial management involves related tasks, including purchasing, keeping records, and managing money. The budgeting process includes four stages: preparation, submission and approval, implementation, and audit and review. Financial management activities support budgeting. Together, skillfully and effectively handled, the two functions ensure that communities make the best possible use of their financial resources. The components of both are shown in the budgeting cycle framework in Figure 12–1.

Budgeting and financial management serve various purposes, especially planning, control, efficiency, and accountability. Budgets constitute and outline a plan governing operations and service delivery. Budgets and financial techniques control what departments can do and how they can do it. Operating efficiency is increased by careful management. Making decisions and plans publicly and reporting on their financial consequences promote accountability. Given its purposes, the annual budget is the single most important policy document in any given year.

Budget preparation

Budget preparation never stops, as individuals gather and interpret information for future budgets while they are in the midst of operating the current budget. However, community governments formally begin preparing a specific budget with a budget "call" or "call letter" issued to operating agencies by the chief administrative officer. The call may set forth executive policy guidelines and technical instructions on how to prepare budget requests. It may also include particular forms, specific instructions on how to fill out forms, and a calendar spelling out who does what when.

Specific forms and information requested vary according to community ordinances, executive preferences, and state legal requirements, but they generally include forms for estimates of expenditures and revenues. The policy guidelines may set forth service priorities for the coming year and deal with raises for personnel, position vacancies, and estimates of the impact of inflation on prices. Policy guidance may be financial (limit all requests to 98 percent of the current budget), substantive (emphasize services related to economic development), or procedural (clear all capital equipment requests with the chief administrator's office).

A budget calendar facilitates meeting deadlines associated with preparing, reviewing, and adopting the budget. Figure 12–2 illustrates a sample budget calendar. State legal requirements determine key dates on a calendar, for example, when a fiscal year begins and ends, when budgets have to be adopted, and when proposed budgets have to be published. Starting with state requirements as a framework, a budget calendar also specifies internal actions and deadlines. State law may require that a budget hearing be held a specified amount of time before the budget's final adoption, but community officials must specify the actual times and places for such hearings.

Revenues The two sides of a budget, revenues and expenditures, have to work together. Early in budget preparation, key officials review the revenue situation and prepare initial revenue estimates. States restrict and regulate revenue sources. Although practices vary, most community governments rely on intergovernmental aid, property taxes, and user charges for the bulk of their revenues.

The revenue book

A community government revenue book should include a current list of all legally available revenue measures with a legal authority reference. The bulk of the book is a listing of current revenue measures with a historical record of rates and revenue raised. The listing includes administrative details (e.g., what office collects revenues and their due dates); legal limits on rates; and any special circumstances (e.g., tax abatements). A revenue book allows officials to see what has been done in the past and what might be done to increase revenues in the future. Revenue books can be started by organizing current and historical revenue records and by securing or developing lists of legal revenue sources. Often, state associations can provide such lists.

Officials review the revenue situation in general and specific terms. The general question asks how well revenues are holding up. Too often in recent years, the answer has been "Not as well as in the previous year." The specific questions deal with how much revenue can be expected from each source.

Figure 12–1 Elements of budgeting and financial management.

Before the fiscal year	During the fiscal year	After the fiscal year
Preparation, submission, and approval of budget	**Implementation**	**Audit and review**
Revenue estimates Expenditure estimates Capital budget Budget review Budget approval	Budget administration Accounting Revenue administration Purchasing Treasury management Debt management Risk management	Financial and budget reports Audits Budget review

Many officials find revenue flows insufficient to support community services adequately. This situation derives from many circumstances: increasing service demands, inflation, reduced federal and state aid, increasing state mandates, and changes in state revenue laws (e.g., exempting classes of property or sales from taxation). In dealing with revenue concerns, a revenue book, described in the accompanying sidebar, is helpful. Communities commonly raise revenues from the sources discussed below.

Property taxes

Property taxes have long been the primary source of community government revenues. The primary base is real property (i.e., land and things attached to the land); personal property taxes (i.e., moveable things) are generally collected only on registered vehicles.

Property taxes are especially noteworthy in at least three respects. First, the base upon which the tax is levied, property, is inventoried and assessed by government officials. This provides the most precisely defined tax base of all revenue measures. Second, every year communities explicitly decide how much to collect in property taxes—in addition to revenues from other sources—to fund operations and then set a tax rate to produce that amount. All other taxes use established tax rates, and the amount collected depends on variations in the tax base (e.g., sales or income).

Figure 12–2 Sample budget calendar.

Date	Activity
May 1	Send call letter for proposed expenditures and revenue estimates to department and office heads.
May 1 to July 1	Department and office heads prepare detailed work programs and expenditure estimates and make relevant revenue estimates.
Before July 1	Review revenue situation for policy changes.
July 1	Expenditure proposals and revenue estimates due to executive or chief administrator, who reviews them and may make adjustments.
July 15	File proposed budget with clerk; provide notice of proposed budget to public; provide notice of budget hearing to public; and provide notice of public meeting.
July 22	Hold budget hearing; hold council or board meeting to review and make any changes in budget; pass appropriations ordinance; and levy taxes.
July 29	Both municipalities and counties file budget with state office; municipalities file budget and tax levy with county clerk.
July 30	Department and office heads informed of expenditure authority granted in budget appropriations.
July 31	End fiscal year
August 1	Begin fiscal year. Implement budget: collect and spend money according to budget and other community and state requirements and fulfill collateral requirements, such as entering budget information into accounting system, treasury management, and the like.
Between August 1 and July 31	Supplemental budget actions: additional or reduced expenditures, transfers of money between funds, and temporary borrowings.
July 31	End fiscal year
After July 31	Prepare annual financial reports; engage external auditor; do budget review.
December 1	Complete financial audit and submit audited annual financial reports to state office for budget year ending July 31 of same year.

Third, even though most local government units rely on property taxes, community governments face the most criticism of these taxes, despite the fact that educational units such as school districts typically collect much more revenue. Community officials can respond only by continually pointing to the community government's share of the local property tax compared with the amounts received by other local government units.

Despite frequent criticism, property taxes have a number of desirable characteristics. States allow their use; they have been used historically, which makes them more acceptable; there is a lot of property, which makes them broad-based; they are locally administered; and they produce a fairly steady and substantial stream of revenue.

The undesirable characteristics of property taxes include high administrative costs; their consistent ranking as one of the most unpopular taxes; poor tax assessment; the possibility that they are regressive; and the antidevelopment effect of taxing increased property values. If given a choice, many community governments would opt to rely more

Figure 12–3 Sample property tax bill for local governments and special entities serving DeKalb County, Illinois.

DEKALB COUNTY REAL ESTATE TAX BILL FOR 1992

CHARLOTTE SUNDLY COUNTY COLLECTOR SYCAMORE, ILLINOIS 60178

ACRES	PARCEL NUMBER		TAX CODE	TAX RATE	TOTAL TAX
	08-15-479-007	5	DK-12	8.3643	3540.86

Hofman, James & Lynne

1505 Brassie Place
DeKalb, IL 60115

EQUALIZED VALUATION: 45,833
HOMESTEAD EXEMPTION (OVER 65): 0
HOMESTEAD EXEMPTION LIMITED: 3,500
NET VALUATION: 42,333
SOLD AT TAX SALE
FORFEITED TAX

FAIR CASH VALUE: 137,500

You may pay this bill at most Dekalb County Banks or at the Collector's Office, 110 E. Sycamore St., Sycamore, IL. 60178
Do not detach stub if paying in person. 1.5% interest per month, or any part thereof, added after due date. Mail payments must be postmarked on or before due date to avoid penalty.
Personal checks not accepted 30 days prior to tax sale.

2nd INSTALLMENT DUE DATE: SEPT. 1, 1993
2nd INSTALLMENT TAX: 1,770.43
ABATEMENT: 5494
INTEREST: 5/21/93
COST
TOTAL DUE

RECEIPT FOR TAXPAYER

1991 RATE	1991 AMOUNT	TAXING BODY	1992 RATE	1992 AMOUNT
.8137	459.98	COUNTY	.7290	308.63
.0669	37.82	IMRF	.0735	31.11
.1017	57.49	SOCIAL SECURITY	.1030	43.60
.0287	16.22	FOREST PRESERVE	.0303	12.83
.1646	93.05	DEKALB TOWNSHIP	.1583	67.01
.2097	118.54	DEKALB ROAD & BRIDGE	.2766	117.09
.2422	136.91	CITY OF DEKALB	.2295	97.15
.1258	71.11	IMRF	.1107	46.86
.0926	52.34	SOCIAL SECURITY	.0932	39:45
.0786	44.43	POLICE PENSION	.0756	32.00
.1059	59.86	FIRE PENSION	.0989	41.87
.2673	151.10	DE KALB LIBRARY	.2446	103.55
.3985	225.26	DE KALB PARK	.3759	159.13
.0143	8.08	IMRF	.0044	1.86
.0190	10.74	SOCIAL SECURITY	.0261	11.05
5.0293	2842.96	SCHOOL DISTRICT 428	4.9674	2102.85
.0757	42.79	IMRF	.0728	30.82
.0757	42.79	SOCIAL SECURITY	.0728	30.82
.5355	302.71	CC 523 KISHWAUKEE	.5227	221.27
.0595	33.63	DE KALB SANITARY	.0641	27.14
.0294	16.62	IMRF	.0198	8.38
.0148	8.37	SOCIAL SECURITY	.0151	6.39
8.5494	4832.80	TOTAL	8.3643	3540.86

PLEASE RETAIN THIS CARD FOR YOUR INFORMATION
SEE REVERSE SIDE FOR FULL INSTRUCTIONS

PARCEL NUMBER 08-15-479-007

COUNTY EQUALIZATION VALUES

NON-FARM LAND	14113
NON-FARM BUILDINGS	31720
TOTAL	45833
STATE MULTIPLIER	
NON-FARM	
45833 X 1.0000	45833
TOTAL	45833

LATE PAYMENT SCHEDULE LISTED BELOW - INCLUDING 1.5% PER MONTH PENALTY.
1ST INSTALLMENT
AS OF JUNE 15 1796.99
AS OF JULY 15 1823.54
AS OF AUG. 15 1850.10
AS OF SEP. 15 1876.66
2ND INSTALLMENT
AS OF SEP. 2 1796.99
OCTOBER - TAX SALE

Self-addressed, stamped envelope and receipt portion of tax bill required for receipt.

Formerly included in each tax district, itemization of pension and retirement funds are now required by law to be separate. The law is written on the reverse side of this bill.

CHANGE OF MAILING ADDRESS AND INSTRUCTIONS (See Reverse Side)

heavily on other, more attractive tax measures; however, states generally retain those measures for themselves. Property taxes will continue to be disliked, criticized, and used for the foreseeable future.

Sales taxes

Sales taxes produce the second greatest amount of tax revenue for community governments. Communities levy taxes generally on retail sales of goods (general sales tax) or upon specific categories of goods and services (selective sales taxes). General sales taxes parallel state measures and are usually state administered. Selective sales taxes are most often levied on public utility services, motor fuels, and nonessential or "sinful" goods and services (e.g., alcoholic beverages, tobacco products, amusements, lodgings, and restaurant meals). Sales tax rates are a percentage of the sales transaction; different rates are used for various tax measures (e.g., general sales at .01, telephone at .0025, and hotel rooms at .03).

Business activity taxes

Business activity taxes vary widely. They include taxes on gross receipts, number of employees, occupation, and inventory. Gross receipts taxes resemble sales taxes but are levied on businesses. Employee head taxes are assessed at a given amount per employee. Occupation taxes are levied upon persons engaging in a specific occupation (e.g., pawnbroker, tree surgeon). Inventory taxes are a personal property tax applied to businesses.

The use of income taxes is permitted in one or more community governments in about a fifth of the states in the United States, but they generally are used by only the largest communities. They are a major source of revenue where used, but other states are not likely to allow their use soon.

Intergovernmental revenues

The proportion of community government revenues represented by intergovernmental aid and the actual purchasing power of the aid keep declining.

Federal and state policymakers in recent years have been reducing the portion of their budgets devoted to intergovernmental aid, grants, and shared revenues. Some specific programs have been eliminated, others have been consolidated, and still others are administered through state programs. The key change is that the rate of increase in intergovernmental aid has been less than the rate of inflation and the increase in overall federal and state budgets. The dollar amount of intergovernmental aid keeps increasing, but the proportion of community government revenues represented by this aid and the actual purchasing power of the aid keep declining.

The two primary types of grant are project and formula grants. Project grants are narrow in scope and are awarded for a specific period of time after an application process, often competitive, has been followed. In social services, examples are a pregnancy counseling program, a program to give electric fans to elderly poor people, and a program to cultivate ethnic awareness. Formula grants are broader in scope and generally are awarded for ongoing programs. They are available to all community governments meeting legally specified criteria (e.g., income support and community development programs). In addition to the revenues they receive from federal and state grants, local governments may also receive money from shared revenues. These are monies from specific revenue measures shared by states with community governments (e.g., retail sales, motor fuel, or income taxes).

User charges

User charges and fees are paid for a wide variety of services and privileges; other common names for charges are *fee*, *license*, and *permit*. Charges vary by the amount of service, whereas fees are generally set at a certain level. Figure 12–4 lists numerous examples.

User charges and fees help local governments to measure, and they may also reduce, service demand. Political pressures against tax increases make it easier to collect money from user charges. However, they do not always cover the total costs of services; shortfalls may be intended, or they may occur by accident. When charges and fees do not cover costs, the community government often subsidizes services. Subsidies for cer-

Figure 12–4 Types of local government fees, charges, and licenses by service areas.

Police protection
Special patrol service fees
Parking fees and charges
Fees for fingerprints, copies
Payments for extra police services at stadiums, theaters, and circuses

Transportation
Subway and bus fares
Bridge tolls
Landing and departure fees
Hangar rentals
Concession rentals
Parking meter receipts

Health and hospitals
Inoculation charges
X-ray charges
Hospital charges, including per diem rates
Ambulance charges
Concession rentals

Education
Charges for books
Charges for gymnasium uniforms
Concession rentals

Recreation
Green fees
Parking charges
Concession rentals
Admission fees or charges
Permit charges for tennis courts
Charges for specific recreation services
Picnic stove fees
Stadium gate tickets
Stadium club fees
Park development charges

Sanitation
Domestic and commercial trash collection fees
Industrial waste charges

Sewerage
Sewerage system fees

Other public utility operations
Water meter permits
Water services charges
Electricity rates
Telephone booth rentals

Housing, neighborhood and commercial development
Street tree fees
Tract map filing fees
Street lighting installations
Convention center revenues

Commodity sales
Salvage materials
Sales of maps
Sales of codes

Licenses
Advertising vehicles
Amusements (rides at fairs)
Billiard and pool halls
Bowling alleys
Circuses and carnivals
Coal dealers
Commercial combustion
Dances
Dog tags
Duplicate dog tags
Electrician—first class
Electrician—second class
Film storage
Foot peddlers
Hucksters and itinerant peddlers
Heating equipment contractors
Hotels
Junk dealers
Landfills
Loading zone permits
Lumber dealers
Pawnbrokers
Plumbers—first class
Plumbers—second class
Pest eradicators
Poultry dealers
Produce dealers—itinerant
Pushcarts
Rooming houses
Secondhand dealers
Sign inspection
Solicitation
Shooting galleries
Taxis
Taxi transfer licenses
Taxi drivers
Theaters
Trees—Christmas
Vending—coin
Vault cleaners
Sound trucks
Refuse haulers
Sightseeing buses
Wrecking licenses

tain services or persons may serve the public interest; for example, subsidies for recreational facilities are justified as a means of promoting the physical and social development of youth and of reducing demand on police services. Subsidies for citizens who are economically less well off are justified as a means of ensuring fair access to services.

However, unintentional subsidies may occur when the costs of services and payment levels are not regularly reviewed. The community government—and taxpayers—then absorb costs that could conceivably be reduced or recuperated by adjustments in charges. Therefore, reviewing and revising charges on an annual or biennial basis is a good practice.

In some cases, local governments may actually earn a profit from charges and the excess revenues may be used to fund general operations. Community governments have relied more and more on charges in recent decades. However, it is not possible to obtain ever-increasing amounts of money from them.

Beach maintenance

In order to help fund cleaning and maintenance of its beachfront, Port Hueneme, California (20,500), charges homeowners a special assessment. The tax, which affects approximately 1,200 homeowners, ranges from $66 to $184 per home. Because homeowners closer to the beach benefit more from a clean, well-kept beach, the tax is based upon each home's proximity to the beach. The budgeted receipts of $400,000 fund almost half of the community's beach maintenance costs, including landscaping, irrigation, and beach cleaning.

Source: *The Guide to Management Improvement Projects in Local Government,* vol. 16, no. 1 (Washington, DC: ICMA, 1992), no. MGT-7.

Debt and minor revenue sources

Borrowed money allows community governments to acquire long-term capital assets and to cover short-term gaps between other revenues and expenditures. It is usually considered poor practice, and in many states may be illegal, to use borrowed funds to pay current operating expenditures.

Fines, forfeitures, and gifts supply a minor portion of community revenues. Special assessments are taxes levied against particular parcels of property when the property is benefited by a specific public project (e.g., street lights and sidewalks).

Estimating revenues and expenditures

Despite the imperfect character of estimates, estimating revenues and expenditures is essential to budget preparation and deliberations. It is preferable to estimate expenditures high and revenues low, as spending too little or having too much revenue generally are not problems.

Revenue estimates

Revenue estimates are made for each revenue source—for example, retail sales, utility charges, fines for parking violations, building permits, or recreation fees. The central finance or chief administrator's office usually estimates the largest revenues and those collected centrally (e.g., intergovernmental aid and taxes). Departments that collect lesser revenue sources often estimate those revenues.

Accurate forecasting of revenues is critical, because estimates that are too high can result in year-end deficits or service cutbacks during the year. Generally, communities estimate revenues by using some sort of trend analysis or expert opinion technique. Trend analysis techniques assume that future events will be similar to past events. Current factors such as the state of the economy and recent legal changes are also taken into account. Trend analysis works best when a large number of events take place (e.g., taxes and charges). Readily available computer software facilitates the use of trend analysis.

Expert opinion requires one or more persons who render an opinion on a future outcome. An expert is anyone with the greatest knowledge of or most experience with a particular revenue source (e.g., for dog licenses, the administrator of the animal shelter). This type of technique applies especially to intergovernmental revenues that have not yet been approved.

Expenditure estimates

Increasingly, communities are realizing that budgets should show what the community government proposes to do.

Operating units prepare estimates of their expenditures for the upcoming fiscal period based on the guidelines in the budget call. It is usually assumed, unless otherwise communicated, that agencies will continue, in a general sense, to do what they currently do. The two parts of the expenditure-estimating enterprise are determining what actions to propose for the next year and what they will cost.

What community agencies propose to do is not always visible in expenditure estimates. Many community governments use a lump-sum or line-item budget format that does not specify what will be done. Lump-sum budgets simply show a total dollar amount estimated for each department or major expenditure category; a line-item budget lists items that the department hopes to buy (e.g., four police cars) along with prices of items, but it does not relate the purchase of these items to the department's goals.

Increasingly, communities are realizing that budgets should show what the community government proposes to do and are using budget formats that specify planned activities, projects, or goals. They may use performance, program, or zero-base budget formats, which relate planned accomplishments to spending levels. Features from other approaches may be combined with lump-sum or line-item budgets.

As agencies make their plans, the primary variables are anticipated revenues, current services, the desirability of new services, and the likely level of demand for existing services.

As community agencies estimate costs, they have to determine how many of what specific items (e.g., personnel, equipment, and supplies) are required and what their price will be. Larger expenditures justify greater estimating effort. Most estimating starts with the levels in the current-year budget. Unless policies change or current numbers prove insufficient, the numbers of items are assumed to be adequate for the next fiscal year. This applies to most items.

Informed opinions on price movements form the basis of price estimates. The cost of personnel, the largest part of community budgets, is set by community decisions or negotiation. Cost-of-living and other raises can be precisely calculated, though they cannot be known with certainty until the governing body approves them. The general practice is to estimate some price increase.

Categories for estimating expenditures include funds, organizational units, functions, objects of expenditure, and accounts. Funds (which are discussed later in the chapter in the section on accounting) are used to account for particular kinds of financial activities of a community government (e.g., a library fund). All budgeted financial transactions, including approved expenditure estimates, are recorded in one or another fund of the accounting system.

Organizational units are the operating agencies of the government (e.g., the police department). They usually estimate their own expenditures in the budget preparation process. Function refers to such categories as general government, public safety, public works, health/welfare, and culture/recreation.

Objects of expenditure (things bought), are either line categories or line items. Line category refers to general categories of expenditure such as personnel, supplies/materials, other services/charges, and capital items. Line item refers to particular items such as overtime, labor costs, gasoline, a particular consulting contract, or a dump truck.

Accounts are subdivisions of funds, usually organizational subdivisions and line categories and items. An accounting system is likely to be organized, for example, along the following pattern: a fire department

Figure 12–5 Street maintenance account from the city of Greenbelt, Maryland, Proposed Budget, FY 1993-94.

STREET MAINTENANCE
PUBLIC WORKS
GENERAL FUND

ACCOUNT EXPLANATION

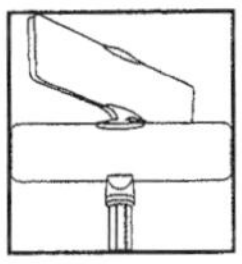

Public Works crew members repair and maintain over 24 miles of city streets. New construction, reconstruction, resurfacing, curb replacement, patching and repairs on all streets are charged to this account. Snow removal costs are also budgeted here, as are expenditures for maintaining sidewalks, public parking facilities, and storm sewers and cleaning roadsides.

PERFORMANCE MEASURES	1990/91 Actual	1991/92 Actual	1992/93 Estimated	1993/94 Estimated
Street mileage (as of December)	24.05	24.38	24.38	24.38
Maint. cost/mile (except street lighting)	$51,586	$35,468	$57,954	$36,302
Street lighting cost/mile	$3,375	$2,812	$3,281	$3,364
State shared revenues per mile for maintenance	$13,746	$14,179	$15,669	$16,140
Street resurfacing (sq. yds)	18,450	17,049	0	0
Curb and gutter (lin. ft.)	550	6,900	460	550
Sidewalk construction (sq. ft.)	4,630	27,063	10,600	10,000
Handicap ramps constructed	6	6	25	15
Tons of asphalt purchased	704	750	500	550
Tons of road salt purchased	200	300	360	400
Tons of roadside trash	160	300	N/A	N/A
Full Time Equivalents (FTE's)				
Street maintenance	7	6	6	6
Specialty operations	5.7	5	4	4

MANAGEMENT OBJECTIVES (MBO's)

1. Develop standard work schedule to program work required, monitor time and labor expended, and establish work measurement standards.
2. Continue the development of a current inventory of City streets, sidewalks, curbs and gutters with condition and replacement needs assessment.
3. Bring City facilities into compliance with non-structural requirements of ADA by installing ramp access to City buildings, curb rampings, and handicap-size parking spaces.

account that includes fire prevention, fire suppression, and emergency medical services subunit accounts that include personnel expenses accounts that include salaries and benefit accounts. The accounts in a community government's accounting system match the information categories used in its budget.

Figure 12–6 From the city of Greenbelt, Maryland, Proposed Budget, FY 1993-94.

	1990/91 Actual Transac.	1991/92 Actual Transac.	1992/93 Adopted Budget	1992/93 Estimated Transac.	1993/94 Proposed Budget	1993/94 Adopted Budget
WASTE COLLECTION AND DISPOSAL - ACCT. NO. 350						
PERSONNEL EXPENSES						
16 Waste Collection	$175,394	$153,129	$149,800	$157,800	$157,600	
17 Recycling Incentives	217	0 0	0	0	0	
18 Special Pickup	0	0	0	0	0	
25 Rep./Maint. Vehicles	6,233	8,116	10,500	10,500	10,500	
28 Employee Benefits	34,989	33,468	37,100	37,600	38,600	
Total	$216,833	$194,713	$197,400	$205,900	$206,700	
OTHER OPERATING EXPENSES						
33 Insurance	$7,670	$7,105	$8,200	$6,700	$6,700	
34 Other Services	115,579	110,185	163,000	156,600	175,000	
37 Public Notices	410	214	300	300	300	
48 Uniforms	2,338	2,016	2,400	3,200	3,000	
49 Tools	976	4,809	4,500	4,500	4,500	
50 Motor Equipment Maint.	39,555	26,198	38,000	38,000	38,000	
51 Radio Equipment Maint.	0	244	300	300	300	
55 Office Expenses	87	1,118	200	200	200	
71 Miscellaneous	10	145	100	300	100	
Total	$166,625	$152,034	$217,000	$210,100	$228,100	
CAPITAL OUTLAY						
91 New Equipment		$58				
94 Interfund Transfer - Replacement Fund	$25,110	$24,400	$13,900	$13,900	$5,000	
Total	$25,110	$24,458	$13,900	$13,900	$5,000	
TOTAL WASTE COLLECTION	$408,568	$371,205	$428,300	$429,900	$439,800	
REVENUE SOURCES						
Service Fees	$271,602	$273,160	$278,000	$276,000	$281,000	
Landfill Disposal Rebate	116,564	137,487	161,700	161,700	156,300	
Recycling grant - County	27,260					
Sale of Recyclable Materials	633	0	500	500	500	
TOTAL REVENUE	$416,059	$410,647	$440,200	$438,200	$437,800	
Excess (Deficiency) of Revenues over Expenditures	$7,491	$39,442	$11,900	$8,300	($2,000)	
Quarterly residential service fee required as of Jan. 1 of each year	$31.50	$31.50	$31.50	$31.50	$31.50	
Percent change	1.8%	10.6%	2.8%	1.9%	-0.5%	

Performance, program, and zero-base budget formats

A *performance budget* format shows departmental proposals for what will be done with resources in terms of functions, activities, or projects (e.g., the vehicle repair and crime investigation functions, trash collection by the ton and street sweeping by the mile activities, and the project for resurfacing 15th Street). Line items are specified for the various functions, activities, and projects. The services performed—outputs—are the focal point of this budget format. Performance budgeting is associated with concern for efficient operations; attention is directed to what is done at what cost.

A *program budget* format shows departmental proposals for what will be achieved or accomplished by different programs, which are sets of organized activities directed to particular goals (e.g., crime solution and clean street programs). Program budgeting focuses attention on goal attainment or effectiveness and predicts specific outcomes (e.g., particular numbers of crimes solved or clients successfully served).

A *zero-base budget* format resembles the other two budget formats in that outputs or outcomes are specified in budget proposals. Zero-base budgeting uses decision units, decision packages, and ranking. A budget is divided into decision units within each of which a ranked series of decision packages are proposed. Each decision package includes a description of outputs or outcomes, a list of line items, the cost of the package, and perhaps a justification. Attention is focused on priorities and choices as spending occurs only for decision packages that are explicitly chosen from those presented.

These three ways of budgeting sound wonderful in theory because they are rational. Unfortunately, in practice, the price paid for this characteristic is high in terms of the great amounts of time and paper needed to collect and process information. Nevertheless, many concepts from these approaches may be implemented separately, as has been done successfully in many jurisdictions.

Source: Adapted from Richard J. Aronson and Eli Schwartz, eds., *Management Policies in Local Government Finance*, 3d ed. (Washington, DC: ICMA, 1987), 153-156.

Capital budgeting

Many communities devote special attention to capital improvement projects, usually in a separate capital budget that shows planned projects for four or more years into the future. Because these projects take years to plan and build, last a long time, and cost large sums, they require careful advance planning. Typically, communities consider plans over a period of several years, developing priorities and arranging for the needed funds. Capital budgeting creates a forum in which to undertake advance planning, to relate projects to revenues over a period of years, and to evaluate projects in terms of community priorities. The portion of the capital budget that relates to spending in the forthcoming budget year is incorporated into the annual operating budget.

Communities frequently finance capital projects through borrowing and intergovernmental aid. Debt financing allows communities to raise revenues over a longer time for such projects and ensures that people benefiting from the projects pay for them through taxes and other payments.

Budget submission and approval

After initial preparation, budget requests are reviewed, revised, and approved by department heads, chief administrators, and the elected governing body. Reviews focus on technical and policy issues, especially in regard to expenditures. Technical issues concern the accuracy of the estimates of revenues and expenditures (e.g., tax bases, items to be purchased, and prices). Policy issues concern the appropriateness of particular revenue and service decisions. Because requested expenditures always exceed available revenues, the review process always requires hard decisions to reduce initial expenditure requests.

The chief administrator or executive takes final submissions from operating departments and makes revisions to prepare an executive budget that includes a comprehensive listing of revenue and expenditure estimates for the upcoming fiscal year along with past years' figures and a general policy statement.

The executive budget proposal is then submitted to the legislative body, which reviews it, especially through public hearings; makes revisions as it sees fit; and approves the budget, often in the form of an appropriations ordinance and a property-tax levy ordinance.

Budget implementation

During the fiscal year, budget administration and other financial management activities ensure that the community receives the best possible return for each dollar collected and spent. These activities include accounting, revenue administration, purchasing, treasury management, debt management, and risk management.

Budget administration

All department managers as well as the chief administrator are responsible for the details of budget implementation. Generally, budget responsibility means implementing policies for service provision. Budget administration requires many specific tasks. First of all, the chief administrator communicates to departments the extent of their authority to spend money; this authority may be constrained by expenditure controls. Second, actual revenues and expenditures are monitored and compared with budgeted figures in order to determine whether budget plans have to be changed. Third, when unexpected events transpire, revisions of budget plans deal with the new circumstances. Fourth, procedural and substantive expenditure controls are implemented. One common procedure is a pre-audit in which a finance office reviews and approves each expenditure, determining whether it has been authorized by the budget and approved funds are still available. Travel and training expenditures are frequently subject to special approval.

Accounting

Accounting systems collect and report financial information used for budgeting and financial decision making. It is generally recommended that all accounting be performed by a central finance office or department. Accounting systems record information in specific categories. The key information categories include funds, account types, balances, reports, and accounting basis.

Funds

Funds are used to divide and to group financial records into useful sets. In community governments, many revenues are restricted to specific uses; separate funds make it possible to show that restrictions were followed.

Most government accounting takes place within funds. Budget documents show the division of finances by funds. For example, a library may budget and account for monies in two funds: a library operating fund into which the revenue from a special property tax levied for the support of the library is recorded (general library expenditures) and a library special projects fund to record the revenues and expenditures for projects funded by grants and contributions from the Friends of the Library. Budget documents show what revenues go into which funds and from which funds monies are expended. The three groupings of funds are governmental, proprietary, and fiduciary.

Governmental funds are used to account for governmental services; specific fund types are general, special revenue, debt service, capital project, and special assessment. Communities use one general fund, usually the largest, to account for most revenue sources and for most general government expenditures.

Transactions are recorded in other funds only for specific reasons. Special revenue funds are for restricted revenues: for example, road grants from the state are recorded in the highway fund along with associated expenditures to make it easier to show that the monies from particular revenues are used as required. A debt fund is used to hold and pay out monies for general long-term debt. Capital project funds are for the revenues and expenditures of specific projects (e.g., Jail Capital Project Fund). Special assessment funds account for special assessment projects.

Proprietary funds are used to account for business-like services, that is, those for which a charge is collected from whoever uses the services or purchases a good. Enterprise funds are used when the public is served and charged (e.g., for water and sewer services). Internal service funds are used when one agency (e.g., a copy center or motor pool) supplies services to other agencies and the other agencies pay for the service out of their budgets. In both cases, rationing and pricing of services take place because of the limited or finite amount of resources available: for consumers, it is just a question of whether they are willing to pay for the service. Revenues, units of service produced, and the costs of providing services are recorded. Service costs can be allocated to users on a per-unit basis.

Fiduciary funds account for the use and control of other people's money. Both trust and agency funds involve situations in which a community government handles money for other people (e.g., a perpetual care cemetery trust fund).

In addition to funds, two account groups list general long-term debt and general fixed assets. This information is helpful in budgeting and financial planning.

Account types

Within each fund, separate accounts are used to collect information on specific transactions. A transaction is any event about which one wants to collect information. The primary types of accounts are assets, liabilities, fund balance, budgeted revenues and expenditures, and actual revenues and expenditures.

Asset accounts are for things owned (e.g., cash). Liability accounts show what is owed to others (e.g., bills or a bank loan). Fund balance accounts primarily show net balances between accounts. Budgeted revenue and expenditure accounts, called estimated revenues and appropriations accounts, record the approved budget in the accounting system. Actual revenue and expenditure accounts record those amounts for comparison with budgeted amounts.

The different account types hold the information required and vary widely in specific details. Revenue accounts are typically organized by revenue source; expenditure accounts, by organizational units and objects of expenditure. Budget categories and accounts have to match so that budgets and actual financial actions can be compared easily and accurately in order to monitor community finances and make financial decisions.

Balances

Balances refers to amounts recorded in particular accounts. The balances may result from a series of transactions affecting one account (e.g., the cash account balance resulting from receipts and disbursements), or they may be the difference between two or more other accounts (e.g., an account balance indicating how much money can still be spent on library books is the difference between the library books appropriations and expenditure accounts).

Reports

Most officials use regular monthly, quarterly, and annual accounting reports. Reports show balances for particular periods and points in time at different levels of detail. For example, most department heads get a monthly expenditure report that shows departmental expenditures in particular accounts for the previous month. In addition, such reports indicate total expenditures for the fiscal year up to the end of the month, total appropriations, and remaining expenditure authority for the fiscal year. Elected officials typically get summary reports on total revenues and expenditures.

Accounting basis

Basis refers to when transactions are "recognized" as having occurred (i.e., when an accounting entry is made). The use of a particular basis determines precisely when revenues and expenditures are recorded in the accounts as having occurred; more than one basis may be used simultaneously. The same situation can be reported in a variety of ways. It is essential in dealing with financial reports to know what basis is being used. Community governments may use different bases for different funds. Four common bases include cash, accrual, modified accrual, and encumbrance.

It is essential in dealing with financial reports to know what basis is being used.

The *cash basis* is the simplest. A transaction is recognized when money moves; money is collected or sent to pay a bill. Its weakness is that it can be manipulated to produce misleading reports by speeding up or delaying bill payments.

Accountants prefer the *accrual basis*. Transactions are recorded when an obligation is incurred; an obligation is incurred when a bill is sent, a service rendered, or a good delivered. This method produces much more accurate reports, although the bookkeeping is much harder and more time-consuming. The *modified accrual basis*, which means the accrual basis is used for expenditure and not revenue accounts, is often used for governmental fund types because it is not possible to predict government revenues with desired accuracy.

The *encumbrance basis* is used only for expenditures and reflects when a decision or commitment to spend has been made. The advantage of this basis is that it provides the earliest possible record of spending decisions and thus provides the best possible budgetary control. It also requires more complicated accounting and reporting.

Internal controls

Internal controls are features of accounting systems that are designed to ensure accuracy and to safeguard public resources. Generally, these controls involve formally specified and divided responsibilities, systematic procedures, and regular reviews of accounting records. Typical controls include requiring that a person who has no part in making cash receipts or disbursements reconcile monthly bank account records; the use of prenumbered accounting forms; the use of checks to make all payments; and requiring a responsible official to approve by signature such things as checks, payrolls, invoices, purchase orders, and cash deposits.

Revenue administration

Revenues should be collected as efficiently as possible. First, adequate information must be provided to those from whom revenues are collected. For example, property owners must be informed clearly about the way their taxes are calculated and when they must be paid. Revenue bases have to be located and their value assessed; payers of revenue must get a bill indicating what they owe. Actually collecting money takes much time and effort. Compliance with applicable laws has to be ensured. Appeals may be appropriate in some cases (e.g., valuation of property for property taxes). Enforcement efforts are required when people do not pay willingly.

Purchasing

The goal of purchasing is to buy the right things at the best possible price in an approved manner. Successful purchasing generally results from formal regulations, regular procedures, and centralization. Appropriate regulations should be adopted by the governing body. Such regulations guide purchasing procedures and specify such details as the general duties of different officials (especially the purchasing agent); the dollar amount above which competitive bids are required (the bid limit); informal price gathering; conditions under which emergency purchases can be made; and disposal of obsolete equipment and materials.

Operating procedures are best based on written regulations. These procedures govern such tasks as preparation of specifications, solicitation of formal and informal bids, preparation of purchase orders, inspection and testing of goods, making of payments, and handling of exceptions to normal purchasing procedures.

Regardless of a community's size or form of government, all purchasing responsibilities should be centralized in one office. This approach saves money through bulk-purchasing price advantages, reduced costs for small purchases, and control over inventories. It also minimizes delayed deliveries and rush orders. Other benefits include systematic inspection of delivered goods for quantity and quality; standard specifications to ensure the suitability of purchases; discouragement of favoritism; and encouragement of greater competition among prospective vendors. A centralized system works best when there is close cooperation with operating departments.

Cooperative purchasing, in which several governments collaborate in making their purchases, has been increasing in recent years because it promises significant savings to small governments through large-scale bulk purchasing. Community governments organize such efforts or avail themselves of state purchasing pools in which states allow local units to take advantage of bulk state purchasing.

Treasury management

Treasury management seeks to maximize the advantages and minimize the costs from the flow of monies into and out of bank accounts. It is usually achieved by placing responsibility for managing the government's cash resources under the direction of one person.

The first requirement of good treasury management is to have money available to pay bills when they become due. After that, treasury management seeks to maximize returns on investments and discounts for early payment of bills, and to minimize debt and financial service costs. Cash flows are forecast, and plans made accordingly to pay bills, invest monies, or borrow monies. A treasury management system involves bringing in revenues as soon as possible and delaying expenditures as long as reasonably possible. Taking discounts for early payments may be the best use of community money.

Investment has enjoyed soaring popularity as an additional source of community government income. One crucial investment technique is the use of interest-bearing checking accounts. Generally, government income is maximized by using one checking account to serve all of a government's funds rather than having a separate account for each fund.

Internally pooling money into one or a few bank accounts is also preferred for investment purposes. External pooling is accomplished through state-sponsored or other local government investment pools. Money should be invested only for as long as it is not required to make payments. As a general rule, funds that will not be needed to pay bills within thirty days should be invested to earn more interest. All such investments should be completely safe. Generally, the longer the investment period and the larger the investment, the greater the investment income.

Debt costs are minimized by limiting the time and amount of debt. Financial service costs are minimized by shopping around among banks for the best total package of checking, borrowing, and investing services.

Debt management

Debt management concerns the use of borrowed money. Borrowing money should neither be shunned nor used excessively. In many cases, communities fail to borrow even when it would be to their advantage to do so. Debt burdens should not exceed communities' ability to repay them. Increasing amounts of short-term debt or increases in indebtedness for three consecutive years are two signs of possibly excessive debt. Decisions on borrowing require careful review of legal authority, proper procedures, financial capacity, and the appropriateness of the purpose of borrowing. Borrowing occurs through a bidding or negotiated process. Generally, smaller borrowings are negotiated and larger ones are bid.

In many cases, communities fail to borrow even when it would be to their advantage to do so.

Community governments manage both short- and long-term debt. Short-term debt includes borrowing to cover a shortage of money and to finance the purchase of assets under the terms of lease-purchase agreements. When communities do not have enough money to pay bills while waiting for revenues to arrive, they borrow to pay bills (such borrowing is often called tax anticipation warrants). Short-term loans in anticipation of revenues should not exceed expected revenues.

Lease-purchase agreements have become popular in recent years as a way of avoiding referendum requirements and general obligation debt limits and as a way of purchasing assets without paying or acknowledging their full price in a given year. Communities pay for equipment or buildings on a yearly basis for a specific period and own the items at the end of the period. Lease-purchase agreements should not be used excessively because they have higher interest costs and can overburden a community.

Long-term debt, usually for large amounts, falls into the categories of general obligation and revenue bonds. General obligation bonds constitute a commitment to repay borrowed money using any and all revenue sources and assets of the community. Their use is limited to activities that serve a governmental purpose, and their interest cost is the lowest available. Revenue bonds usually pledge only certain revenues toward repayment. They commonly finance facilities that generate revenues (e.g., water and sewer systems). Revenues from the service charges must be used to repay the debt. Because of the lesser commitment to repayment and greater risk of default, such bonds carry higher interest costs as well as numerous specific requirements (e.g., no free utility service).

Managing debt means that all details associated with borrowing agreements are being met. Making sure that money is available and submitted for repayment is obvious. Other details may include maintaining financial reserves, making reports, and accounting properly for operations.

Risk management

Risk management seeks to identify situations that could impose large, avoidable costs or liabilities and then to take steps to prevent or minimize the likelihood that they will occur. It starts with identifying risks from accidents, thefts, fires, equipment breakdowns, and liability suits, both from employees and from persons affected by government services. Once identified, such risks can be classified into categories based on their frequency and severity, which facilitates decision making about strategies for dealing with risks.

High-frequency and high-severity risks should be targeted for reduction. The usual means of doing so include minimizing risk exposure through sensible alteration of practices (e.g., training all employees how to lift things); transferring risks to other parties; in rare cases abandoning an activity; and making provisions to pay damages that do occur.

Once risks have been identified, classified, and minimized, communities must prepare to pay the potential financial consequences of remaining risks. Insurance is one way of paying for risks. Self-insurance practices, when sensible, include paying for minor risks out of current operating revenues; funding a designated risk payment account or fund in which monies are accumulated to pay for larger losses; and participating with other governments in a multijurisdictional risk financing pool.

An ongoing risk management program requires regular reviews of the effectiveness of existing policies and constant identification of new risks. Centralization of risk management responsibility in one person or office is best. A formal policy statement is helpful and good recordkeeping essential.

Audit and review

After a fiscal year, budget implementation ends, but budgeting responsibilities continue. Community governments make annual financial and budget reports, undertake audits, and review the just-expired budget year to evaluate successes, failures, and ongoing concerns. All three areas work together.

Financial and budget reports

As part of ensuring their accountability to citizens, community governments report on concluded budget years. The primary means of reporting is the annual financial report, which displays accounting information for a fiscal year. For each fund for the fiscal year, these reports show actual expenditures and revenues, and the ending balances in asset, liability, and fund balance accounts. Additional information includes budgeted expenditures and revenues, information on general fixed assets and general long-term debt, and any other important details (e.g., pension liabilities and funding). States typically require that these reports be filed with a state office. Financial information reported on a yearly basis comes from the annual financial report.

Community reports about budgets highlight major concerns. These reports focus attention on major capital projects, unexpected expenditure requirements, revenue increases or shortfalls, and the overall financial position of the community. Such reports may be broken down into detailed departmental or functional area reports. They may appear by themselves or as part of a comprehensive annual community report.

Audits

Audits are reviews of financial records by persons from outside the community government. These reviews have several purposes; each purpose raises different questions that yield different answers. The kinds of audits are financial, management letter, compliance, performance, and program.

Financial audits, which account for the overwhelming majority of audits, involve a review of accounting records to determine whether the community is using "generally accepted accounting principles" (GAAP). If it is, the community gets an audit report letter that says that its annual financial reports were prepared in accordance with GAAP and that they "present fairly" its financial information. This means that the accounting procedures used should result in accurate reports. If it is not in compliance, the letter notes specific exceptions or generally says that the auditor can offer no opinion.

Management letters, the next most common audit component, are conducted in conjunction with financial audits at additional expense. These letters, especially the first few times they are used, provide extremely detailed reviews of internal controls for safeguarding community resources and the accuracy of accounting records.

Compliance, *performance*, and *program auditing* are used much less. Compliance auditing reviews whether administrative and legal procedures have been followed; some federal grants require this kind of audit. Performance auditing concerns efficiency, and program auditing concerns effectiveness.

Budget review

Finally, after the end of the fiscal year, the chief administrator should review how the actual revenues and expenditures fared relative to the budget adopted at the beginning of the fiscal year. When chief administrators and department heads use formal objectives to guide operations, the focus should be on their accomplishment.

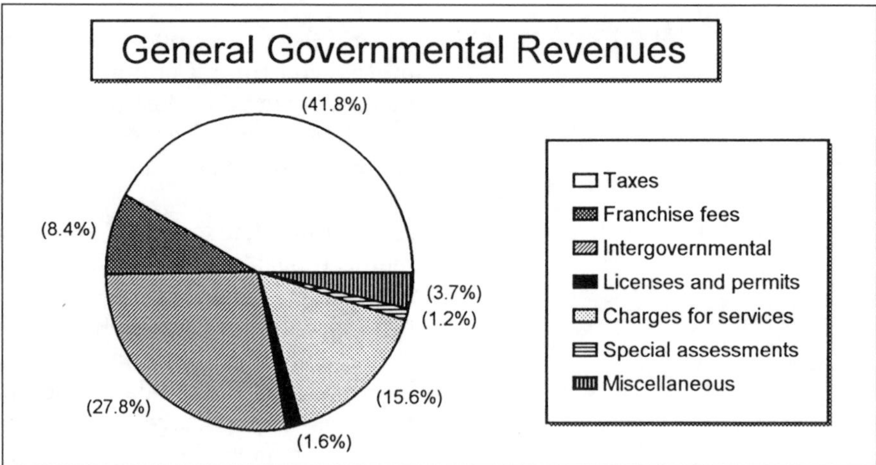

Figure 12–7 Summary of general governmental revenues for the fiscal year ended June 30, 1993, from the annual financial report of the city of Gresham, Oregon.

Revenues	Amount	Percent of Total	Increase/ (Decrease) from 91-92	Percent of Increase/ (Decrease)
Taxes	$12,255,451	41.81	$1,131,074	10.17
Franchise fees	2,456,285	8.38	326,992	15.36
Intergovernmental	8,134,032	27.75	1,640,597	25.27
Licenses and permits	475,369	1.62	(360,069)	(43.10)
Charges for services	4,570,601	15.60	3,862,591	545.56
Special assessments	348,286	1.19	165,835	90.89
Miscellaneous	1,070,348	3.65	(274,180)	(20.39)
Total	$29,310,372	100.00%	$6,492,840	

Annual budget reviews take place in two contexts. First, right after a fiscal year ends, a community's administrative and political leadership can analyze that fiscal year for lessons to be learned. For example, unexpected expenditures can be reviewed for the likelihood of future difficulties. Second, during the preparation and submission and approval stages, community officials review past budgets to find answers to questions concerning the budget under consideration.

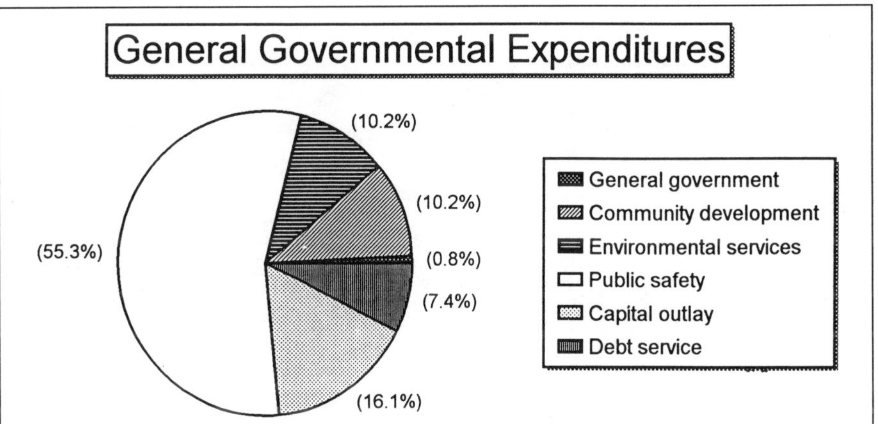

Figure 12–8 Summary of general governmental expenditures for the fiscal year ended June 30, 1993, from the annual financial report of the city of Gresham, Oregon.

Revenues	Amount	Percent of Total	Increase/ (Decrease) from 91-92	Percent of Increase/ (Decrease)
Current:				
General Government	$ 217,967	0.77	$ (38,055)	(14.86)
Community Development	2,893,203	10.25	(2,522,957)	(46.58)
Environmental Services	2,881,739	10.21	2,881,739	100.00
Public Safety	15,607,882	55.27	1,306,190	9.13
Capital Outlay	4,548,755	16.11	1,735,307	61.68
Debt Service:				
Principal Retirement	1,059,036	3.75	35,305	3.45
Interest	1,028,842	3.64	57,729	5.94
Total	$28,237,424	100.00%	$3,455,258	

Afterword

Many students of government believe that budgeting and financial management are the single most crucial functions of management. It is in the budgetary process that the most critical decision of all is made: how much effort to devote to each service function. It is in budgeting that the ultimate policy decisions are made, priorities are established, resources are allocated, and service levels are determined.

Financial management is also critical. It is in handling the public's money that the public administrator's discharge of what Woodrow Wilson called "the sacred trust" is most evident and most easily monitored. Good financial management often means the difference between good government and mediocre government, between long-term fiscal health and future fiscal crisis.

In addition, budgeting and financial management are the tools that enable the government administrator to respond to public insistence that government "do more with less" and sustain or even expand services without increasing either taxes or spending. In short, good financial management is essential to good government. ■

13 Personnel Management

Experienced community administrators know that despite the election-year rhetoric of political candidates, governments cannot be run exactly like businesses. Government is about societal values as much as it is about efficient service provision, and nowhere is this more true than in the management of personnel. For example, the increase in the number of households in which both parents work outside the home has prompted some community governments, as well as private employers, to make a greater effort to accommodate the needs of working parents. Some have liberalized leave policies, instituted job-sharing arrangements, and subsidized child care or established on-site child-care centers. Moreover, the Family and Medical Leave Act of 1992 specifies circumstances in which employers must grant leave to allow employees to care for family members. Societal values thus have as much influence on the personnel practices of community governments as do concerns for efficiency and effectiveness.

Personnel management is arguably the most critical activity in community government—critical because the provision of government services depends on the efforts of a broad spectrum of government employees. Ensuring that these employees fulfill their responsibilities in an effective manner is part of the personnel function. As O. Glenn Stahl, a noted expert on public personnel administration, said, "Personnel administration . . . is the totality of concern with the human resources of an organization."

Successful personnel administration requires the assurance that treatment of government employees is fully consistent with societal values, as well as effective use of sophisticated management tools and techniques. It means adhering to the tenets of affirmative action; ensuring equitable treatment of women, as required by law; and showing respect for diverse opinions, life-styles, and cultural backgrounds. Community government personnel managers must also be prepared to confront the effects in the workplace of major social problems such as alcoholism, drug abuse, and AIDS.

To excel at personnel management, community government leaders must combine practical knowledge with a high level of sensitivity to the concerns of others and an awareness of social trends. This chapter seeks to provide an overview of the critical-knowledge areas of public personnel management while alerting the reader to value-laden issues that may need special consideration. Of course, individual readers decide what values are most important in their community.

The application of personnel management techniques in individual circumstances is highly complex. The outcome of a particular situation is affected by the interaction between issues and values, on one hand, and a wealth of information that may be interpreted in a variety of ways on the other. Moreover, interested parties often argue for a particular interpretation because of their personal stake in the situation.

Merit as a guiding principle

The merit principle has its roots in a reform movement that flourished in the United States in the late 1800s after President James A. Garfield was assassinated by a dissatisfied patronage seeker. Merit-based personnel systems typically possess the following traits:

Employees are recruited, selected, and promoted on the basis of their relative abilities, knowledge, and skills. Entry-level jobs are open to all qualified applicants.

Compensation is equitable and adequate.

Employees are given whatever training is necessary to ensure optimum performance.

Employees are retained on the basis of the adequacy of their performance, are given opportunities to correct inadequate performance, and are discharged only when inadequate performance cannot be corrected.

Fair treatment of applicants and employees is ensured in all aspects of personnel administration, without regard to political affiliation, race, color, national origin, sex, or religious creed, and with proper regard for their privacy and constitutional rights as citizens.

Employees are assured protection against political coercion and are prohibited from using their official authority to interfere with, or affect the results of, an election or a nomination for office.

In many community governments merit principles are incorporated into a system of rules and regulations known as a civil service system, although civil service systems can be established without merit as a major consideration. Merit-based personnel systems in community governments tend to be associated with other changes, such as adoption of the council-manager form of government. These "reformed" governments place a greater emphasis on the recruitment of professionally trained employees, who are insulated from political pressures. Despite the broad-based success of the reform movement, however, political patronage is an accepted part of personnel practices in many large cities and in a wide array of counties. Where political patronage still flourishes, whether applicants are hired or employees advanced tends to depend on their relationship with key political leaders. These governments are easily identified by the high turnover that accompanies a change in leadership.

A changing view of merit

The term *merit* can be misleading because it tends to imply a high level of performance. Ironically, in many cases merit principles and civil service regulations have become synonymous with poor performance. Merit protection and civil service regulations were established to prevent political abuse, but today they often protect employees who are not performing at an acceptable level. As a result, even the term *civil servant* has developed a negative connotation. Not only does excessive protection mar the image of government service, but it also limits management control.

Many local governments have reacted to these problems by increasing management control over the personnel function and bypassing civil service regulations in favor of new approaches that reward employee excellence and achievement. Often called simply "merit systems," these new approaches use personnel policies to promote higher work quality rather than to insulate workers from political pressures. By doing so, they seek to restore the traditional meaning of merit and restore public confidence in community government.

Organizing the personnel function

The organization of the personnel function is highly related to concerns for merit and management control. For example, in the past a higher proportion of community governments possessed an independent personnel board or civil service commission that had total responsibility for the personnel function. Today modern local governments use one of the following three models:

A central personnel department or a single director with full authority over the personnel function

A central personnel department or a single director with an independent personnel board or civil service commission with limited functions

Decentralization of the personnel function into individual departments.

The first two approaches are currently the most popular. Decentralization of the personnel function to the department level is used only in a limited number of small cities and counties.

The declining emphasis on civil service commissions reflects the desire for greater management control as well as the increasing complexity of the personnel function. Managing a personnel system in a modern community government requires a trained professional with a thorough knowledge of legal requirements and specialized management tools.

Position classification

Position classification is the cornerstone of effective management of the personnel function in community governments. It organizes essential information about how work is done in the organization so that the information can be used in personnel operations. Similar positions are grouped under common job titles according to the type of work performed, the level of difficulty and responsibility involved, and the qualifications required.

For classification purposes, every position consists of a group of duties and responsibilities assigned to an employee. A class is a group of positions that (1) are similar in duties and responsibilities; (2) require the same qualifications in education and experience; (3) can be filled through similar testing procedures; and (4) can be assigned the same job title and salary range. The description of duties, responsibilities, and qualifications of positions in the class is called the class specification. The classification as a whole takes in (1) all the classes and class titles that have been established; (2) the specification of each class; and (3) the procedures for maintaining the position classification plan.

Properly prepared class specifications are essential for establishing pay scales; recruitment, selection, and promotion procedures; training programs; performance evaluation criteria; and labor-management relations. Class titles and specifications provide a uniform terminology for discussing positions, keeping records, and preparing systematic budget requests for personnel services. Class specifications help clarify how positions within the organization relate to one another and provide information needed to compare internal rates of pay and rates relative to other jurisdictions. In addition, class specifications are useful in compiling personnel statistics and conducting management studies.

Professional personnel administration

Historically, employees were not highly valued in organizations. The personnel function consisted of collecting time sheets and doing the payroll and, in some cases, administering benefits. Today, organizations have come to realize that the human resource is their greatest commodity, and with this realization, personnel administration has taken on a more comprehensive meaning and become a much more complex task.

Along with time sheets and payroll, human resource officers may attend to the issues of compensation, management-employee relations, recruitment, job classification, training, employee evaluation, and policy and procedure administration, among others. Larger organizations may hire specialists in each of the areas listed above, who report to the human resource director; in smaller organizations, the human resource officer may not have an in-house staff and may therefore rely on outside consultants to assist with technical issues such as job classification systems and the evaluation process.

Professional human resource officers come from a variety of academic backgrounds. Colleges and universities have only recently begun to establish degree programs in personnel administration; some institutions now offer a master's degree in the field. There are also several professional associations that provide training. The Society for Human Resource Management sponsors two certification programs: the Professional in Human Resources program, for those with four years' experience in an exempt-level human resource position, and the Senior Professional in Human Resources program, for those with eight years' experience.

Other organizations offer certification in specific areas of human resource management. For example, the American Compensation Association offers the Certified Compensation Professional program. Candidates for certification must complete nine courses and pass the exams for each. The International Society of Certified Benefits Specialists offers the ten-course Certified Employee Benefits Specialist Program. Upon successful completion of these programs, candidates receive a certificate and may use a professional designation such as C.C.P. (Certified Compensation Professional).

In addition to the services of a professional human resource officer, many organizations need to have access to an attorney. Complex issues such as terminations, labor negotiations, or compliance with federal legislation such as the Fair Labor Standards Act or the Americans with Disabilities Act may require legal expertise. In summary, human resource professionals need a combination of education and experience in the field, as well as access to outside consultants and attorneys, to be most effective.

The challenge of job classification

Position classification is a specialized technique, and it should be performed by a trained and experienced person. Position classification reflects the value placed on different jobs, making classification plans subject to legal challenges. An example is the controversy that developed over "comparable worth" during the 1980s. The principle of comparable worth holds that the pay associated with different jobs must correspond to the value of the job to the organization, and not to the sex or other characteristics of typical workers holding the jobs. From a legal perspective, the comparable worth movement has become bogged down in the complexities of establishing the true value of different jobs and job activities.

Given the ambiguities surrounding this issue, it is not surprising that few community governments have comparable worth policies. The only strong exception to this rule appears to be the state of Minnesota, where many cities and counties have them.[1] Although comparable worth has yet to have a major impact upon the personnel practices of local governments, the case illustrates how societal changes influence the personnel function.

Developing a position classification system

The first step in classifying a position is usually developing a questionnaire that asks employees in great detail about every aspect of their work. The questionnaires are analyzed and used to group positions into common classes. Work audits are later used to verify responses. A preliminary allocation of positions is then made to the appropriate classes, and specifications are written for each class. Each specification contains (1) a descriptive title; (2) a description of the nature of the work; (3) examples of the work; (4) a summary of duties and responsibilities; and (5) a statement of required qualifications.

Meetings are held with department heads and supervisors to discuss the specifications and review the tentative allocation of positions to their respective classes. Any necessary adjustments can be made at this time. Individual positions are allocated to the appropriate classes on the basis of existing duties, responsibilities, and place in the organizational hierarchy. Individual employees are notified of the proposed allocation of their positions and are provided an opportunity to comment on the allocation.

The complexity of developing or modifying a position classification system and the legal and political consequences of such a system make the task one usually assigned to professionals with special training and experience. When completed, the classification system is usually adopted by the council either in a separate ordinance or as a part of a more comprehensive personnel ordinance.

Figure 13–1 Steps in developing the position classification plan.

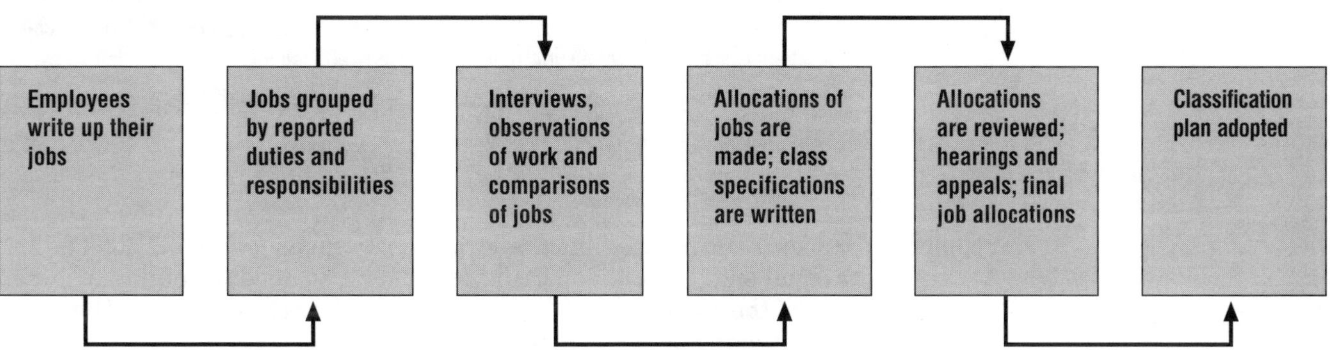

Implementing the system

The classification plan also includes rules for its own interpretation and maintenance. Rules cover such issues as the definition of terms, allocation of positions to classes, amendment of classes and class specifications, and procedures for changing personnel and financial records to conform with the classification plan. An appeals procedure is essential in order to protect the integrity of the plan, and each employee must be provided an opportunity to appeal his or her job allocation.

No classification plan can be expected to remain static. Class specifications need to be reviewed and revised periodically to ensure that the requirements are job-related and do not discriminate against minorities, women, or other protected groups. Periodic reviews also serve to keep management abreast of changes in the nature of the work, the number of positions, the number of employees performing specific duties, and changes in the skills needed by workers. Changes in organizational structure and in the scope and level of services provided also affect the classification plan.

Personnel experts recommend a complete reclassification study every five or six years, supplemented by periodic review of the plan, particularly when revisions of an accompanying pay plan are contemplated. Supervisors should initiate reclassification studies before implementing pay-plan changes in order to avoid paying employees improperly. Whenever employees work outside classifications, morale and liability problems can be expected.

Hiring new employees

Placing a person on the payroll of a community government generally follows a recruitment and selection process that may take only a few days or stretch out over months. Recruitment involves seeking out prospective employees for a job; selection involves choosing a person from the list of applicants to receive a job offer.

Local governments must approach the recruitment and selection process carefully. If it is done properly, the workforce of a community government will be more productive and efficient; if not, the cost in litigation and nonperformance can be enormous. Finally, community governments have an obligation to hire scrupulously and to avoid even the appearance of favoritism or discrimination.

Compensation for college

To recruit and maintain a well-educated workforce, Brentwood, Tennessee (16,000), compensates employees for taking undergraduate-level courses and completing degrees related to their jobs. Judged on an individual basis, employees whose job descriptions do not require a college degree may be compensated $50 per month for each year of college they have completed. The supplement does not apply to graduate programs or to those whose job requires a college education.

Source: *The Guide to Management Improvement Projects in Local Government*, vol. 16, no. 3 (Washington, DC: ICMA, 1992), no. PRM-15.

Recruitment

Recruitment policies must address basic salary considerations as well as equal employment opportunities. They also need to define the dimensions of the search for suitable candidates. For example, should the search be limited to persons already employed in the government or residing in the community, or should it be broadened to encompass talent beyond the community's boundaries?

Considerable imagination and initiative are needed in developing a recruitment program. The individual responsible for recruitment needs to be well acquainted with job requirements, sources of qualified candidates, and the many laws and regulations governing recruitment and selection.

Position descriptions and requests from the hiring agency for specific skills (for example, proficiency in use of a particular word processing program) are used to prepare a public job announcement that includes the title of the position, a brief description of duties, the salary range, a statement of the minimum education and experience required, the method of application, and the closing date for filing the application.

Once the announcement has been prepared, it must be publicized. It is a good practice—often required by law—to post announcement of examinations and job vacancies where employees can see them. Advertisements are usually placed in newspapers of general circulation as well as in local papers. To demonstrate their good faith effort to avoid discrimination in employment, many governments insert the phrase "Equal Opportunity Employer" in their advertisements.

Job openings

Largo, Florida (62,000), encourages its employees to file interest cards if they would like future consideration for employment in positions for which the city is not currently recruiting. The postcard-sized form lists the individual's name and address on one side and position information on the other. If an opening occurs in that position within six months, the postcard is forwarded as notice that an application form must be completed by a specified deadline for further consideration. The technique has proved to be a cost-effective way of notifying employees of openings for positions in which they are interested.

Source: *The Guide to Management Improvement Projects in Local Government*, vol. 15, no. 1 (Washington, DC: ICMA, 1991), no. PRM-4.

In the case of professional and technical positions, job advertisements are usually placed in those professional journals, newsletters, or periodicals that accept them. Some professional associations operate placement services that bring together employers and potential applicants. Other sources of assistance in recruitment include the American Society of Public Administration, the International City/County Management Association, the National Association of County Officials, local chambers of commerce, trade associations, public and private employment services, and state municipal leagues.

As applications for the position are received, an effort should be made to keep applicants informed of the status of their application. Those who are ineligible should be notified immediately. If there is to be another stage in the recruitment process, such as an examination, all qualified applicants must be notified of the date, time, and place.

Selection procedures

Any standard used in deciding who is hired can be considered a test. Personal employment history and background information as described on the application form, personal interviews, oral and written examinations, performance tests, evaluations of education and experience, reference checks, physical examinations, and psychological testing are commonly used. Written tests are particularly useful for evaluating technical knowledge and writing skills. However, most written employment tests do not evaluate a candidate's personal skills, attitudes, or level of motivation, which are the factors that most frequently affect job performance. Interviews, background checks, assessment centers, and certain psychological tests are all additional ways to determine which candidate is most likely to succeed.

Several commercial firms design and market a wide variety of personnel tests, but a test should not be chosen simply on the basis of a description in a catalogue. Because testing is a specialized field, community government officials should always seek expert advice on the preparation and validation of tests; unless the validity of a test has been established, the results are open to legal challenge. The National Public Service Accreditation Board, established by ICMA as a professional, nonprofit service to accredit tests used for selecting, hiring, promoting, and certifying public employees, provides technical assistance and program support in this area to local governments and other public sector employers.

Videotaping interviews

Brentwood, Tennessee (16,400), has employed a company to videotape job applicants. Instead of paying to transport its seven finalists for an open position, the city prepared a list of twenty-five interview questions and used a private firm to videotape thirty-minute interviews at its offices around the country. After viewing the tapes, the city invited two candidates to the city for personal interviews and final selection. The procedure cost a total of $800, substantially less than the cost of air fare and lodging.

Source: *The Guide to Management Improvement Projects in Local Government*, vol. 16, no. 1 (Washington, DC: ICMA, 1992), no. PRM-3.

The testing process must be carefully managed so that federal laws on discrimination in hiring are not violated. Some critics charge that civil service tests are inherently discriminatory because they assume the point of view and values of white middle-class culture. Other complaints are that these tests are not job-related and that they frequently are not subjected to objective validation studies. Recent court decisions and rulings by fair employment practices authorities have resulted in a movement to reconsider testing during the selection process. Community governments must take great care to ensure that their testing procedures are consistent with current legal requirements.

Affirmative action

The passive prohibition of discriminatory practices is insufficient to ensure equal opportunity. To achieve the goal of equal employment opportunities for all, community governments are expected to initiate affirmative action programs that include practical plans to be developed and vigorously pursued at every level.

Affirmative action efforts usually require special recruitment techniques to solicit applications from minorities, women, and disabled individuals. The more common recruitment techniques tend to be inadequate for these groups. Techniques that have been used to recruit among minorities include the use of minority newspapers and radio stations, door-to-door recruiting, posters, job fairs, neighborhood bulletins, and cable television. Extensive use can also be made of church groups, fraternal societies, community action groups, and organizations such as the National Forum for Black Public Administrators, the Urban League, the National Association for the Advancement of Colored People, and the Hispanic Network. Schools, employment and training programs, and employment agencies can also be useful. Groups selected for affirmative action, whether minorities, women, or disabled persons, require outreach strategies tailored especially for them.

College loans

To increase the number of college-educated, minority officers in its police, fire, and park departments, University City, Missouri (40,000), offers four-year college scholarship loans. Qualifying applicants earn money and on-the-job experience while pursuing their college degrees. Upon completion of their degree, candidates have 20 percent of their loan forgiven for each year of full-time service in the city's employment.

Source: *The Guide to Management Improvement Projects in Local Government*, vol. 16, no. 4 (Washington, DC: ICMA, 1992), no. PRM-23.

Efforts to improve employment opportunities for women, minorities, or disabled workers need not conflict with merit system concepts. Outreach recruitment programs, job restructuring to increase job competition among minority-group applicants, on-the-job training for upward mobility, and similar affirmative action steps are consistent with true merit principles and the pursuit of excellence in employment.

Communities undertaking an affirmative action program encounter a number of barriers: budget limitations; inadequate numbers of applicants; public resistance; inability of applicants to pass tests (the fairness and relevance of which must be called into question); civil service restrictions; and resistance from employees and employee organizations and supervisors. A firm commitment from top management is necessary to overcome these obstacles.

Figure 13–2 Checklist for orientation of new employees.

New Employee Checklist
Full Time/Full Benefits

- ☐ Job description reviewed
- ☐ I.M.R.F.
- ☐ Life insurance
- ☐ Hospital benefits
- ☐ W-4 forms
- ☐ Personnel manual and receipt
- ☐ T.B. X-ray form
- ☐ I.D. card
- ☐ Demographic
- ☐ Fingerprint form
- ☐ Background check form
- ☐ Pay schedule
- ☐ I.C.M.A. form
- ☐ Racial diversity
- ☐ U.S. savings bonds
- ☐ Credit union
- ☐ Immigration form
- ☐ HIV policy and statement
- ☐ EAP
- ☐ Personal data form
- ☐ Village recycling program
- ☐ Hours, workweek, weekends
- ☐ Overtime requirements
- ☐ Job evaluation
- ☐ Probation period
- ☐ Pay increases and promotions
- ☐ Vacations/holidays
- ☐ Unpaid and emergency leave policy
- ☐ Rest periods
- ☐ Seniority/job posting
- ☐ Work rules and regulations
- ☐ Discipline procedures
- ☐ Telephone calls
- ☐ Attendance/punctuality
- ☐ Dress code
- ☐ Parking information
- ☐ Sexual harassment policy
- ☐ Grievance procedure

Non-Harassment Policy

All employees have the right to a work environment free from intimidation and harassment because of their sex, race, age, religion, ethnic origin, handicap, marital status, and military discharge. Any physical, verbal, visual, or sexual harassment is prohibited. Employees should report any complaints to their immediate supervisor, department head, or human resources officer.

I acknowledge that we have discussed all the above.

Employee's signature/Date ______________________

Human Resource Department/Date ______________________

Evaluating employee performance

Community governments must be committed to the job success of every employee. A newly hired person cannot be merely turned loose with instructions in one hand and tools in the other. Employees represent a valuable resource; they require proper orientation and training to reach their potential. Community governments must create management systems that provide adequate supervision while encouraging high levels of performance. Correct use of appropriate evaluation tools is critical to this effort.

The performance evaluation system should include a probationary period. Successful completion of the probationary period should be determined by a thorough performance evaluation; similar evaluations should be conducted of all employees on at least a yearly basis. Regular evaluations give management a chance to reiterate organizational goals and expectations and allow employees to learn more about what constitutes effective performance and how they can improve their work habits.

Performance evaluation should be closely linked to mechanisms for promotion and disciplinary action. Employees whose performance is inadequate should be given constructive criticism; improvement should always be encouraged and recognized. When they cannot be avoided, disciplinary actions must be fair, documented, and consistent with laws or labor contracts. Few aspects of a supervisor's job call for more tact, good judgment, common sense, and fairness than handling a disciplinary action.

Figure 13–3 Disciplinary action checklist.

1 Prior to disciplinary action:

- ☐ Have expected standards of performance been communicated to the employee?
- ☐ Is management rule/policy known and properly promulgated to the work force?
- ☐ Was a thorough investigation conducted, to determine the facts and degree of violation?
- ☐ Was the employee given opportunity to respond to the allegations?
- ☐ Quality of evidence: did the management's "judge" obtain substantial and compelling evidence?
- ☐ Severity of infraction: is this an infraction that routinely receives oral reprimand for first offense, suspension, or discharge?

2 Corrective/progressive discipline

- ☐ Is this a first offense?
- ☐ If so, is the violation serious enough to warrant punishment?
- ☐ Was the employee counseled or advised regarding continued conduct?

3 Were management rules/policies applied fairly and uniformly?

- ☐ No discriminatory or preferential treatment
- ☐ Back-up support from "other cases" inter/intra-firm (i.e., other employees treated thus for similar or same violation).
- ☐ Have all published procedures been followed?

The design of a performance evaluation system is important because it is considered a test under federal guidelines. It is subject to the same validity standards as any procedure used in the employee selection process. Despite the challenges, however, a well-designed performance evaluation system can encourage employees to cooperate in pursuing community goals. During evaluation, the supervisor and employee together can develop job performance objectives that reflect and help attain the broad goals of the government's mission statement and strategic plan.

"Get Caught" campaign
Florence, South Carolina (30,000), sponsors a "Get Caught" campaign that encourages local residents to report city employees they "catch" providing good service. Employees who are "caught" are recognized before the city council, given a special token, and given an opportunity to participate in a lottery for bonus vacation hours.

Source: Thomas W. Edwards, Jr., City Manager, Florence, South Carolina, 1993.

Formal methods of evaluation

Different approaches—ranging from the relatively simple to the very complex—are used to evaluate performance. The utility and even the legality of them all are threatened by their subjectivity (the rating received by an employee can vary widely depending on who is doing the rating) and their validity (they may not measure job-related performance). The inability to establish the validity of the methods used for performance evaluation could leave community governments vulnerable to legal challenges. At a minimum, community governments should make sure that any rating scales in use pertain strictly to job requirements. Also, they should take steps to ensure that all supervisors understand the problems associated with rating scales and the importance of objectivity. Ideally, all supervisors should base their rating upon standards uniformly applied to all employees in similar positions.

Simple methods

One of the most commonly used techniques involves a multiple-choice format of rating scales and checklists that requires the grader to judge employees on personal traits such as punctuality, cooperativeness, dependability, and general job performance. The evaluation forms usually have room for supervisors to elaborate upon checked-off responses. These forms take a minimum amount of time to fill out, and they are easy to score. However, they often reflect the evaluator's biases, and their validity is therefore particularly prone to challenge.

Multiple-choice rating scales often reflect the evaluator's biases, and their validity is therefore particularly prone to challenge.

A related approach that is commonly used is a narrative-based evaluation system that calls for a written evaluation of employees that is not structured by specific questions. Written narratives provide more detail about employee behaviors than do rating scales. Although the extra information provided by these narratives can be useful for guiding employee behavior, the same cautions noted for rating scales still apply. Any written comments about the suitability of employees must clearly relate to their job responsibilities.

Complex methods

More sophisticated performance evaluation systems are specifically designed to ensure that all employees are evaluated against carefully developed performance standards. These systems ask for an evaluation of each employee's work in relation to objectives or goals. This "management by objectives" approach is becoming increasingly popular in community governments.[2] It seeks to achieve a strong association between employee goals and objectives and the overall goals and objectives of the organization; such strategic thinking is becoming increasingly important.[3]

Fairness Virtually all performance evaluation plans have come under attack as being unfair, impossible, or useless. There is little agreement about the most effective rating system, and even good systems may be used improperly or ignored by community government leaders. Supervisors often assign average or satisfactory ratings to their employees regardless of their performance. Moreover, salary increments often go into effect automatically, despite ratings. Not uncommonly, supervisors file disciplinary charges against employees to whom they have given high performance ratings in the past. These charges are often dismissed when an appeals officer sees inconsistent treatment by a supervisor.

The mere existence of a performance evaluation system does not guarantee that it will be effective. Any performance evaluation

The employee evaluation process

Employee evaluation should be a constructive approach to improving employee performance and productivity. It should help to attain the following objectives:

- Identify employees who are capable of assuming greater responsibilities and deserving of promotion
- Strengthen the selection and training programs
- Determine employee productivity bonuses
- Keep the supervisor aware of employees' job performance
- Assist the supervisor in counseling employees
- Improve communication between management and employees
- Encourage employees to work toward their own self-development.

Comparison of an employee's performance with the requirements of the job is an important part of the evaluation. The review should answer the following questions:

- How well did the employee perform the job overall?
- What are his or her strengths, abilities, and potential for growth?
- What are his or her weaknesses and problems? What seem to be the reasons for them?
- What appears to be the most likely area for development?
- How can the employee bring about the required improvements?
- How can the supervisor help the employee improve?

To serve a constructive and practical purpose, the performance evaluation should

- Be understood and accepted by the employee
- Be the basis for plans to help the employee improve
- Recognize the employee's strengths as well as weaknesses
- Help the employee understand what is expected of him or her and how success will be measured.

A principal difficulty in employee evaluation is lack of objectivity. Errors that the supervisor should recognize and try to avoid are

- The tendency to allow a single personality trait to influence judgment on other factors ("the halo effect")
- The tendency to base evaluations on actions in the recent past or on one dramatic incident
- The tendency to translate abilities not used in the present job into a higher evaluation than performance justifies
- The tendency to translate potential usefulness and growth into a higher evaluation than present performance warrants
- The common tendency to rate everyone as average or a little above average.

The following rules can be useful in overcoming the errors listed above:

- Collect and record evidence throughout the entire evaluation period.
- Evaluate employees according to their job levels.
- Base the evaluation on the employee's actual performance apart from any consideration of estimated potential.
- Do not allow the individual's good or bad performance in one area to influence the total evaluation.
- Do not allow personal feelings to dominate the evaluation.

The evaluation process should conclude when the supervisor has covered all the points he or she intended to cover; when the employee has had an opportunity to review the points made, respond, and release any tensions that may exist; when a plan of action has been cooperatively developed; and when a natural stopping point has been reached. The supervisor should reassure the employee of the supervisor's continuing interest in the employee's progress and indicate willingness to discuss matters of concern at any time.

system is only as good as the supervisors involved. Adequate training is necessary to ensure that supervisors are able to fulfill their responsibilities.

The right to due process

The notion of "fairness" is critical in all personnel activities. In addition to performance evaluation, it is especially critical in disciplinary and termination actions. In such cases, employers must follow due process. The U.S. Supreme Court has ruled that no public employees may be denied a constitutional right, including property rights to their job, without due process. The court has set down the following steps as an articulation of due process:

- Timely advance notice of the action contemplated by the government and reasons for that action
- An opportunity for persons affected by the proposed action to respond through a hearing
- The right to present evidence
- The right to confront adverse witnesses
- The right of cross-examination
- The right to be represented at the hearing by counsel
- The right to have a decision based solely on applicable legal rules and the evidence adduced at the hearing
- The right to an unprejudiced decision maker
- The right to a statement from the decision makers regarding the reasons for the decision

The government's attorney should always be consulted before any action is taken to discipline or discharge an employee.

Employee compensation

No matter how performance evaluations are handled, for employees the bottom line is pay. Even if they derive nonfinancial awards from their job, employees view pay as a sign of their ultimate worth to their employer. Pay levels can be judged in two ways, by internal equity and external equity. Internal equity is based on pay comparisons within an organization and external equity on comparisons with employees in other organizations.

Failure to maintain both types of equity can have serious negative implications for the job satisfaction of employees. Disgruntled employees are likely to exhibit diminished performance and are more likely to leave an organization. Simple fairness requires that leaders in community government develop an equitable pay plan; they also must adhere to a number of statutory requirements.

Legal requirements

Employers abuse pay equity when they allow considerations of age, sex, race, and other non-merit factors to influence individual salary decisions. In response, many legislative and judicial remedies have been developed to ensure that employers observe basic principles of pay equity.

The Fair Labor Standards Act (FLSA) was expanded by a 1985 U.S. Supreme Court decision to cover wage and recordkeeping practices of local governments. It requires that all covered employees receive the minimum wage; that hourly employees must receive overtime or "comp time" when they work more than a 40-hour week; and that records of hours worked and pay be kept at least three years for all employees. Maintaining compliance with this law is especially difficult for community governments because of the irregular work hours of employees such as police officers and firefighters.

Other federal laws that forbid employment discrimination affect compensation practices. The Equal Pay Act of 1962 requires that men and women receive equal pay for equal work that is performed under similar working conditions, but it exempts pay differentials resulting from seniority or merit.

The Civil Rights Act of 1964 (Title VII), which forbids discrimination based on non-merit factors, has been interpreted in a number of court cases to require equal pay for comparable jobs. Different jobs can be considered comparable if there are strong similarities in job requirements.

Figure 13–4 Steps in developing the pay plan.

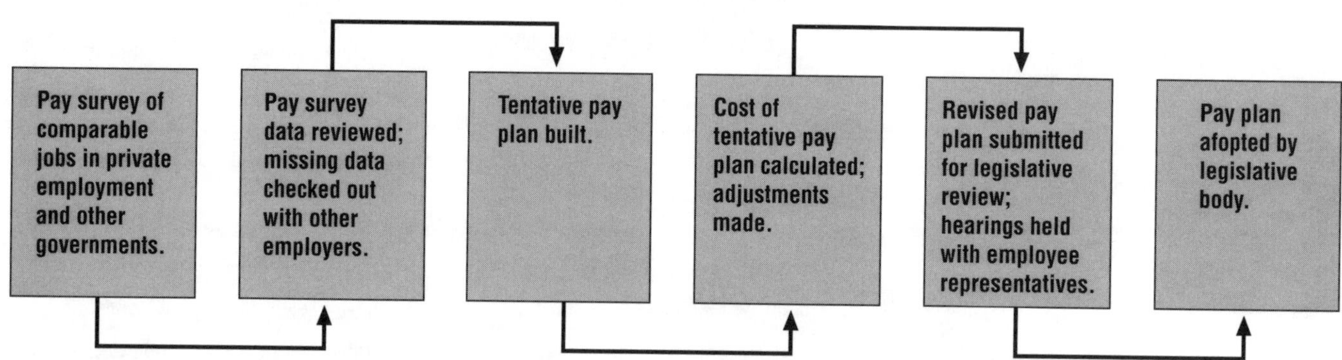

The Age Discrimination in Employment Act of 1963 requires employers to give older employees the same pay as younger ones for the same work. It also prohibits employers from using pension plan provisions to force older employees to take early retirement.

Linking pay and performance

Many local governments are taking steps to create a stronger link between compensation and employee performance. The goal is to reward top employees and encourage excellence. One popular approach is the use of pay-for-performance plans that offer broad pay ranges for different levels of individual performance. Also, some community governments are offering performance bonuses to individuals or groups who demonstrate noteworthy achievements.

Although the logic of linking pay and performance is compelling, attaining this objective requires overcoming some major barriers. Most important, lean budgets and political considerations may prevent community governments from providing meaningful monetary rewards for all of their top performers. Compromises that spread funds too thinly or ignore some deserving employees can do more harm than good.

Another problem is that enhancing the link between pay and performance increases the responsibilities of supervisors because they must decide who gets a pay increase and who is left out. This fact can certainly create conflict between supervisors and their subordinates and possibly between employees who see themselves as competing for monetary rewards.

Given the problems that may result, community government should not rush to adopt a pay-for-performance program. Success is likely to depend on taking the time to educate employees and supervisors about their responsibilities under the plan and the types of benefits that result from their cooperation.

Despite the challenges, however, community governments are likely to demonstrate considerable interest in pay-for-performance programs over the next decade. As the economy becomes more service oriented, public expectations for high-quality service are likely to increase. Community governments have to find ways to reward their best employees if they are going to meet those standards.

Employee benefits

Besides a paycheck, employees of local governments receive a benefits package. Some benefits are required by federal law, such as social security, workers' compensation, and unemployment compensation, but others are currently discretionary. The additional benefits typically include health care and pension provisions.

Health benefits

The high cost of health care puts community governments in the difficult dilemma of containing costs while providing a high level of health services. Currently, benefits experts are strongly supporting the concept of "managed care" as the most effective strategy for reducing costs. This strategy requires employers to take an active role in monitoring any activities that can increase health care expenditures. Some community governments have developed extensive programs to improve the health of employees by helping them to lose weight, reduce stress, quit smoking, or reduce injuries.

Managed care programs also prompt employees to become more cost-conscious consumers of health care, for example by requiring employees to share a larger portion of costs through deductibles, coinsurance, or copayments. Deductibles refer to the initial fixed costs of services that employees are responsible for paying before employer-financed benefits apply. Coinsurance refers to employees paying a fixed percentage of health care costs above the level of the deductible. Copayments refer to fixed payments by employees for health care services (e.g., $5 per prescription).

Advocates of managed care also stress the importance of negotiating agreements with health care providers to reduce costs. The idea is for a large employer or a group of cooperating employers to negotiate lower prices for higher volumes of employees. Even small single jurisdictions may be able to develop mutually beneficial relations with individual physicians. Although developing relationships with what are called "preferred providers" offers the promise of reduced health care costs, such arrangements are not easy to develop. First, community governments need to acquire access (usually through a third party) to a highly sophisticated database to get the type of information needed to negotiate with providers. Second, they must then find ways to encourage their employees to visit the designated providers for treatment. Because this usually involves switching their family doctor, employees are often not eager to make the change.

Given the complexities of the health care environment, local governments are advised to seek out the help of trained benefits experts. Larger jurisdictions can develop the capacities of their own staffs, but smaller jurisdictions have to choose carefully from among the many third-party services available in the health care market.

Encouraging employee wellness

To encourage employee wellness and increase productivity, Dunedin, Florida (38,000), pays its employees to stay well. All hourly, non-salaried employees can earn a lump-sum bonus of $300 if they do not take any sick leave during a year, and they receive $100 if they use less than eight hours of leave. Part-time employees who take no sick leave receive a prorated bonus according to the number of hours they work. Of the city's 452 employees, 44 percent received bonuses in 1990-1991.

Source: *The Guide to Management Improvement Projects in Local Government*, vol. 16, no. 3 (Washington, DC: ICMA, 1992), no. PRM-17.

Employee dental care pool

Convinced that its dental insurance plan was not cost effective, Akron, Colorado (1,599), canceled its dental insurance and created a town employee dental pool. The town determined the average amount spent for premium expenses in the previous three years and allowed eligible full-time employees a premium of $386 per year. Each year, any money left over in the amount set aside is used to reimburse, on a pro-rated basis, employees whose expenses exceeded the $386 allotment. Any money still remaining is carried over into the following year. In effect since 1989, the dental program has saved money for both the town and its employees.

Source: *The Guide to Management Improvement Projects in Local Government*, vol. 15, no. 3 (Washington, DC: ICMA, 1991), no. PRM-22.

A regional health care coalition

Local governments and school systems in the metropolitan Washington, D.C., area began to feel the health care insurance pinch dramatically in 1987 when premiums to provide health care insurance to municipal employees rose as much as 70 percent. Through the establishment of a regional health care coalition, participants realized tremendous savings.

A working group met monthly with an independent consultant to identify and more thoroughly understand problem areas, the requirements of a joint program, and the political realities of working with so many organizations. Negotiation, information gathering, and group education took almost one year to complete.

Of the fourteen participants, five determined it was in their interest to formalize the health care coalition and begin the process of managing the program. The following were membership requirements:

Being a regional public sector employer

Committing to remain the program for two years

Offering only the selected health care plan to employees

Ensuring that employees make contributions toward their health care insurance costs.

Upon entering into this agreement, most participating governments and schools realized a premium savings of 30 percent to 40 percent over the previous year's costs. The following year, premiums increased by 18 percent, due in large part to inflation in the cost of medical services. Even with this increase, costs remained significantly below the rates of the previous two years.

Source: "Regional Strategies for Local Government Management," *MIS Report*, vol. 24, no. 3 (March 1992).

Pension benefits

All employees want to feel that they and their families are financially secure. Pension benefits, generally described in terms of retirement, are meant to provide that security. As with health benefits, however, many community governments are forcing employees to take greater responsibility for achieving this end. There are two typical pension program patterns, defined benefit and defined contribution programs.

Defined benefit programs, the traditional pattern, make provision for benefit payments by community governments to employees or their families upon retirement, disability, or death. The payment levels are usually determined by the reason for the payments, wages during a particular period, and the length of employment service. Employees frequently, but not always, contribute to funding these programs through payroll deductions. Vesting, which means that employees acquire legal rights to benefits from pension programs, typically comes after a predetermined number of years of service. This practice, along with benefits that are paid at a higher rate for later years of service, tends to reduce employee turnover.

This kind of pension program has significant administrative burdens. Employers are responsible for designing programs; creating pension funds, which are used to collect and invest monies; determining benefit eligibility; and making payments.

Defined contribution programs provide for employee retirement through payments to third parties, who establish retirement investment accounts for each employee. In many cases, employers also provide disability and life insurance. Payments are based on each employee's salary, and sometimes require an employee as well as an employer contribution. Payments are made to the third party, who administers all aspects of the retirement package. Retirement benefits to employees depend crucially upon the amounts of money contributed to their accounts and the investment performance of the program. The responsibilities of community governments for this kind of retirement program are minimal and clearly defined.

Underfunding and weak investment performance have created concerns over the ability of some local governments to meet their pension obligations.

Problems in community pension programs in recent years have created a number of changes. Unexpectedly high costs have given impetus to the redesign of program features. Underfunding of pension funds and weak investment performance have created concerns over the ability of some local governments to meet their pension obligations. Employees have often found it difficult or impossible to transfer the money in their accounts to a new pension fund if they change jobs; the resulting lack of employee mobility has also been seen as a problem to be corrected.

Common responses to such problems include lowering benefit responsibilities of community governments, increasing costs imposed on employees, striving to improve funding levels and investment performance, and providing portable pension programs that allow employees to retain participation in a pension program when they change employers. Although each of these responses can be managed in the context of defined benefit programs, many community governments have switched to defined contribution programs because they appear to solve most of the problems, especially future employer responsibilities. Of course, employees are then more at risk because they must cover more exigencies themselves.

Employee unions

Many local governments struggle with pressures from employee unions, greatly increasing the challenge of managing their personnel. The first step in dealing with unions is to develop formal personnel policies and rules. Once this task has been completed, the community government is in a much better position to bargain. Should an employee organization be recognized, a number of other steps will become necessary, such as the designation of a bargaining unit, preparations for negotiation, development of a strike contingency plan, and the administration of a labor contract.

The bargaining relationship

In states that have comprehensive labor relations statutes, local government officials must become familiar with their provisions. Where state legislation does not exist, community governments should be prepared, if necessary, to adopt an employee relations ordinance that covers all aspects of the bargaining relationship. Such an ordinance generally will recognize the right of employees to join and be represented by a union. Other matters to be covered include

A procedure for handling grievances

Rules relating to the activities of the union representatives

A prohibition of strikes or a specification of conditions under which they are permissible

A listing of unfair labor practices

The procedures to be followed in handling an impasse in negotiations.

The bargaining unit

When an employee organization has demanded recognition or when employees themselves have requested the right to organize, membership in the bargaining unit must be carefully defined. The government must also evaluate the impact of the union's suggested structure on the current management structure and identify positions, usually supervisory and managerial, to be excluded from the unit.

In states with comprehensive labor relations laws covering the public sector, the state agency administering the statute usually is responsible for assisting community governments in determining bargaining units and conducting all aspects of the labor relations program. Where such statutes do not exist, the administrator should seek expert advice from other state agencies or local government associations, because it is extremely difficult to change a unit once it has been established. Fragmented bargaining units can impose demands on the employer and make it difficult to keep benefits and working conditions uniform.

After the bargaining unit has been determined, the administrator must provide for an election in which affected employees can decide by secret ballot whether they wish to be represented by the unit. Where a state labor relations agency does not exist, assistance with conducting the election may be obtained from the American Arbitration Association or the state mediation service.

Management has a responsibility to participate in the pre-election campaign—a responsibility always exercised fully in the private sector—to explain to employees the implications of union membership. Although management is prohibited in most states from threatening the loss of jobs or benefits or misrepresenting important facts, it can and should provide factual information. Before getting involved in such an election, however, management should seek and follow expert legal advice to protect itself from accusations of unfair labor practices.

Labor-management negotiations

When a community government recognizes an employee organization, the chief administrator must become acquainted with all facets of negotiations. These include determining who will serve on the negotiating team, preparation for negotiations, physical arrangements for and scheduling of meetings, evaluation of proposals, methods of preparing counterproposals, strategy and tactics, and preparation of the written agreement.

Ordinarily, because of staff limitations, the administrator and the local government's legal counsel must assume responsibility for the negotiations. Usually it is advisable to obtain the assistance of a law firm specializing in labor-management relations.

Preparing for negotiations

Negotiators representing employees are often much better prepared than the management team.

Direct participation in labor negotiations by members of the governing body is not advisable. As policymakers, elected officials should limit themselves to determining allowable limits on policies being negotiated and to considering the recommendations of the officials who have been designated to meet with employee representatives on a continuing basis. The governing body must, however, be kept informed of the progress of the negotiations.

The negotiating team may consist of the chief negotiator, the finance officer, the government attorney, and the official or officials affected by the negotiations. In a team approach, alternates must be designated so that the negotiating sessions will not be interrupted should a particular member of the team be unavailable. Even a small community government should consider retaining a labor-relations consultant if no staff member is skilled in negotiations, because many costly and irreparable mistakes can be made.

Considerable homework is required before negotiations. The negotiator and the negotiating team must determine the management position and work out the tactics they will use. (Negotiators representing the employees are often much better prepared for negotiations than is the management team.) Suggestions should be solicited from supervisors and department heads on matters that might arise during the negotiations. A review of past grievances will also help to determine possible problem areas. Data must be gathered on past and present wages and fringe benefits, recruitment and retention experience, budgets and revenues, and the distribution of employees by classification, work location, and wage. Information on the current personnel practices of other local governments in the area is essential.

Reaching agreement

Any final agreement must be put into writing. Contract drafting is a vital and complex aspect of collective bargaining. Both union and management should help draft the language of the contract. Contract preparation can be simplified if agreement is reached on the phrasing of each clause during the negotiations. If the municipal attorney or administrator has had little or no experience in drafting contracts, a qualified consultant should be retained for this purpose. Mistakes in a first contract will be difficult to rectify in later ones, and a poorly written or ambiguous contract will lead to problems in administration.

Because not all negotiations result in agreement, it is essential that the administrator be acquainted with the various alternatives available for resolving disputes—especially mediation, fact finding, and arbitration. Other alternatives include nonstoppage strikes (in which work continues, at a slower rate), partial strikes, public referendums, votes of union membership on the employer's last offer, and court actions that might lead to injunctions, fines, or penalties. A well-prepared contingency plan for coping with all forms of work actions—including strikes, the spread of "blue flu" (using sick leave to avoid reporting to work) among the uniformed services, speedups or slowdowns, and mass resignations—can minimize the impact of work actions on the community. A plan of this type should be developed well before starting the negotiations.

Contract administration

Once a contract has been approved by both sides, the task of contract administration begins. Well-trained and informed supervisors are the key to effective contract administration. Copies of the contract should be distributed to all department heads and supervisors. Orientation sessions—to give the supervisors a thorough understanding of each provision and how it affects them and their work—are also available. Skillful handling of complaints in the early stages can prevent serious problems from developing during the contract period. Supervisors, whose suggestions can be of great importance in preparing for future negotiating sessions, should be encouraged to keep records of grievances as well as recommendations to revise clauses of the contract that are costly or ambiguous.

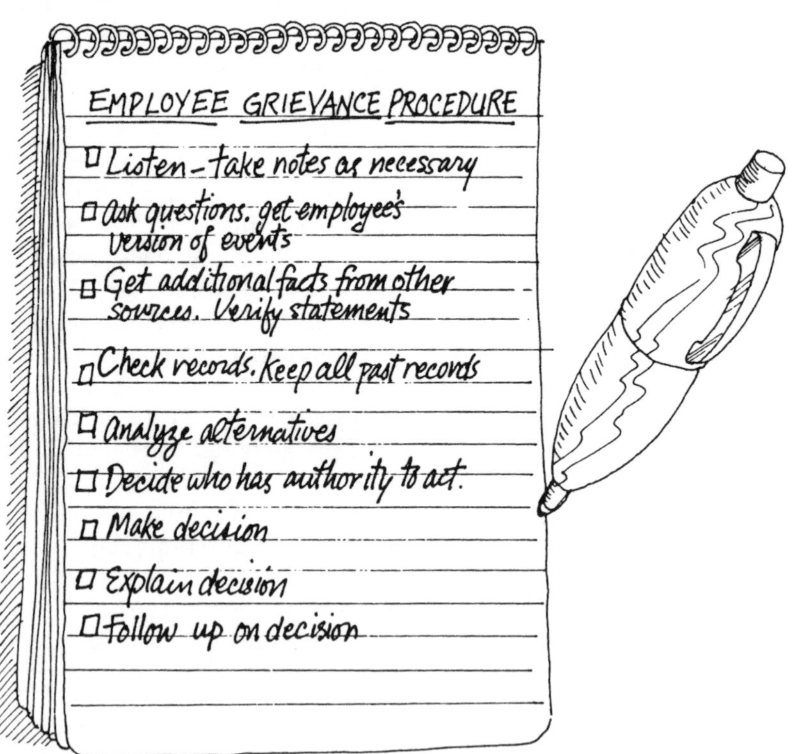

Figure 13–5 Suggested steps in processing employee grievances.

The contract generally describes a grievance procedure for resolving questions of interpretation and application. When such procedures are not negotiated as part of the contract, a formalized grievance procedure should be established to clarify and interpret personnel policies and practices. Employee participation in the formation of a grievance procedure is essential.

Most grievance procedures consist of three to five steps, including successive reviews, as needed, by the line supervisor, the division head, the department head, and either the personnel officer or the representative of the chief administrative officer. Some grievance procedures provide for arbitration of disputes. Many establish grievance committees, consisting of employee and management representatives, to resolve disputes. An employee with a grievance always has the right to choose a representative to be present at any or all stages of the grievance procedure. Careful definition of the channels to be followed and of definite and reasonable time limits ensures prompt consideration and adjustment of grievances.

Career development and training

Training helps maintain the effectiveness of personnel, ensuring that employee efforts are consistent with established goals and objectives and that employees are able to meet new challenges. A commitment to training expresses a concern for the long-term welfare and productivity of employees serving the community. Training can be expensive in the short run, especially when lost work hours are considered, but failure to provide needed training is even more expensive in the long run, causing both lower productivity and more frequent and costly mistakes. Training can remain cost-effective if maximum use is made of existing organizational resources.

Employee training library

San Mateo, California (79,000), has established a training library in the city manager's office. The library, which contains a wide variety of city- and management-related topics, is available for individual use by city employees for personal training and development. Employees are encouraged to donate training and conference tapes to the collection. An updated catalogue of all materials is periodically circulated to all management personnel and elected officials.

Source: *The Guide to Management Improvement Projects in Local Government,* vol. 14, no. 1 (Washington, DC: ICMA, 1990), no. PRM-9.

Determining needs

Training needs can be identified through discussions with supervisors, diagnostic tests, and employee interviews. Department heads and supervisors should always play a prominent role in defining training needs and recommending courses and personnel to be involved.

With the growing concern for providing equal employment opportunities, training may be used to prepare economically and educationally disadvantaged persons for permanent types of employment. Training for the disadvantaged involves the improvement of job skills and work habits. Remedial education opportunities can be provided in cooperation with nearby schools or colleges.

Technological, social, and legislative changes often require employees to develop new skills and point up the need for in-service restraining programs. For example, special training may help employees cope with the introduction of computers into the workplace or gain a better understanding of the meaning of sexual harassment. Also, the increasing incidence of labor-management collective bargaining in the public sector has created a need for labor relations training for management and supervisory personnel.

Class catalogue

Ocala, Florida (42,000), gives its employees a comprehensive training catalogue listing formal and informal classes, workshops, and seminars offered by the city and a local university. The city pays for the employees to attend the university workshops. Employees also receive a calendar listing of available programs to help them in scheduling their own training efforts.

Source: *The Guide to Management Improvement Projects in Local Government*, vol. 14, no. 1 (Washington, DC: ICMA, 1990), no. PMR-1.

Program implementation

From analyses of training needs, objectives can be defined and policies established. Policy decisions need to be made on many matters, including (1) which employees should receive training first; (2) what balance should be sought between training in administrative skills and in technical skills; (3) how much time should be devoted to each kind of training; (4) whether training should be conducted on or off the job; (5) whether leaves of absence should be granted for training; (6) what the relationship, if any, should be between training and promotion or salary increases; (7) whether training should be optional or required; and (8) whether tuition-refund and education-incentive programs should be developed.

Off-the-job training can involve lectures, conferences, case studies, demonstrations, role playing, field trips, and problem-solving sessions. To meet specific requirements, a program can be tailored from a multitude of approaches. The small community government may find it desirable to initiate a tuition-refund program that encourages employees to take advantage of educational programs offered by community colleges and other institutions.

Training resources and facilities include public schools, colleges, or universities that offer in-service training programs; professional associations; and technical institutes. In cooperation with colleges, state municipal leagues often offer a variety of training programs for local government officials. University extension divisions and government research bureaus are other valuable sources of employee training programs.

Benefits of training

Benefits resulting from training may include increased skills, new ideas, improvements in work behavior, success in promotional examinations, and better government-citizen relations. Information to document such benefits can be obtained from attitude surveys, on-the-job observations, standardized tests, long-term studies of trainee behavior, interviews with supervisors and employees, and performance reports.

Because of limited government funds and the difficulty of documenting the often intangible benefits of training programs, careful evaluation is necessary. A program evaluation should

Examine the methods used to select trainees and to measure trainee response to the training material

Assess learning of information or skills

Evaluate attitudinal or behavioral changes

Examine the effectiveness of training techniques

Determine the relevance of the training to the work situation.

Training resources in your community

The enterprising community interested in the professional development of its employees can find numerous sources of assistance in achieving its training objectives. Degree programs, credit courses, noncredit courses, and training workshops are frequently offered by local universities and colleges. Community colleges are particularly good sources of training assistance; frequently they will design special training programs to fit the needs of a particular local government at little or no cost.

Local municipal leagues sometimes offer special training programs for government employees, or they can direct local government officials to other organizations that have such courses. Many professional associations, such as those listed in Chapter 1 of this book, offer training courses and programs. Professional consultants are also willing to assist with training programs.

Many communities will find a wealth of training expertise within the ranks of their own employees. In-house training programs—those in which employees help train their fellow employees—offer a particularly effective training format, because they involve people working with friends and colleagues.

Walnut Creek, California (60,500), trains employee volunteers to conduct workshops for other employees on professional and technical skills including team building, writing skills, leadership, public speaking, stress management, and assertiveness. After being screened and selected as trainers, thirteen employees complete fifteen days of intensive training before training other employees.

Source: Adapted in part from *The Guide to Management Improvement Projects in Local Government*, vol. 16, no. 1 (Washington, DC: ICMA, 1992), no. PRM-4.

Other approaches to employee development

The efforts of contemporary community governments to improve employee performance do not end with career development and training. Increasingly, effective community administrators are now working in partnership with their employees to find new ways to help them, not only to improve in their work, but also to increase their sense of personal fulfillment and satisfaction. The notion is that happy employees—employees who have positive self-images and who are able to manage stress in their personal lives and balance the demands of home and job effectively—will also be better employees, in all respects.

Efforts to achieve these goals include alterations in work requirements, flexible benefits, employee assistance programs, new initiatives to serve the special needs of disabled employees, and modifications in work rules and patterns to accommodate employee family obligations without sacrificing work accomplishment. Although the link between these creative approaches and genuine productivity improvements is not clearly established, such efforts may make an important contribution to employee job satisfaction. This can be an important consideration to those community governments that must compete with high-paying private companies for skilled employees.

Alterations in work requirements

Alterations in work requirements are sometimes allowed to enable employees to achieve a better balance between work and family demands, or simply to enable an individual to achieve more personal satisfaction from the work environment. Such alterations include flex-time, job sharing, job enhancement, at-home work assignments, and virtually any other arrangement that meets employee needs without unduly burdening the employer. These alterations cannot be applied to all jobs, but they have been productive in a surprising number of different occupations.

Flex-time

Flex-time allows employees to make alterations in their work schedule. With flex-time, employees may be allowed to come to work earlier or later as long as they are available during designated core hours. Such flexibility can help meet the family demands on single parents or two-career families, or simply enable individuals to schedule more of their working hours during their most productive periods of the day.

Under another flex-time arrangement employees may be given the option of working four longer days instead of five regular days each week. Such scheduling has proven popular with many in nursing and clerical occupations for it enables them to reduce child-care and commuting costs.

Job sharing

Job sharing is an arrangement in which two employees fulfill the responsibilities of one job. This plan can fit the needs of working parents who have valuable skills but lack the time to meet the requirements of a full-time job. It may also be popular with older workers who want to reduce their work hours but are not ready for retirement.

Job sharing

Novato, California (45,000), has used job sharing to advantage since the middle 1970s. For example, it employs two professionals with graduate degrees in an administrative position. Recruiting was conducted in the same manner as for a regular position, but the job was advertised on a job-share basis. In addition to attracting high-quality applicants, the city benefits because each person brings different skills to the position and, together, the two do a better job than a single individual could. In addition, the job share provides professional talent that can be used to help fill temporary vacancies in other departments. The city has had to pay only incidental extra costs for an additional work station and for memberships in professional associations. The city's contribution to benefits is split between the two employees.

Source: *The Guide to Management Improvement Projects in Local Government*, vol. 15, no. 2 (Washington, DC: ICMA, 1991), no. MGT-12.

Job enrichment

Job enrichment is an approach that involves changing the tasks performed by particular employees in order to increase their opportunities for new responsibilities, personal achievement, growth, and advancement.

At-home work assignments

Some employers have found that both employee satisfaction and productivity can be improved by permitting employees to perform some of their work assignments at home. The arrangement gives parents and homemakers more control over their home and family and, when combined with flexible work hours that enable the employee to work during the quiet hours of the day at home, increases productivity by freeing the employee from the disruptions and interruptions that are a normal part of workplace routine.

Flexible benefits

Community governments can help employees meet personal or family needs by offering a choice of benefits. In these programs, employees typically take a minimum package of benefits, which may consist of basic life insurance, short-term disability insurance, a week of vacation, and hospital and medical coverage (in cases in which coverage is required, it can be waived if the employee provides documentation of comparable coverage from another source, such as a spouse's employment).

Working women
Muskegon, Michigan (40,300), formed a seven-member committee to evaluate programs, services, and conditions for women working for the city. Gathering information from all women employees, the committee found employee interest in flexible benefits, training on sexual harassment policy and procedures for filing complaints, an on-site exercise program, improved restroom facilities, on-site day care, and increased education and training.

Source: *The Guide to Management Improvement Projects in Local Government*, vol. 17, no. 1 (Washington, DC: ICMA, 1993), no. PRM-2.

Employees are then given an additional level of fringe benefit coverage from which each individual can design a personal program from such options as increased vacation time, more life insurance, dependent health coverage, dental coverage, additional sick or personal leave time, child-care assistance, or an investment program. Sometimes, employees can choose still more benefits that they purchase through payroll deduction. Such "cafeteria" type options tailor job benefits to each individual employee's lifestyle and personal responsibilities; as a result, they add to employee job satisfaction without additional employer costs.

Employee assistance program

Some of the toughest decisions facing community administrators involve employees whose work performance is suffering because of some type of personal problem. Although managers should not attempt to become in-

Employees' personal problems
Personal problems may dramatically affect job performance, so supervisors should be alert to the symptoms of such difficulties. But it is important for supervisors to realize that they can address these symptoms *only* if job performance is inadequate.

No matter what the supervisor knows or suspects about an employee's personal life, the supervisor must be very careful *not* to say to an employee with performance problems, "I think your performance has deteriorated because of [name of personal problem]." Rather, the supervisor who suspects a personal problem should allow the employee to bring up the matter.

The supervisor should focus simply on performance deterioration while encouraging the employee to talk out and identify the basic cause of the problem by asking something like, "Is there anything I should know about your performance problem? You're aware that we do have an employee assistance program."

If the employee does speak of a personal problem, the supervisor must resist the urge to diagnose, define symptoms, or become clinically involved; such involvement has led to litigation. The supervisor must also resist the urge to become emotionally involved. He or she may certainly recommend counseling, but cannot require it; the only thing the supervisor can require is standard performance.

Source: Adapted from John Matzer, Jr., ed., *Advanced Supervisory Practices* (Washington, DC: ICMA, 1992), 43-44.

volved in the personal problems of an employee, they should not look the other way when an employee is no longer performing effectively. This is especially true when the problem threatens the safety and security of the public, or when the employee has job security protected by personnel rules, a union contract, civil service regulations, or simply a past record of good performance.

Substance abuse

Because of the destructive effects of drug and alcohol abuse and because employees go to great lengths to hide this type of problem, even from themselves, it is one of the most difficult personal problems that community administrators face.

The first step toward dealing with employee substance abuse is the development of a written policy, communicated to all employees, making it clear that any form of substance abuse is unacceptable.

In some cases, a second step may be to develop a drug testing program to enforce the policy. Testing of employees whose job performance may affect public safety (e.g., those who work in public transportation) is generally more accepted than random testing of employees. However, drug testing is a sensitive and complex issue; managers should act cautiously and should seek both legal advice and guidance from professionals in this field before attempting to institute a program.

Testing can be used as a pre-employment screening device, as part of routine physicals, or in cases where there are strong indications that an employee is under the influence of drugs or alcohol. Any efforts in this area should be accompanied by a well-defined, sympathetic yet force-

Figure 13–6 Drug and alcohol screening policy from the *Personnel Manual for the Village of Oak Park*, Oak Park, Illinois.

APPENDIX IV DRUG/ALCOHOL SCREENING POLICY

Effective May 1, 1989, drug and alcohol screening will be performed as part of the health evaluation of all potential full-time regular employees. If the initial screening result is positive, the result will be confirmed by a second, more sophisticated laboratory method on the same specimen.

Pre-placement Screening:

All potential full-time regular employees shall, as part of the pre-placement health evaluation, undergo drug/alcohol screening.

1. **Alcohol:** A level in excess of 50% of the State of Illinois Intoxication Level in effect at the time of screening would disqualify the applicant from employment.
2. **Drugs:** It is the position of the Village of Oak Park that since no specific research exists to correlate at what level a drug makes a specific person incompetent and unable to function, evidence of any drug other than *supported prescribed* drugs would disqualify the applicant from employment.

Failure to provide an authentic urine or blood specimen at the time of examination or to sign the necessary consent for drug/alcohol screening with authorization to release test results to the Village's Personnel Director would disqualify the applicant from employment. Applicants are not permitted to retake the screening except as may be recommended by the West Suburban Hospital Medical Center Occupational Health Network for technical reasons.

Employees may also be sent for a health examination based on poor worker performance, poor attendance, actions or slurred speech which is uncharacteristic of the individual, involvement in an accident, or other basis for reasonable suspicion that an employee is under the influence of drugs or alcohol.

ful strategy for dealing with the problem when drug or alcohol abuse is discovered.

Before taking disciplinary action, most employers give troubled employees at least one chance to rehabilitate themselves. Employee assistance programs, which offer assessment, professional counseling, referral, treatment, and education, can help employees in this process. Community governments may choose to offer their own employee assistance program or use existing private or public providers.

Financing treatment for substance abuse
City employees in Redmond, Oregon (7,000), who need and cannot afford rehabilitation for drug or alcohol problems, can borrow from the city the money needed to pay the difference between the total cost of treatment and the portion paid by the city's health insurance. The one-time-only program provides an interest-free, four-year loan with monthly payments of at least $85 made through payroll deduction.

Source: *The Guide to Management Improvement Projects in Local Government*, vol. 15, no. 1 (Washington, DC: ICMA, 1991), no. PRM-3.

Mental health services

Substance abuse is not the only cause of personal problems. Employees suffer from other problems as well, such as excessive personal stress, a difficult divorce, or other types of family problem. Statistics indicate that over half of all adults now experience some form of mental or emotional illness during their lives, and the increasing tension and stress in the American life-style are making such conditions more common. This means that most employees—even most of the best employees—will experience periods on the job when their work suffers from personal problems.

To minimize their losses from such periods, more and more employers, even in small organizations, are now retaining health care professionals to provide employee education and counseling and to diagnose and treat employees needing help. (Diagnostic and treatment costs are typically provided, within limits, by health insurance programs.) Most communities are now served by a nonprofit community mental health center that will provide such services. Private clinical psychologists and psychiatrists can also be employed for this purpose.

The special needs of disabled employees

Over the years, many community governments have made special efforts to meet the needs of disabled workers. However, most of these efforts are minor compared with what the law now requires. The Americans with Disabilities Act of 1990 has expanded the 1964 Civil Rights Act (which originally outlawed discrimination on the basis of race, religion, sex, or national origin) to cover physically and mentally disabled individuals, including AIDS and cancer patients and recovering substance abusers. Due to the vagueness of the law, the full scope of the difficulties that may qualify as disabilities will not be known for some time; presently it appears that even smoke sensitivity and anxiety may qualify. There can be little doubt that finding new ways to accommodate the special needs of disabled workers will become one of the major personnel issues of the 1990s.

Strictly speaking, the law specifies that employers must not discriminate against disabled employees and that they must make "reasonable accommodations" to meet their needs. Disabled employees need only perform the "essential" functions of a job with reasonable proficiency to be eligible for legal protection. Accommodations that may be necessary to meet the needs of disabled employees include job restructuring, modified work schedules, acquisition of new equipment or devices, and modification of examinations, training materials, and policies. Local governments could be required to provide special computer equipment or readers for the visually impaired or amplifiers and hearing aids for employees who have difficulty hearing.

Although the initial implementation of this legislation may cause major difficulties for local governments, it will help to open new doors for disabled Americans and ensure full utilization of the skills and abilities that these individuals possess. The Senate Committee on Labor and Human Resources estimates that there are forty-three million disabled Americans and that two-thirds of those who are of working age are unemployed. Community administrators will play a major role in offering these individuals the opportunity to work. An additional impact of this legislation will be to increase the importance of employee development efforts for all types of employees.

Accommodating employees' family obligations

Public policy is increasingly concerned with the ramifications of the movement from one-wage-earner families to two-wage-earner families that has occurred in American society during the last half century. The movement, which originated in the labor shortages of World War II, has increased life-style options, professional opportunities, and socioeconomic equality for women.

Sick-child care

Alameda County, California (1.2 million), developed the Alternative Child Care Assistance Program to assist county employees in caring for sick children and thereby reduce parental stress and employee absenteeism. The program reimburses 90 percent of child-care expenses up to a maximum of $350 per year when alternative child-care arrangements are required. Parents who cannot secure care providers for sick children are referred to local agencies for help. The program generates a positive response from employees, improves morale, and demonstrates the county's support of families.

Source: *The Guide to Management Improvement Projects in Local Government*, vol. 17, no. 1 (Washington, DC: ICMA, 1993), no. PRM-3.

Public policy has come under pressure to address the impact of the two-wage-earner family on family life.

The movement has generated public policy concern over resulting changes in the labor force and modifications needed in public and private sector employment practices. Some local governments have struggled to meet the needs of employed parents by establishing day-care cooperatives or providing subsidies. More recently, public policy has come under pressure to address the impact of the two-wage-earner family on family life. The Family and Medical Leave Act of 1992 resulted from such pressures, but it did not address all of the issues caused by changes in employment patterns. Continuing employment-related problems confronting families include increased levels of family stress, breakdowns in family communication, inadequate child-care options, increasing levels of concern over child development and discipline, and the dissolution of extended family support systems.

The past fifty years have witnessed the expansion of employment opportunities for many citizens. The decades ahead will find increasing attention focused on ways to reconcile work and family life so that employment opportunity and worker productivity will support rather than threaten the quality of personal and family life.

The other approaches to employee development discussed above, and especially such practices as flex-time, job-sharing, at-home work assignments, flexible benefits, and counseling programs are increasingly emphasized as partial means of preserving the quality of family life while maintaining existing employment opportunities. The persistence of concern over family life, however, suggests that even these tools need both wider application and support from methods not yet devised. Employers will be under increasing pressure in future years to modify their work requirements in ways designed to foster stronger, healthier employee families.

Afterword

Neither the best elected officials nor the best administrative talent can produce good government. To be sure, good government requires good leadership, but good leadership can accomplish little unless it is supported by competent, dedicated staff. Just as the proverbial army can go only as far as its foot soldiers take it, an organization can accomplish only what its staff can produce. Ultimately, the quality of an organization can be measured by the quality of its staff.

In the latter half of the twentieth century, local governments have used two very different criteria to select staff. Traditionally, these governments stressed local residence as a prerequisite for employment. Although there is merit in hiring people who are familiar with the community, there is also risk, particularly when employing people for positions requiring specialized knowledge. The time is gone when the Jacksonian notion that "all citizens are equally qualified to hold any government job" was valid.

More recently, with renewed public demand for government honesty and effectiveness, community governments have stressed hiring "the best and the brightest" talent available. Communities today search widely for job applicants who have specialized training and experience. Local residence is considered a bonus, not an overriding consideration in the quest for quality.

The best and the brightest employees are recruited and retained through a professionally operated personnel system consisting of a number of discrete facets, including recruitment and promotion on the basis of merit; regular performance evaluation; competitive salaries and benefits; training to expand skills and encourage personal development; and a well-documented and clearly understood framework of rules and regulations.

Personnel management has undergone many changes during the last decades of the twentieth century. Unionization has become a fact of life in many communities. Equal opportunity has become a standard expectation; government staffs now comprise persons of different ethnic groups, races, and sexual orientations. As staffs evolve, the emphasis on personnel management must evolve, too. Not only must opportunities be made equal, but so too must conditions in the workplace. This means that community governments must work proactively to ensure that employees are understanding of and sensitive to diversity and that they strive to make the workplace a pleasant place for all.

Personnel management must also adapt to the changing needs of employees. Workplaces must be made flexible and responsive to a growing variety of needs; they must be accessible to disabled employees; and they must be sensitive to employees' home and family pressures.

Studies indicate that worker productivity is linked to the satisfaction of such individual concerns; a community government cannot overlook any consideration that will increase employee productivity. Personnel remains a critical function and a field of growing complexity posing complex challenges to those who manage government. ■

---

[1] Joseph N. Cayer, "Local Government Personnel Structure and Policies," in *The Municipal Yearbook 1991* (Washington, DC: ICMA, 1991).

[2] Gregory Streib and Theodore Poister, "Established and Emerging Management Tools: A Twelve Year Perspective," in *The Municipal Yearbook 1989* (Washington, DC: ICMA, 1989), 45-54.

[3] Streib and Poister, "Strategic Planning in U.S. Cities: Patterns of Use, Perceptions of Effectiveness, and an Assessment of Strategic Capacity," *American Review of Public Administration* 20 (March 1990): 29-44; Gregory Streib, "Strategic Decision Making in Council-Manager Governments: A Status Report," in *The Municipal Yearbook 1991* (Washington, DC: ICMA, 1991), 14-23.

14 Communication

Communication, both internal and external, is essential to achieving the mission of all local governments; they cannot function effectively without it. Although local governments have been concerned with publicity and public relations for most of the twentieth century, the definition of communication has expanded to encompass a broad range of other ideas and activities. In this chapter *communication* means the organized efforts of community governments to convey and receive information and meaning to and from citizens, employees, and others. This expansion reflects the growing recognition of the need for all government employees to exercise communication skills in all their dealings with citizens and fellow workers and of the need for communication between public officials and citizens to be a two-way process.

The need for two-way communication is especially important at a time when local government resources are strained because of reductions in federal and state support, unfunded federal mandates, and citizen opposition to tax increases. If citizens are shown why they may have to make a choice between increased property taxes or cuts in services; if they are made aware of government efforts to increase efficiency in order to achieve more with fewer resources; and if they are invited to participate in deciding which services to maintain, reduce, or cut, they are far more likely to support public officials' decisions and actions.

Without public support, even the most efficient government services cannot succeed: police officers cannot enforce the law unless they enjoy the cooperation of the citizens served; public health workers cannot vaccinate children against disease if suspicious parents will not bring their children to public health centers. Public support does not occur automatically because services are provided. Rather, it is the result of successful two-way communication between the public officials who provide public services and the citizens who use those services. Not only must citizens be informed about available services, but public officials must also be kept informed about citizens' needs and preferences.

The changing environment

Two decades ago, local newspapers were far more influential in covering local government than radio and television; this is no longer the case. Newspaper readership has dropped sharply, and newspapers now devote far more space to less demanding stories and features. Today, running an article or feature story about the community government in the local paper does not guarantee that citizens will get the message; sole reliance on print media is insufficient for the information age. Most people now get their information more quickly and directly from radio and television, often in bits and pieces devoid of context or explanation. In addition, people's attention spans are shorter; they do not read as much as they used to; and they get messages through many more channels than they did a generation ago.

A wide range of local media and sources of information now exists; some examples are suburban newspapers, neighborhood newspapers, shoppers' guides, government-access channels on cable TV, local cable news stations, all-purpose telephone numbers for information on local government services, libraries, community centers, civic associations, access to county board agendas for anyone with a personal computer and a modem, community government newsletters, radio and television broadcasts, information counters in government office buildings, and information kiosks in shopping malls. Although it may not be possible or desirable for smaller communities to use all the above means, most now use at least some of them.

Soliciting citizen input

To show area residents the inner workings of city government and foster citizen comments and suggestions, the city of Hickory, North Carolina (25,000), holds "town meetings" monthly during the summer. Citizens are taken on a guided bus tour of city facilities while employees describe the proposed capital projects regarding the city's water, sewer, and transportation systems; discuss the community's infrastructure and financial issues; and demonstrate opportunities associated with planned growth, aggressive land use regulations, and progressive economic development. Each town meeting lasts approximately four hours and reaches more than thirty residents.

Source: *CitCom* (July-August 1993) Washington, DC: ICMA.

Other forms of communication—with governing boards, other governments, employees, and community groups of all kinds—have changed equally dramatically. Managers, department heads, and other key employees in community government must comply with open meeting and privacy laws, meet with advocacy groups armed for verbal combat, work with full-time governing bodies engaged in administration, and engage in endless one-on-one and small-group encounters. They must also have the ability to work with tools that range from the notepad and pencil to the communications satellite.

Elements of communication

Communication has become more open, pervasive, targeted, and local, and information technology has added unprecedented accessibility, speed, feedback, and control. Managing communication requires knowing about its elements. These include content, format, access, coverage, and distribution.

The content of community government news is usually focused on particular groups or interests. While all-purpose stories continue, especially those about elections and budgets, most stories and features now cover specific groups, such as elderly citizens; specific areas, such as identifiable neighborhoods or communities; and specific interests, such as hobbies and historic preservation.

Increasingly, printed materials are produced by using inexpensive methods and simple formats. Desktop publishing is used to create newsletters, public service announcements, informational flyers, and similar materials.

Information exchange and public feedback are sought aggressively. Speakers' bureaus are promoted, and volunteers are used to the extent that policies and ethics will allow.

Speakers' bureau

A speakers' bureau is one communications tool that almost any local government can make available to citizens on request.

As part of its public information and education efforts, the city of Dubuque, Iowa (60,200), developed a comprehensive speakers' bureau to communicate information to citizens about what city employees and the local government do to maintain the quality of life in Dubuque. The program, which makes available names and background information for speakers from all walks of city government, includes more than fifty contacts in more than one hundred topic areas, ranging from city finances and zoning enforcement to book talks and gardening. Program listings are packaged in an attractive booklet, available to citizens upon request. The booklet is organized by twenty-three city areas, and each listing includes the primary contact, his or her title, a brief description of each individual's professional and educational background and interests, and the topics on which the individual is qualified to speak. Some listings also include suggested audiences and information on speaker availability.

Source: "Public Information: Educating and Communicating," *MIS Report*, vol. 23, no. 3 (March 1991).

Community governments with diverse populations are expanding information coverage to include non-English-speaking residents, especially Asians and Hispanics, and preparing materials in two or more languages. Large-print materials for the visually impaired individuals and audiovisual materials for those who cannot read are being developed.

Finally, information is distributed to those most likely to have an interest in it: neighborhood news to neighborhoods; special interest news to clubs, churches, and other groups; and major developments to newspapers, radio, and television.

Mission and responsibilities

Effective communication is a primary responsibility of elected officials, managers, assistant managers, the public information officer, and department heads, but it is also the responsibility of every local government employee. The community government has a mission of service to all community residents, and the manager must ensure that all employees understand the government's mission and how their jobs relate to it.

Elected and appointed officials most often represent the local government to the media and the public, but employees constantly relay their perceptions of the government, its mission, and their role in helping to achieve that mission to the public both when they are on and off the job. Officials must foster the attitude that all employees are the government's public relations agents. Officials and employees alike should be perceived by the public, including the media, to be knowledgeable (professional), reliable (they do what they say they will do), assertive, and open.

Cornerstones of communication

Experience in interpersonal communication over more than half a century has highlighted several cornerstones upon which to build effective communication. These cornerstones provide the foundation for both internal and external communication.

The first is openness, the basis for trust and credibility. Openness has been facilitated by federal and state freedom of information and open-meeting laws and by electronic systems that make it remarkably easy to gain access to computer systems and files.

The second is listening. Effective listening depends on empathy and interaction.

The third is suspension of judgment, which means trying *"to see the expressed idea and attitude from the other's point of view, to see how it feels to them, to achieve their frame of reference."*[1]

The fourth is feedback, which provides signals that messages have been received and understood. It is a significant part of management planning, implementation, evaluation, and control.

The final cornerstone is understanding. To communicate means to share and to agree on the content of the message.[2]

If the entire local government staff understands the importance of these cornerstones, communication within the local government organization, with the public, and with other jurisdictions is likely to be effective.

Elected officials

In general, local elected officials set the tone for the local government and provide the essential political backing for administrators and rank-and-file employees. Council or board members are the most visible and well-known local government officials, and they receive much of the applause—or abuse—from individual citizens and community groups.

Figure 14–1 Every employee represents the city or county government; to some people, he or she *is* the government.

Figure 14–2 It is important for community governments to communicate with young citizens as well as adults. The city of West Des Moines, Iowa, organizes a student government day every year. In 1993, students from a local elementary school attended a council meeting at which each student was matched with a local government official who explained the proceedings.

Members of the legislative body are at the crossroads of opinion, influence, and advocacy. Because these officials spend a great deal of time in formal and informal hearings on many subjects, such as major zoning problems, public works proposals, revitalization plans for the business district, and conflicts between different groups in the community, they must be attuned to public opinion and attitudes. As legislators, they must confront the dilemma of a citizenry that demands more services but also wants taxes cut. Conveying to citizens the difficulty—perhaps the impossibility—of achieving both goals at the same time presents elected officials with a major communications challenge.

Public officials must recognize the important role of the general public—and public opinion—in forming and carrying out public policy. Support for public policies must be developed through the continuous and widespread participation of all groups in the community. Participation is achieved, for example, through hearings, citizen surveys, and debates, during policy consideration and through feedback from citizens after policy implementation.

Elected officials are the spokespersons and representatives of the community government on all major issues. In addition to communicating with the public in their own community, they are also responsible for communication with officials from other jurisdictions. For example, they may negotiate with the elected officials of a neighboring community on a plan for joint service delivery (although administrative officials work out the details). Or they may appeal to state and federal officials for help during a disaster.

Administrative officers

Because the local government's principal administrative officers have a special responsibility for helping to develop policy and for implementing it, they have a special responsibility to keep in constant communication with elected officials and the public. Ultimate responsibility for communication must rest with the chief administrative officer. Unless the chief administrator has a strong sense of the need for good public relations and communication tools, methods, and skills, an effective communication program is not likely to develop or continue.

In communicating with his or her governing body, the chief administrative officer must ensure that elected officials have the information they need and are not caught unaware by citizens or the press. Administrators should ask elected officials frequently what kinds of information they want to receive. On the other hand, because of the sheer volume of written briefings, letters, memorandums, proposals, reports, and studies, managers have to select what information to pass on to elected officials. However, they have a responsibility to be fair and impartial and should not attempt to influence policy by overemphasizing or downplaying certain information. They should also make sure that all members of the governing body have equal access to information. Good communication between elected and appointed officials requires that they have formal and informal, personal means of conveying information, and it depends on mutual respect and trust.

Because they have the responsibility for service delivery, administrators have a major obligation to take the initiative in disseminating information about government programs and services and in establishing effective communication concerning those programs and services with the public. They also have a major responsibility for ensuring that all citizens' voices are heard as they work with elected officials to establish policy.

An informative city calendar

The department of parks and public works in the city of Portland, Maine (population 62,670), sees communication with citizens as the responsibility of all the department's employees.

Formerly, department employees used press announcements and mailings to inform citizens of items such as changes in snow removal schedules and dates for pickup of heavy objects (e.g., old appliances and furniture). The department's employees found that citizens did not always see the announcements in the newspapers and that the frequent mailings were expensive, so they brainstormed to come up with better ideas for informing the citizens of the department's services.

Street foreman Robert Giampetruzzi suggested that the department produce a calendar to give citizens information about the department's twenty-seven divisions and to inform them of the schedule for various services. The first calendar was produced in 1990 by a team consisting of the assistant city manager, the department director, and some of the department's employees.

After two years, the calendar was so popular that it evolved into a city calendar rather than just a department calendar. It now has a different theme each year, and includes information such as council members' names, districts, and phone numbers; dates for elections, council meetings, and payment of taxes; statistical data; summer recreational activities; and parking locations.

Source: Donna Gilbert, Senior Administrative Officer, Department of Parks and Public Works, Portland, Maine, 1993.

Audiences

A generation ago, community governments concentrated their communications efforts on one audience, the general public, which was personified in "John Q. Public," a homogenous "everyman" who was a lot like community government managers. The social upheavals of the 1960s, especially the citizen participation movement, changed that approach. Poor citizens and those who were not well educated discovered that they, too, could organize to be heard. Citizen participation expanded from staid citizen advisory committees, churches, and service clubs to include community associations, block groups, and advocacy groups. During this time, elected officials discovered that the administrative background of policy proposals was interesting and political. They demanded to be included in the information loop. Coupled with the growth of employee unions and a service economy, multiple audiences came to the fore.

The government workforce

Community government employees constitute an important audience that should be reached through internal as well as external channels. Employees should not have to rely on the news media to keep up to date on community government activities. They cannot do a good job in public relations if they do not know what is going on. The employees' understanding of what is happening in the organization (and why) is a significant factor in the success of their customer service efforts.

Managers, department heads, supervisors, and other employees communicate face-to-face much of the time, but they also use phones, two-way radios, computers, telenetworks, letters, memos, bulletin boards, and employee newsletters. Such communication is so constant that it is taken for granted, but it is a process which, to be effective, requires training, supervision, and control. Communication affecting the workforce can also be contentious. For example, how much monitoring of employee communications can or should be attempted to control union proselytizing? Employee statements to news reporters? Papers prepared by employees for professional meetings? Effective communication is often a life-and-death matter for police and fire services.

The media The quality of the interaction between the community government and the media is determined to a great extent by the community government. Officials must respect the role that the media play in safeguarding the democratic process, and they must be cooperative partners in an active relationship with the media. Each medium has its characteristics, which are discussed later in this chapter in the section entitled "News media."

Figure 14–3 A calendar produced by the department of parks and public works in Portland, Maine, provides residents with information on community events and the department's services.

JULY

SUNDAY	MONDAY	TUESDAY	WEDNESDAY	THURSDAY	FRIDAY	SATURDAY
ISLAND HEAVY ITEM PICKUP (H. I. P.) Little Diamond - 7/18-20; Great Diamond - 7/21-24; Cliff - 8/1-7 (Reminder: Peaks H.I.P. - 9/19-25) • Please separate material by type (metal/white goods; tires; wood brush, etc.) • Please separate regular household rubbish from H. I. P. items				1	2	3
4 INDEPENDENCE DAY CHANDLER'S BAND FORT ALLEN PARK GAZEBO, 7:30, 874-8791	5 (HOLIDAY OBSERVED)	6 Monday and Tuesday rubbish routes will be picked up today CONCERT IN DEERING OAKS PARK (Seacoast Wind Ensemble), 7:30 PM, 874-8791	7 Council Meeting, 4 pm and 7:30 pm, Cable Channel 39 FOLK CONCERT, WESTERN PROM (Darien Brahms), 8 PM, 874-8791	8 CHILDREN'S SHOWS (Jugglers Troy & Rod), DEERING OAKS PARK, 12:30 PM, 874-8791	9	10
11	12	13 CONCERT IN DEERING OAKS (New England Electronic Quintet), 7:15 PM, 874-8791	14 FOLK CONCERT, WESTERN PROM (Driftwood), 8 PM, 874-8791	15 CHILDREN'S SHOWS, DEERING OAKS PARK, 12:30 PM, 874-8791 CHANDLER'S BAND FORT ALLEN PARK GAZEBO, 7:30, 874-8791	16	17
18 CLASSICAL CONCERT WILDE CHAPEL EVERGREEN CEMETERY 3 PM, 874-8791 ——LITTLE DIAMOND	19 Council Meeting, 4 pm and 7:30 pm, Cable Channel 39 ISLAND H.I.P.——	20	21 ——	22 CHANDLER'S BAND FORT ALLEN PARK GAZEBO, 7:30, 874-8791 ——GREAT DIAMOND	23 ISLAND H.I.P.——	24 ——
25	26	27 CONCERT IN DEERING OAKS PARK, (The Pinetones) 7:00 PM, 874-8791	28 FOLK CONCERT (Marianne Chatterton), WESTERN PROM, 7:45 PM, 874-8791	29 CHILDREN'S SHOWS (Singers Julie and Brownie), DEERING OAKS PARK, 12:30 PM 874-8791	30	31

AUGUST

SUNDAY	MONDAY	TUESDAY	WEDNESDAY	THURSDAY	FRIDAY	SATURDAY
1 ——	2 Council Meeting, 4 pm and 7:30 pm, Cable Channel 39 ——	3 CONCERT (Devonsquare) IN DEERING OAKS PARK, 7:00 PM, 874-8791 ——	4 FOLK CONCERT (Slaid Cleaves), WESTERN PROM, 7:40 PM, 874-8791 CLIFF ISLAND H.I.P.	5 CHILDREN'S SHOWS (Songs with the Whoose Family), DEERING OAKS PARK, 12:30 PM, 874-8791 ——	6 ——	7 ——
8	9	10 CONCERT IN DEERING OAKS PARK (Jazz Workshop Orchestra), 6:45 PM, 874-8791	11 FOLK CONCERT, WESTERN PROM (Lisa Gallant), 7:15 PM, 874-8791	12 CHILDREN'S SHOWS, DEERING OAKS PARK (Funny Man Glen Dwyer), 12:30 PM, 874-8791	13	14
15	16 Council Meeting, 4 pm and 7:30 pm, Cable Channel 39	17	18	19	20	21
22	23	24	25	26	27	28
29	30	31	**Riverside landfill is open Saturdays until November 20, 1993** **REMINDER: City Hall's Treasury Division no longer sells land fill (dump) permits. So, when you are ready to purchase your land fill permits, visit Carol Polisky of Parks & Public Works, 55 Portland Street. For fees, see page 18. Questions? Call 874-8494**			

Page 3 **1993**

Community associations and groups

Even small communities are likely to have a bewildering variety of formal and informal groups: the chamber of commerce, service clubs, churches, homeowners' associations, historical societies, sports fans, elderly citizens, library patrons, and many more. Although many groups are not highly structured, most are cohesive enough to organize quickly if their interests are threatened.

In most communities, it is not difficult to compile comprehensive rosters of groups according to geographic area and interest by consulting directories and talking to knowledgeable persons. Such rosters will provide a plethora of audiences. The question then is, "How do we put this together on a community basis?" The first step is to look at the characteristics of the community.

Is the community small and homogenous? If so, differences in ethnic origin, race, education, and income are usually minimal, and most communication channels are self-evident.

Is the community split between two contesting groups? A common example is the rapidly growing community where old-timers and newcomers battle over land development issues. Communications have to be scrupulously balanced to minimize accusations about government bias.

Is the community a mosaic of a highly visible, affluent class; multiple, shifting factions of minority groups; one or two highly visible immigrant groups; and an underclass that exists outside the other groups?

The evolution of government communication

The growth of government communication has paralleled the growth of services and professionalism in government, as these highlights show:

1913 The U.S. Civil Service Commission announced its first examination for a publicity expert.

1917 President Woodrow Wilson appointed the Committee on Public Information in order to mobilize public support for World War I, an effort that was highly successful.

1922 National Publicity Council for Welfare Services was founded under the auspices of the Russell Sage Foundation to publicize the work of social work agencies.

1923 Social scientists at the University of Chicago began pioneering work in attitude measurement, voting behavior, and other forms of social research, a precursor of public opinion polling and its many offshoots in advertising, marketing, fund raising, political campaigns, community surveys, and other fields.

1933 The New Deal era brought an explosion in public relations activity with radio broadcasts, newsreels, the Gallup and Roper polls, and sophisticated political campaign management.

1942 The Office of War Information (OWI) was established early in World War II to mobilize public support. The most successful effort was the production of war-related film documentaries. Later reorganized, the OWI evolved into the U.S. Information Agency.

1947 Public Relations Society of America was organized.

1951 The Bureau of the Census used Univac I (Universal Automatic Computer) for data processing, the first large-scale application of computers beyond scientific and engineering applications.

1964 International Business Machines announced its "360" series of computers with unified computer architecture and modular components, a major step in making computer programming instructions readily transferable among small, medium, and large computers facilitating the development of information systems.

1968 A National Academy of Engineering study panel on urban communications projected the telecommunication infrastructure for wired cities with telephones, cable, and interactive telecommunication networks.

1970 The information age: citizen attitude surveys, graphic identification programs, cybernetics, telecommunications, the citizen participation movement, interpersonal communication, information technology, niche communications, the public information officer, communication management.

Here the search is for communication methods that take specific messages to the different groups.

A demographic analysis of this kind helps identify both the organized and the unorganized segments of the community so that communications can be more effective, economical, and targeted.

Figure 14–4 Audiences and communication methods.

Checklist of publics	Information outlets
Associations/professional groups	Print and broadcast media, speakers' bureau, slide shows, brochures, public meetings
Business/chamber of commerce	Newsletters, print/broadcast media, exhibits
Churches	Print/broadcast media, speakers' bureau, slide shows, quarterly reports
Neighborhood action groups	Print/broadcast media, speakers' bureau, brochures, public meetings
Cultural groups	Print/broadcast media, brochures, speakers' bureaus, direct mailings
Education groups/schools	Speakers' bureau, slide shows, brochures
Elderly	Speakers' bureau, direct mailings, print/broadcast media
Financial institutions	Direct mailings, newsletters, print/broadcast media
Fraternal organizations	Speakers' bureau, print/broadcast media, brochures
Industrial/labor groups	Speakers' bureau, print/broadcast media, public meetings, quarterly reports
Homeowners	Print/broadcast media, door-to-door dissemination
Military/veterans	Speakers' bureau, brochures, print/broadcast media
Minorities	Print/broadcast media, public meetings, neighborhood meetings, brochures, speakers' bureau, door-to-door dissemination
Political groups	Print/broadcast media, public meetings, speakers' bureau, quarterly reports
News media	Releases, meetings, news conferences, brochures, quarterly/annual reports, newsletters
Sports groups	Print/broadcast media, brochures, posters/fliers
Civic groups/clubs	Speakers' bureau, slide shows, print/broadcast media, brochures
Youth groups	Speakers' bureau, broadcast media, slide shows, brochures

Individual citizens

Communication with individual citizens is one of the most common, but least understood, functions of community government. Its importance has grown dramatically with the increase in computerized recordkeeping and databases and in onerous requirements pertaining to tax payments, building permits, and a myriad of other government transactions.

The inevitable errors of omission and commission that ensue lead to one-on-one encounters by telephone and in person to get information, confirm information, and register complaints. Customer service is a useful and widely understood term for working with citizens, usually on a personal basis, to resolve problems. Citizens expect to be

Treated with dignity and respect

Given reliable information

Dealt with politely

Given individual attention

Given explanations, not excuses

Sent to the correct person or office when referrals are necessary.

Figure 14–5 It is good public relations to let people know in advance when public improvements or repairs are scheduled.

These expectations seem simple and obvious, but everyone has anecdotes about government employees who were indifferent, rude, uninformed, careless, and hostile. It is management's responsibility to ensure that employees give people the same message under similar circumstances, treat citizens equally, handle one-on-one and small-group encounters professionally, and convey the values of the community. For many people, exposure to community government comes in little bursts of activity: getting a building permit, paying a water bill, getting a dog license, filing an application for a zoning variance. Good customer service means giving individual attention to these and many other kinds of interactions and exercising appropriate customer service skills.

Customer service skills are a means of achieving effective interpersonal communication that can be developed and strengthened through on-the-job training in dress, personal demeanor, nonverbal communication, listening, dealing with angry individuals, behaving with courtesy, eliciting information, *and* providing correct information directly or through referrals to other sources. Sometimes the best answer may be "I don't know, but I'll help you find out."

The public information officer

As mentioned previously, the chief administrative officer has ultimate responsibility for the community government's communication. He or she may designate one person as a public information officer. Ideally, this position is filled by a full-time public relations professional, but smaller communities often cannot afford a full-time person. If this is the case, someone in an existing position (such as an administrative assistant, the clerk, a department head, or the human resources officer) may be assigned the public information function. The duties described below form, to a greater or lesser extent, part of this person's job description.

The job title *public information officer* (PIO) is widely used and well understood in government, but the position may be labeled director of public affairs, director of community relations, or director of communication. Typically, the position involves primary responsibility for working with media, especially newspapers, and conveying information back and forth between the media and the community government.

With the growing complexity and divisiveness of intracommunity relations, however, the work has evolved to encompass a broader range of duties: monitoring internal communications; monitoring legal requirements and ethical standards for open meetings and public access; training employees and elected officials; and evaluating the public impact of the work of the community government. Media relations, internal communications, and communications planning are the most important management responsibilities of the public information officer.

When a community has a designated information officer, citizens and the news media can go directly to that person for accurate information: the PIO can verify media stories and squelch rumors. However, the existence of a public information officer does not reduce the public relations responsibilities of other elected or appointed officials. Rather, the PIO serves as a source of expert assistance to the other officers as they handle their individual internal and external communication responsibilities.

A public relations checklist for government workers

Provide the best service possible.

Look constantly for ways to improve service and reduce cost.

Creating good will toward local government is the responsibility of every government employee.

Keep up-to-date in the use of new equipment and new methods for carrying out the work of your unit.

Learn as much as you can about all jobs that relate to your unit.

Respond to taxpayers' questions promptly, courteously, clearly, and accurately.

Listening to what citizens are saying about local government is as important as telling them about it.

Schedule work at times that will inconvenience the smallest number of persons.

Warn people before service is to be interrupted or delayed.

Handle complaints in a systematic way.

Alert superiors to policies that are difficult to enforce or that create additional problems.

Do not take criticisms from citizens personally.

Maintain equipment, grounds, and buildings in good condition.

Remember that it is each employee's responsibility to make a good impression on citizens; this, in turn, gives citizens a good impression of government.

Small, simple courtesies to citizens can have long-lasting positive effects.

Avoid taking breaks in public areas.

Learn everything you can about all aspects of government services so that when friends, neighbors, and others ask questions, you can either answer the questions or refer the people to the right sources.

Media relations

The PIO is responsible for planning news media policies; supervising directly the release of information on major stories; and coordinating inquiries, interviews, and meetings between reporters and community government officials.

Claremont, California, a city of 35,000, recognizes the importance of these functions. The Community Information Office, headed by the Community Information Coordinator, has been established as a "central information center with an individual responsible for the coordination of public affairs and media relations."[3]

The responsibilities of the Community Information Office in Claremont are illustrative. They include supervising the preparation and distribution of "nonroutine" media releases; helping reporters gain access to city officials and employees; helping city departments and elected officials prepare media releases and handle media questions; and, on a stand-by basis, serving as the public information center "when the emergency operation center is activated by the city manager."[4]

Other responsibilities might include helping reporters locate obscure records; defining the latitude that subordinate employees have in releasing information; and providing informal training sessions on information policies, legal requirements for both open records and privacy, and media practices and customs with respect to deadlines, quotes, and news conferences.

Internal communications

As previously mentioned, local government employees cannot do a good job of communicating with the public or providing customer service if they do not know what is going on within the organization and are not familiar with its mission, policies, and goals.

Managers and the PIO need to practice what they preach when they communicate with employees. An employee newsletter and bulletin boards are essential, but insufficient. In addition, internal communication may be facilitated by employee incentives (letters of commendation, informal notes, staff recognition, and the like) that provide visible evidence of management interest, electronic mail, print media, and communications training.

Communications planning

The PIO is a communications consultant for community government officials. In addition to disseminating information and handling publicity, he or she sees that communication facilitates program and service delivery. This means that every service and program should be planned with built-in mechanisms for disseminating information and receiving feedback.

When should information be distributed? How much effort should be directed toward the media? Elected officials? Employees? Community associations and other special groups? What format should be used? How much will it cost? How can feedback be obtained? Although the public information officer is the major resource for communications planning, implementation, feedback, and evaluation, this does not relieve elected officials, chief administrators, department heads, and other key employees from their responsibilities in this regard.

Communication is too important for agency heads to divorce themselves from the process. They may delegate broad authority for directing communication activities to a communications director or public information officer, with whom they work closely, but agency heads and their top management team must remain involved in setting, implementing, and evaluating communication policy and performance.[5]

Information management

In well-run organizations, information is managed. This does not mean concealing, distorting, or falsifying information; it refers, rather, to questions of timing, information load, and the ways that information is put together. The decision to issue, or not to issue, an annual report is a familiar example. The timing for release of the budget is another. The level of detail in financial reports is a third. The control of information is particularly relevant to news reporters. Who speaks for whom? A workable answer is suggested by the city of Claremont, California:

Every attempt should be made by department heads or their designees to respond promptly and accurately to all media inquiries. Department directors and identified management level staff are authorized to serve as liaison to media representatives regarding policy issues. Nonmanagement staff may respond to routine, factual information relating specifically to their function.[6]

Perhaps the most important rule in information management is that most information must be accessible. This is reinforced by federal law (the Freedom of Information Act) and by state statutes that mandate open meetings and public access to government records. Citizens have a legal right to open government, and news reporters consider it both their right and their duty to report on anything they deem newsworthy. Therefore,

The decisions, thoughts, and even life styles of public officials and administrators are far more likely to receive public scrutiny than is true for their business sector counterparts.[7]

Heartland Free-net Inc.

Heartland Free-net Inc. is a not-for-profit organization sponsored by community-minded institutions and businesses that provides a public computer system free of charge to people and organizations in Central Illinois.

The system can be accessed by any user who has a personal computer and a modem. By dialing a local number, the user can access information that historically has been difficult or impossible to obtain. Individuals can visit the system or they can become Registered Users. Visitors can read any item in the system; registered users can send mail to and receive mail from other registered users, and they also can request information from expert Information Providers. The categories of information available are as follows:

Community calendar Includes schedules for and information related to community events, such as programs at the Peoria Civic Center.

Public square An open, public forum.

Administrative center Provides instructions on using the system, updates, passwords, and registrations.

Business connection Provides information on businesses in the area.

Education center Describes pre- and post-secondary educational opportunities and continuing education programs.

Tax clinic Provides local tax information; question-and-answer area.

Government center Provides information about local governments in the area.

Legal center Covers legal topics; question-and-answer area.

Social services center Describes organizations and services available to the public.

Library center Provides library information and reference services.

Medical center Covers medical issues; question-and-answer area.

Free-net users' mail Allows registered users to send and receive mail from other registered users.

Source: Adapted from public information folder distributed by Heartland Free-net, Inc., P.O. Box 5873, Peoria, Illinois 61625.

Communication methods

The two most important communication principles for managers have been set forth in a basic text on public relations:

> *Effective communication must be designed for the situation, time, place, and audience.* It means careful selection of media and technique. . . *Advances in technology and specialized media are opening up a wealth of possibilities for serving the needs of special audiences.* Practitioners would be well advised to think in terms of smaller and more circumscribed patterns of communication.[8]

This quote stresses, first, that communications of all kinds are usually developed for specific applications. Even news releases are intended mostly for specific groups. Second, the wide range of methods makes it much easier and more effective to tailor and target communications. The information tools most commonly employed by community governments are news releases, newsletters, public service announcements, and direct mail. Other less frequently used tools include radio and television; cable television, speakers' bureaus; films, videotapes, and other audiovisual material; and electronic bulletin boards.

Communications of all kinds are usually developed for specific applications.

Many other methods are available, however. The range of printed information includes pamphlets and flyers, annual reports, directories, newspaper inserts, special reports and booklets, newspaper ads, newsletters, news releases, media kits, fact sheets, and utility bill inserts. In the audiovisual field, the possibilities include films, slides, videotapes, audiotapes, cable television, and radio and television programs. Still other methods include speeches, informal personal reporting, and special events. The PIO is a valuable source of advice to managers on the targets, tools, and methods that are applicable to a particular communication goal.

Communication volunteers

A highly effective means of communication is using volunteers, often as block leaders, to help in educational and promotional activities for recycling old waste. Volunteers can explain and promote the correct separation of cans, bottles, and newspapers for recycling; proper setouts of waste for curbside collection; and reasons for regulations for tree branches, furniture, boxes, cartons, and other bulky items. These volunteers help on a continuing basis to keep their neighbors informed.

For example, a corps of neighborhood block leaders in Boulder, Colorado, distributes newsletters to residents, staffs booths at county fairs, and sponsors recycling events. Block leaders in Durham, North Carolina, talk to their neighbors about how to participate in curbside recycling and in workshops on preparing lessons for elementary schools.

Source: Adapted from Public Technology, Inc., Urban Consortium Environmental Task Force; and ICMA, *Recycling Lessons Learned* (Washington, DC: ICMA, 1991), 22-23, 34, 43, 54, 74.

News media

Newspapers and especially radio and TV work within a system that values speed and immediacy, the live event, the contentious proposal, the scandal, and the personal side of a story. It is an outlook that often deletes background information and critical details. Local officials therefore need to understand the nature of the media and to do all they can to provide reports with adequate and accurate information.

Community government should be proactive, providing user-friendly procedures for obtaining hard news, suggesting stories and interviews for follow-up coverage on major events, and steering reporters to the wealth of human interest stories that every community has. By seeking persons other than public officials to "carry" the news, community government can present the positive side of government.

Roles and relationships

Public officials and news reporters have different jobs to do. Both seek to inform the public, but each does so for a different reason. Public officials are concerned with generating public understanding and support. Reporters see themselves as not only reporting the news but also as guarding the public interest by maintaining surveillance of community government affairs.

Public officials should resign themselves to the fact that often reporters are imbued with investigative zeal. The best defense is open, honest, and well-run government. The backup is scrupulous observance of open records and open-meeting requirements, and patience with reporters' endless requests for information.

Differences in perception and mission affect relations between local government officials and the media. Even when mutual understanding of these different roles exists, public officials must be resigned to a certain amount of news media disagreement and criticism. However, it is possible to achieve good working relations, mutual respect, and fair coverage when elected and appointed officials (and especially information officers) follow a few simple guidelines.

First, know what's going on in the government and have all relevant facts. Credibility with reporters suffers when public officials are not sure of the answers to reporters' questions. If answers are not readily available, public officials should get them as soon as possible and call the reporters back. Prompt answers are important to reporters who are facing deadlines.

Differences in perception and mission affect relations between local government officials and the media.

Second, provide adequate background information to buttress the facts. Reporters will understand the situation better, and write about it more accurately, if they are given enough relevant information.

Third, avoid off-the-record information. Although such information is useful for giving reporters background and increasing understanding, there should be compelling reasons for going off the record. It must be clearly understood beforehand what information is off the record and what is on the record.

Fourth, avoid "no comment." It is better to explain why the information cannot be revealed and indicate when the information will be available.

Fifth, balance competing media demands from newspapers, radio, and television. Deadlines and information requirements are different from one medium to another.

Sixth, never forget media deadlines. An on-time story may make page 1; a too-late story will be run the next day on an inside page or will be killed. For radio and television, a too-late story may never be used. Awareness of the reporters' time constraints, and an honest effort to provide them with the needed information in time to make their deadlines, can do much to improve working relationships with the media.

Finally, truthfulness and candor are mandatory. Trust forms the basis for respect.

A particularly important part of media relations is facilitating coverage of meetings of elected councils and boards, other boards with legal authority (such as zoning boards), and various citizen advisory committees. Observing three simple rules will meet most media needs for providing coverage.

1. Prepare a weekly calendar of community government events showing dates, times, and locations of council and board meetings, public hearings, tax filing deadlines, recreation classes, special events, and so on. Be sure the calendar is sent to editors and reporters for all media.

Figure 14–6 In 1993, one of the primary goals of the mayor of Brea, California, was to increase citizen involvement in the leadership of the city. The council hosted a series of town hall meetings at which citizens discussed ideas and concerns with their elected officials. This two-sided fact sheet provided citizens with follow-up information.

MAY 1993

Town Hall Today *is designed to provide you with follow-up information to issues raised at last week's Let's Talk Brea Town Hall Meeting. As always, the Brea City Council is interested in keeping you informed about issues affecting your city today.*

We would like to once again express our appreciation for your input and encourage you to attend City Council meetings on the first and third Tuesdays of each month at 7:00 p.m in the Council Chambers of the Civic & Cultural Center.

City Council Reaffirms Major Goals

Mayor Dunlap reaffirmed Council commitment to the Brea community by highlighting three major goals: Increase citizen involvement in city leadership; ensure long-term economic vitality and enhance quality of life.

In addition to establishing town hall meetings, Council has taken a number of steps to increase accessibility to our government. You may leave a message for the mayor anytime day or night by dialing the new 24-hour hotline at (714) 671-4488; the mayor has instituted weekly office hours on Monday mornings and steps have been taken to provide better access to Council study sessions and other meetings at the Civic & Cultural Center. To enhance communication with the school district, the mayor has appointed a community liaison.

Council and staff are working diligently to maintain existing revenues, seek ways to raise new revenue and attract quality businesses to give a jolt to the local economy.

Discussing the Sphere of Influence (SOI), Mayor Pro Tem Parker stressed its potential impact, explained what the project entails, why it's important to you as a Brea resident and how you can get involved. *(see map and story next page).*

Recession and State Cuts Harmful to California Cities

The lingering recession plus proposed budget cuts from the State have put California cities in a bind this fiscal year.

In Brea the recession has greatly impacted city revenues from sales and property taxes and development fees. Brea faces a current shortfall of 1.5 million dollars in anticipated revenues. To make up this shortfall, Brea has further streamlined its operation, imposed a hiring freeze and left positions unfilled.

California State officials have estimated that the State budget deficit will exceed $10 billion in fiscal year 1993-1994. To help balance its budget the State's lawmakers have proposed to take at least $2 billion in local property tax revenue from California cities.

If the State has its way, Brea may lose another $4 million this year, bringing the total taken from Brea to more than $12 million since 1981.

Brea, as well as other California cities, have made tough decisions to overcome recessionary times and prior State cuts, yet city services are still potentially at risk.

If you'd like your voice heard, please call or write Governor Pete Wilson at: 1st Floor, Capitol Building, Sacramento, CA 95814. Phone: 916/445-2864; Fax: 916/445-4633. For more information on the budget, please call Doug Stevenson in the City Manager's office at 714/671-4416. The current Video Brea Line airing on Channel 3, as well as the May issue of Brea Line, the City's official newsletter, both have detailed stories on Brea's budget situation.

FOR MORE INFORMATION CALL CITY OF BREA COMMUNICATIONS AND MARKETING AT (714) 990-7725

2. Mail council and board agenda materials several days in advance of council and board meetings. If there is no time, hand deliver the materials to various offices.
3. Return all phone calls promptly. Remember the deadlines.

Characteristics of the media

In addition to bearing in mind the general guidelines above, local officials need to be familiar with the characteristics and needs of specific media.

Newspapers

Newspapers are still the first line in local government news coverage because they provide in-depth reporting and a permanent record that is seldom matched elsewhere. On small newspapers, only a few reporters may provide the paper's total news coverage. The community government assignment usually goes to a beginning reporter, which may be deflating to community officials but provides a new opportunity to build rapport and mutual respect. The reporter learns about the community's problems and issues and the political background that influences local policies. Community officials learn about news priorities, deadlines, and production requirements.

The reporter's judgment on news value should be respected. He or she knows what would be of general interest to most readers. Because newspapers must compete for people's time with radio, television, movies, sports events, and leisure activities, they may have a tendency toward sensationalism in some news stories. Because a story that is unread is of little value to anybody, reporters must use their judgment on how to make the story interesting. Controversy makes news. Public officials should resign themselves to this fact and exercise patience and restraint in their responses to newspaper treatment of news and feature stories.

What to do when a reporter calls

The local government and the media share responsibility for accurate and timely news coverage. When a newspaper, radio, or television reporter calls, certain guidelines, such as those developed by the city of Claremont, California, are useful:

Always assume that all your statements are quotable.

When you do not know the answer to a surprise inquiry, tell the reporter that you will call back.

Listen carefully to the question. The reporter may have made incorrect assumptions, and you will need to give clearer background information before answering the question.

Do not argue with reporters.

If interrupted in mid-thought, proceed with your original answer before answering the new question.

Challenge any effort to put words in your mouth.

If you do not know the answer, say so. If you cannot divulge information, state why in a matter-of-fact way.

Be positive, not defensive.

Always tell the truth.

Source: City of Claremont, California, *Media Relations Policy Manual* (Claremont, CA: City of Claremont, 1990), 5, 6, 7.

Most communities are served by only one local newspaper and public officials should bear this in mind when dealing with the publisher or editor. The situation does not call for subservience or servility, but it does warrant making every effort to establish and maintain a good working relationship.

Radio

News for radio presentation must be gathered in a different manner and reported in a different framework from newspaper coverage. Radio news coverage is very brief: A typical fifteen-minute newscast may include local news for only three minutes, or 20 percent of the time. Of the three minutes for local news, perhaps seventy to eighty seconds will be available for reporting on developments in local government. Analysis and interpretation are rare.

In contrast to newspapers, which usually have a broad, general audience, radio audiences are fragmented. Radio stations cater to varied groups and interests: listeners may prefer country and western, rock, or classical music; ethnic programming; all news or call-in shows; and so on.

Radio stations can offer unique opportunities to reach particular segments of the public.

These different radio formats are often accompanied by different policies and practices covering news reporting. Some stations have reporters who will cover a local government beat in a fashion similar to newspapers. Other stations limit their news coverage to wire-service copy; some will not even report local news. The most important radio outlets for community governments are all-news stations and those that give extensive coverage to public affairs. These stations will usually welcome news releases from community governments to balance their coverage of regional and national news.

To obtain news coverage from radio outlets, the information officer must vary methods of contact with radio news staffs according to the format and staffing of the individual stations. Because of their distinct audiences, radio stations can offer unique opportunities to reach particular segments of the public, and news releases and announcements can often be tailored to the specific audience each station serves.

Television

Television news coverage has to be immediate, and the time limitations are rigid. Local television stations, however, can provide visually appealing coverage for events such as sports contests, award ceremonies, kite-flying jamborees, and building dedications and tours. Television audiences are much harder to define than radio and newspaper audiences, but that does not preclude efforts to reach viewers through visually oriented special events, coverage of council and board meetings, news conferences, and public hearings.

Cable television in particular provides an excellent opportunity for community government to communicate with citizens. Cable TV is more than a substitute for antennas that bring network TV into individual homes. It is a transmission medium that communicates voice, video, and data with good quality, at high speed, and in large volume. Further, the communications can be sent from a central station to individual homes and offices, and then back again.

Even in small communities, cable TV can cover proceedings of governing bodies and committees; disseminate information on driver training, fire prevention, job openings, temporary street closings, and solid waste collection schedules; facilitate citizen surveys, at-home work, field reports, and other interactive modes; channel digital (nonvideo) information for meter reading, traffic control, police reports, and other government activities; and provide dedicated channels for police patrol, emergency services, traffic control, and many other public safety activities.

Publicity

A large part of the management job is to convey facts, news announcements, and other forms of information to the various audiences described earlier in this chapter. This section reviews management responsibilities for publicity, the community efforts to attract attention and provide news and other kinds of information.

The publicity tools that are generally available to community governments are printed information, audiovisuals, and special events. Each can be used, even in small communities. The choice depends on the audience, of course, but also on other factors such as time, cost, local resources, staff, and number of people to be reached.

The printed word in one form or another is likely to be the backbone of community publicity. Although audiovisuals and telecommunications are growing in importance, the printed word is still, for many purposes, the simplest, most economical, and best understood medium. The range of choices is large: pamphlets, flyers, annual reports, special reports, newsletters, newspaper ads, news releases, posters, and others. Those most commonly used are probably pamphlets, flyers, annual reports, and newsletters.

Figure 14–7 A partial list of uses of cable TV in small communities. The list is for demonstration purposes only and is not intended to be exhaustive or limiting in any way.

One-way cablecasting

1. Proceedings of boards, councils, and committees
2. Dissemination of information and education to citizens, including: driver training and safety; fire prevention; traffic information; emergency warnings; consumer information; city public relations; job information

Interactive (two-way) modes

1. Service delivery; client interviewing and screening; problem solving; polls, citizen surveys; information gathering; paramedic functions; magistrating of prisoners
2. Administrative: field reports; at-home work; technician training; procedural updates; conferences

Regional interconnection

1. Regional meetings of municipal officials and special associations
2. Regional emergency alerts

Digital (nonvideo) information

1. Meter reading
2. Traffic surveillance and control
3. Fire early-warning systems
4. Burglar alarm systems
5. Computer data interface
6. Linking computer local area networks (LANs)

Use of dedicated video and data channels

1. Fire monitoring surveillance
2. Security monitoring of government buildings
3. Reserved emergency channel
4. Traffic control
5. At-home work programs
6. Police magistration

Pamphlets and flyers contain sets of facts, the presentation of which can be tailored to any literate audience. Although pamphlets can be expensive, they usually are low in cost and easy to prepare. Flyers (one-page sheets of information) are especially good when the information to be conveyed is simple, short, and factual.

Annual reports may be required by state law; in any case, they are desirable because they provide a permanent, historical record. The major considerations in developing such reports are production costs (high cost does not guarantee good results), selection of coverage (a community overview often is sufficient), and distribution (again, the cost can be formidable).

Newsletters should be simple in format and low in cost. They supplement newspaper coverage by announcing new programs and services, highlighting special events, and providing information on the budget, tax dates, license application deadlines, and council and board meetings.

Figure 14–8 When Imperial Highway in Brea, California, was being widened between 1992 and 1994, the city kept the community informed of the project's progress and helped local businesses affected by the construction. This flyer offered the businesses free advertising in a holiday gift guide produced by the city.

You've asked for assistance in advertising your business during construction—so here it is! As part of its continuing communications and marketing efforts to help merchants during the widening of Imperial Highway, the City of Brea will produce a holiday gift guide to promote Imperial Highway businesses during this critical shopping season.

All businesses located within the Imperial Highway widening project are eligible to participate. Each business will receive a **free 1/10 page ad.** The Holiday Gift Guide will be inserted into the Orange County Register on Wednesday, November 24, December 1 and 8. Your ad will reach over 80,000 shoppers within our region at no cost to you*! Copies will be available to merchants for individual distribution.

To participate, simply fill out the information below and attach the logo, graphic, etc., that you want included in your ad. A limited amount of space is available for businesses who would like to purchase additional ad space. Rates are listed below and include your 1/10 page ad "credit." To purchase a larger sized ad, please be sure to place a check by the desired ad size and enclose your check, payable to the Orange County Register.

Imperial Highway Holiday Shopping Guide Advertising Form

Friday, October 1 is the deadline to return this completed form (with payment if ordering additional ad space). Due to space limitations, additional ad size orders will be determined on a first come basis.

Name of Business ____________

Business Address ____________

Telephone ____________

Person to contact regarding this ad ____________

**Yes!* I would like to increase my 1/10 page advertisement to:

- ☐ 1/8 page $17
- ☐ 1/4 page $67
- ☐ 1/2 page $168
- ☐ 1 page $370

See reverse side for approximate ad sizes.

***Note:** Horizontal vs. vertical ad dimensions are based on availability. One proof will be provided prior to publication and must be returned with corrections/changes within two working days of receipt or we reserve the right to use creative judgment and proceed with production.*

Ad copy to read: ____________

Figure 14–9 The city of Brea, California, produces and airs local programming over its government access channel. The programming includes live broadcasts of city council meetings, council meeting agenda previews, coverage of community events, and educational programs. When programming is not being aired, a twenty-four-hour electronic community message board operates.

Audiovisuals include slides, films, videotapes, audiotapes, radio and television programs, and cable television. They have the powerful advantages of immediacy and the intimacy of visual and aural exposure. They also have the drawbacks of high cost (in some cases, very high cost) and a short life span.

Special events—centennial observances, dedications, and festivals—are a good way of promoting community government unobtrusively by stressing history and a sense of place so that people can take pride in their community. Festivals have become popular in many places to recognize cultural and ethnic diversity in a positive manner.

Information technology

Not long ago a local government was at the forefront of the computer revolution if it had a mainframe computer on which citizen survey results could be tabulated. Today, citizens can punch answers to survey questions directly into their telephones; the information is automatically transmitted to a database, and the results are tabulated and available within a short period of time. With the information highways proposed by the Clinton administration, citizens and city hall will be able to communicate regularly and immediately. Using computers, for example, city hall will transmit auto registration renewals to citizens, who will in turn transmit payment directly to city hall. Public access to computerized city records will herald the real beginning of the 24-Hour City Hall.

Information technology encompasses systems used to develop, process, store, and transmit messages; computer hardware and software; and the equipment and services of outside suppliers, especially the local telephone company. Technological changes drive other changes in information handling both within a community government and in communication with the public.

Among small cities, 50 percent or more use computer technology for budget analysis, budget development, finance, utility services, personnel, and law enforcement, as well as for other programs. Forty-three percent of small jurisdictions used local area networks (LANs), and at least a few make use of some of the more progressive technologies, such as the 24-Hour City Hall, video arraignments, and fingerprint identification systems (see Figure 14–10).

As information technology has become less expensive and more accessible, it has also introduced a complex set of issues that have caught the attention of local governments. No longer is the use of technology limited to one or two local government departments. The information contained within the systems is not only extensive but often sensitive and potentially damaging if misused. If someone who opposes a new

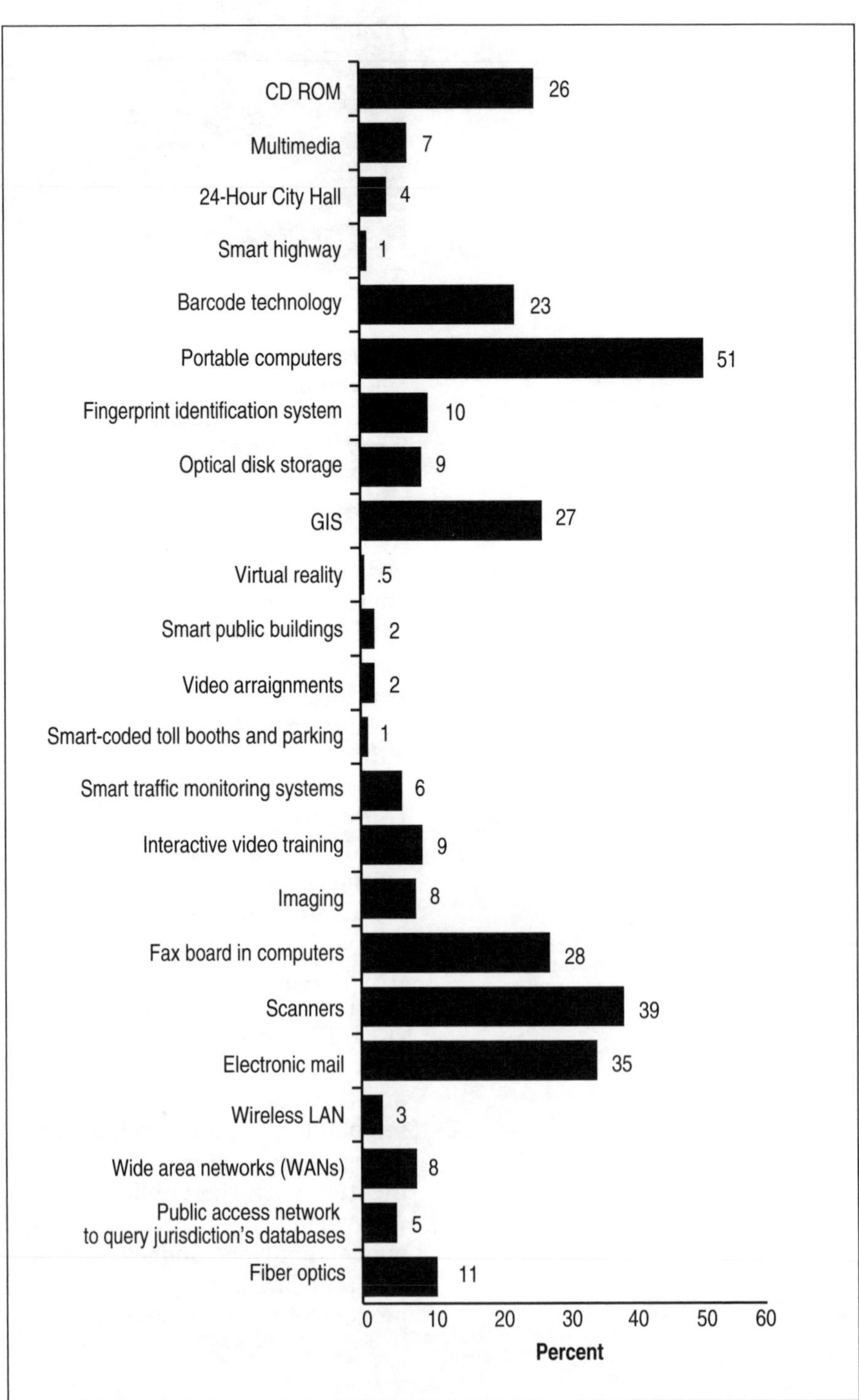

Figure 14–10 Progressive technology applications in cities under 100,000.

The local government manager must assume a significant role in information planning because the reach of technology extends across all local government activities.

local program or policy gains access to the details before they are complete, bad publicity can influence public opinion before the program is presented. During the budget process, preliminary figures can be damaging, particularly during an election year. Moreover, an electronic equivalent of "stuffing the ballot box" may be devised. Security, privacy, and ownership are among the many concerns that must be addressed.

There are also issues of purchasing, planning, and access. MIS or data processing functions used to be limited primarily to programming and report generating. Today, MIS is usually responsible for information planning, system standards, purchasing, equipment performance standards, training, systems evaluation, and local area networks.[9] The local government manager or administrator must assume a significant role in information planning because the reach of technology potentially extends across all local government activities. Lack of planning can be catastrophic, both programmatically and financially. Guidelines for management responsibility are shown in the following checklist:

Centralize responsibility for information planning in the office of the chief administrative officer.

Develop an information master plan, and update it annually.

Develop goals and objectives for plans, systems, and standards with employee task forces so that employees have a stake in successful operations.

Establish standards for common information system elements (names, addresses, dates, and so on).

Provide training in technologies.

Require understandable systems and documentation.

Establish systems and procedures so that information can be accessed easily by employees and the public.

Develop policies and rules for the kinds of information that must be open to the public and the kinds of information that must be kept private.

Establish security measures to protect data.[10]

Public electronic network
Santa Monica, California (95,000), uses its Public Electronic Network (PEN) to maintain contact with its citizens. PEN features an electronic bulletin board of city information, electronic mail for communication between city hall and residents, and computer conferencing. Users can also access the city library's card catalog and databases of city and social services. A city jobline, television guide, and information on beach events, earthquake safety, recycling tips, park and recreation schedules, and library news are available twenty-four hours a day. The system is accessible without charge from any home or office computer or from thirty-five public terminals and can support up to sixty-four simultaneous users. In its first year, 2,000 residents accessed the network over 52,000 times.

Source: *The Guide to Management Improvement Projects in Local Government*, vol. 15, no. 4 (Washington, DC: ICMA, 1991), no. CCR-25.

Telecommunications is the general term used to describe the range of devices used by public and private organizations for information transfer: two-way radios, computers and their peripherals, telephones (which include an extraordinary subset of targeted features and services), cable television, Telex, facsimile (fax) machines, and Telenet, Internet, and other communication networks that are based on radio frequency (RF), fiber optics, coaxial cable, and digital formats.

Videotex is of special interest to local governments because it provides quick, interactive, and easy-to-use public access to community government information. By video, telephones, and computers, Videotex links users with such information sources as court dockets, library catalogs, customer service information on utility bills, tax payments, building permit applications, land title searches, and locations and schedules for public school events.

Ethics of communication

Communication does not exist unless meaning is shared. Trust facilitates sharing, but there is no trust unless it has been earned through knowledge, reputation, experience, and performance.

The trustworthiness (or lack thereof) of the communicator permeates all communication, including reports, news conferences, speeches, training programs, publications, audiovisual materials, databases, and agendas. Evidence of his or her integrity is present or absent in the material selected, the material withheld, the questions that are asked, the veracity of the presentation, the vocabulary employed, and the timing of the release of information.

Lack of trust develops in the relations between reporters and government officials when officials omit key facts, use confusing language, resort to euphemisms, and use the terms *classified* and *privileged* as escape hatches. Communication in community government is not nearly as complex and contentious as it is in the federal government and some state governments, but emotionally charged situations may develop during public hearings, meetings of community governing bodies, administrative hearings, and one-on-one encounters between employees and citizens. Examples of the issues that can come up at such times are zoning variance applications, budget hearings, property tax proposals, dog ordinance enforcement actions, street and road improvements, and changes in work requirements for persons on welfare.

The obligation for ethical communication behavior rests with community officials. They control information and therefore are responsible for observing criteria for truth, clarity, openness, and fairness. Truth is more than not lying. It also means not concealing or distorting information. It requires telling others when information cannot be revealed because of privacy laws or for other good reasons, which should be explained.

Deliberately using polysyllabic words and professional jargon with people of limited education is unethical.

Clarity means that meaning—what the message says—is jointly understood. Deliberately using polysyllabic words and professional jargon with people of limited educational background is unethical. It may postpone, but it will never eliminate, a problem. Clarity means also pointing out the pros and cons, when pertinent; explaining consequences; going over points a second time, when needed; interpreting professional and technical terms, when such terms must be used; and answering questions in a manner that does not intimidate or patronize.

Openness applies to all audiences and is generally a legal requirement at all levels of government. It must be balanced, however, with equally compelling legal requirements for privacy and security. Openness obviously applies to relations with the public and the media, but it applies also within the organization.

Subordinates owe it to their superiors and elected officials to inform them, even of bad news, so that problems can be addressed. . . .Likewise, superiors owe subordinates enough information so that subordinates can do their jobs competently and avoid administrative or even legal trouble.[11]

Fairness means that administrators and other key employees should not exploit the advantages they have in communicating: primary information sources, access to documents, preparation of agendas, and control of computer-driven databases.

Administrators and other key employees should not exploit the advantages they have in communicating.

A common complaint of members of councils and boards is that they cannot judge administrative proposals effectively because managers and department heads decide what information to include in agendas, reports, and other materials submitted to them. What has been left out? How relevant is the omitted information? There is no categorical answer. Administrators must exercise professional judgment tempered by ethical standards and ensure the ready availability of further information any time elected officials ask for it.

Garnett describes three other kinds of situations in which managers, department heads, and other professionals have an advantage:

Relying solely or primarily on formal written reports and testimony. Public hearings are a form of communication in which well-educated citizens may have an advantage. Hearings can inhibit citizen participation for those who lack reading, oral comprehension, and speaking skills. This puts less-educated, less-organized groups at a severe disadvantage at meetings of community governing bodies and at public hearings. This can be mitigated by neighborhood meetings in a variety of informal formats.

Exploiting language and terminology.

Using knowledge of persuasion to unfair advantage. Research shows that less-educated people are more susceptible to propaganda methods. These people may lack the vocabulary, reasoning skills, and background to cope with dogma, half-truths, exaggerations, and other unethical forms of persuasion.[12]

Afterword

The late twentieth century has been dubbed the information era. Communication has evolved from two-way exchanges by mail, telephone, and telegraph to an array of electronic media, modes, and systems—we live not only in the media era but also in the telecommunications era, the digital/binary era, and the network era.

News reporting and audience attention have shifted sharply from newspapers to radio and television; organizational communication is much more two-way and shared; and information technology is changing established work practices. In the technical sense, information and data can be pinpointed, are easily accessed (both legally and illegally) from databases and other sources, and are ubiquitous.

Communication planning is mandatory to cope with these and other changes described in this chapter. Planning includes media relations, analysis of community associations and groups, employee training, frank and open discussions with elected officials about information access, and evaluation of communication methods. Prudent community government managers are developing policies and procedures that recognize changes such as the need and desirability for some employees to work at home (telecommuting); work stations with personal computers that are linked together (the only constraint is cost); the competition between departments to buy the latest in computer hardware and software; and the need to balance legal and ethical requirements for open meetings and open records with the equally compelling need to respect privacy rights.

The public information officer is a major resource for elected officials, managers, and other key persons in the rapidly changing communication environment. The PIO is no longer just a news source and publicity agent. Today the PIO—more than anyone else in the community government—must have the background and perspective to see how news, messages, and other forms of information interact.

Communication in its many forms is easy to evade and subvert. The evasion and concealment that have characterized too much of government over the past two decades have led to unprecedented public cynicism and distrust. Community governments can lead the way in improving public perceptions by fostering ethical practices in all forms of communication. It will be a major step, in the words of the National Commission on the Public Service, toward "rebuilding the public service." ■

---

1 Phillip V. Lewis, *Organizational Communication: The Essence of Effective Management*, 3rd ed. (New York: John Wiley & Sons, 1987), 154. Emphasis in original.

2 Abstracted and excerpted from Lewis, *Organizational Communication*, 149-59.

3 City of Claremont, *Media Relations Policy Manual,* 2.

4 Ibid.

5 Garnett, *Communicating for Results in Government*, 137.

6 City of Claremont, California, *Media Relations Policy Manual* (Claremont, California: City of Claremont, 1990), 3. Available from International City/County Management Association as a Clearinghouse Report.

7 James L. Garnett, *Communicating for Results in Government* (San Francisco: Jossey-Bass, 1992), 17.

8 Scott M. Cutlip, Allen H. Center, and Glen M. Broom, *Effective Public Relations*, 6th ed. (Englewood Cliffs, NJ: Prentice-Hall, 1985), 275. Emphasis in original.

9 For an overview of the changes in MIS departments in state and local government, see Rob Gurwitt, "The Defrocking of the Computer Priesthood," *Governing* (April 1992): 57-62.

10 Much of this section has been based on experiences and evaluations reported by four cities and one county: City of Long Beach, *Telecommunications 2000*; City of San Diego, *Communication and Information Master Plan* (San Diego, California: Office of the City Manager, 1990); and *Information Master Planning Sampler* (Sarasota, Florida; Mercer Island, Washington; and Genesee County, New York). All three publications are available from International City/County Management Association as Clearinghouse Reports.

11 Garnett, *Communicating for Results in Government*, 240.

12 Ibid., 241-43.

15 Intergovernmental Relations

Much of the change facing community governments today has a profound impact on their relationships with other levels and units of government, the nonprofit sector, and for-profit organizations. This chapter deals with two separate but interrelated sets of relationships: intergovernmental management (IGM) and intersectoral management (ISM).

IGM concerns relationships that exist between the community government and other local governments of all kinds, the state government, and the federal government. These relationships are often complex and involve legal, political, and financial considerations. However, although IGM relationships are of key concern to community government managers, ISM relationships have emerged as equally important. ISM concerns relationships between the community government and both nonprofit organizations (often referred to as the *third sector*) and for-profit organizations (the private sector). Communities are working increasingly with nonprofits and for-profits in activities related to both service delivery and economic development.

The organization of the chapter is meant to convey the dynamic nature of today's intergovernmental and intersectoral relationships. The chapter focuses initially on how the management environment has changed in recent years, then describes how relationships have changed between community governments and federal and state governments, among community governments, and between community governments and nonprofit and for-profit organizations.

The chapter then discusses the characteristics of city and county governments within the IGM/ISM system and the various IGM/ISM approaches to service delivery, ranging from interlocal agreements to contracting or transferring services. It closes by exploring the emerging roles of communities within the IGM/ISM environment that is developing as the twenty-first century approaches.

The changing environment

Today, community governments are increasingly confronted with external changes over which they have little control. Terms such as *turbulent environment* and *future shock* convey the sense of rapid change facing individuals and organizations. Chapter 1 of this book summarized those changes, focusing particularly on economic changes, demographic changes, changes in urban patterns, technological changes, political changes, and ideological changes. All of these affect the challenge to management, but some have particular relevance to the tasks facing IGM/ISM relationships.

Citizen demands and attitudes

Perhaps most significant, the current pattern of citizen demands is forcing governments to look for new ways to deliver services. Three strands interwoven into that pattern of demand are particularly relevant. First, demands for public services by increasingly narrow interest groups have added to the pressures for local government action. Second, citizen opposition to tax increases—particularly in property taxes—to support these services has grown significantly. Third, local residents are increasingly active in opposing the location of public facilities—ranging from solid waste disposal sites to homes for the developmentally disabled—close to their homes. This resistance has added two new terms to government jargon—NIMBY (Not In My Backyard) and LULU (Locally Unwanted Land Use)—and created problems in the local policymaking process. Recommended solutions to citizen demands frequently call for new forms of IGM/ISM action.

Economic change

In addition to the era of government austerity and retrenchment noted in Chapter 1, several other economic trends are forcing communities to deal with economic issues on a regional basis, thus increasing the pressure for innovation and creative interaction among counties, municipalities, and the nonprofit and for-profit sectors of the economy.

One is the continuing decline in manufacturing jobs, with a concurrent shift of jobs from the industrial to the service sector of the economy. Seven of ten jobs are now in the service sector, which includes a wide range of concerns such as insurance, medicine, education, legal services, financial services, information processing, and consumer services. With this shift, more lower paying and part-time jobs have replaced the higher paying manufacturing jobs of the past. Threatening to even large communities, such trends pose a special threat to smaller communities with a less-diversified economic base. For rural communities that have been heavily dependent on production of raw materials (agriculture, forestry, mining), this shift can be devastating.[1]

At the same time that traditional manufacturing jobs have declined, there has been a significant shift from a national to a global economy. The effects of globalization cannot be overestimated. Economic pressure on businesses to increase domestic competitiveness is strong; communities, in turn, are pressured to reduce regulatory controls, provide financial support, and help increase and improve worker skills. Even when such commitments are made, the ability of communities to depend on the loyalty of companies has disappeared as international competition drives businesses to abandon uneconomical plants and facilities and relocate corporate headquarters with little concern for historical ties to location.

Small communities—counties as well as municipalities—cannot address such trends alone. Community governments must work with other governments in the region, with private sector employers and industrial development groups, with educational institutions, with regional planning agencies, and with professional and trade associations of all kinds to address problems relating to business retention and development, site location, financial incentives to private firms, worker training and retraining, and supportive public services.

Changing federal and state relationships

Changing conditions have also altered the relationships of municipalities and counties with the federal and state governments.

Federal–local relations

The key change is that the rate of increase in intergovernmental aid as a percentage of federal outlays has remained stagnant or declined since 1975. The reduction or elimination of such staple programs as general revenue sharing (often the only direct federal aid received by small cities and counties), community development block grants, comprehensive employment and training, economic development administration grants, urban development action grants, and wastewater treatment grants have changed the federal–local relationship.

The federal government has also eliminated provisions in the federal tax code that helped community government budgets. Federal action has greatly restricted the use of industrial revenue bonds (which are exempt from federal income taxes), eliminated the deductibility of state sales taxes (affecting the ability to raise revenue from this source, because taxpayers now find the tax less acceptable), and applied a federal gasoline tax to fuel used in public vehicles.[2]

The federal government has eliminated provisions in the federal tax code that helped community government budgets.

While federal dollars and tax code support for local services were disappearing, federal regulatory control continued unabated. Environmental Protection Agency regulations require cities and counties to meet strict guidelines for the disposal of solid waste and have forced thousands of landfills to close. The Clean Air Act and Clean Water Act require communities to comply with more stringent requirements for air and water quality, but offer no financial help. One estimate predicted that, for the smallest communities, the increased cost of federal water quality standards could equal $170 per household by 1996.[3]

The passage in 1990 of the Americans With Disabilities Act (ADA) has increased hiring-process requirements for localities with more than twenty-five employees to ensure that "qualified individuals with disabilities" are not discriminated against. The Internal Revenue Service issued revisions to regulations that further complicate how municipalities issue tax-exempt bonds, notes, and other obligations. Other examples of federal action exist with respect to transportation, hazardous waste management, the criminal justice system, health services, and the ability to regulate businesses.[4]

Sedona, Arizona, and the U.S. Forest Service

Sedona, Arizona (7,300), and Coconino National Forest have entered into the first cooperative agreement between a city and the U.S. Forest Service. The city and the Forest Service agreed to work together to protect the beauty, environment, and recreational facilities in the 6,455 acres of red rock forest land within and surrounding the city. The city agreed to consult early and often with the Forest Service in developing zoning regulations, ordinances, and infrastructure plans that may affect the lands, and both parties agreed to hold regular meetings and share correspondence. The agreement is the first step towards intergovernmental cooperation in the areas of planning, zoning, and transportation.

Source: *The Guide to Management Improvement Projects in Local Government,* vol. 16, no. 1 (Washington, DC: ICMA, 1992), no. MGT-3.

State involvement in intergovernmental relations

A survey of national, state, and local government experts found three major trends affecting the role of state governments in intergovernmental relations.[5] First, the state role has become more prominent. The ascendancy of the state has occurred as increased capacity and professionalism in state government have enhanced state ability to handle new demands, demands created in part by the reduced role of the federal government in assisting localities financially.

Second, state governments also face increasing federal regulation, which allows them less latitude to govern. The federal government has

Each state has different legal, historical, and cultural experiences that drive its relationships with community governments.

increased the use of state governments as intermediaries for federal programs and regulations. In the case of the community development block grant program, states must ensure that communities are meeting all federal requirements ranging from standards for labor and lead-paint removal to those concerning acquisition of property, relocation assistance to persons displaced, and assessment of the environmental impact of proposed projects and activities.[6] In other areas, such as environmental protection, states have the option of developing their own procedures within federal guidelines or shifting that responsibility back to the federal government.

Third, the extent to which individual states have assumed or desire to assume more responsibility in the intergovernmental system is neither uniform or certain, despite the trends mentioned above. Each state has different legal, historical, and cultural experiences that drive its relationships with community governments.

The "Green Brigade" of Haut-Rhin, France

The "green brigade" of the Alsace region is a collaborative effort of 184 communities and the regional government of Haut-Rhin. Most of the funds for the thirty-six guardians of the environment, who operate out of six command posts, come from the regional government of Haut-Rhin with modest contributions by local communities based on their size.

The task of the rangers, popularly known as the green brigade, consists of monitoring compliance with environmental laws and ordinances, reporting violations, tracking down offenders, and sensitizing the public to environmental concerns. The brigade currently controls seven jeeps, twelve motorcycles, two snowmobiles, two trucks, and twenty-seven horses.

Source: Adapted from *Public Innovation Abroad* (October 1992): 6.

The state–local relationship is also greatly affected by the fiscal constraints that states have placed upon local governments. Although fourteen states have implemented legislation to help pay for costs incurred by community governments in implementing mandates, such efforts are often minimal in relationship to the actual financial impact.[7] In addition, states are still reluctant to grant increased taxing power. Counties are particularly restricted; they are often limited to the property tax—the slowest growing and most administratively burdensome of all major tax sources. Almost 80 percent of own-source tax revenue for counties comes from property tax, and almost 60 percent of all county revenue derives from either property tax or state government transfers.[8]

The combination of federal and state regulatory and fiscal mandates has made it particularly difficult for communities to respond to local demands. As much as 60 or 70 percent of some local government budgets comprises mandated funding, leaving little flexibility to meet other needs.

Fragmentation of service delivery

Just as state–local and federal–local relationships have been changing, so too have interlocal relationships. Almost 30,000 special districts exist today, compared with roughly 24,000 in 1972. This explosion in limited-purpose jurisdictions has resulted from state limitations on annexation by localities, state limitations on local taxing and borrowing powers, and service demands that cross jurisdictional boundaries.

States have allowed the creation of alternative delivery systems to meet these demands. Although the ability of cities and counties to raise revenue locally through increased taxing authority has been limited, alternative structures with separate taxing powers have been created to provide services. Fire districts, sewer districts, school districts, and road districts have often prospered through separate property tax and special assessment powers.

In addition to the fragmentation of community government services, responsibilities have shifted between and among governments, particularly cities and counties. According to one writer, "It is no longer unusual to find counties running what used to be city jails or libraries or zoos, or repairing roads within municipal boundaries."[9]

Community governments in the IGM/ISM system

Even as their interactions with federal and state governments grow more complex, community governments find their own operations expanding in both the number and complexity of their service responsibilities.

Growth of municipal responsibilities

Municipal governments have traditionally had the broadest range of responsibility for neighborhood services. They have focused their resources on public safety (police and fire services), public works, public utilities, libraries, and parks and recreation. In recent decades, clearly regulatory functions promoting public health and safety have become key municipal responsibilities; zoning, subdivision control, and housing are now often seen as primary municipal functions. New areas of responsibility range from economic development to social services, primarily a state and county responsibility in the past; the range of activity in each of these areas is extensive.

Changing role of county governments

Although municipal governments have transformed their roles and responsibilities to meet increasingly complex demands and expectations, county governments may be undergoing the greatest change.[10] Traditionally, counties have acted as agents of the state to provide services in areas such as tax collection, education, public safety, welfare, courts, and roads. Recently, counties have moved actively into areas such as economic development, environmental control, housing, and recreation facility operation.

Common elements of cities and counties

In reaction to both external and internal trends, the traditional boundaries between cities and counties have blurred. Increasingly, demands for services cut across jurisdictional lines. Environmental issues such as solid waste collection and disposal, water supply and wastewater treatment, and hazardous waste disposal are area-wide problems.

Public safety is another area that is seeing significant change. Whereas historically municipal police departments and county sheriff's offices have been separate and often even antagonistic toward one another, today services such as 911 services and criminal detention require increased cooperation. Other examples of cross-over responsibilities include mass transportation, social service delivery, solid waste management, economic and community development, and provision of cultural facilities and services.

IGM and ISM approaches to service delivery

The tremendous changes and demands placed on community governments since the 1980s have required new service delivery approaches. These approaches fall into two categories: innovations in IGM and the increasing role of third-party providers.

Figure 15–1 Selected alternative service delivery approaches and evaluation criteria.

Alternative service delivery approaches

1. Contracting with other governments
2. Contracting with private organizations
3. Franchises
4. Joint public/private activity
5. Joint-powers agreements and shared, multijurisdiction performance
6. Formation of special service districts
7. Grants/subsidies
8. Self-help and volunteerism
9. Regulatory and taxing authority
10. Fees and charges to adjust demand
11. Reduction of demand

Evaluation criteria for selection of alternatives

1. Cost of the government service
2. Financial cost to citizens
3. Choice available to service clients
4. Quality/effectiveness of the service
5. Potential distributional effects
6. Service continuity/disruption
7. Feasibility/ease of implementation
8. Potential overall impact

Innovations in IGM

Innovative IGM approaches to service delivery are found in interlocal agreements and state–local agreements.

Interlocal agreements

Interlocal agreements have existed for a long time. What has changed is the number of agreements and their nontraditional and innovative nature. These arrangements operate in a number of different ways.

Agreements may be developed through an existing organization. Councils of governments (COGS), for example, have become a major facilitator of agreements; all but four states have some form of COG, and more than five hundred exist throughout the United States.[11] In the metropolitan Chicago area, smaller communities use COGs to receive assistance and funding for problems that are too large for single municipalities to handle; in Alabama, Lee and Russell counties, working through a COG, pushed the creation of a joint landfill contract; and in Virginia, a COG developed an agreement for regional wastewater treatment.

Some COG structures operate within municipal boundaries. Oak Park, Illinois, for example, participates as a member of the Oak Park COG, which includes the presidents or CEOs of the village, school districts, township, library, and park district. This group reviews possible joint action in both service delivery and revenue collection.[12]

Regional organizations such as economic development districts also help coordinate and organize interlocal agreements. In Nebraska such organizations have been used to promote joint-purchasing agreements and planning and facility development for solid waste management. Ad hoc joint agreements have expanded to include a wide range of services, such as emergency medical services, hospitals and health services, libraries, economic development activities, social service delivery, recycling, refuse collection and disposal, and parks and recreation facilities.

Finally, through contracting or informal arrangements, cities and governments are providing services to constituents of other local jurisdictions. For example, Salem, Oregon, contracts with surrounding community governments to provide 911 emergency phone services; Scottsbluff, Nebraska, provides building inspection services for Gering, Nebraska, and police services for Terrytown, Nebraska; and San Joaquin County, California, contracts with Sacramento County for the provision of landscaping services on a project-by-project basis.[13]

Partnership program pays off

The city of Temple City, California (31,000), has found that participating in cooperative programs with other local jurisdictions has allowed the city to comply with mandated programs, maintain or increase services to residents, and save general fund monies. The city currently is involved in six such joint ventures:

A joint advertising program with eight San Gabriel Valley cities for economic development. The cost: $500 per city in contrast to over $5,000 per city if executed individually.

Implementing two joint recreation programs with the Temple City Unified School District. Through these cooperative arrangements, the city can offer an extensive array of otherwise financially infeasible recreational opportunities.

Participating in the San Gabriel Valley Joint Powers Authority which allows the city to share the cost of complying with the California Integrated Waste Management Act. Savings: over $50,000.

Participating in the San Gabriel Valley Air Quality Consortium, to share the cost of the development of state-mandated air quality controls. Savings: over $35,000.

Continuing membership in the San Gabriel Valley Animal Control Authority, consisting of eight cities that contract for animal control services. Savings: several thousand dollars a year.

Source: Adapted and reprinted with permission from *Western City*, the monthly publication of the League of California Cities (January 1993): 11.

State–local agreements

States have had to expand their relationships with community governments as federal participation in local service delivery has declined and as demands on localities have grown to exceed their ability to finance them. The following list, developed by the Coalition to Improve Management in State and Local Government, identifies a number of areas in which states can assist community governments:[14]

Simplify the process for adopting home rule and optional statutory charters.

Enact or amend state legislation/regulations to facilitate intergovernmental and intersectoral cooperation.

Provide for local government agreements, consolidation, "piggybacking," or other forms of shared services.

Pass legislation that permits and encourages organization of councils of governments.

Establish information services including state-regional-local communication networks.

Provide joint state–local purchasing or other services.

Support local government service institutes or other technical assistance programs at state universities and community colleges.

States have increased their interaction with local subdivisions; efforts to help local governments finance expensive environmental projects have recently taken place in states such as Florida (water management), Georgia (regional water reservoirs), Oregon (hazardous household waste), and Maine and Nebraska (solid waste management).[15] To stimulate local economic development, many states have given community governments increased flexibility by identifying selected areas within their borders as enterprise zones. Other areas of assistance include providing technical assistance and support to cities and counties through state community-affairs agencies; overseeing the allocation of grant funds; coordinating programs that affect local governments; and piggybacking on statewide purchasing agreements.

ISM: The role of third-party providers

Community governments are actively shifting many services to third parties (i.e., private, for-profit organizations and nonprofit organizations).

Contracting with the private sector

The privatization of the delivery of public goods and services has stirred considerable debate. Privatization historically has been limited to areas in which internal capacity was lacking, where costs and benefits could be easily defined, and where political control was seen as less critical. More recently, it has been used as a means to reduce service delivery costs.

The benefits most often associated with privatization include cost saving, more efficient and effective use of resources, shifting labor costs, reduced start-up costs, increased service flexibility, and reduction of risks associated with liability. However, there are some significant drawbacks to privatization. These include opposition by public employees, lack of sufficient competition for services, lack of evidence of the effectiveness of private alternatives, legal constraints, and loss of control.[16] Many critics also claim that private firms provide services for less cost by exploiting workers: private employers often make little or no provision for such fringe benefits as health insurance and retirement programs.

Although communities can shift the delivery of services to others, responsibility remains with local officials.

The loss of control is a key concern for public officials as they seek to ensure accountability. Although communities can shift the delivery of services to others, the responsibility for the quality and cost of those services remains with local officials.

In the past, the services most likely to be contracted were garbage collection, building and grounds maintenance, vehicle towing and storage, and street and road repairs.[17] However, the realities facing many community governments today have forced them to consider privatization as an alternative for a wider array of services including transportation, human services, and health care services. For example, in Jefferson County, Colorado, a private lease-purchase agreement helped finance a $30.2 million jail facility.[18]

Contracting with the third sector

Although a great deal has been written about privatizing public services, less well-known is the shift to the use of nonprofits to deliver programs. As cities and counties have become more involved in nontraditional program activities, they have also come to interact much more with nonprofit organizations. These relations are often quite different from those associated with the private sector. Nonprofits by their very nature serve some purpose other than the generation of profits for shareholders; insofar as they carry out public purposes, they often share characteristics of government organizations. The range of third sector organizations is staggering—from those that mirror private sector counterparts (e.g., hospitals) to those that have no private sector parallel (e.g., The Urban League).

Day-care partnership
Visalia, California (61,000), established a unique public-private partnership to solve the problem of lack of convenient, affordable day care in the community. Under the arrangement, the Building Industry Association used funds it raised from its membership to build a day-care center on school property to be operated by the YMCA. The project offered a new day-care facility, helped the YMCA provide day care at reduced costs, and answered onsite needs for the school district without increasing demands on transportation, safety, and time associated with off-site facilities.

Source: *The Guide to Management Improvement Projects in Local Government*, vol. 15, no. 1 (Washington, DC: ICMA, 1991), no. LHS-1.

Nonprofit organizations often work directly with community governments in areas such as social services, mental health care, job training, economic development, and recreation. Maricopa County, Arizona, and the state of Arizona worked together to deliver a victim compensation program through a nonprofit foundation; Prince Georges County, Maryland, contracted with a nonprofit hospital to increase services to economically disadvantaged citizens.[19]

Management challenges and roles

The emerging IGM and ISM environment poses new barriers to, and demands new skills from, managers who want to optimize their success in this area of growing importance.

Barriers to success in IGM and ISM

A number of constraints or barriers exist that limit the ability of managers to cope with the tremendous changes that will sweep through community governments in the 1990s and beyond. For local managers to accomplish their goals, they must act to lessen or eliminate these barriers.

The focus on autonomy and procedures

A key concern of many public managers is protecting and expanding the autonomy of their organizations.[20] Real and perceived external threats can result in managers focusing more on turf than on accomplishing goals. In community government, this creates serious problems because of the highly complex and fractionalized system of government that exists. Solving problems often requires a regional approach that is not always possible when the primary concern is protecting turf.

In addition, local governments have a tendency to focus less on outputs and outcomes and more on inputs and regulations. Behavior often focuses on procedures (e.g., making sure proper steps are followed in advertising for bids or issuing public notices for condemning property), which may stand in the way of accomplishing goals and objectives.

Although certain procedures and regulations are necessary and proper, they should not take the place of goals nor of improving the performance of government in achieving its tasks. The key is to strike a balance between goals and procedures. Recent attention on "reinventing" and "reengineering" government has shown community governments increasingly moving toward a performance-based system of service delivery. Such trends are likely to continue in the future.

Employee resistance
Where states allow local government employees to bargain collectively, community government managers face increasing resistance from public employee unions as managers attempt to change organizational responses to the trends identified earlier in this chapter.[21] The most common points of contention include a resistance to changing the organizational structure to increase efficiency (e.g., moving police and fire operations into a cross- trained public safety department); contracting with third parties to deliver services; building merit- and performance-based incentive systems into personnel policies; and increasing the diversity of the public workforce.

Citizen activism
Increasing activism on the part of citizens has both positive and negative impacts on community governments. The barriers created by activism include resistance to public facilities such as sanitary landfills and wastewater, correctional, and social service facilities and increasing opposition to tax and debt increases for new capital facilities. Although it is encouraging that citizens are taking an increased interest in community government, some of that interest results in opposition to government activity.

Limited financial resources
The ability of community governments to finance necessary public services is becoming more limited. Citizen opposition to higher taxes and bond issues; reduced federal aid; the failure of states to provide revenues for mandated programs; and increasing pressure on states to fund education, Medicaid, and other human service programs all restrict the ability of local governments to raise revenue. Each of these, combined with the unwillingness of many state governments to increase the ability of local subdivisions to tap alternative revenue sources, such as sales and income, make the effort to finance government challenging. Any federal government use of a sales or value-added tax only compounds this problem.

Legal constraints
Federal and state preemptions of local authority greatly restrict the local manager's ability to respond to constituent needs and concerns. For example, contracting for services in a more responsive manner may be prohibited by state laws requiring formal competitive bidding. The ability to alter labor force allocations or responsibilities may be prohibited by state labor relations statutes. Even the color of the lights on police cars may be controlled by state law. Furthermore, the exposure of public officials to liability has exploded in the past decade; sovereign immunity has largely disappeared and with it protection from litigation based on actions taken by community government.

Even the color of the lights on police cars may be controlled by state law.

Technology problems
In many local governments, technology is driving decisions rather than decisions driving technology. The ability to do more sophisticated types of cost analysis because of computer technology, for example, does not

mean that the application of such a technique leads to better decisions. Decisions may be worse if the basic assumptions of the analysis are faulty to begin with.

As the information highway becomes a reality, it may well change how governments relate to each other.

Sharing information across federal, state, and local governments is increasingly complex. Fiber optic technology has led to new, rapidly developing information networks. How such networks will affect communication between and among governments is still unknown. Some states are linking city and county governments to area networks to share information. However, other states see this technology as a way to better audit and oversee community government functions or to shift responsibilities. As the information highway becomes a reality, it may well change how governments relate to each other.

Political leadership

Finally, a barrier to success in intergovernmental relations that may have the most serious impact is the escalating turmoil surrounding local political leadership. Public discontent has swelled since the 1970s, leading to sunshine laws and public disclosure requirements that discourage many citizens from running for local office. The rise of special interests has led to an increase in the number of citizens running for local elective office to support a narrow concern rather than to serve the broader public interest. These trends have led to a reduced pool of potential elected officials, more recall elections, and a higher turnover rate among those who do serve. They have also increased the job turnover rate among professional managers in community governments.

Skills for managing IGM and ISM relations

Surmounting these barriers to IGM and ISM activities requires the development of skills that have not previously been part of the public manager's repertoire (e.g., marketing skills) and refinements in other, more familiar skills (e.g., contract management). Skill development in at least nine different areas is needed.

The ability to *build coalitions* to develop alternative delivery systems is a key skill for the future. Recent use of ad hoc and permanent matrix structures to combat local drug trafficking has proven highly successful. For example, in many communities, representatives from the county sheriff's office, various city police departments, the state highway patrol, the Federal Bureau of Investigation, and the federal Drug Enforcement Agency have worked to implement drug enforcement programs on a countywide basis.[22]

Intergovernmental emergency services team

Recognizing the need for special police expertise not feasible in a small community, Lake Forest, Illinois (16,000), joined forces with about twenty other local governments in Lake County, Illinois (480,000), to form an emergency services team consisting of representatives from each agency. Team members, who must qualify through special tests and evaluation, receive extensive training to enable them to operate as a unit. The combined tactical unit operates, in any particular case, under the command of the affected agency. Because costs are shared and each individual agency's commitment is small, the tactical unit is practical and cost effective.

Source: *The Guide to Management Improvement Projects in Local Government,* vol. 15, no. 1 (Washington, DC: ICMA, 1991), no. PS-5 and *The Chicago Tribune,* August 23, 1993, p. 8.

The complexity of the relationships facing community governments demands *negotiation and mediation skills*; they are a prerequisite to success for community managers. The ability to build consensus, manage conflict, and handle difficult policymaking processes is vital to operating in an IGM/ISM environment.

The ability to understand and manage statutory and regulatory processes has become a necessity as well; almost every aspect of IGM/ISM incorporates legal processes and procedures. Providing services through a delivery mechanism that includes many different public, private, and nonprofit organizations requires close attention to *administrative law.*

The rise in use of nonprofit and for-profit organizations and other governments to deliver traditional local government services raises the importance of *contract management.* Today, many of the public services for which communities are responsible are provided by outside entities. Managers must build their capacity to locate, solicit, contract, and manage services provided by nongovernmental organizations. This includes the ability to measure contractor performance effectively and to articulate service outputs and outcomes as part of the contract. Communicating effectively, mastering details, protecting the agency against liability, understanding statutory requirements, evaluating and understanding the political environment, and assessing contractor honesty, capacity, and motives accurately are all keys to success in this area.[23]

Knowing how to influence federal and state policy decisions is of critical concern to managers whose communities will be affected by them.

Citizens are often confused about what public services are available, who is responsible for them, and, if problems arise, where to seek assistance. Increasingly, managers must communicate this information to the public. They must also have the skills necessary to solicit citizen's input, assess their needs and concerns successfully, and help policymakers take constructive action to address those needs and concerns.

Skills in *marketing* and *public relations* may be crucial to stem the declining image of local government. Today's local managers must aggressively solicit ideas and support from their constituents and actively communicate what the government does and why. A number of key areas for a manager to explore include consumer behavior, including market segmentation and marketing to each segment; evaluating the direction, intensity, and breadth of marketing needed; determining the timing of the marketing effort; learning how to acquire and use marketing information; estimating and forecasting market segments; and gauging future demand for services.[24]

In addition to their efforts in marketing and public relations, community leaders have to become more actively involved in *communicating with elected state and federal representatives.* Barriers to successful local government action are often created in state legislative chambers and in Congress. Financial restrictions, new regulations, and mandates emanate from Washington and fifty statehouses. Knowing how policies are formed and implemented and how to influence policy decisions is of critical concern to the managers whose communities will be affected by them.

Local elected officials can lobby their elected federal representatives directly or work through organizations such as the National Association of Counties (NACO), the National League of Cities (NLC), the U.S. Conference of Mayors (USCM), and the National Association of Towns and Townships (NATaT). All of these organizations actively lobby Congress and federal agencies in support of community concerns.

State leagues of municipalities and counties and local councils of governments provide similar support to local officials in lobbying at the state level. Both the national and state organizations work closely with local officials to develop and campaign for policies that support community efforts. These organizations spend a substantial amount of their time opposing legislation that would restrict local government authority.

Local appointed officials may need to become involved in such lobbying activities if requested to do so by their governing body. However, in the case of ICMA members, whose code of ethics requires them to refrain from partisan political activities, their role should clearly be one of supporting, and working on behalf of, the local community's elected officials to implement the governing body's policies.

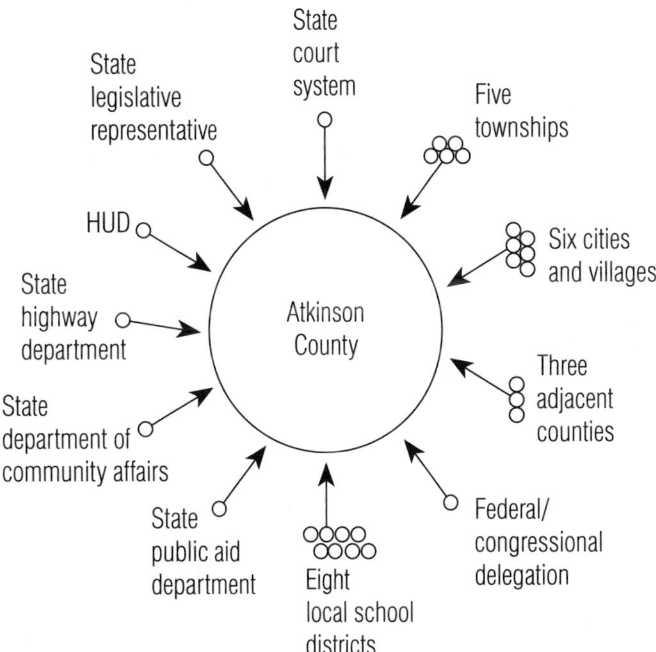

Figure 15–2 Many government departments and agencies can provide advice and information on questions in intergovernmental management for the chief administrator and department heads. Here is the hypothetical example of Atkinson County, which can draw on legislative, executive, and judicial agencies at all levels of government from neighboring cities and counties to the regional and national offices of the U.S. Department of Housing and Urban Development in Washington, D.C.

With the above caveat in mind, local government managers can no longer exempt themselves from nonpartisan political interaction with leaders at the state and federal level. They must actively pursue issues in cooperation with their national and state associations; work to build functioning legislative coalitions between the various municipal and county professional associations; and work directly with state and federal elected representatives and their staffs.

Because private economic activity stimulates economic wealth and expands the tax base, many city and county officials see their role in *economic development* increasing. The role of the local government manager in this field is discussed in Chapter 5.

The ability to *manage technology* and its organizational impact will become more important in the future. Not only does technology affect what happens within cities and counties, but it is playing a growing role in how communities interact with each other, other governments, and the private and nonprofit sectors.[25] The state of Nebraska recently instituted a statewide computer network in every county courthouse to link city and county governments with state government for purposes of data collection, retrieval, and analysis. Current plans include interactive uses for everything from vehicle licensing to tracking child support payments.

New communications technologies, such as satellite communications and laser optic telecommunication lines, will make technology a driving force in IGM/ISM.

Finally, a skill that is critical for community government managers is the ability to *manage change* and to operate effectively in an increasingly turbulent environment. Tools that have gained increasing prominence in managing change are strategic planning and total quality management (TQM). Strategic planning and management are tools that allow organizations to gauge environmental change and adjust goals, objectives, strategies, and actions to position the organization more effectively to meet service demands. TQM focuses on building a customer orientation within the organization and building employee responsibility and capacity to produce quality services. Other tools such as action research, program evaluation, management by objectives, and program budgeting all focus on improving the capacity to manage change.

Afterword

To be a community government administrator is more difficult, complex, and challenging today than ever before. A major reason is the extraordinary changes that have occurred in the relationships among government units, private businesses, and nonprofit organizations.

The twentieth century has witnessed two major revolutions in the intergovernmental relations of community governments. For much of the first half of the century, community governments were largely alone in their work. Community governments had sole responsibility for meeting all the public service needs of their residents (except those for local schools). Then, at mid-century, the local government scene became crowded with players. Counties and municipalities were joined by a myriad of new units of local government—special districts of all sorts—and supplemented by special authorities of their own creation, all sharing in the task of delivering a growing variety of services.

Now, late in the century, the business of government is changing again. Nongovernmental organizations and not-for-profit agencies as well as profit-seeking businesses have further enriched the mix of organizations seeking to meet demands for public services. In many instances, community governments have found that they can improve service delivery, cut costs, or both, by privatizing government functions (i.e., by using the services of these new, nongovernmental entities). This, in turn, has created a need for government managers who understand and are skilled at handling intersectoral relations as well as intergovernmental relations.

Managerial success in the coming decades requires managers who understand the intergovernmental and intersectoral climate in which their community operates and who have developed the skills to exploit this climate for the advantage of local residents. Such skills are thus a new requirement in the portfolio of competencies needed for managing government. ■

---

1 Sara Mills Mazie and Mollier Sizer Killion, "Growth and Change in Rural America: The Experience of the 1980s and Prospects for the 1990s," in *Rural Community Economic Development,* ed. Norman Walzer (New York: Praeger, 1992), 1-13.

2 John Thomas, "Financing County Government: An Overview," *Intergovernmental Perspective* (Winter 1991): 11-13.

3 Margaret Kriz, "Effluent, Not Affluent," *National Journal* (March 25, 1989): 742.

4 Thomas, "Financing County Government."

5 Robert Gage, "Key Issues in Intergovernmental Relations in the Post-Reagan Era: Implications for Change," *American Review of Public Administration* 20 (September 1990): 155-174.
6 Barbara Todd, "Counties in the Federal System: The State Connection," *Intergovernmental Perspective* (Winter 1991): 22.
7 W. John Moore, "Crazy Quilt Federalism," *National Journal* (November 26, 1988): 3001-3005.
8 "City & State 2000," *City and State* (January 4-17, 1993): 30.
9 John Herbers, "17th Century Counties Struggle to Cope with 20th Century Problems," *Governing* (May 1989): 42-48.
10 Donald C. Menzel et al., "Setting A Research Agenda for the Study of the American County," *Public Administration Review* 52 (March/April 1992): 173-180.
11 Coalition to Improve Management in State and Local Government (CIMSLG), *Improving Local Services Through Intergovernmental and Intersectoral Cooperation,* Special Paper 5 (1992), 70-76.
12 Comments by Neil Nielson, Village Manager, village of Oak Park, Illinois, 1992.
13 CIMSLG, *Improving Local Services.*
14 Ibid.
15 Ibid.
16 Susan MacManus, "Government Contracting and Procurement: A Critical Process for Both the Public and Private Sectors," paper presented at the Annual Meeting of the American Society for Public Administration, April 1992.
17 Jean Dimeo, "Can Privatization Help Stretch the Local Dollar?" *American City and County* (September 1991): 26-29.
18 Elizabeth Voisin, "Privatization and Prisons," *City and State Magazine* (1990).
19 CIMSLG, *Improving Local Services.*
20 James Q. Wilson, *Bureaucracy* (New York: Basic Books, 1989).
21 CIMSLG, *Improving Local Services.*
22 Timothy Dempsey and Marty Bilek, "The BARK for Law Enforcement," unpublished manuscript, Douglas County Sheriff's Office, Omaha, Nebraska, 1991.
23 John A. Rehfuss, *Contracting Out in Government* (San Francisco: Jossey-Bass, 1989).
24 Philip Kotler and Alan Andreasen, *Strategic Marketing for Non-Profit Organizations* (Englewood Cliffs, N.J.: Prentice-Hall, 1991).
25 Barry Bozeman and Jeffrey D. Straussman, *Public Management Strategies: Guidelines for Managerial Effectiveness* (San Francisco: Jossey-Bass, 1990), 108-134.

16 Issues Facing Community Government

As the end of the twentieth century approaches, community governments are returning to their traditional role as governments of last resort in confronting the problems of the society they serve. They respond to the crises that affect individual residents; they ultimately determine the quality of life in the neighborhood; and they perform these tasks in the face of political demands for lower taxes and less public spending.

However, although local governments are re-assuming their traditional role, there is nothing traditional about the policy problems they must resolve or the technologies and strategies they must employ to resolve them. Given the changes outlined in the first chapter of this book, community governments will fail to discharge their public trust if they attempt to rely only on traditional methods to deal with traditional responsibilities.

Although the role of community governments in the future may be traditional, many of their responsibilities will not be. As the chapters in this book emphasize, community residents today expect a far broader range of public services, and the delivery of those services requires much more sophistication, knowledge, creativity, and public accountability than has been the case in decades past. The business of community government—the delivery of community services—has ceased to be a task that civic-minded and talented residents can undertake on a part-time basis. In today's complex and interdependent world, specialized knowledge and skills are essential to perform even traditional roles in an adequate manner.

The issues facing community government will certainly grow even more complicated in the years ahead. The chapters of this book have attempted to highlight forthcoming challenges as well as the traditional complexities faced in delivering community services. Several common themes have recurred: the role of community growth and development, the importance of technological innovation, the evolving pattern of intersectoral sharing of service responsibilities, and the urgent need for professionalization of staff. Because of their central importance, this chapter will restate these themes, emphasizing their broader, long-term implications for the daily business of governing the nation's small cities and counties.

Growth and development

Chapters 4 and 5, which deal with planning and economic development, focus on the processes and problems relating to community growth and development. They presume a continuing need to manage growth, accommodate changing populations, and sustain the economic vitality of the community. And, indeed, all communities have a continuing need to address these concerns regardless of whether they are experiencing population growth or decline.

Yet there are already clear indications that planning and development must be—and are—concerned with more than economics. Increasingly, life-style considerations are becoming dominant in community policymaking. Neighborhoods and sometimes whole communities are now being designed to appeal specifically to particular kinds of people: to retired persons; to young, upwardly mobile professionals; to families; to vacationers; to business owners and professionals fleeing urban density; or to persons with disabilities or special needs.

Planning and development are concerned with more than economics.

Other communities are centered around particular kinds of activity; examples of such communities are those that revolve around a regional shopping center, college campus, upscale shopping area, office park, resort community, or medical center. Still other communities are now being designed to promote particular living patterns, for example, by combining sidewalks and grassy areas with street patterns in ways that discourage auto use in order to promote more interaction among neighbors. The motivations behind such community designs are many. Research has found, for instance, that community opposition to growth is frequently motivated by residents' desire to protect a community's family-oriented life-style.[1]

Different kinds of communities develop from different strategies. Efforts to develop a particular kind of community life-style or ambience require community consensus regarding development objectives, a long-term strategy to achieve those objectives, and a commitment of years of effort to accomplish the task.[2]

Citizen suggestions

Hobart, Australia (47,000), incorporated citizen input in the process of designing its North Hobart Townscape Project by sponsoring two public design workshops in which community residents were taken on tours and given plans, pens, and cameras to encourage their comments. Other methods used included a colorful caravan in the street staffed by the plan's artists and two public exhibitions of the design proposal. Citizens proposed sculpture festivals, multicultural festivals, traffic management proposals, sign control, public artworks, and landscaping. Citizen input helped to foster a high level of community approval of the final design as well as a heightened sense of community ownership and pride.

Source: *The Guide to Management Improvement Projects in Local Government,* vol. 17, no. 3 (Washington, DC: ICMA, 1993), no. LD-18.

Management of community growth and development in the future, then, will be a much more complicated and involved task for those communities that wish to promote a particular life-style as well as accomplish certain economic objectives. The communities that successfully achieve their objectives will be those that combine local leadership and professional development expertise.

Technological innovation

The genius of the American people, displayed in community governments as well as in business, consists in producing and adapting to new technologies—new ways of doing things. Although new information technologies are most visible at present, innovations in people-oriented technologies abound, as can easily be seen by perusing the "Nuts and Bolts" section of the *ICMA Newsletter*.[3] One example of a new technology reported there is the use of teddy bears by police officers to facilitate their interactions with small children. Such new people-oriented technologies are evolving with increasing frequency; they prove that, in government, people do matter. The focus in this chapter, nonetheless, is on information technologies because they represent a radical departure from past practice and promise to have the most far-reaching and permanent effect on community government in the years ahead.

Much of the work of community governments involves information; thus, the changes in information technologies now under way portend great changes for these governments. The key question is how the changes will affect them. It seems likely that the consequences of new information technologies will be new services, different work processes, and new challenges.[4]

New services

New services already available in some communities include communication with citizens via voice mail systems, dedicated cable television channels, and computer terminals, some of which are installed in public facilities. Automatic teller machine cards are being used by welfare recipients to draw out public assistance payments in cash, and inspection services are being scheduled by clients over the telephone through a computer that produces schedules for the inspectors.[5]

Two of many examples of new services currently possible but not yet in common use include library operations conducted over telephone lines, with "books" and music loaned in temporary electronic forms, and personal alarm systems used for fire, police, and health emergencies.

Differences in work processes

The new technologies change work processes in many ways.[6] First, the new technologies speed up work by processing information faster; one consequence is a greater sense of time pressure for workers. Second, the new technologies link formerly separate areas of work into one integrated system (e.g., emergency dispatch systems have replaced separate dispatchers for police, fire, and emergency medical services). In addition, the new technologies can lead to the creation of new systems (e.g., public health and safety systems will be developed that link information from health departments, building inspections, fire prevention programs, public works files, and police traffic systems).

Third, the new technologies will make most workers more interdependent (as they require information provided to them by others) and these technologies can vastly increase the quality of work performed (e.g., the greater volume of systematically developed data will help engineers and planners produce more accurate and helpful reports). Fourth, the new technologies produce "greater control over people for managers and professionals and greater control over jobs for clerical and administrative workers." Fifth, the technologies facilitate choices in organizational structure. Whatever the structure chosen, people work more reliably using the new technologies, partly because of the monitoring capacity, but even more because of the satisfaction they will derive from the ability to do a better job.

New challenges

The challenge facing community governments will be to select the most suitable of the new information technologies from the many possible choices and to integrate them with current operations.

Successfully meeting this challenge will require judgments about the service needs of the community, decisions about which services to implement, and estimates of the costs and positive results of new services. For cost reasons alone, few communities will try to implement all or most of the possible new services. Estimating costs presents the greatest difficulty; the major cost may be ongoing personnel costs rather than the purchase price of hardware.[7]

In addition to considering the cost of adopting new information technologies, it is essential to consider other factors, as managing changes in work processes is a major challenge. Training and retraining are obvious requirements that are too frequently underemphasized when new information technologies are adopted. The design of work processes and the relationship between tasks assume greater importance than before. Top-level managers must recognize the need to support supervisors and managers as well as workers during times of transition; managers and supervisors can be overlooked too easily. Generally, personnel requirements will change over time; changing requirements gradually, and retaining current employees whenever possible, is usually beneficial.

Intersectoral service provision

Just as rapid changes in technology promise to alter the management of local governments, so too does the expanding role of intersectoral relationships. The paradox of an increasing demand for broader and greater levels of service combined with a stagnant or shrinking per-capita revenue base has led many administrators to explore alternative service delivery systems. Of the options, contracting with non-governmental organizations to deliver specific services is now widely regarded as an alternative that offers both a less expensive and a more efficient method of supplying many local government services. Thus, growing numbers of community governments are turning toward the private and nonprofit sectors to deliver a wide variety of services.

Public works contract

Mustang, Oklahoma (11,000), has reduced its public works costs by more than $200,000 a year through an operations, management, and maintenance contract with a private firm. The city found that through contracting out its public works (functions that include water and wastewater plants; water distribution and collection; meter reading; garbage collection; animal control; and street, park, and ground maintenance) it could take advantage of both technical and financial advantages.

Source: "Privatizing Public Works," *American City and County* (September 1993): 48-56.

A number of advantages are cited for such arrangements, chiefly reduced personnel costs. Non-governmental organizations are claimed to have greater flexibility, which enables them to use only the persons with the skills required; employ part-time and temporary workers on an as-needed basis; and provide less extensive and expensive fringe benefit packages.

The ability of service contractors to supply services across jurisdictional boundaries is another appeal of intersectoral agreements. Contractors are able to provide service to multiple jurisdictions, thereby allowing them to take advantage of economies of scale that are not available to individual units of local government. These economies of scale may allow the contractor to provide services at less expense, spread equipment costs over many jobs, employ more skilled workers, and employ more current technologies.

Animal control contract
In response to citizen concerns over the unfair and inadequate enforcement of animal control and rabies laws, Fulton County, Georgia, negotiated a contract with the Atlanta Humane Society, a private nonprofit organization, to establish an animal control division to serve the county and cities within the county. The animal control division enforces leash, license, cruelty prevention, animal nuisance, and rabies control laws. The county pays half the cost of the contract, with the remaining half divided (on a prorated basis) among the nine cities participating in the contract.

Source: *Service Delivery in the 90s: Alternative Approaches for Local Government* (Washington, DC: ICMA, 1989), 9.

Local governments may find it easier to tap into new technology through intersectoral relationships.

Tapping into current technologies through the intersectoral relationship can also be a benefit. A lack of sufficient resources and any number of "higher" priorities have historically caused local governments to lag behind the private sector in the adoption and use of new technologies. Because this historical pattern is likely to continue and technology is changing at an ever-increasing pace, local governments may continue to find it easier to tap into new technology through intersectoral relationships.

Finally, intersectoral relationships, especially with the nonprofit sector, will continue to fill a void in the health and human service area, especially in providing services that do not generate enough revenue to provide a profit for the private sector or to cover the costs government would incur. The nonprofit sector has traditionally filled the void in these areas, providing the needed services and raising the money to pay costs not covered by available government funds. With an increasing need for social service intervention to serve or to bring about change in individuals and society, nonprofit organizations will continue to provide services in areas such as homeless shelters, food pantries, senior centers, and mental health and medical clinics.

The expanding role of intersectoral relationships promises to challenge more than ever the interpersonal skills of the local government administrator. To manage successfully under the circumstances described, the administrator will need to strengthen his or her communication skills. The arts of negotiating, bargaining, and coalition building must all be added to the administrator's repertoire of management skills if local governments are to take full advantage of the possibilities in the intersectoral arena.

Staff professionalization

Chapter 1 referred to the growing role that professionalization can and should play in providing responsive community government and in delivering community services. Subsequent chapters have consistently reinforced this theme, providing evidence to support the notion that good community government today requires

Strong, forceful elected officials who focus their time and energies on the tasks of building citizen support for government, formulating policies governing community development and services, and ensuring government service delivery that adheres to community standards of responsiveness and efficiency

Professional managers who serve as the link between elected leaders and government employees, advising the former of policy and program needs and directing the performance of the latter so that it is consistent with stated policies and fulfills established objectives

Trained, competent employees who are masters of their craft and who accept the challenge to be fully professional in their work by combining a continuing program of professional education and development with responsive and efficient performance of their responsibilities.

The community governments that most successfully meet these three requirements will, over time, be most effective in responding to citizen needs and in achieving the community's life-style goals. They will be the governments that govern best.

Ultimate responsibility for securing the "best" government resides with elected officials. Ensuring the professional quality of government staff is the single most significant action elected officials can take to achieve excellence.

A change in political culture

Complicating all of the attempts to manage community governments will be an emerging change in the nation's political culture. The years between 1960 and 1990 witnessed a major shift in cultural expectations, a shift toward greater emphasis upon the rights of the individual and away from the obligations of citizenship. The nation's traditional sense of individual responsibility for collective well-being diminished. By 1994, that pattern appeared to be changing: demands for restrictions on smoking, gun control, welfare reform, and universal health protection were all indicative of a changing sense of cultural priorities, of less sensitivity to individual desires, and of a growing concern for the social consequences of individual behavior.

As this shift in cultural emphasis gains momentum, the impact upon community government will probably be severe. Easy to anticipate will be the demands for more and different services: for the enforcement of no-smoking policies; for expanded public delivery of health services; for adjustments in welfare policies (and the subsequent need to deal with those individuals whose personal benefits are diminished or lost in the process). Less easy to anticipate will be more subtle changes, such as challenges to cherished individual rights in the name of community well-being. Government workers, both policymakers and street-level bureaucrats, may well be confronted with the need to formulate and enforce policies that strike a new balance between individual and collective rights and well-being. This may present community governments—and, indeed, all governments—with new and complex issues involving the preservation of the nation's democratic values.

Afterword

There are some distinct similarities between the operations of professional sports teams and community governments. Both require a high level of professional talent and skill; both require strong, consistent leadership. Neither will succeed when an individual leader (owner, mayor, county executive, manager) attempts to dominate; both can succeed only when leaders build and rely on teamwork, both in organizational management and in the field. Community governments need elected leaders who will work together toward common goals, and they need professional managers who build teamwork in the field. These team-building jobs are both equally vital to organizational success.

Community government will be challenged in the future more than it ever has in the past. Success in meeting the challenges will be more dependent than ever before upon the sensitivity of elected leaders to citizen desires; upon the staff's professional vision and technical competence; and upon the organization's ability to adapt to changes in citizen demands, in service requirements, in service delivery methods, and in the use of modern technology.

No longer will the Jeffersonian maxim, "That government governs best which governs least," hold true. In the future, the government that governs best will be the government that makes the most effective and efficient use of the human resources available to it. Acquiring such resources, and using them well, is the first and foremost requisite for those who will succeed in managing the nation's small cities and counties. ■

---

1 Reiko Habe, "Community Growth Gaming: A Survey Method," *Environment and Behavior* 21 (May 1989): 298-322.

2 A good, albeit brief, survey of some of these tools and strategies is provided by John M. DeGrove, ed., *Balanced Growth: A Planning Guide for Local Government* (Washington, DC: ICMA, 1991).

3 Published semi-monthly by ICMA.

4 James L. Perry and Kenneth L. Kraemer, "The Implications of Changing Technology," in *Revitalizing State and Local Public Service: Strengthening Performance, Accountability, and Citizen Confidence*, ed. Frank J. Thompson (San Francisco: Jossey-Bass Publishers, 1993), 225-245.

5 Perry and Kraemer, 228-229.

6 This section is based on Perry and Kraemer, 229-232.

7 John W. Swain and Jay D. White, "Determining the Productivity Effects of Information Technology: Maybe, Maybe Not," in *Handbook of Public Productivity,* ed. Marc Holzer (New York: Marcel Dekker, 1992), 643-663, especially 659-660.

For Further Reference

1 The Challenges of Community Government

Ammons, David N., and Charldean Newell, *City Executives.* Albany: State University of New York, 1989. An exploration of city executives based on a survey of 527 mayors, city managers, and other top executives in city government. Comparisons of city executives with managers in other organizations display similarities and differences in regard to work environment and management characteristics. The book's audience ranges from practitioners to students of government and administration to interested citizens.

Newell, Charldean, ed. *The Effective Local Government Manager.* 2d ed. Washington, DC: ICMA, 1993. Focuses on the role of local public executives as leaders. Discusses what managers do and how they can do it more effectively as they interact with a diverse community, the governing body, local government employees, and other governments. Covers developing and implementing policy, improving productivity, strategic planning, economic development, conflict resolution, and the manager's career. Draws on the experience of seasoned local government executives and offers numerous real-world examples. Special attention is given to the pressures and responsibilities of a public job and to the need to nurture relationships.

Frederickson, H. George, ed. *Ideal and Practice in Council-Manager Government.* Washington, DC: ICMA, 1989. Result of the National Conference on the Study of City Management and the Council-Manager Plan, this collection of research papers addresses the future role and responsibility of the professional manager with respect to economic development, innovation, and technological change. The papers offer empirical data on managers' activities, leadership roles, skills, and values within the council-manager environment.

Mosher, Frederick C. *Democracy and the Public Service.* 2d ed. New York: Oxford University Press, 1982. A revised edition of a widely read text that examines the problems of fusing governmental administration and democratic requirements. Contains a new chapter on management theories and public personnel administration and expanded discussions of collective bargaining and affirmative action programs.

Paul, Amy Cohen, ed. *Managing for Tomorrow: Global Changes and Local Futures.* Washington, DC: ICMA, 1990. An outcome of the FutureVisions Consortium focusing on the critical issues facing local governments in next decades. The articles offer analyses concerning demographics, economic globalization, technology and information management, human capital and resources, public service, and governance from a grass roots to a global perspective. Two themes connect the articles: first, the future needs to be studied; and second, applying what we learn can result in a better world.

Rutter, Laurence. *The Essential Community.* Washington, DC: ICMA, 1980. The report of the ICMA Committee on Future Horizons of the Profession, exploring forces that will affect cities, counties, and councils of governments in the last two decades of the twentieth century and management strategies to deal with them.

Stillman, Richard J., II. *The Rise of the City Manager.* Albuquerque: University of New Mexico Press, 1974. An authoritative interpretation of the development of the city management profession, examining the city manager as a central figure in the American community and placing manager professionalism in the context of historic national values and culture.

Svara, James H. *Official Leadership in the City.* New York: Oxford University Press, 1990. An extensive examination of the roles of city executives in both mayor-council and council-manager governments, the book confronts the challenges and conditions facing today's city leaders. Breaking inaccurate stereotypes, the author looks at the governing process to provide practical models and methods for effective conflict management and the promotion of cooperation in local government.

2 The Legal Aspects of Community Government

Adrian, Charles R. *State and Local Governments.* 4th ed. New York: McGraw-Hill, 1976. A basic text on the importance of state and local governments in the provision of services and the formulation of policy. Also covers metropolitan reorganization and costs of decision making.

Bromage, Arthur W. *Introduction to Municipal Government and Administration.* 2d ed. New York: Appleton-Century-Crofts, 1957. A text on the politics, principles, and practices of municipal government that addresses the interaction of administrative skill and representative democracy.

Hardy, Paul T., and J. Devereux Weeks. *Personal Liability of Public Officials Under Federal Law.* 4th ed. Athens: Carl Vinson Institute of Government, University of Georgia, 1988. A concise review of the current status of personal liability of state and local officials and employees under the Civil Rights of Act of 1871 (42 *United States Code* Section 1983).

Harney, Donald F. *Service Contracting: A Local Government Guide.* Washington, DC: ICMA, 1992. A detailed guide to service contracting for the practitioner that includes guidelines and tips for preparing bid documents, negotiating with providers, and monitoring the contract.

Hill, Melvin B., Jr. *State Laws Governing Local Government Structure and Administration.* Athens: Institute of Government, University of Georgia, 1978. A resource guide that covers the extent to which state laws govern the structure and administration of local governments in the United States. The form of government, annexation and consolidation, local elections, administrative operations and procedures, financial management, and personnel management are examined.

The Municipal Year Book. Washington, DC: ICMA, 1982, 1988, 1989, 1991, 1992. A valuable source of city and county data and developments, much of which is presented as tables, municipal and county profiles, and directories. Also includes discussions of personnel and management issues.

Leach, Richard H., and Timothy G. O'Rourke, *State and Local Government: The Third Century of Federalism.* Englewood Cliffs, NJ: Prentice Hall, 1988. A text that aims at providing sufficient knowledge of the structure, powers, and issues of state and local government to meet present-day challenges. Topics covered include history, formal bases of power, role of the people, functions, organizational and operational arrangements, and finance.

National Civic League. *Model County Charter.* Rev. ed. Denver: National Civic League Press, 1990. A model to be used as a guide in preparing a county charter. Provides for a substantially integrated county government, a representative policy-determining body, a single administrative head, appointment by the head of principal administrative officers, a substantial degree of flexibility in administrative structure, and modern fiscal management procedures.

Pine, John C., and Robert D. Bickel, *Tort Liability Today: A Guide for State and Local Governments.* 1st, 2d, and 3d eds. Washington, DC: Public Risk Management Association and National League of Cities, 1986, 1991, 1992. A state-by-state analysis of state law governing the liability of government units and public officers and employees.

Svara, James H. *Official Leadership in the City.* New York and Oxford: Oxford University Press, 1990. A book that examines the roles of mayors, council members, and administrators in the urban government process and strives to identify ways for practitioners to improve performance.

Weeks, J. Devereux, and Paul T. Hardy, eds. *Handbook for Georgia County Commissioners.* 3d ed. Athens: Carl Vinson Institute of Government, University of Georgia, 1992. Written primarily for newly elected county commissioners in the state of Georgia, this book is an extensive guide to county government that reviews important provisions of state and federal law and provides practical information on and suggests criteria for judging a county's performance in numerous areas.

Weeks, J. Devereux, and Emily Honigberg, eds. *Handbook for Georgia Mayors and Councilmembers.* 2d ed. Athens: Carl Vinson Institute of Government, University of Georgia, 1984. Written primarily for newly elected mayors and city council members in the state of Georgia, this book is an extensive guide to municipal government that reviews important provisions of state and federal law and provides practical information on and suggests criteria for judging a municipality's performance in numerous areas.

3 The Office of the Clerk

Software Reference Guide. Washington, DC: ICMA, 1993. Contains descriptions of more than 900 software programs available for use by local governments. Also included in the guide is a resources section containing information on publications, databases, networks, and organizations that local governments can turn to for technical assistance.

International Association of Clerks, Recorders, Election Officials, and Treasurers (IACREOT). *The News.* Quarterly. Camden, NJ: IACREOT. A forum for the exchange of ideas and information among county officials. IACREOT also publishes a number of brochures on issues of concern to members of the organization.

International Institute of Municipal Clerks. *News Digest.* Monthly. San Dimas, CA: International Institute of Municipal Clerks. Articles on developments and changes in the municipal clerk's profession. IIMC also maintains a Management Information Center for immediate assistance on problems facing the clerk's office; thousands of sample ordinances, covering most areas of regulation; technical bulletins on agendas, indexing and filing, records disposition, and computer applications; and a reference library of materials concerned with the clerk's position.

Norris, Donald F. *Microcomputers and Local Government* 3d ed. Washington, DC: ICMA, 1989. Provides an excellent introduction to the types and uses of computer hardware and software in local government organizations. Also discussed are likely issues of importance, the effects that microcomputers will have on an organization, and microcomputer policies.

Spraggins, Peggy A., et. al. *The Municipal Clerk's Office in Ohio: A*

Study of Duties, Professionalism, and Innovations. Kent, OH: Center for Public Administration and Public Policy, Kent State University, 1993. The results of research documenting information about the duties and functions of the municipal clerk in Ohio. Provided is information regarding those who serve as clerks in Ohio and their duties; innovations in the clerk's office; and the enhancement of professionalism in the clerk's office.

Using WordPerfect 5.2 for Windows. Carmel, IN: Que Corporation, 1993. This book is an example of the many reference documents available to those interested in becoming involved or more skilled in the use of one of the word processing systems available for computers. In this case the text deals with WordPerfect 5.2 for Windows. Similar reference documents are available for almost every word processing software package.

4 Planning

Ford, Christina, James Lopach, and Dennis O'Connell. *Planning Small Town America: Observations, Sketches and a Reform Proposal.* Chicago: American Planning Association, 1990. How to survive while doing small town planning. Many truths here.

Getzels, Judith, and Charles Thurow, eds. *Rural and Small Town Planning.* Chicago: American Planning Association, 1980. Useful introduction to policies, community settings, rural public transportation, infrastructure, zoning, and subdivisions.

Godschalk, David R. *Constitutional Issues of Growth Management*. 2d ed. Chicago: American Planning Association, 1979. Good, though somewhat dated, overview of growth management systems and the constitutional issues used to challenge these programs.

Jones, Bernie. *Neighborhood Planning: A Guide for Citizens and Planners.* Chicago: American Planning Association, 1990. Doing plans with neighborhood groups and carrying them out.

Krieger, Alex, and William Lennertz, eds. *Andres Duany and Elizabeth Plater-Zyberk: Towns and Town-Making Principles.* New York: Rizzoli, 1991. A collection of neo-traditional town plans and studies.

Levy, John M. *Contemporary Urban Planning*. 2d ed. Englewood Cliffs, NJ: Prentice-Hall, 1991. Good basic textbook on the practice of planning.

Mandelker, Daniel R. *Land Use Law*. 2d ed. Charlottesville, VA: Michie, 1988. An excellent, comprehensive single-volume treatise on American planning and zoning law.

McClendon, Bruce W. *Customer Service in Local Government: Challenges for Planners and Managers.* Chicago: American Planning Association, 1992. Peppery, occasionally preachy, proposal on how to revamp planning so that it responds to and satisfies consumers.

So, Frank S., and Judith Getzels, eds. *The Practice of Local Government Planning*. 2d ed. Washington, DC: ICMA, 1988. The comprehensive text on the planning process at the local level. Very clear treatment of capital budgeting.

5 Economic Development

Bartik, Timothy J. *Who Benefits from State and Local Economic Development Policies?* Kalamazoo, MI: Upjohn Institute, 1991. The most authoritative analysis of the costs and benefits of economic development incentives for communities and states. This single report reviews all existing research on the impact and effectiveness of incentives and conducts a new analysis showing that incentives do have a positive impact on local economies in many cases.

Blakely, Edward J. *Planning Local Economic Development: Theory and Practice.* Santa Monica, CA: Sage Publications, 1989. Provides an excellent review of theories and techniques applied to local economic development. Especially helpful in understanding the rationale for different types of strategies.

Bowman, Ann, O. *Tools and Targets: The Mechanics of City Economic Development.* Washington, DC: National League of Cities, 1987. Very useful review of activities by local governments to support economic development. Good information for activities by communities of different sizes and budgets.

Economic Development Program, Cleveland State University. *Marketing Cities in the 1980's and Beyond.* Chicago: American Economic Development Council, 1989. Reviews marketing strategies employed by a representative sample of large, medium, and small communities across the country. Practical information on how to develop and evaluate economic development promotion programs.

Farr, Cheryl. "Encouraging Local Economic Development: The State of the Practice." In *The Municipal Year Book 1990.* Washington, DC: ICMA, 1990. Provides an excellent overview of what priorities local governments have set for economic development and the array of techniques and programs used to achieve these priorities. Good background reading for any community starting a new program.

Hatry, Harry, Mark Fall, Thomas Singer, and Blaine Liner. *Monitoring the Outcomes of Economic Development Programs.* Washington, DC: The Urban Institute, 1990. One of very few practical guides on how communities can evaluate the impact of different types of economic development program. The book identifies performance monitoring measures for six different types of programs, including export trade, business retention and attraction, marketing, job training, and financing assistance.

Heenan, David A. *The New Corporate Frontier: The Big Move to Small Town, USA.* New York: McGraw-Hill, 1991. Provides the corporate perspective on why smaller communities are more attractive as business locations. Several case studies of large corporations growing and relocating to small towns across the country.

Kolzow, David R. *Strategic Planning for Economic Development.* Chicago: American Economic Development Council, 1991.

Lessinger, Jack. *Penturbia.* Seattle, WA: SocioEconomics, 1991. Provides an analysis of why population and jobs continue to move away from central cities beyond nearby suburbs to "outlying areas." The role of infrastructure and community quality of life are two factors discussed.

Martin, Lawrence L. "Bidding on Service Delivery: Public-Private Competition," *MIS Report,* vol. 25, no. 11 (November 1993). Discusses how local governments use competition to make public delivery of services more efficient. Cases highlight actual practices including problems and pitfalls of public-private competition.

Thomas, G. Scott. *Life in America's Small Cities.* Buffalo, NY: Prometheus Books, 1990. Calls attention to the advantages of living and working in 219 smaller non-metropolitan communities across the country. The book ranks these locations based upon economic, social, and quality-of-life factors.

Urban Land Institute. *State and Regional Initiatives for Managing Development: Policy Issues and Practical Concerns.* Washington, DC: Urban Land Institute, 1992. Discusses growth management strategies followed by communities and states. The book describes several examples of how regional cooperation by local governments is contributing to more orderly and equitable development in regions.

6 Public Works

American Public Works Association. *Public Works Today: A Profile of Local Service Organizations and Managers.* Chicago, IL: APWA, 1990. Based on a survey of more than 2,400 public works directors from the United States and Canada. This is the third decennial survey from APWA. The latest organizational and managerial characteristics are listed by region and locality size.

Ball, Norman. *Building Canada: A History of Public Works.* Toronto: University of Toronto Press, 1988. This is a history of public works in Canada focusing on bridges, roads, mass transit, rail and waterways, irrigation and flood control, water distribution and wastewater treatment, solid waste, public buildings, and airports.

Barker, Michael. *Rebuilding America's Infrastructure: An Agenda for the 1980's.* Durham, NC: Duke University Press, 1984. This book includes the Choate book (see Choate reference) then builds on it, offering an agenda for action.

Bingham, Richard D., et al., *Managing Local Government: Public Administration in Practice.* Newbury Park, CA: Sage Publications, 1991. The first section examines local government management functions. The second section focuses on direct local service delivery, including public works as well as public housing, economic development, community development, public safety, and recreational and cultural services.

Choate, Pat, and Susan Walter. *America in Ruins: The Decaying Infrastructure.* Durham, NC: Duke University Press, 1983. This is the book that brought the infrastructure issue to national attention. It clearly describes deteriorating facilities, declining investments, fraud and waste, capital budgeting, and the allocation of public works responsibilities.

Congressional Budget Office. *New Directions for the Nation's Public Works.* Washington, DC: U.S. Government Printing Office, 1988. Documents the federal government's changing role in highways, mass transit, aviation, water transportation, and wastewater treatment. Proposes some comprehensive strategies.

Cristofano, Sam M., and William S. Foster, *Management of Local Public Works.* Washington, DC: ICMA, 1986. The sixth edition in ICMA's series on public works planned and developed with the cooperation of the American Public Works Association.

Grigg, Neal. *Infrastructure Engineering and Management.* New York: John Wiley and Sons, 1988. This book is a good primer in project management. It uses many water-related examples.

Houlihan, Barrie, ed. *The Challenge of Public Works Management: A Comparative Study of North America, Japan, and Europe.* Brussels, Belgium: The International Institute of Administrative Sciences, 1992. Investigates organization, financing, and management practices in public works in Canada, United States, Japan, Netherlands, Sweden, Italy, England, and Wales. Separate chapters examine the provision of roads and bridges and water and wastewater treatment in those countries.

Knorr, Edward L., et al. *Good Practices in Public Works.* Chicago: American Public Works Association, 1988.

National Council on Public Works Improvement. *Fragile Foundations: A Report on America's Public Works.* Washington, DC: U.S. Government Printing Office, 1988. This book is the final report from the joint Presidential-Congressional Council that produced the highly publicized Report Card on the Nation's infrastructure. It highlights the recommendations of the council and the nine books produced supporting the report's findings.

National Council on Public Works Improvement. *The Nation's Public Works: Defining the Issues.* Washington, DC: U.S. Government Printing Office, 1986. This report developed the framework for *Fragile Foundations.*

Office of Technology Assessment, Congress of the United States. *Delivering the Goods: Public Works Technologies, Management, and Financing.* Washington, DC: U.S. Government Printing Office, 1991. Looks at the national issues pertaining to our ability to adopt new public works technologies and methods currently used to finance and manage them.

Office of Technology Assessment, Congress of the United States. *Rebuilding the Foundations: A Special Report on State and Local Public Works Financing and Management.* Washington, DC: U.S. Government Printing Office, 1990. This report examines the intergovernmental framework for rebuilding the nation's infrastructure. Separate chapters highlight both the states' role and local governments' role in rebuilding, fiscal capacity, and effort.

Rosen, Howard, and Ann Durkin Keating. *Water and the City: The Next Century.* Chicago: Public Works Historical Society, 1991. This edited book contains thirty-seven perspectives on the future of water supply, wastewater treatment, and stormwater management.

Schmandt, Jurgen, et al. *The New Urban Infrastructure: Cities and Telecommunications.* New York: Praeger, 1990. This book examines the newest form of urban infrastructure: telecommunications. It discusses local governments' role in the telecommunication business with case studies of twelve cities in the United States, Mexico, and Canada.

7 Leisure Services

Bannon, Joseph J. *Current Issues in Leisure Services*. Washington, DC: ICMA, 1987. Written from a management perspective, this text focuses on some of the more difficult and controversial personnel, programming, and fiscal management issues facing leisure service administrators. It is a part of ICMA's Practical Management Series.

Crider, Ralph, and Sondra Kirsch. *Revenue Policy Manual.* Arlington, VA: National Recreation and Park Association, 1990. Based on the experience of park and recreation practitioners, this manual offers a practical approach for developing and implementing an effective revenue policy.

Hultsman, John, Richard L. Cottrell, and Wendy Hultsman. *Planning Parks for People.* State College, PA: Venture Publishing, 1991. A comprehensive text/reference for planning, designing, and rehabilitating park and recreation areas. It is based on the belief that park planning and design should emphasize a balance between the needs of people and the need to maintain and protect the resource.

McLean, Janet R., James Peterson, and Donald Martin. *Recreation and Leisure: the Changing Scene.* 4th ed. New York: John Wiley, 1985. A basic text in parks and recreation with chapters pertaining to various aspects of the history, operations, and diverse interests composing this field of service.

Murphy, James F., William Niepoth, Lynn Jamerson, and John Williams. *Leisure Systems: Critical Concepts and Application.* Champaign, IL: Sagamore Publishing, 1991. A contemporary perspective of leisure services as a system. It is a blending of theory and practice with particular attention being given to the issues of planning, staffing, and management.

National Commission on Libraries and Information Science Annual Report. Washington, DC: U.S. Government Printing Office, published annually since 1972. Established as a permanent and independent agency of the federal government in 1970, the commission attempts to be a forum and provider of information for the library and information science community. Its annual reports consider such items as recent legislation affecting libraries, trends in operations, and reports of various task forces created by the NCLIS.

Recreation, Park and Open Space Standards and Guidelines. Arlington, VA: National Recreation and Park Association, 1983. A collaborative effort of planners and park and recreation specialists, this document contains recommendations on the number and type of facilities needed in communities based upon the population patterns, the space requirements of specific activities, and the methods by which communities can adequately plan their park and recreation spaces.

Pankratz, Daniel B., and Valerie Morris, eds. *The Future of the Arts: Public Policy and Arts Research*. New York: Praeger, 1990. This collection of essays attempts to address basic issues: what is the future of arts in the United States and what role should social science research play in determining that future through formulation of public policy? It discusses trends, ideology, and current policy positions from both a local and national perspective. Of particular interest are those essays related to the future of the arts and to participation in the arts by minorities and elderly citizens.

8 Human Services

Agranoff, Robert, et al., eds. *Coping with the Demands for Change within Human Services Administration.* Washington, DC: American Society for Public Administration, 1977.

Anderson, Wayne F., Bernard J. Frieden, and Michael J. Murphy. *Managing Human Services.* Washington, DC: ICMA, 1977. Discussion of local government human service activities with extensive use of case studies. Comprehensive review emphasizing program ideas for local governments.

Cooper, Ronald S. *FLSA: The Public Employer's Guide.* Washington, DC: ICMA and Steptoe & Johnson, 1993. Contains the latest information on court rulings, Department of Labor opinions, and requirements for compliance. It includes letters of opinion written by the Wage and Hour Board, examples of applications of FLSA to common situations, appendices with pertinent regulations and statutes, question and answer sessions to address the most commonly asked questions about FLSA.

Dluhy, Milan J. *Building Coalitions in Human Services.* Newbury Park, CA: Sage Publications, 1990.

Flynn, John P. *Social Agency Policy.* 2d ed. Chicago: Nelson-Hall, 1992. Comprehensive policy analysis for local community human services with extensive case illustrations.

Gans, Sheldon P., and Gerald T. Horton. *Integration of Human Services: The State and Municipal Levels.* New York: Praeger, 1975.

Hagen, J. J., and E. Hutchinson. "Who's Serving the Homeless," *Social Casework* 69 (1988): 491-497.

Hasenfeld, Yeheskel, ed. *Human Services As Complex Organizations.* Newbury Park, CA: Sage, 1992. Analyzes human services organizations with particular reference to both their internal characteristic structure and leadership and the political environment in which they exist.

Melaville, Atelia I., Martin J. Blank, and Gelareh Asayesh. *Together We Can: A Guide for Crafting a Profamily System of Education and Human Services.* Washington, DC: U.S. Department of Education, U.S. Department of Health and Human Services, 1993. A book developed to help communities improve coordination of education, health, and human services for at-risk children and families. To correct the current fragmented, inefficient service delivery system, the book advocates a radical change in the system that encourages a holistic approach in treating the problems of children and their families; easy access to comprehensive services; early detection of problems and preventive health care services; and flexibility in the use of federal and state funds.

National Association of Counties. *Human Services Integration at the Community Level: A Six County Report.* Washington, DC: Research Foundation, National Association of Counties, 1974.

Richie, Nicolas D., and Diane E. Alperin. *Innovation and Change In the Human Services.* Springfield, IL: Charles C. Thomas, 1992. Traces the evaluation of human service organizations at Federal, State, and local level with particular emphasis on innovation, change, and further direction.

Rocheleau, Bruce A., and Thomas K. Mackesey. "Utilization-Focused Evaluation: A Case Study from the Human Services Area," *Policy Studies Journal,* vol. 8, no. 7 (1980).

Rocheleau, Bruce A., and Thomas K. Mackesey, "What, Consumer Feedback Surveys Again? A Guide to Improving the Utility of Consumer Evaluation," *Evaluation and the Health Professions,* vol. 3, no. 4 (1980).

Royse, David D. *Program Evaluation: An Introduction.* Chicago: Nelson-Hall, 1992. A practical guide to developing needs assessments and evaluation programs for human services.

Wilson, Marlene. *You Can Make a Difference: Helping Others and Yourself Through Volunteering.* Boulder, CO: Volunteer Management Associates, 1990.

9 Emergency Management

Barton, Bruce E. "Emergency Management: The Economic Developer's Role." Master's thesis. Norman, OK: Economic Development Institute, University of Oklahoma, 1991. A linkage between economic development efforts and emergency management at the local government level.

Drabek, Thomas E., and Gerard H. Hoetmer, eds. *Emergency Management Principles and Practice for Local Government.* Washington, DC: ICMA, 1991. The first comprehensive treatment of emergency management. Covers key issues including mitigation, preparedness, response, and recovery; the roles of the state and federal governments; organizing for emergency management; coordinating community resources; and public sector liability.

"44 CFR Part 206; Robert T. Stafford Disaster Relief and Emergency Assistance Act; Implementation, etc.; Final Rules." *Federal Register* (January 12, 1990): 2284-2318. The official publication outlining regulations for a presidential disaster declaration.

Federal Emergency Management Agency. *Digest of Federal Disaster Assistance Programs.* DR & R-21. Washington, DC: FEMA, June 26, 1989. The Federal Emergency Management Agency publication outlining programs. Good for the practitioner.

Federal Emergency Management Agency. *Guide for Development of State and Local Emergency Operations Plans.* CPG 1-8. Washington, DC: FEMA, October 1985, revised September 1988. Federal Emergency Management Agency guidelines for the preparation of a local government emergency response plan.

Federal Emergency Management Agency. *Hazard Identification, Capability Assessment, and Multi-Year Development Plan.* CPG 1-34. Washington, DC: FEMA, January 1987. Expanded Federal Emergency Management Agency guidelines to assist in the preparation of a local government emergency response plan.

Federal Emergency Management Agency. *Objectives for Local Emergency Management.* CPG 1-5. Washington, DC: FEMA, July 1984. Federal Emergency Management Agency guidelines for the organization and operation of a local emergency management program.

Florida Fire Chiefs Incident Command System Reference Guide. A guideline for incident command structure, staging areas, communication, command post, and terminology.

Hoetmer, Gerard J. "Emergency Management," Baseline Data Reports, vol. 15, no. 4, Washington, DC: ICMA, April 1983. A report of local government disaster experience and attitudes based upon a survey conducted by ICMA in the fall of 1982.

Lerner, Ken. "Governmental Negligence Liability Exposure in Disaster Management," *The Urban Lawyer,* vol. 23, no. 3 (Summer 1991). Good discussion of the legal issues to be considered when planning for emergency management. Although not specific by state, it is a good source for a city attorney and other policymakers.

Livingston, Neil C. "American Bhopals: The Threat of Catastrophic Refinery Accidents and Sabotage to Hydrofluoric Alkylation Units," Washington, DC: The Energy Safety Council, 1992. A revealing overview of the impact of technological disasters within the petro-chemical industry.

McLaughlin, David. "A Framework for Integrated Emergency Management," reprinted from "Emergency Management: A Challenge for Public Administration," *Public Administration Review* (January 1985). Outlines the role of governments in emergency management, organizational structure of Federal Emergency Management Agency, and the components of a successful emergency management program.

National Fire Academy. National Fire Academy Student Manual, "The Incident Command System." Emmittsburg, MD: National Fire Academy, August 1989. An excellent resource for understanding and implementing the incident command system.

National Fire Protection Association. *Developing Fire Protection Services for the Public.* Quincy, MA: National Fire Protection Association, 1989. Chapter 10 provides a model structure for the Incident Command System.

Nudell, Mayor, and Norman Antokol. *The Handbook for Effective Emergency and Crisis Management.* Lexington, MA: Lexington Books, 1988. Written for government and industry. Covers natural disasters, environmental incidents, and terrorism. Good discussion of public affairs management, media relations, and de-briefing procedures.

Ohlsen, Christine, and Claire B. Rubin. "Planning for Disaster Recovery," *MIS Report* vol. 2, no. 7. Defines key elements in the disaster recovery process and guidelines for creating and implementing a recovery plan. Lists of helpful organizations and resources are provided to assist managers in designing a plan.

Prince, Patrick, and Ann T. Phelps. "'Disaster-Proofing' Your People: Caring for the Psychological Needs of Employees." In *The 2nd Annual International Emergency Management Conference Proceedings,* March 17-19, 1992, San Francisco. An overview of the psychological reactions to disaster for both individuals and organizations. Covers phases of response to disaster, factors that influence the degree of impact, predisaster planning, and disaster response and recovery.

Winslow, Francis E. "Caring For Workers and Spontaneous Volunteers: A Local Government Perspective." In *The 2nd Annual International Emergency Management Conference Proceedings,* March 17-19, 1992, San Francisco. A practical discussion of the role of volunteers, including planning for volunteers, registration of volunteers, planning for donations, and volunteer recognition.

10 Police Services

American City and County. Although not aimed specifically at those involved in policing, this periodical regularly discusses topics pertinent to policing. Recent issues have included articles on community policing, alternative options for incarceration, and new technology for public safety departments.

FBI Law Enforcement Bulletin. This periodical publishes articles on numerous topics of concern to police officials, including problems facing today's law enforcement officers, new technologies, and new methodologies of management and human resource development.

Fyfe, James J., ed. *Police Practice in the '90s.* Washington, DC: ICMA, 1989. Discusses issues of primary concern to police officials today. Included are discussions of the mission of police departments, drug enforcement concerns, professionalism, accreditation, and human resource development issues.

Geller, William A. *Local Government Police Management.* 3d ed. Washington, DC: ICMA, 1991. Discusses a wide range of policing issues and concerns. This third edition reflects the changes that have occurred in the practice of policing over the last decade. Administrators and staff are provided with information on such areas as police patrol, crime prevention, traffic control, organized crime, drug enforcement, human resource management, research, planning, performance measurement, and intergovernmental and intersectoral relationships.

Community-Oriented Policing: An Alternative Strategy. Washington, DC: ICMA, 1991. Those interested in learning more about the use of community-oriented policing will find a wealth of information in this volume. Selected readings provide discussions on "innovative strategies and ideas for understanding, developing, and implementing community-oriented policing."

Police Personnel Practices: Education, Participation, and Scheduling. Washington, DC: ICMA, 1991. This special data issue provides the reader with responses to a survey of police personnel practices. Topics include educational incentives, scheduling, and officer involvement in interdepartmental issues. Data is provided on a state-by-state basis, making it easier for the reader to contact departments that have programs of interest.

Mullen, Joan. *The Privatization of Corrections: Issues and Practices.* Washington, DC: National Institute of Justice, 1985. For those facing overcrowded correctional facilities, the author provides a discussion of the private financing, construction, and operation of prisons and jails. Explored are developments in private sector participation in the process.

The Police Chief is a periodical aimed at providing the police executive with information on a wide variety of concerns. Topics have included recruitment, training and development, ethics, management techniques, community policing, performance evaluation, liability, and human resource management.

Swanson, Charles R., and Leonard Territo. *Police Administration: Structures, Processes, and Behavior.* New York: Macmillan, 1983. The authors argue for the importance of integrating structure, process, and behavior in order to create a healthy police organization. Topics include external influences, organizational theory, leadership, communication, decision making, stress, labor relations, fiscal management, and planning. The authors make use of numerous newspaper articles and vignettes that help drive home their views.

Thibault, Edward, Lawrence Lynch, and R. Bruce McBride. *Proactive Police Management.* Englewood Cliffs, NJ: Prentice-Hall, 1985. The authors review the history and structure of law enforcement management and examine several traditional police management models. The models are discussed in the context of a proactive management approach, which argues for police administrators to anticipate occurrences through "planning, effective use of police personnel and resources, and the delivery of a range of services."

Toch, Hans, and J. Douglas Grant. *Police as Problem Solvers.* New York: Plenum Press, 1991. The authors provide an extensive discussion of "problem-oriented policing." Accentuated in the text is the role of the police officer in making more informed, professional judgments. Discussed are issues such as the history and development of this philosophy, the process of defining a problem, addressing the problem, and implementing a solution.

Whitaker, Gordon P., ed. *Understanding Police Agency Performance.* Washington, DC: National Institute of Justice, 1984. This text provides an examination of the process through which police resources are translated into service provision and the impact that service provision has on the community. Also provided is a discussion of models used to assess the performance of police patrol operations.

11 Fire and Emergency Medical Services

American Academy of Orthopaedic Surgeons. *Emergency Care and Transportation of the Sick and Injured.* 4th ed. Park Ridge, IL: American Academy of Orthopaedic Surgeons, 1987. This training textbook covers everything that an emergency medical technician is expected to be able to do according to the 1984 Department of Transportation guidelines. Major section headings include introduction, patient assessment, cardiopulmonary resuscitation, bleeding and shock, injuries, medical emergencies, childbirth, environmental emergencies, psychological aspects of emergency care, patient handling and extrication, and ambulance operations. This book lays out what EMTS have to deal with to do their job.

Coleman, Ronny J., and John A. Granito, eds. *Managing Fire Services.* 2d ed. Washington, DC: ICMA, 1988. This ICMA Green Book covers the nuts and bolts of department management. It also provides treatment of legal issues, cost containment and cost recovery, alternative delivery systems, labor-management relations, code administration and enforcement, and integrated emergency management and planning.

Cote, Arthur E., ed. *Fire Protection Handbook.* Quincy, MA: National Fire Protection Association, 1989. With more than 2,000 pages in 189 chapters, this NFPA handbook provides an extremely detailed treatment of almost any conceivable fire services questions. It is an excellent source for most technical questions, while also providing useful treatment of management concerns.

Federal Emergency Management Agency. *Public Fire Education Planning.* Federal Emergency Management Agency, National Emergency Training Center, National Fire Academy, no place name given, 1983. A training manual for fire safety education.

Fitch, Joseph J., with Rick Keller and Chris Zalar. *Beyond The Street: A Handbook for EMS Leadership and Management.* Solana Beach, CA: JEMS Publishing Company, Inc., 1988. A comprehensive management leadership perspective on setting up and operating EMS services. Includes ten short case studies.

ICMA. *Emergency Medical Services Systems.* MIS Report, vol. 20, no. 11. Washington, DC: ICMA, 1988. This brief MIS report succinctly discusses what services should be provided, how they can be provided, and how various methods of service delivery can affect the costs and quality of service.

jems (The Journal of Emergency Medical Services) is always a good source of information on current and on-going issues in the EMS field.

National Fire Protection Association. This association is a good source for most aspects of fire services.

Office of the Oklahoma State Fire Marshall and Mission Research Corporation. *A Basic Guide for Fire Prevention and Control Master Planning.* Prepared for The National Fire Prevention and Control Administration, U.S. Department of Commerce, 1975. A very basic guide to planning fire protection services.

Scanlon, Raymond D., ed. *Hazardous Materials, Hazardous Waste: Local Management Options.* Washington, DC: ICMA, 1988. This book identifies hazardous materials problems, explains the maze of federal regulation, and shows how community officials can work to minimize hazardous wastes, improve transportation safety, solve facility siting problems, and prepare for accident prevention and emergency response.

Wills, Jane, and Terry Wright, eds. *Volunteer Emergency Medical Systems: A Management Guide.* Blacksburg, VA: Center for Volunteer Development, no date. This book lays out the many activities outside of the realm of emergency medical services that need to be successfully negotiated to make EMS possible. Its topical coverage ranges from fundraising and state licensure to effective leadership and organizing the membership.

12 Budgeting and Financial Management

Allan, Ian J. *Revenue Collection Administration: A Guide for Smaller Governments.* Chicago: Government Finance Officers Association, 1992. Special circumstances of smaller governments are addressed throughout this book, but its comprehensive approach recommends it to governments of any size. Covers organization of the revenue collections office; assessment and billing; accounting, internal controls, and auditing; collections and processing; revenue deposits; enforcement; and evaluation.

Aronson, J. Richard, and Eli Schwartz, eds. *Management Policies in Local Government Finance,* 3d ed. Washington, DC: ICMA, 1987. This Green Book comprehensively covers budgeting and financial management in local government. More than 150 figures, tables, and sidebars expand and illustrate the text.

Bean, David R., Stephen J. Gauthier, and Paul E. Glick. *Governmental Accounting, Auditing and Financial Reporting.* Chicago: Government Finance Officers Association, 1988. Known throughout the government finance community as the "blue book," this publication provides reliable and comprehensive guidance on the practical applications of generally accepted accounting principles for governments. Includes detailed chapters on individual funds and account groups; detailed journal entries; and a complete sample annual financial report that meets the current requirements for the GFOA Certificate of Achievement for Excellence in Financial Reporting.

Bland, Robert L. *A Revenue Guide for Local Government.* Washington, DC: ICMA, 1989. Describes each major source of revenue, its importance in financing services, its advantages and disadvantages, political and policy issues affecting its design and adoption, recommendations for building public support, and administrative issues involved in levying and enforcement.

Gauthier, Stephen J. *Audit Management Handbook.* Chicago: Government Finance Officers Association, 1989. Provides practical, detailed guidance on all aspects of obtaining and managing a financial audit: planning the audit; preparing a request for proposals; and evaluating proposals. Supplemented by a complete model request for proposals. Also covers audit committees; audit contracts; monitoring audit engagements; and audit resolution.

Glick, Paul E. *A Public Manager's Guide to Government Accounting and Financial Reporting.* Chicago: Government Finance Officers Association, 1989. A conceptual overview of the basic principles of accounting and financial reporting. Addresses the full-scope audit; annual financial report; fund equity; interim financial reporting; risk management; internal service funds; and the budgetary basis of accounting.

Government Finance Officers Association has a long tradition of supplying excellent reference materials for local government practitioners. They can be found at 180 North Michigan Avenue, Suite 800, Chicago, IL 60601.

Government Finance Officers Association. *Best of Budgeting: A Guide to Preparing Budget Documents.* Chicago: GFOA, 1993. A comprehensive guide to preparing operating budget documents with examples from city, school district, county, state, and special district budgets. Includes suggestions on how to present policy, financial, and operational data in a variety of formats. Also includes a cross-reference to the awards criteria for GFOA's Distinguished Budget Presentation Awards Program.

Groves, Sanford M., and Maureen Godsey Valente. *Evaluating Financial Condition.* 3d ed. Washington, DC: ICMA, 1994. Uses information already collected for financial planning and management purposes to develop easy to understand graphs that show the effect of intergovernmental mandates on spending flexibility, the real cost of deferred maintenance, the accumulation of unfunded liabilities, and the effects of inflation. Helps to assess how internal management practices and legislative policies—as well as external demographic and economic forces—affect local government's financial health.

ICMA. *The ABCs of Risk Management.* MIS Report, vol. 23, no. 9 (1991). Washington, DC: ICMA, 1991. Describes the five elements in the risk management process: risk identification and analysis, risk treatment options, treatment measures, implementation, and evaluation. Three case studies show risk management plans in action.

ICMA. *The Budget as a Communication Tool.* MIS Report, vol. 20, no. 2 (1988). Washington, DC: ICMA, 1988. Reviews budgets that communicate well and focuses on five key issues: the budget process, manager's letter of presentation, communication with the council, communication with citizens, and presentation of revenue and debt management information.

ICMA. *Strategic Budgeting: A Guide to Financial Stability.* MIS Report, vol. 25, no. 8 (August 1993). Washington, DC: ICMA, 1993. Written by two experts in municipal budgeting, this report takes the reader step by step through the formulation of long-range goals, the connection between the budget and the goals, and the development of a budget document that accurately reflects current programs, community needs, government resources, and external circumstances. The report includes the new GFOA Budget Award criteria.

ICMA. *User Fees: Current Practice.* MIS Report, vol. 24, no. 12 (December 1992). Washington, DC: ICMA, 1992. Describes the different kinds of fees currently being used by local governments as alternatives to taxation, discusses their legal foundation and advantages and disadvantages, and explains how to analyze costs as well as economic and policy considerations before setting fees. Provides comprehensive case study examples, detailing procedures for implementing and updating user fees and giving examples of fees and how they are employed, not only to raise revenue but also to control demand.

Matzer, John, Jr., ed. *Practical Financial Management: New Techniques for Local Government.* Washington, DC: ICMA, 1984. Shows how to evaluate financial condition, formulate written financial policies, assess financial practices and municipal services, conduct revenue surveys, improve revenue collection and forecasting, set priorities for capital programming and financing, and improve local government purchasing.

Reed, B.J., and John W. Swain. *Public Finance Administration.* Englewood Cliffs, NJ: Prentice-Hall, 1990. This textbook covers all major financial management topics in a practical fashion.

Rousmaniere, Peter F., ed. *Local Government Auditing: A Manual for Public Officials.* New York: Council on Municipal Performance, 1979. A primer on audits and auditing that includes many specific examples with detailed explanations, written for local government officials.

13 Personnel Management

Ban, Carolyn, and Norma M. Riccuci, eds. *Public Personnel Management: Current Concerns and Future Challenges.* New York: Longman, 1991. This book offers an overview of a variety of important issues. Of particular interest are discussions of pay-for-performance, sexual harassment, and affirmative action.

Becker, Christine S., ed. *Performance Evaluation: An Essential Management Tool.* Washington, DC: ICMA, 1988. This book offers an in-depth discussion of performance evaluation in community governments.

Bowman, Sarah Y., and Jay M. Shafritz, ed. *Public Personnel Administration: An Annotated Bibliography.* New York: Garland, 1985. An excellent starting place for those interested in learning more about some specific aspect of public personnel administration.

Brock, Jonathan. *Managing People in Public Agencies: Personnel and Labor Relations,* 2d ed. Lanham, MD: University Press of America, 1989. This is an excellent text on public personnel administration. It contains cases useful for training activities.

Cayer, Joseph N. "Local Government Personnel Structure and Policies." In *The Municipal Year Book 1991.* Washington, DC: ICMA, 1991. This article gives an excellent overview of how the personnel function is organized and carried out in city and county governments.

Darnell, Tim. "Drugs and Booze: Combating the Problem," *American City and County* (April 1988): 46-50. A good starting place for those interested in learning more about a couple of tough personnel problems.

Evans, Sara M., and Barbara J. Nelson. *Wage Justice: Comparable Worth and the Paradox of Technocratic Reform.* Chicago: University of Chicago Press, 1989. This book offers insight into the importance of comparable worth and the efforts to develop comparable worth policies in state and local governments in the state of Minnesota.

Hays, Steven W., and Richard C. Kearney, eds. *Public Personnel Administration: Problems and Prospects,* 2d ed. Englewood Cliffs, NJ: Prentice-Hall, 1990. This book provides an excellent overview of some of the most critical issues in contemporary public personnel administration, including compensation and motivation, health care, comparable worth, sexual harassment, and ethics.

ICMA. *Effective Supervisory Practices.* Washington, DC: ICMA, 1984. Teaches supervisory management with special attention to motivating employees, managing change, and developing leadership skills. Also covers communication skills and the budget.

Matzer, John, Jr., ed. *Advanced Supervisory Practices.* Washington, DC: ICMA, 1992. Shows how to maximize employee performance, manage conflicts, supervise project teams, and foster and manage diversity.

Matzer, John, Jr., ed. *Personnel Practices for the '90s: A Local Government Guide.* Washington, DC: ICMA, 1988. The chapters in this book offer some valuable insights into a number of burdensome issues that are likely to cause local government professionals considerable difficulty. These include age bias, managing a multicultural workplace, drugs and drug testing, AIDS, and privacy rights.

Moulder, Evelina R. "Affirmative Action in Local Government." In *The Municipal Year Book 1991.* Washington, DC: ICMA, 1991. Examines the status of affirmative action efforts in city and county governments. The issues examined include the implementation of affirmative action policies, the groups covered by affirmative action policies, the methods used to attract minorities and women, the use of numeric goals, and other critical issues.

Shafritz, Jay M., Albert C. Hyde, and David H. Rosenbloom. *Personnel Management in Government.* 4th ed. New York: Marcel Dekker, 1991. An academic textbook designed for those who need a thorough review of public personnel administration. It offers an excellent discussion of recent legal cases in a variety of areas.

Slack, James. "AIDS, the Local Government Workplace, and the Law." In *The Municipal Year Book 1991.* Washington, DC: ICMA, 1991. This article provides important information on a topic of major importance.

Stahl, O. Glenn. *Public Personnel Administration,* 8th ed. New York: Harper and Row, 1983. This is a classic textbook dealing with public personnel administration. It is a good place to turn for general questions.

Sylvia, Ronald D. *Critical Issues in Public Personnel Policy.* Pacific Grove, CA: Brooks/Cole, 1989. This book offers an excellent overview of major issues in public personnel administration.

Taylor, Robert R., and Lois Smith. "Performance Standards: Developing an Employee Appraisal System to Enhance Productivity in a County Government," *Public Administration Quarterly* (Summer 1987): 217-238. This article offers some interesting ideas on how to establish a performance measurement system.

Thomas, Roosevelt R., Jr. "Managing Diversity: A Strategic Opportunity." In *The Municipal Year Book 1991.* Washington, DC: ICMA, 1991. This article offers some interesting ideas on how to deal with diversity. The author argues that learning to manage diversity will give organizations a strategic advantage in the pursuit of quality human resources.

14 Communication

Wheeler, Kenneth M., ed. *Effective Communication: A Local Government Guide.* Washington, DC: ICMA, 1994. Basic reference on communication in local government. Includes communication with citizens, elected officials, local government employees, and the news media; setting up a communications program; interpersonal communication; effective presentations using print and broadcast media.

Beach, Mark. *Editing Your Newsletter: How to Produce an Effective Publication Using Traditional Tools and Computers.* Manzanita, OR: Coast to Coast Books, 1988. Covers audience identification, budgeting, selection of topics, format, writing, and other aspects of publication.

Claremont, California. *Media Relations Policy Manual.* Washington, DC: ICMA, 1990. Clearinghouse Report. Press relations, news releases, news conferences, public disclosure, media interviews, and coverage of council and board meetings.

Cutlip, Scott M., Allen H. Center, and Glen M. Broom. *Effective Public Relations.* 6th ed. Englewood Cliffs, NJ: Prentice-Hall, 1985. Basic text. Comprehensive, well-illustrated.

Frisby, Michele. *Public Information: Educating and Communicating.* MIS Report, vol. 23, no. 3 (March 1991). Washington, DC: ICMA, 1991. Synopses of media relations programs in Dubuque, Iowa; Eugene, Oregon; Florence, South Carolina; and other local governments.

Garnett, James L. *Communicating for Results in Government: A Strategic Approach for Public Managers.* San Francisco, CA: Jossey Bass, 1992. Excellent guide to internal communication—upward, downward, and lateral—crisis communication, and communication ethics.

Lesly, Philip, ed. *Lesly's Handbook of Public Relations and Communication.* 4th ed. Chicago: Probus Publishing, 1991. Comprehensive reference with forty-eight chapters on wide range of subjects. Useful appendix includes reference sources, associations, glossary, bibliography, and index.

Lewis, Phillip V. *Organizational Communication: The Essence of Effective Management.* 3d ed. New York: John Wiley, 1987. Basic text covering organization theory, systems, verbal and nonverbal communication, media, leadership, group behavior, and related subjects.

Miller, Thomas I, and Michelle A. Miller. *Citizen Surveys: How to Do Them, How to Use Them, What They Mean.* Special Report. Washington, DC: ICMA, 1991. Describes purposes of surveys and how they fit into citizen participation efforts, why they should and should not be done, and what results mean. Guidance on planning, designing, conducting, and reporting credible surveys. Provides average service ratings to be used as benchmarks for evaluating survey results.

Parker, Edwin B., et al. *Rural America in the Information Age: Telecommunications Policy for Rural Development.* Lanham, MD: Aspen Institute and University Press of America, 1989. Policy recommendations for national and state governments that apply to community governments as well as to unincorporated, rural areas.

Public Technology, Inc., and Videotex Industry Association. *Local Government Opportunities in Videotex: A Guide to Communicating and Gaining Revenue through Electronic Services.* Washington, DC: Public Technology, Inc., 1991. How local governments can develop videotex services. Includes five case studies.

San Diego, California. *Communication and Information Master Plan.* Washington, DC: ICMA, 1990. Clearinghouse Report. Shows allocations of departmental responsibilities vis-a-vis the city manager and the San Diego Data Processing Corporation.

Silver, Gerald A., and Myrna L. Silver. *Layout, Design, and Typography for the Desktop Publisher.* Dubuque, IA: William C. Brown, 1991. Fundamentals of layout, copyfitting, type, production, paper, and printing. Covers stationery, newsletters, booklets, ads, folders, and other materials.

Stoner, Randall C. *Practical Promotion: Strategies for Improving Services and Image.* Washington, DC: ICMA, 1992. Special Report. How to promote community government programs and services: special projects, citizen involvement, customer service, external marketing, promoting to hostile audiences, and related subjects.

Swain, John W., and Jay D. White. "Information Technology for Productivity: Maybe, Maybe Not: An Assessment." In Marc Holzer, ed., *Public Productivity Handbook,* 643-63. New York: Marcel Dekker, 1992. How to assess the productivity of information technology innovations.

Zinsser, William. *On Writing Well: An Informal Guide to Writing Nonfiction.* 4th ed. New York: HarperCollins, 1990. Widely used text and reference on major kinds of nonfiction writing.

15 Intergovernmental Relations

Berman, David R., ed. *County Governments in An Era of Change.* Westport, CT: Greenwood Press, 1993. This is one of the first books to focus strictly on county governments. It provides a detailed overview of the development of county government in the United States and provides chapters on authority and structure, legislative operations, intergovernmental structure, and so forth.

Dilger, Robert Jay, ed. *American Intergovernmental Relations Today: Perspectives and Controversies.* Englewood Cliffs, NJ: Prentice-Hall, 1986. This text provides an overview of intergovernmental relations in the United States. It is probably more traditional in its approach, focusing on the political and policy environment surrounding relationships at the local, state, and federal levels.

Honadle, Beth Walter, and Arnold Howitt, eds. *Perspectives on Management of Capacity Building.* Albany: State University of New York Press, 1986. This book reviews capacity building and management from a broad set of local perspectives. It also focuses on a number of intergovernmental elements including human resource management and the federal effects on municipal management capacity.

Howitt, Arnold. *Managing Federalism: Studies in Intergovernmental Relations.* Washington, DC: CO Press, 1984. A series of case studies of various intergovernmental management issues organized along substantive lines. Subject areas include maternal and child health, community development block grants, environmental protection, and surface transportation.

U.S. Advisory Commission on Intergovernmental Relations. *Intergovernmental Perspectives.* Quarterly. Washington, DC: ACIR. This journal provides a wealth of information on intergovernmental issues facing local government jurisdictions.

Wright, Deil S. *Understanding Intergovernmental Relations.* 3d ed. Pacific Grove, CA: Brooks/Cole, 1988. Probably the seminal text in intergovernmental relations. This book provides a historical and conceptual overview of intergovernmental relations and explores a number of specialized topics in IGR including financial management, regulatory policy, redistributive policies, and substantive topics such as health, education, and welfare. ■

About the Authors

David S. Arnold is an editor and writer whose primary interests are public administration and communication in state and local governments. For many years he was on the staff of the International City/County Management Association as editor of the Municipal Management Series and, prior to that, editor of *Public Management* and *The Municipal Year Book.* He holds a bachelor's degree from Lafayette College and a master's in public administration from the Maxwell School, Syracuse University.

James M. Banovetz serves as both Professor of Political Science and Public Administration and Director of the Division of Public Administration at Northern Illinois University and as the Albert A. Levin Chair in Urban Studies and Public Service at the Levin College of Urban Affairs at Cleveland State University.

Professor Banovetz edited the ICMA books *Managing Local Government: Cases in Decision Making* (1990) and *Managing the Modern City* (1971). He has drafted the organization and structure for a number of city governments and has served as a consultant to national, state, and local governments, both in the United States and abroad. A recipient of Ph.D. and M.A.P.A degrees from the University of Minnesota, he has taught at the University of Illinois, Loyola University in Chicago, and the University of Ile-Ife in Nigeria.

Professor Banovetz was awarded the Elmer B. Staats Public Service Career Award by the National Association of Schools of Public Affairs and Administration in 1991 and honorary membership in ICMA in 1978.

Drew A. Dolan is an Assistant Professor of Public Administration and Urban Affairs in the Department of Urban Affairs and Geography at Wright State University. He holds an M.A.P.A. and a Ph.D. in Public Administration and Political Science from Northern Illinois University. He has served as a consultant to municipal and county governments.

Claire L. Felbinger is an Associate Professor of Public Administration and Urban Studies at the Levin College of Urban Affairs, Cleveland State University. She is also the director of the college's Master of Public Administration Program and is the academic coordinator of the largest graduate program in public works management in the country. Dr. Felbinger has written two books and over twenty articles and chapters in books on public works management, urban service delivery, intergovernmental relations, and evaluation research methodology.

Paul T. Hardy is an attorney with the Carl Vinson Institute of Government at the University of Georgia, where he provides legal assistance to state and local governments. He received his undergraduate and doctor of jurisprudence from the University of Georgia. Mr. Hardy has participated in the drafting of local and general legislation, and he has been either the author or co-author of a number of publications and a participant in a variety of programs of importance to state and local governments.

Bob Hart has been city manager of Georgetown, Texas, since 1989. He previously served as city manager in the cities of Pampa, Sweetwater, and Sundown, Texas. He holds a Master of Public Administration degree from the University of North Texas and Bachelor of Science degree from Baylor University.

He is active in municipal affairs and currently serves on the board of directors of the Texas City Management Association, Texas Municipal League, Texas Public Power Association, and the Foundation for Improvement of Local Government. He is a member of ICMA and NCCEM, and has contributed articles to *Public Management* and *The Bulletin,* their respective publications. He has also written for *The International Journal of Mass Emergencies and Disasters.* Mr. Hart was a speaker at the Senior Level Meeting on Awareness and Preparedness for Emergencies at the Local Level, sponsored by the United Nations Environment Programme, in 1988, and currently serves as a lecturer in the Disaster Preparedness Seminar at the Emergency Management Institute in Emmittsburg, Maryland.

Donald T. Iannone is Director of the Economic Development Program at the Levin College of Urban Affairs at Cleveland State University. He has worked in the economic development field for 18 years as an economic planner, chamber of commerce economic development executive, county development executive, business location consultant, policy analyst and researcher, and state and local strategist. He serves on the national boards of the American Economic Development Council and the National Council for Urban Economic Development.

Thomas K. Mackesey is Director of Human Services, Walworth County, Wisconsin. He has directed the development of two integrated county Human Services Departments in Wisconsin. His published work includes consumer feedback survey applications in Human Services. His educational background includes a bachelor's degree in rural sociology, a master's degree in social work from the University of Wisconsin, and a master's degree in Public Administration from Northern Illinois University.

Stuart Meck, assistant city manager and planning director of Oxford, Ohio, is a past president of the American Planning Association. Author of numerous articles on planning and land use law, Mr. Meck holds a B.A. and an M.A. in Journalism and a Master of City Planning from the Ohio State University and an M.B.A. from Wright State University. He is a member of the American Institute of Certified Planners, a licensed professional planner in New Jersey, and a registered professional community planner in Michigan. He has taught planning at Ohio State University, the University of Dayton, Wright State University, and Miami University.

B. J. Reed is David C. Scott Professor and Chairman of the Department of Public Administration at the University of Nebraska at Omaha. Dr. Reed was formerly employed by the National League of Cities, where he directed technical assistance programs for housing, community development, economic development, and transportation. He has also served as the development director of Mexico, Missouri.

Dr. Reed has published articles in journals such as *Public Administration Review*, *American Review of Public Administration*, *The Journal of Urban Affairs*, and *Rural Development Perspectives*. His research interests are intergovernmental management, community and economic development, and public sector budgeting and finance. His most recent books are *Managing Economic Development* and *Public Finance Administration*.

Dr. Reed serves on the board of the Greater Omaha Private Industry Council, the Omaha Housing Authority Board of Commissioners, and the Planning Committee of the Urban League of Nebraska. He received his B.A. and M.S. degrees form Fort Hays State University and his Ph.D. in political science from the University of Missouri–Columbia.

H. Douglas Sessoms is Professor of Leisure Studies and Recreation Administration, University of North Carolina at Chapel Hill. A past president of the Academy of Leisure Sciences, the Society of Park and Recreation Educators, and the North Carolina Park and Recreation Society, he has written extensively on park and recreation issues and has served as a consultant for several universities, and for state and federal agencies, including the Outdoor Recreation Resources Review Commission.

Gregory Streib is Associate Professor of Public Administration and a Research Fellow at the Center for Urban Policy Research at Georgia State University, in Atlanta, Georgia. He has published widely in public administration journals, contributed to a number of books on city and county government, and written chapters for various ICMA publications. He is currently working on several studies dealing with the education needs of local government professionals and a study of the use of pay-for-performance techniques in city and county governments. He holds M.P.A. and Ph.D. degrees from Northern Illinois University.

John W. Swain is Assistant Professor in the Department of Political Science, University of Alabama, Tuscaloosa, where he teaches public administration and public budgeting and financial management. He is the co-author of a textbook on public finance administration and has also written training manuals for local government officials and a number of journal articles. He has worked with community officials in several Midwestern states in a variety of capacities, including that of first coordinator of the secretariat for the Illinois City Management Association. He received a B.A. from the University of New Hampshire and M.A. and Ph.D. degrees from Northern Illinois University.

J. Devereux Weeks is Senior Legal Research Associate with the Carl Vinson Institute of Government at the University of Georgia, where he conducts or supervises legal research for and renders technical assistance to local and state governments. He has published numerous handbooks, articles, book chapters, research projects, and special studies, and also conducts workshops for government officials and employees in Georgia and other states. Mr. Weeks earned his undergraduate and doctor of jurisprudence degrees from the University of Texas. ■

Illustration Credits

Chapter 1 Figure 1–4: Photograph courtesy of the Northwest Municipal Conference, 1616 E. Golf Road, Des Plaines, IL 60016; Figure 1–5: Graph updated by author from U.S. Office of the President, Office of Management and Budget, *Federal Government Finances* (Washington, DC: Office of the President, 1981); Figure 1–6: Courtesy of the city of Brea, Brea, California; Table 1–1 and Table 1–2: Updated by author from U.S. Bureau of the Census, *Census of Governments: 1987*, vol. 1, no. 1, *Government Organization* (Washington, DC).

Chapter 2 Cartoon, p. 39: Reprinted by permission of Johnny Hart and Creators Syndicate, Inc.

Chapter 3 Figure 3–1: Photograph courtesy of Bob Rink, city of Phoenix, Arizona; Figure 3–2: Reprinted by permission of International Institute of Municipal Clerks, 1206 N. San Dimas Canyon Road, San Dimas, California 91773; Cartoon, p. 46: Copyright 1994; reprinted courtesy of Bunny Hoest and *Parade* magazine.

Chapter 4 Figure 4–2: Photograph by Grady Clay reprinted with permission from *Close-Up: How to Read the American City* (Chicago: University of Chicago Press, 1980); Figure 4–5: Photograph by Landis Aerial Surveys, Phoenix, Arizona, reprinted with permission from *Close-Up: How to Read the American City*; Figure 4–8: Plan reprinted by permission of Andres Duany and Elizabeth Plater-Zyberk, Architects, 320 Firehouse Lane, Gaithersburg, Maryland 20878.

Chapter 5 Figure 5–1: Courtesy of the city of Urbandale, Iowa; Figure 5–2: Drawing by David Povilaitis

Chapter 6 Figure 6–1: Reprinted from *Fragile Foundations: A Report on America's Public Works*, National Council on Public Works Improvement (February 1988); Figure 6–2: Reprinted by permission from *The Hole Story: Facts and Fallacies of Potholes*, American Public Works Association (Chicago, 1983); Figure 6–3: Reprinted by permission from Carol Kocheisen, "Study Puts Stormwater Management Costs at $1 Trillion," *Nation's Cities Weekly* (June 22, 1992):9; Figure 6–4: Reprinted by permission of the city of St. Peters, Missouri; Figure 6–5: Photograph courtesy of Bob Rink, city of Phoenix, Arizona.

Chapter 7 Figure 7–1: Photograph courtesy of the city of Davenport, Iowa; Figure 7–2: Photograph by Sy Friedman, Chicago, Illinois; Figure 7–3: Photograph by permission of National 4-H Council, Chevy Chase, Maryland; Figure 7–4: Map courtesy of the city of Clawson, Michigan; Figure 7–6: Photograph courtesy of the city of Bellevue, Washington.

Chapter 8 Figure 8–1: Photograph courtesy of the city of Brea, California; Figure 8–4: Photograph courtesy of the cities of Brea and La Habra, California; Figure 8–5: Photograph by Hallie J. Hamilton, DeKalb, Illinois.

Chapter 9 Figure 9–1: Adapted and reprinted by permission from D.R. Godshalk, *Catastrophic Coastal Storms* (Durham, NC: Duke University Press, 1989); Figure 9–2: Federal Emergency Management Agency; Figure 9–5, Figure 9–6, and Figure 9–7: Photographs courtesy of the city of St. Peters, Missouri.

Chapter 10 Figure 10–3: From Francis R. Kessler and Monte R. Davis, "Police Organization and Management," in *Local Government Police Management* (Washington, DC: ICMA, 1982); Figure 10–5: Photograph courtesy of Fairfax County (Virginia) Police Department; Figure 10–6: Reprinted by permission of the International Association of Chiefs of Police, Alexandria, Virginia.

Chapter 11 Figure 11–1: Photograph courtesy of the city of Southern Pines, North Carolina; Figure 11–2: Photograph courtesy of the city of Raleigh, North Carolina; Figure 11–3: Poster courtesy of the city of Urbandale, Iowa; Figure 11–4: Photograph courtesy of the city of Myrtle Beach, South Carolina; Figure 11–5: Photograph courtesy of the city of Cocoa Beach, Florida; Figure 11–6: Photograph courtesy of the city of Raleigh, North Carolina.

Chapter 12 Figure 12–4: Adapted and reprinted by permission from Selma J. Mushkin and Charles L. Vehorn, "User Fees and Charges" in *Governmental Finance* (November 1977) Chicago: Municipal Finance Officers Association, p.48.

Chapter 13 Figure 13–5: Drawing by David Povilaitis.

Chapter 14 Figure 14–1: Drawing by David Povilaitis; Figure 14–2: Photograph courtesy of the city of West Des Moines, Iowa; Figure 14–5: Drawing by David Povilaitis; Figure 14–10: Graph created with data collected from survey of technology applications in local government conducted by ICMA in 1993.

Chapter 15 Figure 15-1: Reprinted with permission from Harry P. Hatry, *A Review of Private Approaches for Delivery of Public Services* (Washington, DC: Urban Institute Press, December 1983). ■

Index

Municipal Management Series

Managing Small Cities and Counties: A Practical Guide

Text Type

New Century Schoolbook and
Helvetica Condensed

Printing and Binding

McNaughton and Gunn
Saline, Michigan